OPERA PRODUCTION I

A Handbook

Da Capo Press Music Reprint Series

GENERAL EDITOR
ROLAND JACKSON
UNIVERSITY OF SOUTHERN CALIFORNIA

OPERA PRODUCTION I

A Handbook

BY

QUAINTANCE EATON

DA CAPO PRESS • NEW YORK • 1974

Library of Congress Cataloging in Publication Data

Eaton, Quaintance.
   Opera production I: a handbook.

  (Da Capo Press music reprint series)
  Reprint of the 1961 ed. published by University of
Minnesota Press, Minneapolis, under title: Opera
production: a handbook
   1. Opera—Production and direction. 2. Operas—
Stories, plots, etc. I. Title.
[MT955.E25   1974]   782.1'07   73-20232
ISBN 0-306-70635-0

Published by Da Capo Press, Inc.
A Subsidiary of Plenum Publishing Corporation
227 West 17th Street, New York, N.Y. 10011

Manufactured in the United States of America

OPERA PRODUCTION

A Handbook

QUAINTANCE EATON

University of Minnesota Press, Minneapolis

PRINTED IN THE UNITED STATES OF AMERICA AT THE
NORTH CENTRAL PUBLISHING COMPANY, ST. PAUL

Second printing 1962

Library of Congress Catalog Card Number: 61-16843

PUBLISHED IN GREAT BRITAIN, INDIA, AND PAKISTAN BY THE OXFORD UNIVERSITY PRESS
LONDON, BOMBAY, AND KARACHI, AND IN CANADA BY THOMAS ALLEN, LTD., TORONTO

PREFACE

THIS book is designed to be useful to all opera producers, to students, writers, and performers, and also to those who, not actively concerned with the production of opera, nevertheless have a lively curiosity about the art. A book of fact rather than critical judgment, it reveals the many elements that make up more than five hundred operas.

The producer can find in these pages all the information essential for judging which operas are suited to his equipment — or even, by virtue of period, style, and story, to his temperament. How to stage a work is left to him. But by quick scanning he can determine all that is basic for production: the number and importance of settings; the size of orchestra, chorus, ballet; the number of singers, their relative importance and individual requirements. He can learn where to get all musical materials and translations.

Then, if he should want to consult a fellow producer, he can readily discover others who have performed a given work in America. If he wants to see how others throughout the world have mounted a work, he is referred to published photographs, chiefly in the pages of *Opera News*.

The student and writer will benefit from the easy accessibility of facts, clearly presented. Furthermore, the student and writer, together with the general reader, can marvel at the amazing complexity of an opera production.

Historical material anchors the reader in the necessary knowledge of period (when the composer lived, when the opera was first presented, and the time in which the story takes place), source of libretto, and any unusual circumstances of performance or revision. This information, however, has been compressed into capsule form because the book is a practical guide rather than a historical or musicological treatise.

Performers can tell at a glance the suitability of roles to their talents. Vocal and acting demands are set forth; in most cases exact ranges are given, as well as details of other requirements.

In a truly opera-minded society, the so-called general reader would be placed first instead of last. The orchid of opera would be as widely and as lovingly cultivated as the simplest country garden. In spite of the phenomenal growth in opera production, chiefly in workshops and colleges, and the enormous public created by long-playing recordings, America is not yet an operatic country in that all participants in opera production can make a full-time living at it, and that audiences accept opera as a pleasurable matter of course. Failing that desirable state, we can hope that facts about the art we serve will find an audience outside the limited professional circle, if only because they enjoy a peep behind the scenes, which often proves irresistible to even the least knowledgeable. Perhaps by luring novices backstage, and revealing some of those mysteries that are unsuspected from the other side of the curtain, we may gain new customers out front.

QUAINTANCE EATON

Point View, Jamestown, R.I.
July 1961

ACKNOWLEDGMENTS

Opera Production was not so much written as compiled. At various stages the task seemed comparable to leveling a mountain with a teaspoon. It goes without saying that such an effort called for a team — not even Hercules could have seen daylight through that mountain without allies. During some months of trial and error (techniques for unfamiliar procedures evolved slowly), I assembled a small nucleus of willing and able laborers, both by actual contribution and in the value of their suggestions and criticisms. Every paragraph has been distilled painfully from a welter of information and ideas, sometimes undergoing transmutations that left no clear trace of original authorship.

My first debt is to several staunch partners. From the beginning, C. Ray Smith's cool head and concern for clear meaning brushed away many a confusion, while his expert typing provided a comforting sense of security. Gerald Fitzgerald, in long evenings with me after arduous days at his desk at *Opera News*, devoted his sharp eye and fabled memory to checking facts and correcting copy. Conrad Osborne, author, critic, and editor, also rendered valuable editorial service.

Expert opinions of members of the Committee for the Development of Opera had been solicited from early days on portions of the repertoire most congenial to each. But this procedure grew unwieldly as the deadline drew near; busy men all, these opera officials often found their hoped-for inspection difficult if not impossible. Before the pressure mounted too high, however, considerable assistance came from Boris Goldovsky, Douglas Moore, Elemer Nagy (all members of the executive committee), Julius Rudel, and Moritz Bomhard. Mary Ellis Peltz, a stalwart friend and dependable critic, also a member of the executive committee, proved especially helpful in the early stages. John Brownlee and Albert B. Gins of the executive committee also assisted greatly. Besides those already mentioned, other members of the Committee for the Development of Opera are Kurt Herbert Adler, John Anello, Dean Wilfred Bain, James A. Doolittle, Arturo di Filippi, Dr. Herbert Graf, Richard Karp, Mrs. Max Reiter, Professor Frederic W. Stewart, Mrs. Norris Darrell, and DeWitt McLaughlin TerHeun.

Four additional authorities kindly read and approved material: Ignace Strasfogel, assistant conductor of the Metropolitan Opera, who checked the entire Metropolitan repertoire; Walter Ducloux, head of the opera department of the University of Southern California, who looked over the Verdi entries; Dr. Jan Popper, now director of the opera department at the University of California in Berkeley, who gave special attention to Monteverdi's "Orfeo" and other works he has produced; and Felix Popper, of the New York City Opera, who drew on vast knowledge of Richard Strauss to assist with "Die Frau ohne Schatten" as well as other little-known operas. Harry G. Schumer, librarian at the Metropolitan, put his wizard-like memory and storehouse of information to work on checking orchestrations for fourscore and ten operas.

To a valiant quartet of researchers I am in eternal debt. Alan and Martha Wagner (he the purveyor of "Living Opera" over station WNYC in New York, as well as lecturer and critic, and director of program development for CBS-TV; she a former art editor of *Opera News* and a true opera buff) head the list. They chose to delve into the music-dramas of their famous namesake, as well as seeking information in numerous other important directions. Rudolph Fellner, who has written his own book, *Opera Themes and Plots* (Simon & Schuster), was particularly helpful in defining terms and in seeking the essence of musical descriptions, as well as providing material for several operas. Richard Holland, writer and critic, dug in reference libraries and came up with hundreds of facts, figures, and ideas. The earlier research of Daniel Arnstein (particularly in *Opera News* for photographs) and others is also deeply appreciated.

Music publishers were unfailingly courteous and helpful, lending scores freely and submitting cheerfully to endless questions. It is impossible to mention them all, but I cannot refrain from thanking Bob Holton and Michael Sonino of Boosey & Hawkes (the latter now on the staff of *Musical America*); Ruth Roland and Peter Salomone of Ricordi & Co.; Hans Heinsheimer of G. Schirmer; Milton Feist of Mercury (later taken over by Presser, with Arthur Hauser as president); and Phyllis Flick, secretary to Karl Bauer, of Associated, all of whom made their extensive catalogues available for inspection and study. Thanks also are due to John Owen Ward of Oxford, and to Messrs. Greissle (Marks), Michaelis (Peters), Lakond (Southern), Jellinek (Sesac) and Stillman (Leeds) for supplying scores and information. Alfred J. Mapleson, Edwin F. Kalmus, and Louis Aborn (Tams-Witmark) led the way through the maze of the rental business; Dolores Hayward supplied information about translations by the Meads; Elkan-Vogel of Philadelphia answered inquiries about the Durand repertoire; several composers lent their precious manuscript scores. Music librarians, headed by Philip L. Miller at the Central Branch of the New York Public Library, and his wife, Katherine, at the Music Library on 58th Street, proved pillars of strength, as always. In addition to Gerald Fitzgerald, the staff of *Opera News*, headed by Frank Merkling, editor, put files and information freely at the researchers' disposal, as did Raymond A. Ericson, former managing editor of *Musical America*.

The congenial surroundings and agreeable climate of Theodore Erickson's Point View, near Jamestown, R.I., made summer work, both on the manuscript and later on proofs, not only bearable, but even pleasant.

Lastly (and with a sense of climax rather than conclusion), my warm gratitude goes to James S. Lombard, who made the undertaking possible by offering a commission from the University of Minnesota through the Department of Concerts and Lectures, and to Albert B. Gins, who directed the project for him from New York, both of whom showed extraordinary tolerance when the task required more time than anyone had foreseen. And a final word of thanks and appreciation to the University of Minnesota Press, who handled a thorny composition job with expertness and taste, as well as displaying that quality most valued by authors and editors — patience.

Q. E.

FOREWORD

WE BELIEVE that this book will answer a definite need. The suggestion for a readable manual of operatic production was first made at the 1956 Conference held by the Central Opera Service, a department of the National Council of the Metropolitan Opera Association. Those who were present will remember the unanimous burst of approval from over a hundred representatives of opera management which greeted the suggestion, and the applause which followed the statement of James S. Lombard, Director of the Department of Concerts and Lectures of the University of Minnesota, that he felt sure the facilities and financial backing of his institution could be drafted to achieve this result.

As a predecessor to this project, the Central Opera Service had issued a manual in pamphlet form whose immediate usefulness demonstrated the potential value of an expanded volume dealing with such information on opera production as would not speedily become obsolete.

Working with Quaintance Eaton, we, as the executive group of the Committee for the Development of Opera, tried to limit ourselves to material of permanent value. Miss Eaton assembled the facts about 259 operas, long and short, contemporary and standard. She also provided keys to their composers, publishers, translators, and the names of companies which have recently performed them. In addition, vital information about more than 260 more operas appears in an appendix to this manual. Thus the growing roster of American producing companies, now numbering over seven hundred in the United States, may plan their programs with certain knowledge of the material available. It is to be hoped that the publication of this compendium will inspire others to issue annual supplements as the expansion of the operatic scene may require. Meanwhile, we gladly endorse a book of facts that will not grow out of date, but will prove instructive to the amateur as well as the professional opera lover.

Executive Committee
COMMITTEE FOR THE DEVELOPMENT OF OPERA

TABLE OF CONTENTS

SHORT OPERAS

🚩 *Opera Production*

THIS BOOK *is compact — highly condensed and codified. It will be essential, therefore, for the reader to familiarize himself with the method of condensation and codification by reading and perhaps rereading this introduction.*

INTRODUCTION

AFTER many round-robin consultations with members of the supervising committee, it was agreed that this book, if it is to have substantial value, should be a matter of record. The choice of what to include gradually crystallized into a nucleus of time-honored works — those deservedly classed as masterpieces. To this core were added as many representatives of various genres as space permitted.

In the matter of selection, it will prove impossible to please everyone, as always. I expect any number of accusations of sins of omission. There is sure to be a cry: "Why not more Handel?" Lesser-known works of well-known composers will be cited — those of Gounod, Smetana, Wolf-Ferrari, Bizet. Many attractive names did not make our marquee at all — Berlioz, Fauré, Janacek, and Korngold among them.

Since this book concerns itself chiefly with staging, most operas performed only in concert have been regretfully put aside for a possible future supplement, although a few borderline cases are included without demur. Several other tempting categories had to be rejected. Works of Broadway parentage or upbringing (except Gershwin's "Porgy and Bess") were excluded — Bernstein's "Candide" and "West Side Story," Weill's "Street Scene," Blitzstein's "Regina," Moross' "The Golden Apple," and Engel's "The Golden Ladder." Children's operas, too, were omitted. The nearest approach to exceptions are Britten's "The Little Sweep" and "Noye's Fludde" and Hindemith's "Let's Build a Town," in all of which adults play parts.

As for American operas, it would be manifestly impossible to have included all of each season's crop. But a fresh offering by an established composer deserves respect; also, it is possible to uncover buried treasure in the neglected early works of a celebrated man. I am happy to give producers a second look at earlier examples of Moore, Giannini, and Floyd. The standard of multiple or at least repeated performances, at one time suggested as a criterion for inclusion, would have eliminated far too many native pieces that revealed merit upon closer study.

One of the first criteria for performance is the duration of a work: a producer needs to know whether an opera will fill an entire evening or must be paired with another. For this reason, operas are separated in this book into two classifications, long and short, under which categories titles appear alphabetically.

3

For practical purposes the line of demarcation between the long and the short was set arbitrarily at 90 minutes. Operas of a minimum length of one and a half hours have been considered capable of filling an evening. One exception is "Salome," which is customarily paired with another work and is therefore placed among short operas. Another is "L'Amore Medico," which, according to the publisher, is usually performed in double bill. Three operas of less than 90 minutes' duration which I have chosen to put in the long category because they are generally used as a full evening's bill are "L'Amore dei Tre Re" (87 minutes), "The Love for Three Oranges" (85 minutes), and "Wozzeck" (89 minutes).

The ratio of the short to the long operas is 109 to 150. Oddly enough, division by another yardstick shows almost the same proportion: operas that can be considered contemporary number 110, leaving 149 to the past. Of the 110, Americans are responsible for 69. (Battles still rage over the questions: "Who is contemporary?" and "Who is American?" We have determined our designations in making the above comparisons. The stickler for accuracy may amuse himself compiling his own.)

All titles are listed alphabetically in the table of contents under the divisions Long and Short. Both the original titles and their English translations appear, and in a few cases a third title in another language or a variant translation appears. Thus one can find "The Man in the Moon" or "The Portuguese Inn" as well as their originals, "Il Mondo della luna" and "L'Osteria Portoghese." Every effort has been made to avoid ambiguity and to facilitate finding an opera even at the expense of many repetitions.

With but a few exceptions, precedence has been given the original title at the beginning of the discussion of each opera, followed by the English translation, if any, and by any variants.

ABBREVIATIONS:

Amer: American	min: minutes
approx: approximately	opt: optional
arr: arranged, arrangement	orch: orchestra
bklt: booklet	orig: original
chor: chorus	prem: premiere
comp: composer	prep: preparation
conc: concert	publ: published
dial: dialogue	trans: transposed
introd: introduction	vers: version
	voc: vocal

Introductory Paragraph. This includes the name of the composer and his dates; the original language, author, and source of the libretto; the commission, if any; the place and date of the premiere; versions or adaptations; classification of drama and of the structure and style of the music; place and time of the action; number of acts and scenes; over-all timing.

Designation in a dramatic sense is made — "tragedy," "comedy," "farce," etc. — with occasional qualification, such as "historical drama" or "Oriental farce." Where possible, composers' own designations are given: "dramma giocoso" for Mozart's "Don Giovanni," "conversation piece for music" for

4

Richard Strauss's "Capriccio." (Note the absence of such classifications as "opéra comique," "operetta," and "opera seria," which are used only occasionally to clarify a historical reference.)

Musical description or classification proved to be one of the most difficult tasks: to describe structure, style, and mood without resorting to opinion, still preserving the individuality of each opera. Certain formulas resulted after long experiment and discussion.

Structurally, operas are divided into two broad categories: (1) those with mainly set numbers (often specified as arias, duets, ensembles, etc.); these may be separated by recitatives, either patter (*secco*) or accompanied, or they may be closely knit into the orchestral texture; (2) those which are "composed-through," expressed here as "continuous texture," where the orchestral web is unbroken and often of highest importance, and set numbers do not appear or are inseparable from the texture. The presence of overture or prelude and of orchestral interludes is noted.

Unusual difficulties of orchestra are indicated. Harmonic properties are often touched upon, particularly where specific influences are apparent: folk, dissonance, atonality, twelve-tone. The use of leading motives is acknowledged.

Style, when not otherwise labeled, is to be inferred from the description of story, structure, and orchestral and vocal specifications. "Verismo" (the characteristic of the Italian realistic school), is indicated where applicable. "Modern" suffices for certain techniques, in order to avoid lengthy analyses.

Classifications of vocal line include melodious; patterned after speech (I usually avoid the term "parlando"); declamatory; florid. The general description is particularized under individual roles.

I have not attempted to suggest staging beyond the specifications of locale and time; to accept any one authority would be unfair, while to compare several would require more space than is available. A suggestion to publish various ground plans (sketches showing the disposition of scenery and furniture on the stage) was regretfully abandoned for the same reasons.

Background data seldom appear, except in works which have undergone several versions, such as "The Beggar's Opera" and Monteverdi's "Orfeo."

Act and Scene Divisions. This is generally a separate entry for long operas, but is incorporated in the introductory paragraph of many short ones. Where different versions exist, these have been specified if possible.

Timings by Acts. At best, timings are only approximate, as every performance is subject to fluctuation because of cuts or individual tastes. Over-all duration, as well as timing by acts and occasionally scenes, is based upon *Opera News* calculations for the Metropolitan's radio performances, information from the New York City Opera and other companies, and from publishers and composers. In a few cases, no timings were available for various reasons, among them the lack of contemporary performances.

Synopsis of Plot. To write a short synopsis of an opera and keep it clear and sensible is very difficult. To attain to any literary distinction in such writing is virtually impossible. Outlining the story by acts soon proved impractical for reasons of space. Very few operas can be thus clarified in neat

5

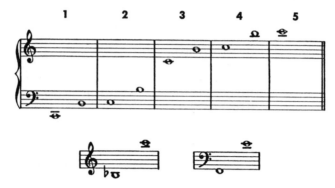

compartments. Furthermore, using space for elaborate plot outlines, particularly of well-known operas, seemed outside the province of this book. Many books exist for this purpose alone and new ones appear each season. Of course, more detail is given for new or unfamiliar operas.

Two basic approaches may be discerned: the dramatic, or blow-by-blow account of the action; and the philosophic, which gives the story line by characterization and motivation. Often a mixture of both seemed appropriate. Occasionally, as for "La Gioconda," there is no solution.

No matter how spare the outline of the plot, I tried to introduce each major character in order to establish relationships and relative importance.

Roles. These are divided into major, lesser, speaking, and bit. The character's name, type of voice, vocal requirements, and range are listed.

Information about requirements for any specific role can be seen at a glance in the sections: *Major Roles, Lesser Roles, Bit Parts.* The type of voice appears in every instance; often special problems are mentioned: the need for agility, sustained tone, high or low tessitura, and so on. The great controversial roles are noted, histrionic demands mentioned in special cases. Speaking and mute roles are indicated. Where no special requirements appear, the role may be presumed to call for average vocal abilities and portrayal of the character as revealed in the synopsis.

The exact compass of a role does not represent the complete picture of a vocal characterization, but it serves as a useful signpost. Extremes of range are most often indicated, together with mention of tessitura and optional notes. Occasionally only the top or bottom extreme is given. Where the range is omitted, no special problem exists.

The accompanying key to range symbols has been simplified from the older method, and employs capital letters throughout, numbering the ranges from 1 to 5, beginning with low C. The upper part of the accompanying illustration is the key to the range symbols. The lower part shows, on the left, a sample soprano range (Bb2 to C5) and, on the right, a sample bass range (F1 to E3).

ABBREVIATIONS:

s: soprano	t: tenor
m-s: mezzo-soprano	bar: baritone
c: contralto	bs: bass

6

bs-bar: bass-baritone	lyr: lyric
buf: buffo	spin: spinto
col: coloratura	dram: dramatic

Chorus. To show the minimum chorus required, the parts have been divided into, for example, SSAATTBB. This means that at some point the score shows two lines each for soprano, alto, tenor, and bass. Occasionally specific information is given about the desirability of large forces, the special duties of the chorus, the division into several choruses, the characters the chorus must portray. The number and complexity of this last requirement will indicate to the producer the necessity for supers, which have not otherwise been specified. The musical importance of the chorus is frequently noted in the introductory paragraph.

Ballet. The genre and the approximate number of dancers required, where available, are listed. The place in the opera and whatever detailed information appears in the score or is known from experience also appear. Interpolated ballets, such as that in the New York City Opera production of Rossini's "La Cenerentola," are mentioned when known. Solo parts are indicated wherever possible.

Production Problems or Notes. Although each producer or director may want to solve his problems for himself, certain problems are inherent in some operas, such as the swimming Rhinemaidens in "Das Rheingold," and various apotheoses, apparitions, and disappearances. Wherever a production problem is implicit in or vital to the story, it is mentioned. Several operas require quick changes of scene during musical interludes of prescribed length; this fact is noted.

Orchestra. Complete instrumentation, including stage requirements, is given (*Stage* means instruments either onstage or behind the scenes). Doubling instruments are shown in parentheses, e.g., 2 fl (picc) means that the second flute doubles piccolo. Wherever possible, the number of percussion players is given rather than a complete list of percussion instruments, although this appears occasionally.

ABBREVIATIONS:

fl: flute	trb: trombone
picc: piccolo	timp: timpani
ob: oboe	perc: percussion
Eng hrn: English horn	sn drum: snare drum
cl: clarinet	xyl: xylophone
bs cl: bass clarinet	vln: violin
bs drum: bass drum	vla: viola
sax: saxophone	vcl: violoncello
bsn: bassoon	cb: string bass
cont bsn: contra bassoon	ten: tenor
hrn: horn	bs: bass
trp: trumpet	P-Yes: piano version authorized
	by composer

Material. Getting the music for performance of an opera may not be so simple as one might imagine. The producer will probably want to rent all the musical materials, as few companies own their own music. How will he go about it?

He will probably approach one of the three large rental agencies in New York or the one in Chicago, or certain New York publishers who rent materials. This applies only to music in the public domain (released from copyright). If the work is still in copyright, the producer will apply to the original publisher (if European, to his American agent). For operas in the public domain, he will pay one fee, a rental, for all materials: orchestra (full) score, orchestral parts, a certain number of vocal scores, possibly chorus parts and chorus score, and occasionally stage guides which offer suggestions for mounting the work.

For copyrighted works he will be allowed to rent the full score and parts for a fee, but will be required to pay an additional performance fee because of the copyright. If the vocal score is already printed, he must buy it in most cases (sometimes the publisher stipulates a minimum number). All prices quoted are subject to change.

If the work is new, and the publisher has not yet determined to bring it out as an addition to his catalogue, the vocal score will be in manuscript or photocopy and must be rented.

If it is a work freshly written, the producer must get materials by negotiating personally with the composer.

If a company is producing an old opera published in a new English translation, that translation will command a performance fee as a copyrighted article. The copyright holder is the translator himself or his publisher as agent. Unpublished translations are covered by the translator's common-law copyright, if the original is out of copyright, or by the copyright on the original.

It is the custom to get all of the material from one source, but occasionally the publisher of a new translation will cooperate with one or another of the rental agencies who will supply score and parts, settling fees between them.

The province of this book is to make as clear as possible the sources of material, rather than to determine the relative excellence of service among the various rental libraries and publishers. The three large rental libraries in New York are (in alphabetical order): Edwin F. Kalmus, Alfred J. Mapleson, and Tams-Witmark (see pp. 248, 250 for addresses). May Valentine maintains a rental library for opera material in Chicago at 20 North Wacker Drive (this information arrived too late to be included elsewhere). The three New York firms will sell music, but their main business is rental.

The firms of Associated, Boosey & Hawkes, Oxford, Peters, Presser (which recently took over the Mercury catalogue, chiefly of French and American operas), Ricordi, and G. Schirmer own large copyright opera catalogues, renting scores and parts and usually selling vocal scores. Several of these firms also rent material that is in the public domain.

Information for this section was obtained from publishers' catalogues; from interviews with publishers, composers, translators, producers and performers; from the *Opera Manual* published by Central Opera Service; from the New York Public Library Music Division and Music Library.

Explanation of the use of abbreviations of publishers' names; of translators and of performing companies as sources of translations; and of libretto information follows:

FS-P: B & H (rent) means that full score and orchestra parts are available on rental from Boosey & Hawkes. (For abbreviations and addresses of publishers, pp. 247–250.)

O Tr: T13 means that another translation is available from Boris Goldovsky, 183 Clinton Road, Brookline, Mass. (For list of translators see pp. 249–250.)

O Tr: (329) means that another translation is available from the company numbered 329, Metropolitan Opera in list of performing companies (pp. 251–262).

Li: Ox (e — Dent) $1.50 means that a libretto is available from Oxford University Press in English translation by Edward Dent at a cost of $1.50.

I have attempted to indicate published translations by including the translator's name in the information about the vocal score; e.g.: VS: B & H (g and e — Martin) $10 means that the vocal score, published by Boosey & Hawkes, is in German with an English translation by Ruth and Thomas Martin and costs $10.

Generally translations not designed for singing have been omitted.

Information about librettos has not always been included, because they mean little to producers unless the work is new and the libretto must be used as a play script. The general rule to follow in reading the section on materials is that although not so marked, all contemporary materials as well as new English translations are copyrighted and subject to performance fees. These are available from the publishers, since the rental libraries handle only material in the public domain, with a few exceptions.

ABBREVIATIONS:

FS: full score	Li: libretto
P: parts (orchestra)	rent: rental
MS: miniature score	e: English
CS: chorus score	f: French
CP: chorus parts	g: German
VS: vocal score	h: Hungarian
Tr: translation	i: Italian
O Tr: other translations	r: Russian

Photographs. In the initial stages of planning, we hoped that reproductions could be included in this book both to guide the producer and to entertain the reader. Eventually the factor of cost forbade their use. References to photographs already published form the most satisfactory substitute. *Opera News* was selected as the main source of illustrations, because of its specialization and incomparable coverage, as well as its thorough and efficient index. The photographs are from *Opera News* unless otherwise specified. For settings or designs, the company or city is listed first, followed by date of issue and page number(s). Occasionally photographs from *Musical America* are listed; these are prefaced by *Mus. Amer.* Lists of photographs of performances of long operas are often broken down by acts, to allow quick reference to particular scenes and designers.

9

Performing Companies. It must be emphasized that this section is neither exhaustive nor definitive and serves merely as a glimpse of the whole picture of opera production in America and as a suggestive guide to the producer. The information came chiefly from the records of the Central Opera Service, which in turn were obtained from the annual surveys in *Opera News.* Additional data were forthcoming from publishers, composers, and producers.

The following limitations were set: if an opera had registered twenty-five American performances or fewer during approximately the past ten years, all of these are listed. Over twenty-five the number in the Central Opera Service records is given, plus the individual performances in the most recent season available. Because this book got under way as the records of the season of 1956–57 became available, this perforce remained the time limit, although many operas were brought more closely up to date.

The numbers in this section refer to the list of performing companies, which shows the companies that have performed the 259 operas in the main section.

A supplementary list of additional operas is appended and contains more than 260 operas, covering some of the kind of information that is in the text proper. This list, with a few exceptions, includes the operas that originally appeared in the *Opera Manual* but were not chosen by the committee for extended treatment here, with the addition of a number from publishers' catalogues that invited attention (Richard Strauss, Dvořák, Kodály, Cherubini, Donizetti, Mozart, Rossini, Orff, Bizet, and others), and several contemporary entries. Whenever possible, the information contained in the *Opera Manual* has been amplified (the size of the orchestra being the most important item to be added). Like the main part of the book, this list is divided into short and long operas. SO, MO, and LO follow operas in the supplementary list where known.

The index by composers, the final element in the book, gives original titles only. It offers, first, a convenient check on the length of the operas: after each title is an L (for long) or an Sh (for short).

As the size of the orchestra often proves a determining factor for producers (especially in workshops), this information is given in the index by composers as a symbol after each title: SO means a small orchestra; MO a medium orchestra; LO a large orchestra. SO includes the chamber orchestra or even smaller ensemble. MO often approximates the usual "Mozart" orchestra or the Rossini orchestra of "Cenerentola." When winds and brass exceed pairs, when the percussion is augmented, or when unusual instruments or stage instruments are added, the orchestra has been designated as LO. The producer will of course want to turn to the opera in question for more detailed study of orchestral requirements.

Bibliography. The original scheme of the book as I outlined it has suffered very few discards. Among these is a bibliography attached to each opera entry. In practice this resolved into endless repetition. I decided to dispense with these references and include them in a single section of this introduction.

The books consulted in pursuit of information for this book and consequently of interest to readers in search of amplification fall roughly into five categories: biographies; histories of opera; collections of opera plots; "read-

10

ers," or other combinations of various features, including analyses; and encyclopedias.

Biographies of the composers of the stalwart operas are standard and well known; it seems superfluous to list Toye's *Verdi* or Newman's *Wagner* at this date. A few recent books, however, proved helpful: Mosco Garner's *Puccini* (Knopf); John N. Burk's *Mozart and His Music* (Random House); and *Virgil Thomson* by Kathleen Hoover and John Cage (Yoseloff).

Grout's *A Short History of Opera* (Columbia) was very helpful. "Combination" books most often to hand were Kobbe (Putnam), Newman (Knopf, now Vintage) and Biancolli (McGraw-Hill).

As for the books of opera stories, they overflow the shelves. Constantly in use were those by Mary Ellis Peltz: *Metropolitan Opera Guide* (with Robert Lawrence, Random House); *Opera Lovers' Companion* (Ziff-Davis); and *Introduction to Opera* (Barnes & Noble). Also Harold Vincent Milligan's *Stories of Famous Operas* (Signet); Henry W. Simon's *Festival of Opera* (Hanover House).

Obscure details often could be found only in the pages of Frederick H. Mertens' *A Thousand and One Nights of Opera* (Appleton), George P. Upton's *The Standard Operas* (Hutchinson, London), Pitts Sanborn's *The Metropolitan Book of the Opera* (Simon & Schuster), Charles Annesley's *The Standard Operaglass* (Brentano's), and Henry E. Krehbiel's first and second *Book of Operas* (Macmillan). Milton Cross's *Stories of the Great Operas* (Doubleday), Rudolph Fellner's *Opera Themes and Plots* (Simon & Schuster), John Tasker Howard's *The World's Great Operas* (Random House), and J. Walker McSpadden's *Operas and Musical Comedies* (Crowell) were often opened.

Requirements and ranges for many opera arias were to be found in Sergius Kagen's *Music for the Voice* (Rinehart). Details about several short operas came to light in Louis H. Huber's *Producing Opera in the College* (Teachers College, Columbia). Valuable ideas came from the pages of Joseph Kerman's *Opera as Drama* (Knopf).

The encyclopedias by Oscar Thompson (Dodd Mead) and Baker (G. Schirmer) yielded facts, while many a missing detail turned up in G. E. Lessing's *Handbuch des Opern-Repertoires* (Boosey & Hawkes), and a doubtful premiere date could be checked in Alfred Loewenberg's *Annals of Opera, 1597–1940* (Societas Bibliographica, Geneva).

🐦 *Long Operas*

LONG OPERAS

⚓ Acis and Galatea

Music by George Frideric Handel (1685–1759). A "serenata" combining two of the composer's works: "Aci, Galatea o Polifemo," text by a Spanish princess, based on Ovid, commissioned for a duke's wedding and performed July 19, 1708; and a masque to a libretto by John Gay, probably performed at Canons in 1720, published in 1730, to which Handel added lines by Pope (both original and translated from Homer), John Hughes, and Dryden, and fitted new music. Premiere revised version: London, 1732. Vocal line extremely florid over conventional harmonies; set numbers, recitative. Overture (Sinfonia). Setting: Sicily in ancient times. Usually given in concert form; little precedent exists for staging. Two acts (approx 120 min).

Synopsis. The Cyclops Polyphemus loves the beautiful nymph Galatea. She rebuffs him, however, for love of a young shepherd, Acis. Polyphemus, in revenge, crushes Acis beneath a boulder, but Galatea in her grief transforms him into a river that bears his name. A character called Damon, not in the original myth, is introduced as commentator.

Roles. GALATEA (lyr s); flexibility required as well as sustained lyricism; D3 to A4. ACIS (t); many difficult florid passages; C2 to A3. POLYPHEMUS (bs or bs-bar); extremely florid; F1 to F3. DAMON (high or counter t or s); F3 to A4.

Chorus. STB. Extreme range for tenors. SATB version by Sir Joseph Barnby.

Orchestra. fl, picc, 2 ob, strings, harpsichord. Mozart vers (1788): fl, picc, 2 ob, 2 cl, 2 bsn, 2 hrn, strings, harpsichord.

Material. FS: Br (Möselerfer – orig) $9. FS-P: Ka (rent). VS: Br (g, e) $9; Gr (No – Barnby vers – e) $2.50; Ox (wom voices, strings, harpsichord – Arnold Goldsborough).

Photographs. Tanglewood: 3.17.41 p. 13.

Performing Companies. 203A (3.16.49). 323 (10.15.51). 211 (3.25.56). 297 (Caramoor) 57–58; 3.24.59. 251A (2.15.60).

⚓ Aida

Music by Giuseppe Verdi (1813–1901). Libretto in Italian by Antonio Ghislanzoni assisted by the composer, from the French scenario by Camille du

15

Locle, after a prose sketch by the Egyptologist Mariette Bey. Commissioned by Ismail Pasha of Egypt. Premiere: Cairo, December 24, 1871. Tragedy. Set numbers barely separated; melodious vocal line over advanced (for Verdi) harmonic structure; highly dramatic accompanied recitatives; large ensembles with chorus. Prelude. Setting: the cities of Thebes and Memphis in Egypt; time, the reign of the Pharaohs. Four acts, seven scenes (152 min).

ACT I i: Great Hall of the royal palace at Memphis (28 min); ii: Temple of Phtha (10 min). ACT II i: Terrace of Amneris' chamber in the palace (17 min); ii: Gate of Thebes (23 min). ACT III: Banks of the Nile (32 min). ACT IV i: Subterranean judgment hall in the palace (31 min); ii: Temple of Vulcan, with vault below (11 min).

Synopsis. Amneris, daughter of the Egyptian King, is in love with Radames, who has been named commander of the Egyptian army to fight the threatening Ethiopians. Radames, however, loves Amneris' slave Aida, daughter of Amonasro, the Ethiopian King. Taken prisoner in the ensuing battle, Amonasro induces Aida to lure Radames into revealing battle plans, but the conspiracy is overheard by Amneris. She denounces Radames, who is condemned as a traitor by Ramfis and the high priests. In his dark tomb Radames discovers Aida, who has hidden herself to die with him.

Major Roles. AIDA (dram or spin s); several arias demand sustained and dramatic singing, often very high tessitura; top C5. AMNERIS (m-s); many highly dramatic passages; Bb4 quite common. RADAMES (dram t); requires both sustained and very dramatic singing; top Bb3. AMONASRO (bar); ranges from sustained legato to explosive outbursts. RAMFIS, high priest of Egypt (bs); top F3. KING of Egypt (bs).

Lesser Roles. PRIESTESS (s or m-s). MESSENGER (t).

Chorus. SSATTTTBBB. Priests and priestesses, soldiers, slaves, prisoners, Egyptian populace, etc. Large chorus necessary.

Ballet. ACT I: Priestesses. ACT II: Dance of the Moorish slaves; ballet in Triumphal Scene. All as large as desired.

Orchestra. 3 fl (picc), 2 ob, Eng hrn, 2 cl, bs cl, 2 bsn, 4 hrn, 2 trp, 3 trb, tuba, timp, perc, harp, strings. *Stage:* harp, band (arranged to fit existing conditions; preferably long so-called Egyptian trumpets).

Production Note. No exact period is specified.

Material. FS-P: Map, Ka, Ri, TW (rent). FS: Br $17.50. CP: Map (i, e) (rent). VS: Ri (i) $6, (i, e) $4, $5, (conc vers) $3; Map (rent); Pet (i, g) $4; G Sc (i, e) $5. Tr: Kenney (T1).

Photographs. Metropolitan: ACT I: 3.17.41 pp. 16, 17, 22; 12.23.46 p. 19; 2.16.48 p. 18; 2.14.49 p. 19; (Gérard) 3.3.52 p. 19; 1.19.53 p. 18; 2.15.54 p. 18; 12.26.55 p. 18. ACT II: 2.26.40 p. 17; 2.14.49 p. 19 (Sc. 1); 3.6.50 p. 18; (Gérard) 3.3.52 pp. 19, 20; 1.19.53 pp. 19, 20. ACT III: 2.16.48 p. 22; 2.14.49 p. 21; (Gérard) 2.15.54 p. 20. Ballet: 12.23.46 p. 4; 2.14.49 p. 20; 3.6.50 pp. 4, 7; 1.19.53 pp. 4, 6, 13. New Orleans: 11.5.45 p. 22. Caracalla: 10.6.47 p. 15. Bob Jones College: 2.16.48 p. 8. Hollywood Bowl: 4.5.48 p. 7. N.Y. City Opera: 11.22.48 p. 14. Covent Garden: 1.10.49 p. 11. Miami: 3.14.49 p. 24. Amato: 10.31.49 p. 21. Flint: 3.6.50 p. 31. Cairo: 12.27.54 p. 14. San Antonio: 3.28.55 p. 14. Naples: 12.26.55 pp. 10, 11.

16

▶ Albert Herring

Music by Benjamin Britten (1913–   ). Libretto in English by Eric Crozier, freely adapted from a short story, "Le Rosier de Madame Husson," by Guy de Maupassant, available in English. The scene has been transferred from Nanterre to Loxford, a small market town in East Suffolk, and from once-upon-a-time to 1900, April and May. Première: Glyndebourne, June 20, 1947. Comedy. Set pieces, recitatives; difficult vocal line over complicated, dissonant accompaniment; short orchestral preludes to each act; orchestral interludes between the scenes of Acts I and II. Three acts, five scenes (137 min).

ACT I i: Morning room in Lady Billows' house (28 min — 2½ min interlude); ii: Mrs. Herring's greengrocery shop (24 min). ACT II i: A marquee set up in the rectory garden (27 min — 4½ min interlude); ii: Same as Act I, ii (18 min). ACT III. Same as Act I ii (33 min).

Synopsis. The village officials meet at the home of the pompous Lady Billows to choose the annual May Queen. But every girl mentioned is accused of some immoral act, and since all parties are sticklers for absolute purity, an impasse is reached. Superintendent Budd solves the problem by proposing a May King, the virtuous, good-as-gold Albert Herring. Albert goes through the ceremony, but a latent rebellion is aroused in him by a liberal dose of rum put in his lemonade by Sid and Nancy, young lovers whom Albert secretly envies. The hero of the day disappears; only his crushed orange-blossom wreath is found. In the midst of the ensuing death watch for him, Albert reappears to disconcert the mourners and to assert his emancipation. A sympathetic kiss from Nancy is his reward. Gaily he flings the offending orange-blossom wreath out over the audience.

Roles. LADY BILLOWS, an elderly autocrat (dram s); florid passages; top Bb4. FLORENCE PIKE, her housekeeper (c). MISS WORDSWORTH, a teacher (s); high, coloratura passages; top D5. MR. GEDGE, the vicar (bar). MR. UPFOLD, the mayor (t). SUPERINTENDENT BUDD (bs). SID, the butcher's shophand (bar). ALBERT HERRING, son of the greengrocer (t). NANCY, the baker's daughter (m-s). MRS. HERRING, Albert's mother (m-s). VILLAGE CHILDREN: Emmie (s), Cis (s), Harry (boy s — the part should be sung by a boy with an unbroken voice, who can act well in a natural urchin manner. If his chest tones are not strong enough, he can change parts with Emmie in the ensembles and in other cases sing the alternate notes provided).

Orchestra. fl (picc, alto fl), ob, cl (bs cl), bsn, hrn, perc, harp, string quintet. Piano for recitatives.

Material. All B & H. FS-P: (rent). VS $15. Li 75¢. Analytical notes 30¢.

Photographs. Glyndebourne: 10.20.47 pp. 22, 23. Aldeburgh: 10.11.48 p. 25; 10.16.50 p. 19. Berkshires: 10.10.49 p. 29. Baltimore: 1.21.52 p. 2. Hartt College: 4.26.54 p. 26. Sadler's Wells: 12.3.56 p. 26. *Mus. Amer.* N.Y. College of Music 6.57 p. 22.

💌 Alceste

Music by Christoph Willibald von Gluck (1714–1787). Libretto in Italian by Raniero da Calzabigi based on the Greek legend as told in Euripides' tragedy. Premiere: Vienna, probably December 26, 1767. Revised French version by Marie-François-Louis Grand-Leblanc, Bailli (officer of the Order of the Maltese Knights) du Roullet. Premiere: Paris, April 23, 1776 (this version more often performed today). Heroic drama. Vocal line built on inflections of speech; continuous texture; short ariosos, recitatives, arias, ensembles, and choruses incorporated. A highly declamatory style of singing is indispensable. Overture. Setting: Thessaly in the era of the Greek legend. The French version has three acts (approx. 130 min).

ACT I i: Outside the palace of Admetus in Pherae; ii: The temple of Apollo — occasionally laid in front of the temple and incorporated into the preceding scene. ACT II: Hall in the palace. ACT III i: Outside the palace — occasionally laid inside the palace and incorporated into the previous act; ii: At the gates of Hades; iii: Outside the palace.

Synopsis. King Admetus of Pherae is dying in his palace while his people pray for him. The priest brings the oracle's word that the King is to die unless someone is willing to take his place. His wife, Alceste, offers herself and is accepted by the gods. Admetus, recovering, discovers his wife's sacrifice; but all his pleas for mercy are in vain. Alceste has almost reached Hades when Hercules bars her way, and with the blessing of Apollo, restores her to earth, to her people, and to her husband.

Major Roles. ALCESTE (dram s); majestic; sustained, vigorous, and very flexible; top B♭4. ADMETUS (dram t); needs strength, facility, animation; top B♭3. HIGH PRIEST (bs-bar); many F3's. APOLLO (bar); top F3. HERCULES (bs); many F3's (this character is omitted in the Metropolitan's English version).

Lesser Roles. THANATOS, god of death (bs) (omitted in the Metropolitan version). EVANDER, a royal messenger (t). HERALD (bs). Four CHORUS LEADERS (s, m-s, t, bs). EUMELOS, ASPASIA, children of Alceste and Admetus (mute).

Chorus. SSAATTBB. Subjects of Admetus, creatures of Hades.

Ballet. As elaborate as desired.

Orchestra. 2 fl, 2 ob, 2 cl, 2 bsn, 4 hrn, 2 trp, 3 trb, perc, timp, strings. *Stage:* trumpets.

Material. FS-P: Pr (rent). VS: Pr (f) $9.25; Ri (i) $7.50, (i, g) $20, $18. CP: Map (rent). Tr: Gutman (Ru).

Photographs. Metropolitan: ACT I: 1.20.41 p. 5 (design); ii: 2.3.41 p. 6. ACT II: 1.20.41 p. 7 (design); 3.3.41 pp. 17, 20; 4.17.50 p. 8. FINALE: 3.3.41 cover.

Ballet: 3.17.41 p. 8. Several scenes: 3.24.52 pp. 4, 15, 18, 19. Boboli, Florence: 1.20.41 p. 13. Naples: 4.1.57 p. 25. *Mus. Amer.* Glyndebourne: 7.58 p. 19. *Performing Companies.* 329 (51–52, 60–61).

🎭 L'Amore dei tre re : The Love of Three Kings

Music by Italo Montemezzi (1875–1952). Libretto in Italian by Sem Benelli. Tragedy of 10th-century Italy, forty years after a barbarian invasion. Premiere: Milan, April 10, 1913. Complicated but consonant harmonies of continuous texture underlying melodious but often extremely demanding vocal line. No overture. Three acts (87 min).

ACT I: A hall in the castle of Archibaldo (31 min). ACT II: A terrace of the castle (38 min). ACT III: The crypt in the chapel of the castle (18 min).

Synopsis. Fiora, formerly betrothed to Avito, Prince of Altura, has been given as the price of peace to the son of Archibaldo, Manfredo, conqueror of Altura. The conflict between her old love and her loyalty to her husband brings about a tragedy, as the blind Archibaldo discovers her rendezvous with Avito and strangles her just as Manfredo returns from battle. Seeking to discover her clandestine lover, Archibaldo poisons Fiora's dead lips. Avito dies from a kiss, but Manfredo, too, chooses this death, refusing to reveal his rival. In a deeper symbolism, the three men personify national love bent on possessing Italy, in the person of Fiora, assuming three aspects of royalty: the pagan chieftain, the man too gentle for authority, and the young man weakened by passion.

Major Roles. ARCHIBALDO, King of Altura (bs); extremes of range E♭1 to F3; requires great dramatic ability, and must be able to lift and carry Fiora after murder. AVITO, a former Prince of Altura (lyr t); top B3. FIORA, wife of Manfredo (lyr s); dramatic passages; needs strong low range to C3, as well as sustained B♭4's, B4. MANFREDO, son of Archibaldo (bar); considerable high tessitura; top G3.

Lesser Roles. FLAMINIO, a castle guard (t). HANDMAIDEN (s). YOUNG GIRL (s). OLD WOMAN (m-s).

Chorus. Onstage: SSAATTBB. Veiled women, men and youths. Offstage: SAATB. Chapel choir.

Orchestra. 3 fl (picc), 2 ob, Eng hrn, 2 cl, 3 bsn (cont bsn), 4 hrn, 3 trp, 3 trb, tuba, timp, perc, celeste, harp, strings. *Stage:* fl, 3 trp, bells.

Material. FS-P: Ri (rent). VS: Ri (i) $10. Tr: Machlis (Ri).

Photographs. Metropolitan: 2.10.41 pp. 14, 15, 17, 19; 1.10.49 pp. 18, 19. Mexico City: 11.2.53 pp. 18–20.

Performing Companies. 329 (48–49). 130 (11.28.55). 443B (1.11.56). 180 (3.8.56).

🎭 Andrea Chénier

Music by Umberto Giordano (1867–1948). Libretto in Italian by Luigi Illica, a fictional representation of a historical character. Premiere: Milan, March

19

28, 1896. Romantic melodrama in verismo style. Score is entirely without key signatures. Accompanied recitatives and set numbers; expansive melodies. No overture. Setting: Paris at the time of the French Revolution. Four acts (111 min).
ACT I: Salon in the Chateau di Coigny, June 1789 (29 min). ACT II: Outside the Café Hottot in Paris, June 1793 (26 min). ACT III: Courtroom of a revolutionary tribunal, July 24, 1794 (41 min). ACT IV: Courtyard of St. Lazare Prison, July 25, 1794 (15 min).

Synopsis. Maddelena di Coigny, a daughter of the aristocracy, is loved hopelessly by her servant, Carlo Gérard, who predicts that very soon his lowly class will rise in revolt against their masters. His aged father is also a menial in the house. Guests gather for a gay party. Emboldened by a thinly disguised diatribe against the aristocracy sung by the poet Andrea Chénier, Gérard pleads for food for some starving peasants. Cruelly rebuffed, he rips off his livery and vows revenge. The Revolution begins; Chénier, at first a hero, comes under suspicion for denouncing Robespierre's excesses. Although urged to flee Paris, Chénier waits to meet the anonymous writer of several appealing letters — the now-destitute but still beautiful Maddelena. Chénier avows his love for her, but Gérard, now a revolutionary leader, prevents their escape. In a duel with Chénier, Gérard is wounded. Remorseful, he bids the lovers flee, then tells his rescuers he does not know who wounded him. Chénier is caught nevertheless, and Gérard, despite his conscience, is forced to denounce him formally. Maddelena offers herself to Gérard if he will help Chénier, but it is too late. The mob demands the poet's death. Maddelena bribes a jailer to allow her to substitute for another prisoner. She and Chénier go to the guillotine together.

Major Roles. MADDELENA DI COIGNY (lyr-spin s); strong personality and voice; C$\sharp$3 to C$\flat$5. CHENIER (dram t); must project poetic quality; frequent high notes; E$\flat$2 to B3. CARLO GERARD (bar); strong dramatic role; B1 to F$\sharp$3.

Lesser Roles. COUNTESS DI COIGNY, Maddelena's mother (m-s). BERSI, Maddelena's mulatto maid (m-s). MADELON, an old blind woman (m-s). PIETRO FLEVILLE, a court poet (bs or bar). MATHIEU, a waiter (bar). INCREDIBLE, a spy (t). ROUCHER, poet and friend of Chénier (bs or bar). MAJORDOMO (bs). ABBE (t). DUMAS, president of the Revolutionary Tribunal (bs). FOUQUIER-TINVILLE, prosecutor of the tribunal (bs or bar). SCHMIDT, a jailer (bs).

Chorus. SSSSAATTBB. Ladies and gentlemen of the court, citizens, soldiers, servants, peasants, prisoners, members of the tribunal.

Orchestra. 2 fl, picc, 2 ob (Eng hrn), 2 cl (bs cl), 2 bsn, 4 hrn, 3 trp, 3 trb, bs tuba, timp, perc, harp, strings. *Stage:* side drum.

Material. FS-P: AMP, Map (rent). VS: AMP (Son − i) $6. Tr: Matz (Ru).

Photographs. Metropolitan: 11.30.42 p. 28; 11.29.54 pp. 19, 20; 4.11.55 cover, p. 4; 12.23.57 pp. 19, 20. Cincinnati: 10.10.49 p. 21. Naples: 12.29.58 p. 24.

Performing Companies. 334 (1952). 443B (52–53). 130 (56–58). 329 (54–56, 57–58, 59–60). 72 (1955).

⚑ Aniara

Music by Karl-Birger Blomdahl (1916–   ). Libretto in Swedish by Erik Lindegren after Harry Martinson's epic poem. Premiere: Stockholm, May 31, 1959. Drama: "a review of man in time and space." Language is replete with new concepts and words. Music embraces many varied styles: twelve-tone, mirror forms, pointillist orchestration, choral polyphony, melody, jazz, and electronic music on tape. Vocal line, often very difficult, usually in small intervals; large skips used in emotional passages. Rhythm is varied and complicated. Brief overture. Setting: The space ship Aniara in Galactic Space; time, the future. Two acts, seven scenes and interlude (107 min).

ACT I i: Galactic Space; ii: Large hall in Aniara; Interlude; iii: The Mima Hall. ACT II i: The Mima Hall; ii: The Hall of Mirrors; iii: The Hall of Light Years; iv: Galactic Space.

Synopsis. The 8,000 passengers in the giant spaceship Aniara form a microcosm of humanity. Unable to return to Earth, which has exploded from radiation, and deflected from their course to Mars, they are doomed to a flight without goal into infinity, and to a meaningless life and equally meaningless death. Phases of passions, power struggles, religious visions run their course through the years. One Dictator succeeds another. In an interlude, the First Chief Technician compares their existence with "a little bubble in God's spirit glass." Influence for good is provided by a kind of animated machine named Mima, which tunes into the universe and communicates through a prophet, the Mimarob, by means of audible and visible symbols (always represented by an electronic sound track). A woman space pilot, Isagel, is another potent force. But Mima, after describing the destruction of the Earth, no longer wishes to live. The Dictator accuses the Mimarob and Isagel of sabotage; they are imprisoned. After years of flight, the human potential has sunk into lechery, religious quackery and foolish regimentation. A new prophetess appears: a Blind Poetess, whose ecstatic song rouses response in the people's hearts. The stern Dictator is replaced by a kinder one and a general amnesty brings Mimarob and Isagel back. But when even the regimented Space Cadets begin to waver from their iron-clad drilling, the Dictator decides that the Blind Poetess must be suppressed. Still, it is her voice that floats over the final denouement; only now she sings of death. The moment arrives when no one is left alive on Aniara.

Major Roles. THE BLIND POETESS (high s); considerable high tessitura; demands strength throughout range. THE MIMAROB (bs-bar); lengthy, taxing role. DAISY DOODY, a chanteuse who remembers the Earth's songs (s). SANDON, a comedian (buf t). FIRST CHIEF TECHNICIAN (high t); considerable falsetto. THE DICTATOR (bar). ISAGEL (dancer).

Lesser Roles. SECOND TECHNICIAN (t). THIRD TECHNICIAN (bar). DEAF MUTE (mute).

Chorus. SATB. As large as possible.

Ballet. As large as possible. Eight solo dancers: YAAL, LIBIDEL, CHEBABA, GENA, and their mirrored counterparts in a lascivious dance.

Orchestra. 3 fl (picc), 3 ob (Eng hrn), 3 cl (bs cl, 2 cl in A), alto sax (E♭

21

cl), 3 bsn (2 cont bsn), 4 hrn, 4 trp (bs trp), 3 trb, tuba, timp, harp, piano, vibraphone, perc (4 players), strings; taped sound effects (Mima's messages). *Material.* FS-P: AMP (Sch) (rent). VS: AMP (Sch) $6.75.

🖤 Anna Bolena · Anne Boleyn

Music by Gaetano Donizetti (1797–1848). Libretto in Italian by Felice Romani. Premiere: Milan, December 26, 1830. Tragedy. Demands the utmost from the principals in vocal effort and dramatic expression. Setting: Windsor Castle, 1536. Two acts, six scenes. Santa Fe version (151 min).

ACT I i: Queen Anne's apartment in Windsor Castle; ii: Castle park; iii: Anne's dressing room (77 min). ACT II i: Anteroom adjoining Anne's prison cell; ii: Vestibule adjoining the Council Chamber; iii: Prison cell in the Tower of London (74 min).

Synopsis. Henry VIII, disappointed that Anne Boleyn has borne him no male heir after he divorced Catherine of Aragon to marry her, looks with favor on Jane Seymour, Anne's closest friend. Anne, unaware of the identity of her rival, confides in Jane, whose conscience disturbs her. But Jane's ambition outweighs her loyalty. As the hunt is assembling, Rochefort, Anne's brother, recognizes Percy, Anne's former fiancé, who has been recalled to court so that Henry can devise a pretext to accuse Anne. The trickery works, for Anne, though unwilling, sees Percy, and when he threatens to kill himself at her refusal of his suit, struggles to prevent him. They are interrupted by the King, who arrests Anne, Percy, and Rochefort. Their fate is sealed, for Anne will not admit guilt and so save herself. Jane reveals that she is the cause of the Queen's plight, and is forgiven after an agonizing scene. Anne forgives everyone before going to her death.

Major Roles. HENRY VIII (bs); flexibility required; extremes of range; G1 to E3. ANNE BOLEYN (s); needs sustained dramatic ability and agility; many florid passages, skips, ornaments; Bb2 to C5. JANE SEYMOUR (m-s); extremely exacting; requires sustained, florid singing and dramatic expression; Bb2 to B4. LORD RICHARD PERCY (t); florid and robust; considerable high tessitura; D2 to C4.

Lesser Roles. LORD ROCHEFORT (bs). SMETON, page and musician of the queen (c). SIR HERVEY, official of the king (t).

Chorus. SSATTB. Ladies-in-waiting, hunters, soldiers, courtiers, officials.

Orchestra. 3 fl, 3 ob, 2 cl, 2 bsn, 4 hrn, 2 trp, 3 trb, timp, perc, strings.

Material. FS-P: Ri, TW (rent). CP: Ri (rent). VS: Ri (i), $17.50. Li: Chester Kallman (Ri) $1.

Photographs. Mus. Amer. La Scala, Act II: 8.57 p. 9.

Performing Companies. 297 (10.8.57). 275 (1959).

🖤 Arabella

Music by Richard Strauss (1864–1949). Libretto in German by Hugo von Hofmannsthal. Premiere: Dresden, July 1, 1933. Romance. Continuous texture, with several arias set into fabric. No overture. Setting: Vienna, 1860. Three acts (143 min).

ACT I: A drawingroom in a Vienna hotel (57 min). ACT II: A sumptuous public ballroom (44 min). ACT III: An open hall, with staircase, in the hotel (42 min).

Synopsis. Count and Countess Waldner, in a perpetual financial crisis, welcome a rich suitor for their daughter Arabella — Mandryka, who has fallen in love with a portrait of Arabella sent to his late uncle by the Count. The stranger is warmly regarded by Arabella, though she begs for one last fling at the traditional Coachman's Ball before marriage. Her sister Zdenka, who has been brought up as a boy to save expenses, secretly loves the young officer, Matteo, who, however, has eyes only for Arabella. At the ball Zdenka gives Matteo a key he believes to be Arabella's, but it is Zdenka who keeps the nocturnal rendezvous, undetected by the ardent Matteo. The family gathers at the hotel after the ball. Mandryka has overheard Zdenka's plot and accuses Arabella of faithlessness. He is about to depart disillusioned when Zdenka appears in feminine attire and explains all. Matteo turns his affections to her, so that both sisters find happiness.

Major Roles. COUNT WALDNER, a retired captain (bs). ADELAIDE, his wife (m-s). ARABELLA (spin s); extremes of range, flexibility, sustained; top B4. ZDENKA (s); high tessitura; touches C5. MANDRYKA, a wealthy Slavonian (bar); dramatic, considerable high tessitura; top G3. MATTEO (t); important B3, several A♯3's. COUNT ELEMER (t), COUNT DOMINIK (bar), COUNT LAMORAL (bs), Arabella's suitors. FIAKERMILLI, a spokesman at the Coachman's Ball (col s); several D5's.

Lesser Roles. FORTUNETELLER (s). From the chorus: WELKO, DJURA, JANKEL, Mandryka's servants; WAITER; ARABELLA'S COMPANION; THREE GAMBLERS; PHYSICIAN; GROOM.

Chorus. SATB. Briefly in Acts II and III. Coachmen, ball guests, hotel residents, waiters.

Orchestra. 3 fl, 2 ob, Eng hrn, 3 cl, 3 bsn, 4 hrn, 3 trp, 3 trb, tuba, timp, perc, harp, strings.

Material. FS-P: B & H (rent). VS: B & H (g) $20. Tr: Gutman (B & H).

Photographs. Metropolitan: 2.21.55 pp. 18, 19; 2.4.57 pp. 18, 19. Munich: 10.17.55 p. 28. *Mus. Amer.* Salzburg: 9.58 p. 6.

Performing Companies. 329 (56–57, 60–61).

🖤 Ariadne auf Naxos · Ariadne on Naxos

Music by Richard Strauss (1864–1949). Libretto in German by Hugo von Hofmannsthal. Original version was designed as a one-act opera to follow Molière's play, "Le Bourgeois Gentilhomme," which Hofmannsthal revised in a version called "Der Bürger als Edelmann" and for which Strauss wrote 11 incidental numbers, preserved in an orchestral suite. The version including the play is seldom performed. Strauss wrote a Prologue for the one-act opera, which is the form generally produced today. Premiere, original version: Stuttgart, October 25, 1912. Premiere, modern version: Vienna, October 4, 1916. Serio-burlesque, which pokes fun at both the heroics of grand opera and the frills of commedia dell' arte in a musical tour de force. Set numbers within continuous texture; melodious but extremely exacting vocal line; difficult ensembles and orchestra. No overture. In the prologue the period is 18th century; in the opera, antiquity. The scene of the prologue, an anteroom in a nobleman's palace, suggesting an improvised backstage; the scene of the opera, the exterior of a cave on the desert island of Naxos (100 min).

Synopsis. A Viennese nobleman has engaged two troupes to perform for his dinner guests: an opera company and a band of commedia dell' arte buffoons. In the bustle of preparation backstage the nobleman's majordomo throws both camps into confusion by announcing that they must perform simultaneously to leave time for fireworks. The young composer, unwillingly making cuts in his precious opera while his teacher tries to pacify both the Primadonna and the Tenor, is momentarily diverted by the charms of Zerbinetta, pert comedienne of the Harlequinade. But despair overcomes him as he sees in the Clowns a pollution of the holy art of music. Nevertheless, the opera goes on: Ariadne, who has been deserted by Theseus and has retired to a desert island to die, bewails the loss of her lover to a trio of sympathetic sprites while Zerbinetta and her followers vainly offer consolation. Zerbinetta in a spectacular aria dwells at some length on her own flexible and receptive attitude toward love. The young god Bacchus, released from the power of Circe, finds in Ariadne another and welcome bondage. She, believing him at first to be Death, goes willingly to his arms. Zerbinetta slyly approves.

Major Roles. ARIADNE (PRIMADONNA) (dram s); short but exacting role; long phrases, skips, extremes of tessitura; G2 to Bb4. BACCHUS (TENOR) (dram t); generally high tessitura, many A3's; range E2 to Bb3. ZERBINETTA (col s); long brilliant aria; C3 to E5. COMPOSER (s); aria includes extremes of range; Bb2 to Bb4, several Ab4's, A4's.

Lesser Roles. MUSIC MASTER (bar); F1 to G3. DANCING MASTER (t); A1 to Bb3. NAIAD (high s); C3 to D5. DRYAD (c); Ab2 to G4. ECHO (s); C3 to B4. HARLEQUIN (bar); F1 to G3. BRIGHELLA (high t); Eb2 to C4. SCARAMOUCHE (t); Eb2 to Ab3. TRUFFALDIN (bs); Eb1 to E3. LACKEY (bs); Ab1 to E3.

Bit Parts. OFFICER (t). WIGMAKER (bs). MAJORDOMO (speaking).

Orchestra. 2 fl, 2 ob, 2 cl, 2 bsn, 2 hrn, trp, trb, piano, harp, harmonium, celeste, timp, perc, strings (6.4.4.2.).

Material. FS-P: B & H (rent). VS: B & H (g) $12.50. Li 75¢. Tr: Sachse (B & H – typescript). O Tr: Mead (Ha). Blatt (215).

Photographs. Los Angeles: 10.31.49 p. 17. Berkshires: 10.29.51 p. 14. Ann Arbor: 4.26.54 p. 27. Juilliard: 11.2.53 p. 17. Salzburg: 10.8.54 p. 11. Central City: 11.1.54 p. 8. *Mus. Amer.* Opera Society, Washington, D.C.: 3.58 p. 15.

Performing Companies. 321 (1947: 3.21.58). 334 (1947: 9.49). 48 (5.49). 198A (2.27.51). 327 (5.19.52). 215 (3.2.54). 323 (3.7.54 – conc; 56–57, 1.2.58). 82 (7.54). 333 (2.27.55). 148 (3.11.55). 76 (8.23.55). 275 (7.56). 127 (56–57). 254 (11.30.56). 496 (12.56). 104 (2.6.58). 527A (2.23.58). 308A (7.11.59).

24

⚜ Armide

Music by Christoph Willibald von Gluck (1714–1787). Libretto in French by Philippe Quinault, based on "Gerusalemme Liberata" ("Jerusalem Delivered") by Torquato Tasso. Premiere: Paris, September 25, 1777. Medieval drama originally in five acts, approximate duration, 150–60 minutes. The opera is laid in Damascus in the 11th century, but as the episode around which the story revolves is purely imaginary, some latitude in production is permissible. Production can be as spectacular as desired, on the basis of the old French spectacle, using stage machinery, etc. Music is intensely dramatic and expressive; accompanied recitatives, set numbers; vocal line alternates between melodious, declamatory, and speech patterns. Overture. An edited English version, produced by the Hartt College in 1957 compresses the three middle acts into one, also reverses Acts III and IV of the original. Approximate duration of this version: 115 minutes.

Two basic sets: 1. Hidraot's palace in Damascus (Acts I, V, Acts I and III in new version). 2. A wood, which is transformed in turn into an enchanted forest and the home of the Furies, then back to the enchanted forest for the three middle acts (scenes) respectively.

Synopsis. Armide, sorceress and niece to King Hidraot of Damascus, has rendered powerless the knights of the Crusade, failing only with Rinaldo. A celebration in honor of Damascus' victory is premature; Aront, the army leader, brings news that Rinaldo has freed the captive knights. Aront dies; the citizens of Damascus cry for vengeance. Rinaldo is exiled, having incurred the wrath of the Crusade commander. He and the knight Artemidor wander into a wood, where under Armide's enchantment they are bound while sleeping. Armide, intending to slay the hero, falls in love with him instead and spirits him away. Torn by guilt at this forbidden passion, Armide summons the Furies to deliver her. Hate is powerless against her great love, but prophesies that Rinaldo will one day leave Armide of his own accord. On their way through the wood to rescue Rinaldo, his friend Ubaldo and a Danish knight successfully resist Armide's demons, who appear in the forms of their loved ones, and find their way to the palace. They persuade Rinaldo to rededicate himself to his mission. He bids farewell to Armide, who in despair orders her demons to fire the palace. She vanishes in the air (or dies in the holocaust).

Major Roles. ARMIDE (dram s); needs sustained classical singing; top A4. RINALDO (t); many passages high tessitura; A2 to G3. ARTEMIDOR (t); top G3. FURY OF HATE (c); animated, vigorous aria; F3 to A4. HIDRAOT (bar).

Lesser Roles. UBALDO (bar). DANISH KNIGHT (t). PHENICE, SIDONIE, Armide's handmaidens (s, s). ARONT (bs). DEMON AS LUCINDA (s). DEMON AS MELISSA (s). NAIAD (s).

Chorus. SATB. Citizens of Damascus, apparitions, furies. Four coryphees as chorus leaders.

Ballet. Victory ballet, gavotte, furies. As ambitious as desired.

Orchestra. 2 fl, 2 ob, 2 cl, 2 bsn, 2 hrn, 2 trp, 3 trb, timp, strings.

Material. FS-P: Map (rent). VS: Map (rent). Tr: Gutman (329); Radford (T14).

Photographs. Hartt College: 3.18.57, p. 32. Group at Central Opera Service meeting (Hartt production): 4.29.57 p. 11. *Mus. Amer.* Hartt College: 3.57 p. 54.

Performing Companies. 94 (2.9.57).

🎭 Assassinio nella cattedrale · Murder in the Cathedral

Music by Ildebrando Pizzetti (1880–   ). Libretto in Italian based on the original text of the T. S. Eliot play by Monsignore Alberto Pizzetti. Premiere: Milan, March 1, 1958. Tragedy. Complex harmonic structure, continuous texture; uses instrumental leitmotifs; mixed styles. Chorus on broad lines, reminiscent of Gregorian modes. Vocal line generally melodious, partly declamatory. Brief orchestral introduction. Setting: Canterbury Cathedral; time, December, 1170. Two acts and an Intermezzo (94 min).

Synopsis. Thomas à Becket, Archbishop of Canterbury, has quarreled with Henry II over the King's right to interfere in ecclesiastical matters, and has fled to exile in France. It is now seven years since his departure, and a chorus of Canterbury women have gathered in the Archbishop's Hall to moan his absence. A herald arrives to inform the women and priests that the Archbishop has returned to England, still unreconciled with Henry but determined to defy him. After Thomas arrives at the cathedral, four tempters try in turn to dissuade him from pursuing his course, but he survives his temptation and reaffirms his trust in God. On Christmas Day, Thomas preaches a sermon on martyrdom to his people, foreshadowing his own death. After this interlude, the four knights sent by Henry to murder the Archbishop break into the cathedral and kill him, later rationalizing their deed and prophesying its historical significance.

Major Role. ARCHBISHOP THOMAS A BECKET (bs); requires high order of dramatic ability; G1 to E3.

Lesser Roles. A HERALD (t). THREE PRIESTS (t, bar, bar). FOUR TEMPTERS (t, bar, bar, bs). TWO WOMEN (s, s). FOUR KNIGHTS (t, bar, bar, bs).

Chorus. SSATBB. Women of Canterbury, priests, attendants.

Orchestra. 3 fl (picc), 2 ob, Eng hrn, 2 cl, bs cl, 2 bsn, cont bsn, 4 hrn, 3 trp, 3 trb, tuba, timp, harp, celeste, perc, strings.

Material. FS-P: Ri (rent). VS: Ri (i) $15.

Photographs. La Scala: 4.7.58 p. 29. Empire State Festival: 10.27.58 p. 11. Trieste: 2.23.59 p. 12. *Mus. Amer.* Milan: 4.58 p. 13. Empire State Festival: 10.58 p. 31.

Performing Companies. 308A (9.17.58 – Amer prem; 7.24.59; Boston Cathedral: 9.25.59).

🎭 Aunt Caroline's Will

Music by Albert Roussel (1869–1937). Libretto in French by Nino (Michel Weber). Premiere: Paris, October 2, 1933. Farce. Set pieces, very free, a few

26

strophic; dialogue. Period can be contemporary, or near past. Three acts (150 min).
ACT I: Drawingroom, with safe and portrait of Aunt Caroline. ACT II: Maternity hospital, waiting room or corridor. ACT III: Lawyer's office.

Synopsis. Aunt Caroline, recently deceased, has left her estate to the first child of any of her three nieces. They have a year's grace, after which the money goes to the Salvation Army if no child is born. Noémie and Christine, married to Jobard and Ferdinand respectively, immediately go to the hospital with fake pregnancies. Their husbands purchase babies from other patients, but their duplicity is exposed. Beatrice, the unmarried niece, reveals a former liaison by which she has had a child, the present chauffeur of the establishment, Noel. All ends happily with Noel dividing the money and marrying Lucine, Aunt Caroline's nurse.

Major Roles. LUCINE (lyr s). The nieces: BEATRICE (m-s), NOEMIE (c), CHRISTINE (s). The husbands: FERDINAND (t); JOBARD (bar); NOEL (t).

Lesser Roles. MAITRE CORBEAU, lawyer (bs). DOCTOR PATOGENE (bs). ERNESTINE, a patient (s).

Bit Part. MME. X, mother of second baby (m-s).

Chorus. SAT. Servants, nurses, pregnant women, stenographers (sizable women's chorus preferable for Act II).

Orchestra. fl, ob, cl, bsn, hrn, trp, trb, timp, perc, strings.

Material. FS-P: Pr (Mer) (rent). VS: Pr (Mer – f, e) (rent). Tr: Milton Feist (T28).

Performing Companies. 343 (8.54 – Amer prem).

🎵 The Ballad of Baby Doe

Music by Douglas Moore (1893–   ). Libretto in English by John Latouche. Commissioned in honor of the Columbia University Bicentennial by the Koussevitzky Foundation of the Library of Congress. Premiere: Central City, Colo., July 7, 1956. Drama based on real characters and events in American history. The music has an American folk flavor, influenced by music of the '90's, and is both light and dramatic in style, increasing in seriousness and intensity; it is strongly rhythmic in many sections. Set pieces, accompanied recitative and dialogue; arias, several men's and women's quartets and other ensembles. Short orchestral interludes between scenes. No overture. Setting: Colorado; Denver and the mining town, Leadville; also Washington, D.C.; time, 1881 to 1899. Two acts, 11 scenes, 10 sets; may be as simple or as elaborate as desired. The final scene may be played in semidarkness with Tabor's "visions" spotlighted. In Central City and N.Y. City Opera version, slides of appropriate historical places and persons are flashed on inner proscenium screen (135 min).

ACT I i: Outside the Tabor Opera House, Leadville; ii: Exterior of Clarendon Hotel; iii: Augusta's apartment; iv: Lobby of the Clarendon; v: Augusta's apartment; vi: Suite in the New Willard Hotel, Washington (70 min). ACT II i: Balcony of the ballroom, Windsor Hotel, Denver; ii: Clubroom, Denver (added since premiere); iii: Matchless Mine, Leadville; iv: Augusta's study; v: Stage of the Tabor Grand Theatre, Denver, 1899 (65 min).

27

Synopsis. Elizabeth Doe, known in the mining town of Central City as Baby, leaves her husband Harvey and goes to Leadville, where she meets Horace Tabor. What begins as a flirtation ends as a deep and abiding love for the man thirty years her senior. Tabor divorces his wife, Augusta, and marries Baby Doe in Washington, shocking capital society because both are divorced. During the following years in Denver, the new Mrs. Tabor is never accepted in society. Augusta, though she has scorned Baby Doe, pays her a friendly visit to warn of the impending collapse of the silver standard and the consequent probability of Tabor's ruin. Tabor shrugs off Augusta's advice and places his hope on William Jennings Bryan, who is running for president on a free-silver plaform. His fortune collapses with Bryan's defeat. Tabor dies a beaten man; Baby Doe alone has not failed him. He has made her promise never to sell the Matchless Mine; thither she retreats when she is left alone and penniless, later to freeze to death. The lights dim . . . the years flow past and a whitehaired woman moves towards the Matchless as the snow falls quietly on her.

Major Roles. BABY DOE (lyr s); a few coloratura passages; extremes of range, several sustained pianissimo D5's. AUGUSTA (m-s); exacting in dramatic force and vocal intensity; extremes of range. HORACE TABOR (bs bar); requires dramatic ability.

Lesser Roles. WILLIAM JENNINGS BRYAN (bs). MAMA MC COURT (c). Four quartets: SAM, BUSHY, BARNEY, JACOB, Tabor's cronies (t, t, b, b); SARAH, MARY, EMILY, EFFIE, Augusta's friends (s, s, c, c); McCourt family at wedding (s, a, t, b); Four Washington dandies (t, t, b, b).

Bit Parts. OLD MINER, PRIEST, DOORMAN AT TABOR GRAND, HOTEL CLERK, PRESIDENT CHESTER A. ARTHUR, MAYOR (t); FOOTMAN, BELLBOY, BOUNCER AT SALOON, POLITICIAN (bar); KATIE (s); MEG (m-s); SAMANTHA, a maid (m-s); TWO NEWSBOYS (t, offstage); ELIZABETH AS A CHILD (s); SILVER DOLLAR AS A CHILD (mime); SILVER DOLLAR GROWN UP (m-s). (Many of these may be doubled or tripled, but preferably not drawn from the chorus.)

Chorus. SATB. Dancehall girls, miners and wives, wedding guests.

Ballet. Dancehall-type ballet in first scene. Wedding guests' dance in Act I iv (both can be done by chorus).

Orchestra. 2 fl (picc), ob, 2 cl, bsn, 2 hrn, 2 trp, 2 trb, tuba, harp, piano, perc, strings.

Material. FS-P: TW (rent). VS: TW (rent); Ch $7.50. Six solo arias available separately (Ch).

Photographs. Central City: 11.5.56 p. 13. *Mus. Amer.* N.Y. City Opera: 5.58 p. 7.

Performing Companies. 82 (7.7.56 — world prem; 7.59). 53 (1956–57). 334 (4.3.58). 48 (12.60).

🎭 Un Ballo in maschera · A Masked Ball

Music by Giuseppe Verdi (1813–1901). Libretto in Italian by Antonio Somma, based on Scribe's libretto for Auber's "Gustave III, ou Le Bal masqué."

28

Premiere: Rome, February 17, 1859. 18th-century Colonial Boston melo-drama, originally set in Sweden but changed because of political censorship. Today frequently played in Swedish setting. Set numbers tightly knit; recitative; elaborate ensembles with and without chorus; subtle musical characterizations. Prelude. Three acts, five scenes (127 min).

ACT I i: Audience chamber of the governor of Boston (21 min); ii: The den of Ulrica, the fortuneteller (29 min). ACT II: A lonely field near the gallows (31 min). ACT III i: Room in Renato's house (24 min); ii: Grand ballroom in the governor's mansion (22 min).

Synopsis. Riccardo, governor of Boston, ignores the warnings by his secretary and friend, Renato, of a plot against his life. He also ridicules the prophecy of the seeress Ulrica that he will be assassinated by a friend. When circumstances mislead Renato into believing that his wife Amelia and Riccardo (who actually are in love with each other) had kept a lover's tryst, he joins the conspirators and stabs Riccardo at a masked ball. Riccardo proves his loyalty to his friend by producing an order already signed that transfers Renato and his wife to England. Commanding a pardon for all conspirators, he dies.

Major Roles. RICCARDO (lyr t); high tessitura; demands ease in articulation; top Bb3. RENATO (bar); highly dramatic passages; sustained G3 for aria. AMELIA (dram s); needs C5 as well as strong low range. OSCAR, page to the governor (col s); high but firm sustained passages; top C5. ULRICA (c or m-s); G2 to Ab4.

Lesser Roles. SAMUEL and TOM, conspirators against the governor (both bs). A JUDGE (t). SILVANO, a sailor (bar or bs).

Bit Part. SERVANT (t).

Chorus. SATTBB. Friends of the governor, conspirators, townspeople.

Orchestra. 2 fl (picc), 2 ob (Eng hrn), 2 cl, 2 bsn, 4 hrn, 2 trp, 3 trb, tuba, timp, perc, bells, harp, strings. *Stage:* string orch and military band.

Material. FS-P: Ri, Map, TW (rent). P: Ka (rent). CP: Map (i, e); Ri (rent). VS: Ri (i) $6; G Sc (i, e — Fuchs) $5; B & H (i, e — Kenney) $3.75; Pet (i, g) $6.50. O Tr: Dent (Ox) $1.50.

Photographs. Metropolitan: 11.20.40 pp. 5–7, cover; 12.9.40 pp. 16, 17; 1.10.44 pp. 18–22. Chautauqua: 10.21.46 p. 4. Univ. of Southern California: 10.31.55 p. 17.

Performing Companies. 129A (2.27.54). 178 (3.25.54). 391 (7.6.54). 329 (54–56, 58–59). 321A (3.16.55, 56–57). 48 (3.18.55). 449 (11.3.55). 298 (10.56). 338 (56–57).

⚜ Der Barbier von Bagdad · The Barber of Bagdad

Music by Peter Cornelius (1824–1874). Libretto in German by the composer, based on "The Arabian Nights." Premiere: Weimar, December 15, 1858. Comedy. Set numbers imperceptibly woven into continuous fabric; generally melodious vocal line; only occasional use of local color; symphonic intermezzo based on muezzin's call to prayer. Setting: Bagdad; the fabled past. Two acts (100 min).

ACT I: At the house of Nureddin (55 min). ACT II: A room in the Caliph's house (45 min).

Synopsis. The wealthy young Musselman Nureddin languishes for love of Margiana, whose old companion, Bostana, promises him an interview. He sends for a barber, the garrulous Abul Hassan Ali Ebn Bekar, who delays him with his chatter. Finally Nureddin gains entry to his sweetheart's house, Abul following close behind. The Cadi, Margiana's father, goes to pray at the mosque but returns unexpectedly to punish a slave. Nureddin hides in a trunk. Abul, believing him to have been murdered, raises such a hue and cry that the Caliph himself comes to investigate. Nureddin is discovered in the trunk, but the Cadi relents at the Caliph's urging and the lovers are allowed to marry. The Caliph engages Abul to entertain him with his fanciful tales.

Major Roles. ABUL HASSAN ALI EBN BEKAR (buf bs); needs great flexibility; brilliant quick patter; good acting. NUREDDIN (lyr t); high tessitura. MARGIANA (lyr s).

Lesser Roles. THE CALIPH (bar). BABA MUSTAPHA, a Cadi, father of Margiana (t). BOSTANA (m-s). THREE MUEZZINS (t, t, b). A SLAVE.

Chorus. SATB. Friends of the Cadi, people of Bagdad, wailing women, the Caliph's entourage.

Orchestra. picc, 2 fl, 2 cl, 2 ob, 2 bsn, 4 hrn, 2 trp, 3 trb, tuba, timp, perc (2 players), harp, strings.

Material. FS-P: Map (rent). VS: Map (rent); AMP (BH − g, e) $6. Tr: Brown (T1); Reese (T31).

Performing Companies. 48 (2.51). 78 (11.21.53).

🎭 Il Barbiere di Siviglia · The Barber of Seville

Music by Giovanni Paisiello (1740–1816). Libretto in Italian by Giuseppe Petrosellini after Beaumarchais' play of the same name. Premiere: St. Petersburg, September 2, 1782. Comedy. Similar to Rossini's opera in story, but less exacting in musical style for singers. Setting: Seville; 18th century. Four acts or two with four scenes (120 min).

ACT I i: Exterior of Bartolo's house. ii: A room in Bartolo's house. ACT II, i and ii: Another room in Bartolo's house.

Synopsis. (See Rossini's "Il Barbiere di Siviglia.")

Major Roles. DR. BARTOLO, a physician (buf bs); demands good acting. ROSINA, his ward (lyr s); coloratura ability needed; top B♭4. COUNT ALMAVIVA, a Spanish nobleman (lyr t); conservative range. FIGARO, a barber (bar); calls for acting ability. DON BASILIO, music master (bar); not an extensive part.

Lesser Roles. GIOVINETTO, Bartolo's servant (t). SVEGLIATO, Bartolo's servant (bs).

Bit Parts. A NOTARY (bs). CHIEF OF POLICE (t).

Orchestra. 2 fl, 2 ob, 2 cl, 2 bsn, 2 hrn, 2 trp (not in Ricordi edition), timp, mandolin, strings.

Material. FS-P: Ri, Pr (Mer), Ka (rent). VS: Pr (Mer — e — Mead) (rent); Ri (i) $10. Tr: Mead (Ha); Kerman (23).
Photographs. Hartt College: 4.7.47 p. 26.
Performing Companies. 302 (2.13.46). 94 (1947). 23 (2.4.55).

🎭 Il Barbiere di Siviglia · The Barber of Seville

Music by Gioacchino Rossini (1792–1868). Libretto in Italian by Cesare Sterbini, after Beaumarchais' play of the same name. Premiere: Rome, February 20, 1816. Comedy. Simple harmonic structure; highly melodious; set numbers, quick patter recitatives. Overture. Setting: Seville, 18th century. Originally in two acts, three scenes. Usually played in three acts (144 min). ACT I: A square in Seville, near Dr. Bartolo's house (40 min). ACT II: A room in Dr. Bartolo's house (51 min). ACT III: Same as ACT II (53 min).

Synopsis. The pretty Rosina is the ward of old Dr. Bartolo, who plans to marry her. To win Rosina for himself, rich Count Almaviva enlists the help of Figaro, barber and factotum of all Seville. Many pranks and much confusion ensue. Almaviva disguises himself first as a drunken soldier with orders to quarter himself in Bartolo's house, next as a young music master to replace Don Basilio, each time winning short tête-à-têtes with his beloved. His schemes always masterminded by Figaro, Almaviva finally succeeds in employing the very notary summoned by Bartolo for his own use to solemnize the marriage.

Major Roles. ROSINA (orig m-s; today sung most often by col s); top C5 (s vers of arias halftone higher than m-s, with additional embellishments). COUNT ALMAVIVA (lyr t); very florid; top Bb3. FIGARO (bar); needs flexible voice of wide range, agile articulation; D2 to G3 (A3 opt). DR. BARTOLO (buf bs); demands character acting and expert vocalization; top F3. BASILIO (bs); spirited comic aria demands facility; C♯2 to F♯3 (usually trans with top E3).

Lesser Roles. BERTA, Dr. Bartolo's housekeeper (m-s or s). FIORELLO, Almaviva's servant (bar); often doubled with Sergeant. SERGEANT (t). AMBROGGIO, Bartolo's servant (bs). NOTARY, MAGISTRATE (mute).

Chorus. TTB. Serenaders, soldiers.

Orchestra. (Orig) fl (picc), ob (picc), 2 cl, 2 bsn, 2 hrn, 2 trp, bs drum, triangle, strings. *Stage:* guitar (often played on harp). 2nd ob in overture; 3 trb, timp in 2nd vers of overture.

Material. FS-P: Ha, Ka, Map, Ri, TW (rent). MS: Br (i) $17.50. CP: Ha (i, e), Map (i) (rent). VS: Ha (e — Mead) (rent); Map (rent); Pet (i, g — orig text, dial) $6.50; Ri (i) $6; G Sc (i, e) $5; B & H (e — Card — three vers: full length; with dial; streamlined) $5. Li: Dent (Ox) $1.50.

Photographs. San Francisco: 10.30.39 p. 23. Old Comédie Française: 2.24. 41 p. 5. Film: 4.21.47 p. 9. Los Angeles: 10.30.50 p. 16. Hamburg: 12.10.51 p. 14. Metropolitan (sketches): 3.1.54 pp. 18, 19, 20; (sets) 3.1.54 p. 17; 12.20.54 pp. 18–20. Buenos Aires: 12.5.55 p. 13.

⟡ The Barrier · Mulatto

Music by Jan Meyerowitz (1913–   ). Libretto in English by Langston Hughes. Premiere: New York, January 18, 1950. Contemporary drama. Occasional use of spiritual and blues ideas. Vocal line patterned largely after speech; a few set numbers, occasionally declamatory; some dialogue, recitative. Very brief prelude; prelude to Act II; interlude between II i and ii. Setting: a Georgia plantation; time, the recent past. Two acts, three scenes: the parlor in Colonel Norwood's plantation house, Albemar (96 min).

Synopsis. Since his wife's death, Colonel Norwood has lived in his plantation mansion with only the company of his negro housekeeper-mistress, Cora, her three children of whom he is the father, and a butler and servant. The Colonel has been liberal according to Southern precepts, sending all three children to school. William is quiet, rather stupid, and well-behaved; Sally, about to return to school, is torn between her black mother and white father; but Robert is all rebellion and pride. Fred Higgins comes from town with the tale that Robert has insulted a white woman and has openly claimed the Colonel as father. Incensed, the Colonel is further inflamed by Robert's arrogant use of the front door. He threatens the youth, who disarms him, strangling him in the heat of the struggle. Robert flees to the swamps, but a posse cuts him off and he is forced to return home. Cora, in a daze of misery, sees a vision acted out before her of the night, thirty years ago, when she first met the Colonel. She and her children continued to live with him even during his marriage to a pale, sickly white woman. Now she believes the Colonel to be one of the posse hunting down their son. Robert returns and goes to her room to hide temporarily. One bullet remains in the gun; he uses it on himself as the mob breaks in the door.

Major Roles. COL. THOMAS NORWOOD (bs); top F♯1 to F3. CORA LEWIS (dram s); A2 to B4. Their children: ROBERT (bar); high tessitura; top F♯3; WILLIAM (bar); top F♯3; SALLY (lyr s); top B4. SAM, butler (t); top A3. (No special vocal difficulties.)

Lesser Roles. FRED HIGGINS (t). LIVONIA, a servant (s).

Actors. TALBOT, overseer. STOREKEEPER. UNDERTAKER. HIS ASSISTANT. OTHERS IN MOB.

Ballet. Young Norwood, Young Cora, The Bride. Offstage voices of Young Norwood and Young Cora sung by Sally.

Chorus. SATTB. (Offstage — optional; can be sung by solo voices.)

Orchestra. fl, 2 cl, bsn, 2 hrn, trp, trb, harp, piano, perc (2 players), marimba, string quintet (may be reinforced). Augmented vers: 2 fl, 2 ob, 2 cl, 2 bsn, 4 hrn, 3 trp, 3 trb, tuba, harp, piano, perc (2 players), strings.

Material. FS-P: Mar (rent). VS: Mar (rent).

Photographs. Columbia Univ. 2.20.50 p. 3.

🎭 The Bartered Bride · Prodaná Nevěsta · Die Verkaufte Braut

Music by Bedřich Smetana (1824–1884). Libretto in Czech by Karel Sabina. Premiere: Prague, May 30, 1866. Lyric comedy with strong nationalistic flavor. Spirited and tuneful; harmonically simple; set numbers, accompanied recitative. Setting: a Bohemian village about 1850. Three acts (118 min).

ACT I: A square in the village (35 min). ACT II: A room in the inn (44 min) ACT III: Same as Act I (39 min).

Synopsis. (Alternate names are in parentheses.) On the patron saint's day of a Bohemian village, the townspeople celebrate, but Marenka (Marie) is unhappy: she has been promised by her parents to Micha's son, Vasek (Wenzel), who is a simpleton. Jenik (Hans), the young man she loves, deepens her despair by seeming to sign her away for money to the marriage broker, Kecal (Kezal). Actually he has bargained that she marry no one but Micha's true son. At the crucial moment Jenik steps forward and reveals that he is Micha's son by a former marriage. Thus he can marry Marenka without breaking her parents' pledge. Vasek is satisfied by being allowed to perform as a trick bear in a traveling circus.

Major Roles. KRUSINA (KRUSCHINA), a prosperous peasant (bar). LUDMILLA (KATHINKA), his wife (s). MARENKA (MARIE), their daughter (lyr s or light dram s); several C5's. MICHA, a landowner (bs). HATA (AGNES), his second wife (m-s). VASEK (WENZEL), their son (buf t); stuttering aria. JENIK (HANS), Micha's son by his first wife (lyr t). KECAL (KEZAL), marriage broker (buf bs).

Lesser Roles. CIRCUS MANAGER (STRINGER) (t). ESMERELDA, gypsy dancer (s). CIRCUS INDIAN (t). TWO BOYS (speaking bit parts).

Chorus. SATB. Villagers, actors, children.

Ballet. Prominent, with special folk numbers: Polka, Furiant, Circus Dance, etc.

Orchestra. 3 fl, 2 ob, 2 cl, 2 bsn, 3 hrn, 4 trp, 2 trb, timp, perc, strings.

Material. FS-P: Map, Ka, Ri (rent). CP: Map (g) (rent); G Sc (e) 75¢. CS: B & H (e) $1. VS: B & H (e — Newmarch) $4; G Sc (e — Farquhar) $5; MPH (e — Bartusek) $4; Pet (g) $7.50; TW (e — Bartusek) (rent); B & H (Harrison, chor-conc vers) $3.75, CS $1.50. O Tr: Blatt (215); Cross and Crozier (B & H); Ronell (522); Glowacki (B & H); Hoffman (148); Kubelik (T1); Loner (T18); MacFarren (T22); Madeleine Marshall (Map); Reese (T31); Warenskjold (38); Levin (T26); Jones (T22).

Photographs. Drawing: 10.16.39 cover. Metropolitan: 3.17.41 p. 5, cover. San Francisco: 10.5.42 cover. Stanford Univ.: 3.18.46 p. 13. Univ. of Texas: 10.29.51 p. 22. Univ. of Kansas: 10.27.52 p. 20. Waukesha: 1.24.55 p. 33 (design). Los Angeles: 3.2.55 p. 15.

Performing Companies. 334 (45–47; 1955). 391 (7.13.54). 532 (1.29.55). 148 (10.14.55). 38 (2.24.56). 99 (5.12.56). 56–57: 187, 215, 440. 72 (1958). 82 (1958). 443B (59–60).

◆ The Beggar's Opera

Music collected and arranged by Johann Pepusch (1667–1752). Libretto in English by John Gay, suggested by writings of Jonathan Swift. Ballad opera; famous musical satire, parody on *opera seria* which damaged both the English government of Walpole and the Italian opera craze, particularly the vogue of Handel. Premiere: London, February 9, 1728. New version (A) by Frederic Austin (1872–1952). Premiere: Hammersmith, 1920. Later version (B) by Edward J. Dent (1876–1957) employing all 69 original songs. Premiere: Birmingham, May 22, 1944. Benjamin Britten's (1913–   ) later version (C), retained 66 of the original songs, placing the setting in a laundry frequented by beggars, as hinted in the prologue, which suggested that the opera was performed in the great room at St. Giles to celebrate the wedding of two ballad singers. Extra dialogue written by Tyrone Guthrie for (C); much original dialogue by Gay omitted. Premiere: Cambridge, May 24, 1948. "Die Dreigroschenoper," adaptation by Kurt Weill (1900–1950); premiere: Berlin, 1928 (see "The Threepenny Opera"). Prologue and three acts (approx 90 min).

PROLOGUE: Spoken by a Beggar and a Player. ACT I: Peachum's house. ACT II: A tavern near Newgate. ACT III: Newgate Prison and a gaming house.

Synopsis. Macheath, the dashing captain of a robber band, has secretly married Polly Peachum, daughter of the leader of the robber gang. Peachum, knowing Macheath's financial state, proposes to end the union and tells Polly that he will deliver Macheath to his friend, the jailer Lockit. Polly informs on her father and warns her lover, but in vain. Macheath lingers too long at an orgy and is arrested. Lockit's daughter Lucy has a violent encounter with Polly at Newgate Prison — Lucy, it seems, has also been taken as a bride by Macheath. Lucy aids the rogue to escape, but again he is discovered and arrested. The judge pronounces sentence, but at the last moment, Macheath is reprieved from the gallows and allowed to go his merry way.

Major Roles. MR. PEACHUM, a fence (bs). MRS. PEACHUM (m-s). POLLY (m-s). CAPTAIN MACHEATH (t). FILCH, in Peachum's employ (t or speaking). LOCKIT (bar). LUCY (s). MRS. TRAPES, the tally woman (c).

Lesser Roles. BEGGAR (speaking). PLAYER (speaking — not in C). MRS. COAXER, POLLY TRULL, MRS. VIXEN, BETTY DOXY, JENNY DIVER, MRS. SLAMMEKIN, SUKY TAWDRY, MOLLY BRAZEN (divided among s, m-s, c). JEMMY TWITCHER, WAT DREARY, MAT OF THE MINT, NIMMING, NED, HARRY PADDINGTON, BEN BUDGE, ROBIN OF BAGSHOT (not in C), CROOK-FINGER'D JACK (not in C) (divided among t and bar).

Chorus. SATB. Beggars, constables, turnkeys, gentry, women of the town, members of the robbers' gang.

Orchestra. (A): fl, ob, harpsichord, strings (viola d'amore and viola da gamba ad lib.). (B): fl, ob, cl, bsn, 2 hrn, strings (ideally 4.4.2.2.1.), harpsichord or piano. (C): fl (picc), ob (Eng hrn), cl, bsn, hrn, perc, harp, strings.

Material. (A and C) FS-P: B & H (rent). VS: B & H (A) $4.50; (C) $10. (B) FS-P: Ox (rent). Voc material: Ox (rent). VS: Ox $4.15.

Photographs. A — National Opera Association, Los Angeles: 4.19.48 p. 29;

34

Univ. of Oregon: 5.1.50 p. 29; Illinois Wesleyan: 11.2.53 p. 18. C — English Opera Group: 2.7.49 p. 8; Vienna: 1.16.50 p. 28; Aldeburgh: 10.16.50 p. 18; Hamburg: 12.10.51 p. 14; Juilliard: 11.2.53 p. 31.

Performing Companies. Version A — 228 (4.25.50). 30 (5.50). 374A (3.1.52). 375A (3.7.52). 475 (5.52). 122 (11.6.52). 161 (2.8.53). 424 (4.27.53). 175A (2.25.54). 302 (4.6.54). 503A (4.54). Version B — 518 (8.15.55 — Amer prem). 179B (5.9.58). Version C — 443A (3.2.50). 321 (3.24.50). 24 (5.24.50). 193B (2.19.53). 390 (5.5.53). 147 (11.16.56). Vers undetermined — 56–57 only: 83, 147, 186, 335, 441, 511.

🗡 La Belle Hélène · The Beautiful Helen

Music by Jacques Offenbach (1819–1880). Libretto in French by Henri Meilhac and Ludovic Halévy. Premiere: Paris, December 17, 1864. Satirical comedy, a burlesque on heroes and heroines of antiquity. Very melodious; set numbers, dialogue. Short overture. Setting: ancient Greece. Three acts.

ACT I: Oracle in Sparta. ACT II: Helen's apartment in Sparta. ACT III: Nauplia, a bathing resort.

Synopsis. The fair Helen has learned from the oracle through Calchas, the high priest of Jupiter, that she is to leave her husband, King Menelaus, and go to Troy with Paris, son of King Priam. She is reluctant to accept her fate, although she does not love her aged husband. Even the appearance of the handsome Paris in the guise of a shepherd does not completely persuade her. At a mock tournament, Achilles, the two Ajaxes, Agamemnon, and others announce themselves pompously and compete for prizes. Paris wins and reveals his identity. Helen is soon in his arms. Menelaus surprises the lovers and raises a hullabaloo, summoning the other Greek kings to his aid. Finally, Menelaus decides to defer to the opinion of the augur of Venus in the matter of his wife's infidelity. A golden galley approaches. The augur proclaims that Helen must go with him; when he is revealed to be Paris himself, Menelaus is furious and calls on the Greek kings to begin the Trojan War.

Major Roles. PARIS (t). MENELAUS (t). HELEN (s); some florid passages; several C5's. AGAMEMNON, King of Kings (bar or bs). ORESTES, his son (t). CALCHAS (bs).

Lesser Roles. PYLADES, Orestes' friend (t). AJAX I, King of Salamis (t). AJAX II, King of Locrien (t). ACHILLES, King of Phtiolides (t). PHILOCOMOS, servant in the Temple of Apollo (speaking). EUTHYCLES, blacksmith (speaking). BACCHIS, Helen's confidante (s or m-s). LEAENA (m-s) and PARTHENIS (s), friends of Orestes. THETIS (m-s or s).

Chorus. SS(or A)TTBB. Important; often onstage; guards, servants, populace, etc.

Ballet. Dancers and flute players.

Orchestra. 2 fl (picc), 2 ob, 2 cl, 2 bsn, 4 hrn, 2 trp, 3 trb, tuba, timp, perc, strings.

Production Problems. Dove flying in with letter for Paris. Ship sailing away.

35

Material. FS-P: Map, Ka (rent). VS: AMP (BB — f, g) $10; Map (rent); Pr (Mer — f) $12.

Performing Companies. 203B (8.4.59).

⚑ Billy Budd

Music by Benjamin Britten (1913–   ). Libretto in English by E. M. Forster and Eric Crozier after the novella of the same name by Herman Melville. Premiere: London, December 1, 1951. Realistic historical tragedy. Although at times very melodious, a complicated harmonic structure and difficult vocal line prevail, over continuous texture. Setting: on board H.M.S. *Indomitable* during the French wars of 1797. Four acts, eight scenes (approx 150–180 min, depending on cuts; NBC-TV production approx 85 min).

ACT I i: (Prologue) Captain Vere's room; ii: Main deck and quarter deck. ACT II i: Vere's cabin; ii: The berth deck. ACT III i: Main deck and quarter deck; ii: Vere's cabin. ACT IV i: A bay of the gun deck; ii: The main deck and quarter deck.

Synopsis. Captain Vere as an old man recalls the story of Billy Budd, a youth impressed into service on the *Indomitable.* Billy incurs the enmity of Claggart, the embittered master-at-arms, who cannot endure the sweet nature that endears the youth to the rest of the crew. Claggart commands Squeak, a corporal, to spy on Billy, and overhear any talk that might be construed as mutinous. Billy catches Squeak rummaging through his possessions, whereupon Claggart bribes the intimidated Novice to do his despicable work. The old seaman Dansker warns Billy of Claggart's enmity, but the boy will not listen. The ship is geared for action against a French frigate, but the mist intervenes and spoils the chase. Vere is confronted now by Billy's supposed crime of treason; Billy, outraged, strikes Claggart dead. In spite of Vere's sympathy and pity, he is forced by the articles of war to call a drum-head court. Three officers find the lad guilty. The men wish to mutiny to save him, but Billy will not hear of it. He swings from the yard-arm, blessing Vere with his last words. Once more the captain meditates on the boy's goodness and his own divided emotions.

Major Roles. (All-male cast.) EDWARD FAIRFAX VERE (t); top A3. BILLY BUDD (bar); warm, flexible voice, several florid passages; top G3; JOHN CLAGGART (bs); top F3. MR. REDBURN, first lieutenant (bar). MR. FLINT, sailing master (bs-bar). LIEUTENANT RATCLIFF (bs). RED WHISKERS, an impressed man (t). DONALD, a sailor (bar). DANSKER, an old seaman (bs). NOVICE (t). SQUEAK (t).

Lesser Roles. BOSUN (bar). FIRST MATE (bar). SECOND MATE (bar). MAINTOP (t). NOVICE'S FRIEND (bar). ARTHUR JONES, an impressed man (bar). FOUR MIDSHIPMEN (boys' voices). CABIN BOY (speaking).

Chorus. TTBB, as large as possible. Several times 8-part; several small roles.

Orchestra. 4 fl (picc), 2 ob, Eng hrn, 2 cl (E♭ and 2nd bs cl), alto sax, 2 bsn, cont bsn, 4 hrn, 4 trp, 3 trb, tuba, timp, perc (5 players), harp, strings.

Production Problem. Sea battle in Act II.

Material. FS-P: B & H (rent). VS: B & H $15. Li: B & H $1.

Photographs. Covent Garden: 12.31.51 p. 14. Indiana Univ.: 12.8.52 p. 3. NBC-TV: 11.24.52 p. 2; 1.7.57 p. 32. *Mus. Amer.*: London: 1.1.52 p. 5. NBC-TV: 11.1.52 p. 17.

Performing Companies. 333 (10.19.52 — Amer prem). 148 (12.7.52).

☙ La Bohème · The Bohemians

Music by Giacomo Puccini (1858–1924). Libretto in Italian by Giuseppe Giacosa and Luigi Illica, based on Henri Murger's novel, "Scènes de la Vie de Bohème." Premiere: Turin, February 1, 1896. Lyric tragedy. Set numbers interwoven into continuous texture; vocal line highly melodious, often patterned on inflection of speech; complex orchestra. No overture. Setting: Latin Quarter in Paris; time, about 1830. Four acts (104 min).
ACT I: An attic studio, Christmas Eve (35 min). ACT II: Square outside the Café Momus (17 min). ACT III: The Barrière d'Enfer (24 min). ACT IV: Same as Act I (28 min).

Synopsis. Mimi, a little seamstress, lives in the building where Rodolfo, a poet, and Marcello, a painter, share a cheerless attic studio. Here their friends, Schaunard, a musician, and Colline, a philosopher, frequently join them. On Christmas Eve, Mimi's candle goes out, and she seeks a light from Rodolfo. It is love at first sight, but destined for tragedy. Rodolfo is penniless, Mimi ill. They separate, as Marcello and his pert Musetta have separated. But Mimi returns to Rodolfo when she is dying.

Major Roles. RODOLFO (lyr t); optional C4 is usually taken in the Narrative, not always at the end of Act I. MARCELLO (bar). SCHAUNARD (bar). COLLINE (bs). BENOIT, landlord (buf bs); often doubled with ALCINDORO. MIMI (lyr s); top C5. MUSETTA, a girl of the Latin Quarter (lyr s); top B4.

Lesser Roles. ALCINDORO, Musetta's admirer (bs). PARPIGNOL, toy vendor (t). CUSTOMS GUARD (bs).

Chorus. SATB, children's chorus (assisted by or replaced by sopranos). Citizens, students, street vendors, soldiers. As large as desired.

Orchestra. 3 fl (picc), 2 ob, Eng hrn, 2 cl, bs cl, 2 bsn, 4 hrn, 3 trp, 3 trb, tuba, timp, perc, xyl, harp, strings. *Stage:* 2 picc, 2 trp (usually doubled), side drum. *Reduced vers:* 2 fl, ob, 2 cl, bsn, 2 hrn, 2 trp, trb, timp, perc, xyl, harp, strings.

Material. FS-P: Ri, Ka, Map (rent). CP: Ri (Dietz) 90¢. VS: Map (rent); Ri (i, e) $4, (i) $10, (e — Dietz) $5, (f) $10, (g) $9; G Sc (i, e — Martin) $6. Tr: Blatt (315); Farquhar (321); Goldovsky (T13); Treash (358); Pleasants (T22).

Photographs. ACT I: Metropolitan: 2.5.40 p. 18; 1.26.48 p. 18; 3.28.49 p. 14; 2.16.53 pp. 19, 21; Gérard sketch: 12.22.52 p. 18. Miami: 10.20.47 p. 12; Indiana Univ.: 5.1.50 p. 28; Frankfurt: 12.6.54 p. 32; Ft. Worth: 4.9.56 p. 29; Amherst: 12.12.55 p. 30. ACT II: Metropolitan: 1.29.45 p. 19; 1.26.48 p. 19; 1.28.52 p. 15; 12.22.52 p. 19; 2.16.53 p. 20. New London Opera Co.:

10.7.46 p. 13; Amsterdam: 11.18.46 p. 10; Illinois Opera Group: 11.18.46 p. 26; Univ. of Michigan: 4.16.51 p. 22; Vienna: 12.8.52 p. 11; Spoleto: 12.20.54 p. 13; Tulsa: 10.31.55 p. 15. ACT III: Metropolitan: 2.5.40 p. 20; 1.26.48 p. 20; 12.20.48 p. 20; Gérard sketch: 12.22.52 p. 19; 2.16.53 p. 20. Italian film: 4.21.54 p. 7; Florence: 3.21.55 p. 5. *Mus. Amer.* San Francisco, Act I: 12.1.58 p. 7.

Performing Companies. Approximately 132. 1956–57 only: 3, 37, 64, 72, 77B, 85, 103, 113, 130, 136, 180, 187, 189, 216, 263, 265, 283, 295, 298, 324, 329, 331, 333, 334, 335A, 338, 344, 354, 366, 368, 391, 437, 443B, 449, 493, 524, 526.

⚓ Boris Godunov

Music and libretto in Russian by Modeste Petrovitch Mussorgsky (1839–1881). After the play by Alexander Pushkin and "The History of the Russian Empire" by Nikolai Karamzin. Premiere: St. Petersburg, January 27, 1874. Historical tragedy. Continuous texture, frequent set numbers interwoven; vocal line often patterned on inflections of speech in a strongly national idiom; many extended and difficult chorus scenes. For many years the only version known was that of Nikolai Rimsky-Korsakov, who rearranged and rescored Mussorgsky's work after the latter's death. This version was first performed in St. Petersburg, November 28, 1896. Nine versions existed as of 1958, some containing scenes absent from the Rimsky version and with orchestrations by various composers. The Rimsky version is still most commonly used, although the Metropolitan Opera in 1953 performed a reorchestration by Karol Rathaus based on Mussorgsky's piano score of 1874 and the 1928 edition of the Russian State Publishing Company. In 1960, the Metropolitan presented a version by Shostakovich (S). The English translation was by John Gutman. Setting: in and near Moscow and in Poland; time, 1598–1605. The Rimsky version (RK) is the basis for the following outline of scenes (159 min).

PROLOGUE i: Outside the Novodievitch Convent in Moscow (12 min); ii: Square in the Kremlin (Coronation) (8 min). ACT I i: Cell in the Convent of Miracles (15 min); ii: Inn near the Lithuanian border (20 min). ACT II: Room in the Tsar's palace (32 min). ACT III i: Castle in Poland, Marina's boudoir (13 min); ii: Palace gardens (16 min). ACT IV i: Forest near Kromy (16 min); ii: Duma, death of Boris (27 min).

Synopsis. Tsar Boris, who has gained the throne after the murder of Dimitri, the young Tsarevitch, is terrified by pangs of conscience. Even the company of his daughter Xenia and his son Fyodor is no consolation. His fears reach a climax as the intriguer Prince Shuisky informs him of the march on Moscow of a pretender. This false Dimitri is a monk, Gregory, who has learned from the ancient Brother Pimen that the Tsarevitch would be about his own age if he had lived. Gregory flees to an inn on the Lithuanian border in the company of a pair of vagabond friars, Varlaam and Missail. Crossing into Poland, the young man enlists the help and wins the hand of the Princess Marina,

38

who is counseled by the Jesuit monk Rangoni to yield for political advantage. Dimitri rides to Moscow through the Forest of Kromy, where a mob has gathered to celebrate the fall of Boris. A Simpleton bemoans the fate of Russia (this scene appears last in a number of versions). Boris, already distraught with visions, is goaded to madness by Pimen's account of the Tsarevitch's miraculous preservation after death, and dies, commending his realm to his son.

Major Roles. BORIS GODUNOV (bs-bar); one of the great and demanding roles of opera; requires extraordinary dramatic ability; some passages of high tessitura; Bb1 to Gb3. FYODOR (m-s). XENIA (s). NURSE (c or m-s). PRINCE SHUISKY (t). BROTHER PIMEN (bs). GREGORY OTREPIEV, later the PRETENDER, DIMITRI (t). MARINA MNISHEK (m-s or s). RANGONI (bar or bs). VARLAAM (buf bs). MISSAIL (buf t). INNKEEPER (m-s). SIMPLETON (t). No special problems of range, but these require vocal characterization and expertness as well as dramatic ability.

Lesser Roles. SHCHELKALOV, secretary of the Duma (bar). NIKITICH, a guard (bs). A BOYAR (t). LAVITSKY and CHERNIAVSKY, Jesuits (bs). OFFICER OF FRONTIER GUARD (bs). MITYUKH, a peasant (bar). A WOMAN (s). Several of these can be doubled.

Chorus. SSAATTBB. As large as possible. Peasants, pilgrims, boyars, nobles, offstage monks.

Ballet. Polonaise in Act III.

Orchestra. 3 fl (picc), 2 ob (Eng hrn), 3 cl (bs cl), 2 bsn, 4 hrn, 3 trp, 3 trb, bs tuba, timp, perc, chimes, harp, piano, strings. *Stage:* 2 trp (usually doubled), chimes, tam-tam.

Material. FS-P: Map (RK); Le (Shostakovich) (rent). VS: Ka (RK — e, g) $7.50; Le (Lamm ed. — r) $15; Ri (RK — Bessel ed. — g, e — Agate) $15; Ri (f, i) $15; Ri (orig. vers, Bessel ed. — r, f, g) $15. O Tr: Collet (Che); Gutman (329); Calvocoressi (Ox). Li: Agate (Ri) 75¢.

Photographs. Metropolitan: 11.29.43 pp. 18–19, 21–22; 4.9.45 p. 12; 3.23. 53 pp. 11, 19–20; 2.22.54 pp. 18–22. San Francisco: 11.5.45 p. 17. Los Angeles: 10.21.46 cover. London: 11.22.48 p. 26; 3.16.53 p. 14. Moscow: 3.23.53 pp. 2, 3. Bloomington: 1.17.55 p. 32.

Performing Companies. 329 (RK: 46–47; Rathaus: 52–54, 55–56, 58–59; S:60–61). 351A (1953). 188 (11.10.54). 78 (1.14.55). 110 (1.29.56). 72 (9.25.56). 130 (11.17.58 in Russian). 180 (57–58). 391 (57–58). 487 (57–58). 333 (3.26.61).

🎭 Capriccio

Music by Richard Strauss (1864–1949). Libretto in German by Clemens Krauss. Premiere: Munich, October 23, 1942. A "conversation piece for music." Melodic elaborations on sophisticated recitation. Two orchestral interludes. Setting: a castle near Paris about 1775. One act (130 min).

Synopsis. During the time of Gluck's operatic reform, a composer, a poet, and a theatrical producer discuss the relative merits of their contributions to

39

the art. The composer and the poet are both in love with the Countess, and each hopes to impress her in his own métier — Olivier with a sonnet from his play, which is rehearsed by the Countess's brother and the famous actress Clairon; Flamand with a musical setting to the poem. The Countess promises to decide between the two — music and poetry — in the shape of her two suitors, but in a long monologue it becomes apparent that she cannot make up her mind. We, too, are left uncertain as the curtain falls.

Major Roles. THE COUNTESS (dram s); youthful Marschallin; some high tessitura; top Bb4. THE COUNT, her brother (bar). FLAMAND (t). OLIVIER (bar). LA ROCHE, a theater director (bs); extremes of range; strongest personality; an extended role; G1 to F3. CLAIRON (c).

Lesser Roles. MONSIEUR TAUPE, prompter (t). ITALIAN SINGERS (s, t). MAJORDOMO (bs). SERVANTS, four (t) and four (bs).

Ballet. Gavotte by a young dancer.

Orchestra. 3 fl, 2 ob, Eng hrn, 3 cl, bs cl, 3 bsn, 4 hrn, 2 trp, 3 trb, timp, perc, cembalo, 2 harp, strings. *Stage:* vln, vlc, cembalo, string sextet.

Material. FS-P: B & H (rent). VS: B & H (g) $15. Tr: Maria Massey (commissioned for Juilliard) B & H. Supplied with vocal score.

Photographs. Salzburg (design): 10.16.50 p. 11. Munich: 12.28.53 p. 12. Berlin: 2.4.57 p. 26.

Performing Companies. 321 (4.4.54 — Amer prem). 275 (1958). 148 (12. 12.58).

🎼 Carmen

Music by Georges Bizet (1838–1875). Libretto in French by Henri Meilhac and Ludovic Halévy, after the novelette by Prosper Merimée. Originally opéra comique (with spoken dialogue). Premiere: Paris, March 5, 1875. For premiere in Vienna (October 23, 1875) Ernest Guiraud wrote accompanied recitatives to connect the set numbers. This version is commonly used outside France. Realistic tragedy. Highly melodious, with Spanish coloration; difficult vocal quintet; several large choruses. Setting: Seville and surroundings about 1820. A ballet with music from Bizet's "L'Arlesienne Suite" and other operas is often inserted in the last act, adding about 9 min. Four acts (140 min).

ACT I: A square in Seville (46 min). ACT II: Lillas Pastia's tavern (38 min). ACT III: In the mountains (36 min). ACT IV: Outside the bullring (20 min).

Synopsis. Carmen, a bewitching gypsy girl, is attracted by the indifference of a young corporal of the dragoons, Don José. She succeeds in making him forget his country sweetheart, Micaela, and his soldier's honor. He deserts to join the smugglers' band to which Carmen belongs. Soon the gypsy discards Don José for the toreador Escamillo, but when she tries to join the victorious bullfighter in the arena, Don José, after an unsuccessful attempt at reconciliation, stabs her to death.

Major Roles. CARMEN (m-s; frequently sung by s with good low register); one of the great controversial roles, requiring imaginative interpretation and demanding great acting ability as well as facile articulation and somber, sustained tones; top A4, with short B4. DON JOSE (lyr-dram t); principal aria range E2 to B♭3. ESCAMILLO (bar); needs B♭1 for Toreador Song. MICAELA (lyr s); sustained; top B4.

Lesser Roles. FRASQUITA, gypsy (s). MERCEDES, gypsy (m-s). LE REMENDADO, smuggler (t). LE DANCAIRE, smuggler (t or high bar). ZUNIGA, captain of dragoons (bs). MORALES, officer (bar).

Chorus. SATTBB, children. Innkeeper, guide, officers, dragoons, gypsies, cigarette girls, smugglers, street urchins.

Ballet. Gypsy dance in Act II; extensive Spanish ballet in Act IV, as elaborate as desired.

Orchestra. 2 fl (2 picc), 2 ob (Eng hrn), 2 cl, 2 bsn, 4 hrn, 2 trp, 3 trb, timp, perc, harp, strings. *Stage:* 2 trp, 3 trb (can be from pit).

Material. FS-P: Map, TW, Ka (rent). CP: Ka, Map, TW (rent). VS: Map, TW (rent); G Sc (f, e — Martin) $6; B & H (Card and Houston) $4.50 (three vers: full-length; opéra comique with dialogue; streamlined or concert); Pet (f) $9. Tr: Martin (G Sc); Carpenter and Norton (Univ. of Oklahoma); Asquith (T1); Foerster (333); Green (82); Goldovsky and Caldwell (T13); Morgan (T16); Merkling (Ru); Pritchard (BMI); Reese (T31); Ryan (T22).

Photographs. ACT I: Metropolitan: (Urban) 3.10.41 p. 15; 10.19.42 p. 13; (Gérard) 3.10.52 p. 15; Hollywood Bowl: 10.21.46 p. 4; Covent Garden: 12.1.47 p. 14; Moscow: 2.2.48 p. 28; Ankara: 4.11.49 p. 11; Jackson, Miss.: 1.16.50 p. 13; La Scala: 2.28.55 p. 11; San Antonio: 2.7.55 p. 30. ACT II: Metropolitan: (Urban) 1.19.42 p. 14; 2.28.49 p. 20; (Gérard) 1.26.53 p. 20; Flint, Mich.: 3.12.51 p. 31. ACT III: Metropolitan (Urban): 1.17.44 p. 20; 2.7.47 p. 21; (Gérard) 4.21.52 cover. ACT IV: Metropolitan: (Urban) 1.17.44 p. 21; 3.19.45 p. 21; 2.17.47 p. 21; (Gérard) 1.26.53 p. 23.

Performing Companies. Approximately 110. 1956–57 only: 1, 2, 16, 37, 56, 64, 136, 140, 148, 180, 182, 197, 216, 244, 264, 283, 318, 324, 329, 334, 347, 369, 391, 435, 442, 464, 495, 502.

🎝 La Cenerentola · Cinderella

Music by Gioachino Rossini (1792–1868). Libretto in Italian by Jacopo Ferretti, based on Charles Guillaume Etienne's three-act libretto for Isouard's "Cendrillon," after the fairy tale. Premiere: Rome, January 25, 1817. Comedy, with sly jibes at human nature woven into the basic fairy story. Set numbers; recitative, patter numbers; many complex ensembles. Melodious, with graceful fioriture, often very difficult for all voices. Overture. Setting: Salerno; time unspecified, but the manners suggest 18th century. Two acts, six scenes (115 min).

ACT I i: Groundfloor room of the Baron's castle; ii: A chamber in Prince Ramiro's palace; iii: Pavilion at the palace (73 min). ACT II i: A chamber in Prince Ramiro's palace; ii: Same as I i; iii: Throne room in the palace (42 min).

Synopsis. Bound by his father's will to marry soon, the Prince hopes to marry for love. Alidoro, a philosopher in the service of the Prince, comes to the Baron's castle disguised as a beggar, to investigate the daughters of the house as possible choices for the Prince's bride. Cinderella receives him warmly, but her two snobbish stepsisters, Clorinda and Tisbe, chase him away. The Prince comes to investigate for himself, changing roles with his valet, Dandini, and falls in love with the kitchen maid. However, as in the fairy story, it is only the two stepsisters who attend his ball. Alidoro plays fairy godmother and sends Cinderella to the party, where she spurns Dandini, confessing that she loves his squire. She gives one of twin bracelets to the disguised prince, who claims her the following day by recognizing it, although she is once more dressed in her rags. Crowned the new princess, Cinderella, out of the goodness of her heart, forgives her cruel stepfather and stepsisters.

Roles. DON RAMIRO, Prince of Salerno (t); considerable fioriture, high tessitura; top C4. DANDINI (bs); needs vocal flexibility as well as acting ability. DON MAGNIFICO, Baron of Mountflagon (buf bs); must command rapid articulation for two extended buffo arias. CLORINDA (s); has one extremely florid aria; top B4. TISBE (m-s). ANGELINA (CENERENTOLA) (c); several coloratura passages and one very florid aria, demands great facility and strength at extremes of range; G2 to B4. ALIDORO (bs).

Chorus. SATB. Courtiers and ladies.

Ballet. The first production at the New York City Opera introduced a comic ballet in Act II to Rossini's ballet music from "Guillaume Tell." Later a conventional ballet was substituted.

Orchestra. 2 fl, 2 ob, 2 cl, 2 bsn, 2 hrn, 2 trp, trb, timp, perc, strings.

Material. FS-P: Ri, TW, Ka (rent). VS: Ri (i) $10. Tr: Kallman (PPC); England and Durbin, Jr. (T27). Gallagher (T9). Jarrett (106A).

Photographs. Glyndebourne: 10.13.52 p. 15. N.Y. City Opera: 11.2.53 p. 18. Houston: 4.5.57 p. 26.

Performing Companies. 80 (8.9.53 – conc). 334 (9.30.54; 3.20.55; 1955–56; 1958). 283 (8.20.54). 358 (2.11.55). 366 (7.55). 36 (3.56; 56–57). 71 (10.20.55). 1956–57: 180, 185, 481.

✍ La Clemenza di Tito · The Mercy of Titus

Music by Wolfgang Amadeus Mozart (1756–1791). Libretto in Italian by Caterino Mazzola, after a libretto (used by Gluck) by Metastasio. Premiere: Prague, September 6, 1791. Historical drama. Arias, duets, ensembles, separated by recitative. Overture. Orchestral interludes if performed in several scenes; possible to perform in one set, omitting interludes. Curjel-Paumgartner version in three acts (original in two), premiere: Salzburg, 1949 (basis for scene division below). Setting: ancient Rome.

ACT I i: Vitellia's house; ii: Atrium; iii: Servilia's house; iv: Vitellia's house. ACT II i: Palatin gardens; ii: Roman square with view of Capitol; iii: Titus' house. ACT III i: Titus' study; ii: In front of Coliseum.

Synopsis. Vitellia, daughter of the late Emperor of Rome, plans revenge on Emperor Titus for his refusal to marry her. She persuades Sextus, who is in love with her, to burn down the Capitol and murder Titus. The latter has

42

loved Sextus' sister, Servilia, but discovering that she is enamored of Sextus' friend Annius, he renounces her and decides to marry Vitellia. The news comes too late to recall Sextus, who commits the arson but refuses to murder the Emperor. Under arrest, Sextus does not reveal Vitellia's part in the conspiracy, but she herself confesses. Titus gallantly forgives everyone, and the opera ends in general rejoicing.

Roles. TITUS (TITO) (lyr t); sustained, flexible but vigorous vocal line; considerable coloratura; E2 to B♭3. SEXTUS (SESTO) (c or m-s); many extremely demanding passages; florid; trill; B♭2 to B♭4. VITELLIA (dram s); needs strength throughout wide range; florid; trill; big skips; A2 (one G2) to B4 (one D5). SERVILIA (lyr s); F♯3 to A4. ANNIUS (ANNIO) (male alto, today sung by t); A1 to A3. PUBLIUS (PUBLIO), Guard commander (bs); B♭1 to F3.

Chorus. SATB. Senators, populace, etc. Unusually important for a Mozart opera.

Orchestra. 2 fl, 2 ob, 2 cl, 2 bsn, basset hrn, 2 hrn, 2 trp, timp, strings.

Production Problem. Burning the Capitol.

Material. FS-P: Ka, Pet (rent). VS: Pet (Curjel-Paumgartner – g, e) $6; (Kogel – i, g) $6. Tr: Goldovsky (T13); Radford (T14).

Performing Companies. 205 (8.4.52). 323 (10.13.52). 302 (4.25.56 – conc).

▶ Le Comte Ory · Count Ory

Music by Gioacchino Rossini (1792–1868). Libretto in French by Scribe and Delestre-Poirson, based on a Picardy ballad which may have a historical basis. Premiere: Paris, August 20, 1828. Comedy. Conventional harmonic structure; abundant delicate melodies; much florid passagework. Accompanied recitatives, set arias and numbers. Setting: Touraine, early 13th century. Prelude. Two acts (109 min).

ACT I: Before the Countess's castle (54 min). ACT II: The Countess's bedroom in the castle (55 min).

Synopsis. Count Ory, a young rake, has been missing a week. His page, Isolier, and his Tutor go to seek him. Outside Countess Adele's castle, from which all the men have set off on a crusade, the searchers come upon a hermit (Ory in disguise) and his crony (Ory's friend Robert) with a group of village girls. Isolier, not recognizing his master, consults the hermit on a matter of the heart, and Ory learns that his page is his rival for the Countess's love. That unhappy lady also consults the hermit, her purpose to seek release from a vow of widowhood, to be free to requite Isolier's love. The Tutor, putting two and two together, guesses that Ory is near, and the deception is uncovered. A letter arrives announcing the end of the crusade and the imminent return of the Countess's brother and other men. Ory determines to make his conquest in the interim. Inside the castle the Countess and her female companions feel safe from Ory and his plots. During a storm a group of "nuns" (Ory, Robert, and friends) seek shelter in the castle. "Sister Colette," again Ory, makes love

43

to Isolier, whom he mistakes for the Countess, and is detected by the page. The Countess resists until the crusaders return, and Ory and his companions are evicted from the castle.

Major Roles. COUNTESS ADELE (s); very florid; high tessitura; Bb2 to C5. ISOLIER (m-s); lyrical quality, high tessitura; C3 to B4. COUNT ORY (lyr t); requires great agility and lightness; extremely high tessitura; C2 to D4. ROBERT (sometimes called RAIMBAUD) (bs); needs facility in passagework; G#1 to G3.

Lesser Roles. RAGONDE, companion to the Countess (c); A2 to F4. TUTOR of Count Ory (bs); F1 to F3. ALICE, young peasant girl (s). YOUNG NOBLEMAN, companion to Count Ory (t).

Chorus. SSAATTBB. Noble companions of the Count, peasants, servants, attendants of the Countess, young girls, pages, heralds, etc.

Orchestra. 3 fl, 2 ob, 2 cl, 2 bsn, 4 hrn, 2 trp, 3 trb, timp, perc, strings.

Material. FS-P: Ri (rent). VS: Ri (i) $10. Tr: Simon (321).

Photographs. Glyndebourne: 10.18.54 p. 26; 10.14.57 p. 30. Berlin: 10.14. 57 p. 5. Tanglewood: 10.27.58 p. 20. Juilliard: 5.4.59 p. 7. *Mus. Amer.* Juilliard: 4.59 p. 30.

Performing Companies. 205 (3.8.58; 8.4.58). 321 (3.13.59). 53 (5.21.59). 468 (4.28.59).

The Consul

Music and libretto in English by Gian-Carlo Menotti (1911–   ). Premiere: New York City, March 15, 1950. Contemporary tragedy with social and political implications. Melodic vocal line interspersed with accompanied and unaccompanied dialogue; several set numbers; frequent dissonance, heavy orchestration. Setting: a European country; time, the present. Three acts, six scenes (114 min).

ACT I i: The Sorel home; ii: The consulate (38 min). ACT II i: The Sorel home; ii: The consulate (49 min). ACT III i: The consulate; ii: The Sorel home (27 min).

Synopsis. In order to save his own life and the lives of his freedom-loving friends, John Sorel is forced to leave his wife Magda, his baby, and his mother, and escape over the frontier. Magda visits the consul's office to obtain a visa so they can join John, but she is thwarted by the necessity for countless documents and papers. Time passes and she makes no progress. The baby dies and John's mother, losing all hope of ever seeing her son again, falls ill and also dies. At the consul's office Magda receives a message from John saying he is returning. To prevent his arrest and that of his associates, Magda sends him a note saying he will not find her alive. She returns home and turns on the gas jets, experiencing hallucinations before she dies. John arrives too late to see his wife, and is arrested by the secret police.

Major Roles. MAGDA SOREL (s); strong voice and personality; B2 to Bb4. JOHN SOREL (bar); A1 to F3. MOTHER (c); needs to display strength of character, warmth; A2 (opt G2) to Ab4. SECRETARY to the consul, a pivotal character in the drama (m-s); Ab2 to G4.

44

Lesser Roles. SECRET POLICE AGENT (bs). APPLICANTS waiting to see the consul: MR. KOFNER (bs-bar); FOREIGN WOMAN (s); ANNA GOMEZ (s); VERA BORONEL (c); NIKA MAGADOFF, MAGICIAN (t); should be able to do sleight-of-hand. ASSAN (bar); glass-cutter and John's friend. VOICE ON RECORD (s).

Bit Parts. TWO PLAINCLOTHESMEN (mute).

Orchestra. fl, ob, cl, bsn, 2 hrn, 2 trp, trb, timp, perc, harp, piano, strings.

Production Problems. Several dream sequences.

Material. All G Sc. FS-P (rent). VS $7.50. Li 75¢.

Photographs. Univ. of Denver: 10.29.51 p. 18; 2.16.53 p. 7. Hamburg: 12.10.51 p. 12. Univ. of Southern California: 2.25.52 p. 15. Univ. of New Mexico: 11.15.54 p. 16.

Performing Companies. 156 (7.51). 87 (9.51). 47 (12.51; 4.53). 435 (4.52). 294A (5.52). 390 (10.52). 334 (1952, 1954). 178 (11.52). 36 and 48 (1952). 193 (5.53). 478 (1953). 154 (2.4.54). 273 (4.54). 503B (10. 15.54). 259 (2.55). 420 (7.19.55; 56–57). 1956–57: 172, 196, 345, 465. 160 (2.12.58).

🎭 Les Contes d'Hoffmann · The Tales of Hoffmann

Music by Jacques Offenbach (1819–1880). Libretto by Jules Barbier from a play by Barbier and Michel Carré, based mainly on stories by E. T. A. Hoffmann. Orchestrated by Ernest Guiraud. Premiere (without Venetian act): Paris, February 10, 1881. Fantasy. Tightly knit sequence of set numbers; accompanied recitative; occasional dialogue; melodious vocal line. Brief prelude. The present French edition, dating back to 1907, is arranged in four acts and five scenes. The shorter Italian and German version and the present Metropolitan version call the five scenes Prologue, Acts I, II, and III, and Epilogue. Some revivals of the original libretto show Acts II and III transposed and the Muse appearing in the Prologue and then adopting the character of Hoffmann's friend, Nicklausse, to protect him during his adventures. Metropolitan version (137 min).

PROLOGUE: Luther's Tavern in Nuremberg (25 min). ACT I: Spalanzani's salon (37 min). ACT II: Giulietta's palace in Venice (27 min). ACT III: Crespel's home in Munich (40 min). EPILOGUE: Same as Prologue (8 min).

Synopsis. The poet Hoffmann meets Councillor Lindorf in Luther's Tavern and addresses him as his eternal evil antagonist. Currently in love with the opera singer Stella (who embodies three women, as he points out), Hoffmann relates to Nicklausse and his other friends the stories of his past loves. Olympia, the first, was but a lifeless automaton whom Hoffmann saw through rose-colored glasses supplied by the mad genius, Coppelius. Giulietta, the second, was a treacherous courtesan who, lured by the offer of a magic diamond, obtained Hoffmann's mirrored reflection for the sinister Dappertutto. The third, Antonia, had been forbidden by her father Crespel to sing, for he knew the exertion would kill her. Nevertheless her love for Hoffmann and the insistent goading of the diabolical Dr. Miracle led her to a fatal outburst of song. The scene reverts to the tavern, where Lindorf takes advantage of Hoffmann's drunken stupor to escort Stella to supper. Only the Muse remains to console her poet.

  · *Major Roles.* HOFFMANN (lyr t); difficult, sustained, extended role; continuous high tessitura; top B3. LINDORF,* COPPELIUS, DAPPERTUTTO, DR. MIRACLE, four manifestations of Hoffmann's evil genius; ideally sung by the same bs-bar. Often DAPPERTUTTO, whose aria, "Scintille, diamant," ranges to F♯3 (G♯3 opt), is cast with a high baritone. Almost always cast separately are STELLA * (speaking); OLYMPIA (col s); agile, top E♭5; GIULIETTA (m-s); and ANTONIA (lyr s); exacting role, high tessitura, top C5 (D5 opt).

  Lesser Roles. SPALANZANI, mechanical engineer, creator of Olympia (t). CRESPEL, Antonia's father (bs or bar). PITICHINACCIO,† lover of Giulietta (t). SCHLEMIL, lover of Giulietta (bs or bar). FRANTZ,† servant of Crespel (buf t). NICKLAUSSE (m-s). A VOICE, the picture of Antonia's mother (m-s). MUSE * (speaking).

  Bit Parts. LUTHER, tavernkeeper (bs or bar). HERMANN (bs or bar), WILHELM (t or bar), and NATHANAEL (t), students. ANDRES,* † servant of Stella (t). COCHENILLE,† servant of Spalanzani (buf t).

  Chorus. SATTBB. Students, guests of Spalanzani and Giulietta.

  Orchestra. 2 fl (picc), 2 ob, 2 cl, 2 bsn, 4 hrn, 2 trp, 3 trb, timp, perc, harp, strings. *Stage:* harp, fl, cl (usually played by pit orchestra), piano (seldom used).

  Production Problems. Quick change from Prologue to Act I and from Act III to Epilogue. Mirror episode in Act II, where Hoffmann's reflection is "stolen." Antonia episode requires sudden materializations and disappearances of Miracle as well as a painting coming to life.

  Material. FS-P: Map, Ka, TW (rent). VS: Map, TW (rent); Pet (f) $8.50; G Sc (f, e) $6. CP: Map (f, e) (rent). Tr: Gutman (Ru); Arundell (T1); Agate (T1); Blatt (215); Fuerst (435); Martin (T15); Warenskjold (38); Hammond (T22).

  Photographs. Metropolitan: PROLOGUE: 2.21.44 p. 18 (design); 11.28.55 p. 18; ACT I: 2.21.44 p. 19 (design); 11.28.55 p. 19; ACT II: 2.21.44 p. 20 (design); 11.28.55 p. 19; ACT III: 2.21.44 p. 22 (design); 11.28.55 p. 20. Pasadena: 12.21.42 p. 10. Florence: 2.21.44 pp. 6, 7. Hartt College: 4.21.58 p. 24.

  Performing Companies. 178 (3.10.48). 390 (11.18.48). 373 (5.50; 4.18. 55). 150A (4.3.51). 333 (5.1.50). 182 (2.52). 351A (1.24.53). 306A (1.25. 53). 241 (2.9.53). 457B (3.53). 124 (10.17.53). 214A (8.25.54). 334 (10. 12.54; 4.7.55). 235 (1.13.55). 1 (2.9.55). 390 (3.13.55). 321A (5.29.55). 16 (7.26.55). 394 (9.25.55; 56–57). 172 (11.10.55). 329 (55–57, 58–59). 435 (5.24.56). 1956–57: 48, 178, 209, 283, 328, 371.

🎭 Le Coq d'or · The Golden Cockerel

Music by Nikolai Rimsky-Korsakov (1844–1908). Libretto in Russian by V. I. Bielski, after a fairy tale by Pushkin. Premiere: Moscow, October 7,

---

* The roles of LINDORF, STELLA, ANDRES, and MUSE are often omitted.
† PITICHINACCIO, FRANTZ, COCHENILLE, and ANDRES can be sung by the same tenor.

1909. Fairy tale with allegorical overtones. Continuous texture with some set numbers; Oriental flavor; elaborate orchestration. Setting: mythical kingdom of King Dodon; time unspecified. Three acts (123 min).

ACT I: Palace of King Dodon (40 min). ACT II: A battlefield in the mountains (43 min). ACT III: Palace of King Dodon (40 min).

Synopsis. King Dodon and his two sons, Guidon and Aphron, are planning the defense of their kingdom when an astrologer arrives, bearing a Golden Cockerel to give an alarm whenever danger is near. Dodon accepts the bird with elaborate thanks, and the Astrologer says he will return for his reward. The Cockerel sounds the alarm; the King sends his sons off to war. At the second alarm, he goes himself. On the battlefield he finds his sons lying dead. Before he can mourn, a large tent appears, and out of it steps the beautiful Queen of Shemakha, singing "The Hymn to the Sun." Dodon, immediately captivated, agrees to marry her. In a golden coach they return to the palace. The Astrologer reappears and demands the queen in payment for the Cockerel. Dodon refuses and kills the Astrologer. The queen then spurns Dodon and the Cockerel swoops down and kills the old king with a blow of its beak. In a peal of thunder Queen Shemakha and the Cockerel disappear, while the people mourn their monarch. The Astrologer, restored to life, steps forth and in a brief epilogue declares the whole story only a fairy tale. He and the Queen are the only realities.

Roles. KING DODON (buf bs); Bb1 to F♯3. PRINCE GUIDON (t); Eb2 to Ab3. PRINCE APHRON (bar); C2 to E3. GENERAL POLKAN (bs); G♯1 to E3. ASTROLOGER (t); instrumental in quality, tessitura abnormally high; E2 to E4 (opt C♯4). QUEEN OF SHEMAKHA (col s); flexibility required, high tessitura; B♯2 to E5. GOLDEN COCKEREL (high s); F3 to C5.

Chorus. SATB.

Ballet. In one version, the entire opera is mimed by dancers while the singers sit on benches ranged at the sides of the stage.

Orchestra. 2 fl, picc, 2 ob, Eng hrn, 2 cl, bs cl, 2 bsn, cont bsn, 4 hrn, 3 trp, 3 trb, tuba, timp, perc (3 players), celeste, xyl, 2 harp, strings.

Material. FS-P: Pet, Se (rent). FS: Le $35. CP: Map (r) (rent). VS: Pet (f, r) (rent); Le (r) $12. Tr: Agate (T1); Agate-Young (72); Drowne (329).

Photographs. Metropolitan: 4.9.45 cover; 3.5.45 pp. 18–20. Philadelphia: 3.5.45 p. 22. Covent Garden: 3.29.54 p. 30; 3.26.56 p. 14.

Performing Companies. 389 (5.54). 72 (10.15.55). 288 (4.19.56). 148 (3.4.61).

✠ Cosi fan tutte · Women Are Like That

Music by Wolfgang Amadeus Mozart (1756–1791). Libretto in Italian by Lorenzo da Ponte. Premiere: Vienna, January 28, 1790. Comedy. Set numbers, recitative; melodious but demanding vocal line. Setting: Naples during the 18th century. Two acts (152 min).

ACT I i: Terrace of a café (13 min); ii: Garden of Dorabella's and Fiordiligi's house (14 min); iii: The ladies' boudoir (33 min); iv: Same as I ii (22 min). ACT II i: Same as I iii (13 min); ii: Garden of the ladies' house (27 min); iii: Terrace (9 min); iv: Banquet hall (21 min).

Synopsis. Don Alfonso, an old cynic, is determined to prove to his two young friends, Guglielmo and Ferrando, that their fiancées, Fiordiligi and Dorabella, are not to be trusted any more than are other women — in other words, hardly at all. With the help of Despina, the ladies' maid, he lays his plot. First he tells them that their lovers have been called up for duty; then he introduces them to two Albanians, who are, of course, none other than Guglielmo and Ferrando. After many inner conflicts the two women succumb to the advances of the "Albanians," forcing Guglielmo and Ferrando to concede defeat. However, Don Alfonso reveals the plot to the two duped ladies and they are reconciled with their original lovers.

Major Roles. FIORDILIGI (s); many florid and dramatic passages with extremely high and low range and wide skips; A2 to C5. DORABELLA (s or flexible m-s); D2 to Ab4. GUGLIELMO (bar); A1 to F3. FERRANDO (lyr t); D2 to Bb3. DESPINA (s), soubrette; C3 to B4. DON ALFONSO, a bachelor (buf bs); A1 to E3.

Chorus. SATB. Soldiers, wedding guests, servants, and boatmen.

Orchestra. 2 fl, 2 ob, 2 cl, 2 bsn, 2 hrn, 2 trp, timp, strings.

Material. FS-P: Ka, Map, Ri, G Sc, TW (rent). MS: Br (e, i) $17.50. VS: G Sc (i, e – Martin) $6; Map (rent); AMP (BH – i, g) $4.50; B & H (i, e – Higham) $5. CP: G Sc 50¢; Map (rent). O Tr: Caldwell and Goldovsky (T13); Mead (Ha); Rosinbum (518); Treash (358); Levin (T26); Stanford Univ. (T22). Li: Ri (i) 50¢; G Sc (Martin) 75¢.

Photographs. Tanglewood: 3.16.42 p. 19. Sadler's Wells: 12.6.48 p. 13. Glyndebourne: 10.16.50 p. 21. Hamburg: 12.10.51 p. 14. Metropolitan: 1.7.52 cover, pp. 20, 21 (Gérard sketches); 4.21.52 pp. 4, 5; 2.2.53 cover, pp. 17–22. Berlin: 10.17.55 p. 9. Piccola Scala: 4.2.56 p. 7.

Performing Companies. Approx 55; 1956–57 only: 8, 9, 16, 32, 56, 72, 120, 148, 176, 188, 275, 313, 338, 368, 378, 397, 402, 404, 419, 496.

🦁 Deseret

Music by Leonard Kastle (1929–   ). Libretto in English by Anne Howard Bailey, based on the story of the Mormons in Salt Lake City. Premiere: NBC-TV, January 1, 1961. Drama. Melodic, occasional passages of dramatic intensity; set numbers embedded in continuous texture; vocal line often patterned after speech; diatonic. No overture; Prelude to Act III. Setting: Salt Lake City, capital of the Mormon empire of Deseret, officially known as the Territory of Utah, in the fall of 1862. One set: Large vestibule of Brigham Young's palatial residence, Lion House, with double doors that lead to an elegant drawingroom, containing a rosewood piano. Three acts (132 min).

Synopsis. Eighteen-year-old Ann Eliza Webb is brought to Brigham Young's home by her parents, who are proud that the Prophet has chosen their daughter as his twenty-fifth wife. Ann Eliza is also elated, and with the natural exuberance of youth she envisions what life will be like when she is Brigham's favorite wife. But she voices doubts: the Lion is old, a great man, what can

48

she offer him? The enamored Prophet promises her that she will be his last love. This is enough to dispel her uncertainties. But meanwhile a new element has entered their lives: Captain James Dee, a Union officer, has come to solicit funds for the Civil War, and is being entertained in Lion House. The young Gentile (the Mormon name for anyone not of their faith) immediately falls in love with Ann Eliza, and she, drawn irresistibly to his youth, gaiety, and ardent attention, reciprocates. But her sense of responsibility to Deseret holds her back, and she plans to go through with the wedding, breaking her promise to meet Dee on the wedding day. At a pre-nuptial gathering, Dee bursts in, telling Ann Eliza that she has taught him a lesson in the meaning of duty. He kisses her so passionately that their love is revealed. The Webbs are angry, but the Prophet, recognizing that Ann Eliza truly yearns for Dee and the world outside, bids her go with his blessing. She will be their messenger to the outside world. This prophecy comforts the Mormons, and they join in blessing the young couple. Brigham Young looks to the wisdom of his first wife, Sarah, in facing the future.

Major Roles. ANN ELIZA WEBB (lyr s); about 18; has several dramatic passages; should be able to play simple hymn on piano; Bb2 to B4, one important C5, one C♯5 (G♯ opt). BRIGHAM YOUNG (bar or bs-bar); aged 60; needs sustained dramatic strength throughout wide range with high tessitura; F♯1 to F♯3. CAPTAIN JAMES DEE (lyr t); young, personable; B1 to C4. ELIZA WEBB (dram s); needs both sustained tone and flexibility; Bb2 to A4. CHAUNCEY WEBB (bar); needs strength and agility; F♯1 to F♯3. SARAH (m-s or c); G2 to F♯4.

Orchestra. 2 fl (picc), 2 ob (Eng hrn), 2 cl (bs cl), 2 bsn, cont bsn, 4 hrn, 2 trp, 3 trb, tuba, perc, celeste, harp, strings.

Material. FS-P: Scu (rent). VS: Scu (rent).

Performing Company. 333 (1.1.61 — prem).

📋 Les Dialogues des Carmélites · The Dialogues of the Carmelites

Music by Francis Poulenc (1899–   ). Libretto in French by Georges Bernanos, adapted to a lyric opera with the authorization of Emmet Lavery; inspired by a novel of Gertrud von le Fort and a scenario of Rev. Father Bruckberger and Philippe Agostini. Premiere: Milan, January 26, 1957. Lyric tragedy. Scenes and interludes are often set numbers by themselves; longer scenes are of continuous texture. With rare exceptions, the vocal line is modeled on the speech inflection; orchestration is basically conservative though generously sprinkled with dissonance. Setting: France, April 1789. Three acts, twelve scenes and five interludes (San Francisco production 128 min).

ACT I i: Library of the Marquis de la Force (17 min); ii: Parlor of the Carmelite convent (10 min); iii: Storeroom of the convent (9 min); iv: Infirmary of the convent (17 min). ACT II i: Chapel of the Carmelites (5 min); Interlude (4 min); ii: Assembly room of the convent (7 min); Interlude (2 min); iii: Parlor of the convent (8 min); iv: Sacristy of the convent (12 min). ACT III i: Chapel (7 min); Interlude (3 min); ii: Library of the Marquis

(5 min); Interlude (2 min); iii: The prison (11 min); Interlude (3 min); iv: Revolutionary square (6 min).

Synopsis. Blanche de la Force joins the Carmelites hoping to escape from the realities of life among the revolution-threatened French aristocracy, though she is forewarned by the elderly Prioress that the order is not a refuge, and that her salvation lies only within herself. Sister Constance tells Blanche of a premonition that they will die together. The Prioress dies and is replaced not by her assistant, Mother Marie, but by an outsider, Madame Lidoine. As the Revolution approaches Blanche is urged by her brother to return to their father, but she refuses. The revolutionary regime orders all religious groups dissolved. In the absence of Madame Lidoine, Mother Marie secures what appears to be a unanimous vow of martyrdom from the sisters. The Carmelites are forced to leave the convent. Blanche returns to her father's home as a servant and refuses Mother Marie's plea to rejoin her sisters. Arrested and sentenced to die, the nuns go to their death singing, and as the last one, Sister Constance, is executed, the repentant Blanche appears and mounts the scaffold to join her companions in martyrdom.

Major Roles. BLANCHE DE LA FORCE (lyr s); young, retiring; C3 to C5. PRIORESS (c); old, feeble quality; A2 to A4. MADAME LIDOINE, second prioress (s); D3 to Bb4. MOTHER MARIE (m-s); high tessitura, strong personality; Bb2 to Bb4. SISTER CONSTANCE (lyr s); high tessitura, youthful quality; Eb3 to C5. CHEVALIER DE LA FORCE (t), Blanche's brother; Eb2 to Bb3.

Lesser Roles. MARQUIS DE LA FORCE, Blanche's father (bar). MOTHER JEANNE, dean of the Community (c). SISTER MATHILDE (m-s). FATHER CONFESSOR of the convent (t). TWO OFFICERS (t, bar). JAILER (bar). THIERRY, a valet (bar). M. JAVELINOT, a physician (bar).

Chorus. SSAATTBB. Eleven nuns S, M-S, C. Officials of the municipality, policemen, prisoners, guards, townsfolk.

Orchestra. 3 fl, 2 ob, Eng hrn, 2 cl, bs cl, 2 bsn, cont bsn, 4 hrn, 3 trp, 3 trb, tuba, timp, perc, harp, piano, strings.

Production Problem. Numerous scene changes.

Material. All Ri. FS-P (rent). VS (f, e — Machlis) $12.

Photographs. La Scala: 3.11.57 p. 10, 11. San Francisco: 10.28.57 pp. 4, 6. *Mus. Amer.* San Francisco: 10.57 p. 3. NBC-TV: 1.1.58 p. 31.

Performing Companies. 72 (10.25.57). 333 (12.8.58).

🗡 Don Carlos

Music by Giuseppe Verdi (1813–1901). Libretto in French by Joseph Méry and Camille du Locle after the play by Friedrich Schiller. Premiere: Paris, March 11, 1867. Revised by Verdi in 1884, libretto in Italian by Ghislanzoni, dropping the first act, which shows the meeting of Elisabetta and Carlos in a forest in Fontainebleau. Premiere of revised version: Milan, January 10, 1884. In a third edition the first act was restored. Historical drama. Texture of unequal intensity, tightly knit; with set numbers of highly melodious character, several very dramatic and expressive, contrasted with more conventional arias.

50

Massive choruses and elaborate ensembles. Brief prelude. Setting: Spain; mid-16th century, the period of Philip II. Four acts, seven scenes (Metropolitan vers — 144 min).
ACT I i: Cloister of the monastery of St. Just (17 min); ii: Cloister gardens of the monastery (35 min). ACT II i: The queen's gardens in Madrid (16 min); ii: Great square before the cathedral of Our Lady of Atocha (17 min). ACT III i: The king's study in Madrid (25 min); ii: A prison cell (14 min). ACT IV: Same as Act I i (20 min).

Synopsis. Don Carlos and Elisabetta de Valois, princess of France, are betrothed; however, for reasons of state the princess is obliged to marry Carlos' father, King Philip of Spain. Carlos confides his love to Rodrigo, Marquis of Posa, who advises him to forget his stepmother and ask for the governorship of Flanders, where he may ameliorate the hardships of the Spaniards' reign. Philip refuses his son's request in great anger. The Princess Eboli, Elisabetta's lady-in-waiting, whose passionate love for Carlos is unreturned, informs the King of Carlos' love for Elisabetta. Philip orders his son thrown into prison and questions the Grand Inquisitor on the propriety of asking for the death sentence. The Inquisitor demands instead that the King denounce Rodrigo, a greater menace because of his liberalism. Philip refuses. Thoroughly embittered, the King rails at Elisabetta for her supposed unfaithfulness. Eboli repents her rash confession and determines to rescue Carlos from prison. She accomplishes this mission in the confusion that ensues after the treacherous shooting of Rodrigo, who has been marked for death as he visits his friend. Carlos and Elisabetta meet in the monastery cloister, where Charles V (or a monk in his guise) steps forward from his tomb to rescue Carlos from the pursuing King and Inquisitor.

Major Roles. ELISABETTA DE VALOIS (spin s); sustained passages; high tessitura; intense climaxes; top B4. PRINCESS EBOLI (m-s); needs dramatic power for great *scena*; C♭3 to C♭5. DON CARLOS (lyr dram t); considerable sustained singing; high tessitura; top B♭3. RODRIGO (bar); many dramatic as well as legato passages; needs good G♭3. PHILIP II (bs); requires acting ability as well as strong, expressive voice; G1 for *scena*. GRAND INQUISITOR (bs); forceful role demanding dramatic intensity, imperious bearing, commanding voice.

Lesser Roles. FRIAR (bs). THEOBALDO, Elisabetta's page (s). COUNT OF LERMA (t). ROYAL HERALD (t). CELESTIAL VOICE (s); high tessitura, top B4. COUNTESS OF AREMBERG (mute).

Chorus. SATB. Courtiers, ladies-in-waiting, citizens, priests, monks.

Ballet. Only in original version.

Orchestra. 3 fl, 2 ob (Eng hrn), 4 bsn (cont bsn), 2 cl, 4 hrn, 4 trp, 3 trb, tuba, timp, perc, bells, harp, strings. *Stage:* military band, organ.

Material. FS-P: Map, Ri (rent). CP: Map (i) (rent). VS: Map (rent); Pet (orig — g) $8; Ri (4 acts — i) $7.50; (5 acts — i) $7.50. Tr: Tucker (T2). Ducloux (T10).

Photographs. Metropolitan: 11.6.50 pp. 19–21, 25 (sketches); (Gérard sets) 3.19.51 p. 19; 4.2.51 p. 6; 3.31.52 pp. 19–21; 12.15.52 pp. 18–20. La Scala (design): 12.15.52 p. 11. Hamburg: 3.2.53 p. 15.

ⓑ Don Giovanni · Don Juan

Music by Wolfgang Amadeus Mozart (1756–1791). Libretto in Italian by Lorenzo da Ponte after Giovanni Bertati's libretto for Giuseppe Gazzaniga's "The Stone Guest" (nearest contemporary setting of the ancient Don Juan legends). Premiere: Prague, October 29, 1787. Subtitled "dramma giocoso," the opera blends comedy, melodrama, and supernatural elements. Highly melodious set numbers, often dramatically florid; both patter and accompanied recitative. Overture. Setting: in and near Seville, 17th century. Two acts, ten scenes (150 to 170 min).

ACT I i: Terrace of the Commendatore's palace (15 min); ii: Street (14 min); iii: Countryside near Don Giovanni's palace (48 min); iv: Terrace before Don Giovanni's palace (15 min); v: Ballroom in Don Giovanni's palace (7 min). ACT II i: In front of Donna Elvira's house (22 min); ii: Courtyard before Donna Anna's house (8 min); iii: Cemetery (7 min); iv: Room in Donna Anna's house (6 min); v: Dininghall in Don Giovanni's palace (20 min).

Synopsis. Don Giovanni, after a long life of amorous conquests, meets defeat in three encounters: with Donna Elvira, whom he has deserted and who has followed him; with Donna Anna, whose father, the Commendatore, he kills in his escape from an unsuccessful attempt at seduction (and who thereupon postpones her nuptials to Don Ottavio); and with the peasant Zerlina, whom he vainly tries to lure from her betrothed, the bumpkin Masetto. All vow vengeance on the Don and his harassed servant Leporello. (Elvira alone weakens in her resolution and attempts reconciliation and reform.) Don Giovanni's destruction and deliverance to hell are effected by the statue of the Commendatore, who had accepted the libertine's joking invitation to supper.

Roles. DON GIOVANNI (bs-bar); one of the great acting roles of opera; demands subtlety and versatility as well as animated singing, a flexible and polished style; G1 to E3. LEPORELLO (buf bs); demands facile articulation; F1 to E3. DONNA ANNA (dram s); florid passages; sustained, heavy, dramatic scenes; F3 to Bb4. DON OTTAVIO (t); exceptionally long-phrased, sustained and florid lines; D2 to A3. DONNA ELVIRA (s); needs agility and great power at both limits of the range; D3 to Bb4. MASETTO (bs or bar); G1 to D3. ZERLINA (light lyr s); C3 to Bb4. COMMENDATORE (bs).

Chorus. SATB. Peasants, noble guests, servants.

Ballet. Minuet and country dances.

Orchestra. 2 fl, 2 ob, 2 cl, 2 bsn, 2 hrn, 2 trp, 3 trb, timp, strings. *Stage:* (preferably) 2 ob, 2 cl, 2 bsn, 2 hrn, 3 trb, strings, mandolin (if player not available, prepared piano). (Minuet in Act I v demands three separate groups of players onstage.)

Production Problems. Quick scene changes; manifestation of statue in

52

cemetery and its appearance in Giovanni's dininghall; simulation of hellfire in II v.

Material. FS-P: Ka, Map, Ri, TW (rent). FS: Br (g, i) $17.50. MS: Pet (i, g) $10, $15. VS: AMP (BH − i, g) $5.50; B & H (i, e − Dent) $4, $5; Ri (i); $7.50; Map (i, e − Martin) (rent); G Sc (i, e) $5. CP Map (i, e) (rent). Li: Dent (Ox) $1.50. O Tr: Mathew (304).

Photographs. Prague, original: 10.21.40 cover. Metropolitan: 3.2.42 pp. 16, 17; 12.4.44 pp. 18–21, 24, 26, 28, 30; 1.1.51 pp. 18–21; 3.8.54 cover, pp. 18–20. Univ. of Michigan: 10.27.52 p. 21. Design: 12.1.52 pp. 18–20.

Performing Companies. 81A (1949). 329 (49–51, 52–55, 57–58). 334 (47–53). 254 (2.12.51). 193 (5.9.52). 290 (11.52). 487 (2.53). 113 (3. 19.53). 361 (7.23.53). 32B (54–55). 449 (3.25.54). 435 (9.24.54). 295 (1.21.55). 460 (1.25.55). 518 (3.8.55). 447 (7.55). 214A (8.3.55). 72 (11.5.55). 304 (1.8.56). 78 (1.13.56). 321A (1.22.56). 202 (1.30.56). 245 (2.12.56). 94 (2.22.56). 281 (3.16.56). 298 (5.29.56). 1956–57: 130, 210, 287, 330.

💈 Don Pasquale

Music by Gaetano Donizetti (1797–1848). Libretto in Italian by Giacomo Ruffini, based on Angelo Anelli's libretto for Stefano Pavesi's "Ser Marcantonio." Premiere: Paris, January 3, 1843. Comedy. Set numbers; vocal line of uncomplicated melodiousness; recitative. Overture. Setting: Rome, early 19th century. Three acts, five scenes (109 min).

ACT I i: A room in Don Pasquale's house (26 min); ii: At Norina's house (15 min). ACT II: Don Pasquale's drawingroom (32 min). ACT III i: Same as Act II (25 min); ii: Garden of Don Pasquale's house (11 min).

Synopsis. Ernesto, the nephew of Don Pasquale, a rich old bachelor, loves Norina, a young widow, and consequently refuses to marry the woman of his uncle's choice. Don Pasquale disinherits Ernesto and decides to take a wife himself. Ernesto's friend, Dr. Malatesta, as a ruse, introduces Norina to Don Pasquale as his sister who has just returned from a convent. The old man marries her on the spot, unaware that the ceremony is a fake. Norina, who until then has appeared all sweetness and innocence, suddenly plays the extravagant hussy, and Don Pasquale soon demands a divorce. Now Dr. Malatesta confesses his plot, and Don Pasquale, happy to regain his freedom, unites Ernesto and Norina.

Major Roles. DON PASQUALE (buf bs). ERNESTO (lyr t); high tessitura; many A3's, top Bb3. DR. MALATESTA (bar). NORINA (s); florid; top D5.

Lesser Role. NOTARY (t, bar, or bs).

Chorus. SATB. Maids, valets.

Orchestra. 2 fl (picc), 2 ob, 2 cl, 2 bsn, 4 hrn, 2 trp, 2 trb, timp, perc, strings. *Stage:* harp (orig. 2 guitars; part usually performed from special harp part or piano with harpsichord effect).

Material. FS-P: Map, Ri, TW (rent). CP: Map (i, e); Ri (rent). VS: B & H (i, e − Kenney) $3.75; Ri (i) $5. O Tr: Dent (Ox); Goldovsky and

Caldwell (T13); Marshall (321); Reese (T31); Mead (Ha); Pagano (T22); Alden (T22). Li: Ri (i) 50¢.

Photographs. Metropolitan: 12.16.40 pp. 16–18 (sketches); 12.31.45 pp. 20–22; 2.6.56 pp. 18, 19, 22. Sadler's Wells: 3.29.54 p. 31.

Performing Companies. 137A (2.23.49). 48 (5.50). 129A (52–53). 351A (1953). 306A (2.15.53). 178 (3.27.53). 287 (5.21.53). 475 (11.53). 327 (4.10.54). 16 (7.22.54). 295 (10.22.54). 378 (11.15.54; 55–56). 66 (1.29. 54). 279A (12.4.54). 334 (3.24.55). 202 (6.4.55; 10.17.55). 321A (3.3.56). 449 (3.8.56). 518 (5.3.56). 391 (7.25.56). 110 (1956). 322 (3.57). 1956–57: 148, 329, 338, 358, 439.

⚏ Die Dreigroschenoper · The Threepenny Opera

Music by Kurt Weill (1900–1950). Libretto in German by Bertolt Brecht, based on John Gay's "The Beggar's Opera." Premiere: Berlin, August 28, 1928. Social satire in European jazz idiom. Melodic; simple harmonic structure with occasional dissonance. Considerable dialogue; songs; a few ensemble numbers. Overture. Setting: the slum and waterfront sections of London, 1837. Prologue, three acts, eight scenes, two interludes (136 min).

PROLOGUE: A street in Soho. ACT I i: Peachum's Beggars' Outfit Shop; ii: An empty stable; iii: Peachum's shop. ACT II i: The stable; Interlude: A street; ii: A brothel in Wapping; iii: Cell in Newgate Prison. ACT III i: Peachum's shop; Interlude: A street; ii: Newgate Prison death cell.

Synopsis. A streetsinger tells of numerous crimes and outrages attributed to the notorious gangleader Macheath. Mr. Peachum, controller of the lucrative London beggar racket, and his wife are concerned over their daughter Polly, who has fallen in love with Macheath. Polly and Mack the Knife have, in fact, been secretly wed, and Macheath's gang celebrates the event in a stable, complete with shoplifted gifts. Polly goes home to break the news to her parents, who insist on a divorce; but Polly is adamant, for she is in love. The Peachums report Macheath to the police. Polly warns her husband to flee. He appoints her head of his gang and hides at the brothel of Jenny, who has been hired by Mrs. Peachum to inform against him. He is captured and taken to prison where Lucy, whom he has also married, upbraids him. Polly enters, and the women quarrel over who is Macheath's true love until Mrs. Peachum removes Polly. Macheath reaffirms his love for Lucy, and she secures his release. Peachum insists that Police Chief Tiger Brown recapture the villain. Jenny reveals his new hiding place, and he is put back in jail. London is in a turmoil over Victoria's coronation. As Macheath is about to be hanged a royal messenger appears with a pardon from the Queen, who has made him a noble and given him a castle. Even the Peachums are pleased.

Major Roles. JENNY (chanteuse-style singer); B2 to F4. POLLY (s); light romantic quality; B2 to G♭4. MACHEATH (t); B1 to A♭3. MR. PEACHUM (bs); C2 to F3.

Lesser Roles. MRS. PEACHUM (m-s); D3 to F♭4. LUCY (s); D♯3 to G♭4. STREETSINGER (t); D2 to D3. TIGER BROWN (bs); G♯1 to E♭3.

Chorus. SATB. Mostly in unison. Beggars, Macheath's gang, whores, constables, warden, etc.

Orchestra. tenor sax (sop sax, bsn, cl), alto sax (fl, cl), 2 trp, trb (bs trb), banjo (cello, guitar), timp, perc, harmonium (celeste), piano (conductor).

Material. VS: AMP (UE – g) $8. *Note:* English version by Marc Blitzstein has revised lyrics but retains identical musical score. "Barbara Song," sung by Polly in the original, is assigned to Lucy in the Blitzstein version. This version will not be published (TW) until after the close of the current production at the Theatre de Lys, New York, and a tour.

Photographs. New York production: 3.9.59 p. 13.

Performing Companies. 212 (6.12.52 – conc). 349 (Blitzstein vers – 3.2. 54; 55–61). 197 (1955). 203A (4.28.55). 366 (8.55).

🎵 The Duenna · Betrothal in a Monastery

Music by Serge Prokofiev (1891–1953). Libretto in Russian by the composer and Mira Mendelssohn, based on Richard Brinsley Sheridan's play "The Duenna." Premiere: Leningrad, November 3, 1946. Comedy. Pseudo-ditties alternate with more extended set numbers and recitative-like passages, often with difficult intervals in the vocal line, but generally based on simple harmonic structure, embroidered throughout with exotic touches. Brief introduction. Setting: Seville, 18th century. Four acts, nine scenes (approx 150 min).

ACT I: In front of Don Jerome's house. ACT II i: Louisa's apartment; ii: Waterfront; iii: Don Jerome's house. ACT III i: Mendoza's lodgings; ii: Don Jerome's house; iii: A convent garden. ACT IV i: A monastery; ii: Ballroom in Don Jerome's house.

Synopsis. Mendoza, a rich, middle-aged fish merchant, is intent on marrying Louisa, the young daughter of the impoverished nobleman Don Jerome. In the end, not only does he find himself married to the duenna who has been impersonating Louisa, but he has also unwittingly helped both Louisa and her brother to marry the mates of their choice.

Major Roles. DON JEROME (light, high t); D2 to A3. LOUISA, his daughter (lyr s); C#3 to B4. FERDINAND, his son (high bar), C2 to G3. MENDOZA (buf bs); A#1 to E3. THE DUENNA (MARGARET) (c); A♭2 to F3. ANTONIO, in love with Louisa (t); D2 to B♭3. CLARA (m-s); in love with Ferdinand; D♭3 to G4.

Lesser Roles. DON CARLOS, friend of Mendoza (bar); C2 to F3. FATHER AUGUSTINE, father superior of the monastery (bar); top E3. BROTHER ELIXIR (t); high tessitura; top B♭4. BROTHER CHARTREUSE (bar); top F3. BROTHER BENEDICTINE (bs); low F1.

Bit Parts. LOPEZ, Ferdinand's servant (t); top G3. ROSINA, Clara's maid (m-s). LAURETTA, Louisa's maid (c). TWO SERVANTS at the monastery (t, t). THREE FISHWIVES (s, s, m-s). THREE MASKERS (t, bar, bar). FRIEND OF DON JEROME (mute); plays the cornet. SERVANT of Don Jerome (mute); plays the bass drum.

55

Chorus. SAATTBB. Nuns, monks, servants, maskers, tradespeople, guests of Don Jerome.

Orchestra. 2 fl (picc), 2 ob (Eng hrn), 2 cl (bs cl), 2 bsn (cont bsn), 4 hrn, 3 trp, 3 trb, tuba, timp, perc, harp, strings. *Stage:* fl, alto sax, strings (Act III); 2 cl, trp, 2 hrn, trb, tuba, perc (Act IV); musical glasses (Act IV).

Material. FS-P: Le (rent). VS: Le (e — Jean Karsavina) $15.

Photographs. Lemonade Opera: 10.25.48 p. 15.

Performing Companies. 321C (1948 — drastically cut vers). 73 (3.59).

📓 Elektra

Music by Richard Strauss (1864–1949). Libretto in German by Hugo von Hofmannsthal, based on Sophocles' play. Premiere: Dresden, January 25, 1909. Classic tragedy. Continuous texture, mostly very dissonant, putting the more conservative passages into strong relief; extensive use of characteristic motives. The vocal line, very difficult technically and musically, is patterned mainly on the inflection of speech. Setting: Mycenae, legendary Greece. No overture. One act: Courtyard in the royal palace (98 min).

Synopsis. Elektra, mourning the murder of her father Agamemnon by her mother Klytemnestra and Klytemnestra's lover Aegisthus, thinks only of revenge. She taunts her mother with a cure for nightmares: murder of someone close. Furiously she threatens Klytemnestra with vengeance by Agamemnon's ghost. Klytemnestra is comforted by the message that Orestes, Agamemnon's son, is dead. Elektra's gentler sister Chrysothemis refuses to join her in revenge. A messenger appears whom Elektra finally recognizes as her brother Orestes. He enters the palace, kills Klytemnestra, and, when Aegisthus arrives, kills him too. Elektra, almost hysterical with joy, dances in final triumph, then dies.

Major Roles. ELEKTRA (dram s); needs great stamina and power throughout wide range; strong personality; G2 to C5. CHRYSOTHEMIS (s); Bb2 to Cb5. KLYTEMNESTRA (m-s); strong dramatic role; very low tessitura; G♯2 to G♯4.

Lesser Roles. AEGISTHUS (t); Eb2 to G3. ORESTES (bar); imposing, weighty tones; Gb1 to Gb3.

Bit Parts. KLYTEMNESTRA'S CONFIDANTE (s). TRAINBEARER (s). OVERSEER OF SERVANTS (s). YOUNG SERVANT (t). OLD SERVANT (bs). GUARDIAN OF ORESTES (bs). FIVE MAIDSERVANTS (s, s, m-s, m-s, c).

Chorus. SATB. Menservants and maidservants (offstage).

Orchestra. 3 fl (picc), 3 ob (Eng hrn), heckelphone, 5 cl (Eb, 2B, 2A), 2 basset hrn, bs cl, 3 bsn, cont bsn, 4 hrn, 4 Wagner tuba, 6 trp, bs trp, 3 trb, cont bs trb, cont bs tuba, 6–8 timp (2 players), perc (3–4 players), 2 harp, celeste, augmented strings. *Reduced vers.* 3 fl, 2 ob, Eng hrn, 4 cl, 3 bsn, 4 hrn, 6 trp, 3 trb, bs tuba, timp, perc (3 players), 2 harp, strings.

Material. All B & H. FS-P (rent). VS (g, e) $12.50. Li (g, e) $1. Tr: Kalisch (B & H). Mason (B & H). Reese (T31).

Photographs. San Francisco: 1.9.39 cover, pp. 2, 8. Metropolitan: 2.18.52

pp. 15, 19; 4.12.54 p. 12. Dresden: 2.18.52 p. 14. Craig design: 1.30.56 p. 12
Naples: 2.13.56 p. 30. Salzburg: 10.14.57 p. 19.
Performing Companies. 329 (51–52, 60–61). 180 (11.55). 1956–57: 240,
285. 281 (57–58).

◪ L'Elisir d'amore · The Elixir of Love

Music by Gaetano Donizetti (1797–1848). Libretto in Italian by Felice
Romani. Premiere: Milan, May 12, 1832. Comedy. Set numbers and recitative. Melodious, often florid vocal line; much quick patter. Brief prelude.
Setting: an Italian village, early 19th century. Two acts (105 min).
ACT I i: Entrance to a farmyard belonging to Adina (20 min); ii: The
village square (35 min). ACT II i: Inside Adina's farmhouse (20 min); ii:
The village (30 min).

Synopsis. The poor and simple peasant Nemorino, unhappy at the rich
Adina's apparent indifference toward him, becomes even more miserable
when she engages in a lively flirtation with Sergeant Belcore. From the itinerant quack doctor Dulcamara, Nemorino buys a love potion (in reality nothing
more potent than wine), with money obtained by selling his services to the
army. His sudden self-confidence so vexes Adina that she decides to marry
Belcore on the spot; still, she delays when Nemorino fails to appear for the
ceremony. She finds him happily drunk and surrounded by girls, who have
heard that he has just inherited a fortune. Spurred by jealousy, she buys
Nemorino's army contract and bestows her hand on him.

Major Roles. DR. DULCAMARA (buf bs); top F3. ADINA (lyr s); needs flexibility; top C5. NEMORINO (lyr t); high tessitura; top A3. SERGEANT BELCORE
(bar); high tessitura; top F3.

Lesser Role. GIANETTA, a young peasant girl (s).

Chorus. SATTB. Villagers and soldiers.

Ballet. A simple dance may be staged at the beginning of Act II i.

Orchestra. 2 fl (picc), 2 ob, 2 cl, 2 bsn, 2 hrn, 2 trp, 3 trb, timp, perc,
harp, piano for recitatives, strings. *Stage:* trp, sn drum, band (usually arranged
for existing conditions).

Material. FS-P: Ka, Map, Ri, TW (rent). CP: Map (i, e) (rent). VS:
Pet (g) $6.50; Ri (i) $7.50.

Photographs. Metropolitan: 12.29.41 pp. 14, 18; 1.31.49 pp. 18–20. La
Scala at Covent Garden: 11.13.50 p. 26. Wexford Festival, Ireland: 3.5.56
p. 32. *Mus. Amer.* Piccola Scala, Edinburgh: 10.57 p. 9.

Performing Companies. 290 (10.25.51). 77B (1952; 9.4.55). 150 (3.18.
54). 33 (2.8.55). 16 (7.29.55). 130 (11.22.55). 37B (4.3.56). 391 (7.22.56).
72 (10.12.56). 1956–57: 64, 388. 329 (60–61).

◪ Die Entführung aus dem Serail · The Abduction from
the Seraglio

Music by Wolfgang Amadeus Mozart (1756–1791). Libretto in German by
Gottlob Stephanie the Younger, adapted from an original libretto by Christoph

Friedrich Bretzner. Premiere: Vienna, July 16, 1772. Comedy, with set numbers, very simple vocal line alternating with bravura arias and dialogue; occasional Turkish influence. Overture. Setting: Turkey, 16th century, but often played in 18th-century dress. Three acts (130 min).

ACT I: In front of Selim Pasha's palace (40 min). ACT II: Pasha's garden (50 min). ACT III i: Square in front of palace; ii: Hall in the palace (40 min).

A version produced by the New York City Opera divides the opera into two acts (95 min), with two scenes each: ACT I i: Outside the palace (37 min); ii: Palace garden (24 min). ACT II i: Outside the seraglio (19 min); ii: Throneroom of the Pasha (15 min).

Synopsis. Belmonte, a Spanish prince, gains admittance to the palace of Selim Pasha, where his beloved Constanza, her maid Blonda, and Belmonte's servant Pedrillo are held captive. Constanza, longing for Belmonte, has continued to spurn the Pasha's suit, while Osmin, the coarse overseer, vainly woos Blonda, who finds solace in Pedrillo's affection. An attempt by the quartet of young lovers to escape begins successfully as Pedrillo persuades the vigilant Osmin to drink himself into oblivion. But it ends in frustration when the overseer rouses himself just in time. The Pasha displays unexpected clemency and allows all four to go.

Major Roles. CONSTANZA (col s); very florid and dramatic; range of chief aria B2 to D5. BLONDA (light s); florid in extremes of range; Ab2 to E5. BELMONTE (lyr t); requires flexibility as well as sustained power. PEDRILLO (light t). OSMIN (buf bs); demands very facile articulation; low D1. PASHA SELIM (speaking).

Bit Parts. A MUTE (mute). KLAAS, a boatman (speaking; often omitted).

Chorus. SATB. Janissaries, slaves, guards. Can be performed offstage.

Orchestra. picc, 2 fl, 2 ob, 2 cl (basset horn), 2 bsn, 2 trp, 2 trb, 2 hrn, timp, perc, strings.

Material. FS-P: Ha, Ka, Map, TW (rent). MS: Br (g) $17.50. CP: Ha (e); Map (i) (rent). VS: Ha (Mead) (rent); B & H (Martin) $3.75; Pet (i, g) $6, (g) $3. O Tr: John Bloch (333); Kallman (334); Stoessel (321). Li: Ox (Dent) $1.50.

Photographs. Bar Harbor, Me.: 10.21.46 p. 9. Metropolitan: 1.3.47 pp. 19–22. Juilliard: 4.17.44 p. 13. Paris Opéra: 10.15.51 p. 17. Sadler's Wells: 4.6.53 p. 13. College of the Pacific: 3.19.56 p. 26. Rome: (design) 3.4.57 p. 12. Washington Opera Society: 3.4.57 p. 33. Toronto: 4.8.57 p. 13. *Mus. Amer.* N.Y. City Opera: 11.15.57 p. 14.

Performing Companies. 329 (1946–47). 326 (5.23.49). 316 (4.14, 5.14, 11.26.49). 323 (3.31.50). 36 (3.50). 287 (4.19.51). 367A (6.6.53). 290A (6.6.53). 214A (7.29.53). 306A (10.11.53). 176 (2.25.54). 487 (5.18.54). 447 (7.27.54). 78 (2.3.56). 254 (5.14.56 – conc). 97B (5.30.56). 302 (5.30. 56). 334 (10.30.57). 333 (10.31.54). 1956–57: 23, 104, 313, 441.

🎵 Esther

Music by Jan Meyerowitz (1913–   ). Libretto in English by Langston Hughes, based on early rabbinical commentaries, the Book of Esther, and

58

Racine's play of the same name. Commissioned by the Fromm Music Foundation. Premiere: University of Illinois, March 17, 1957. Biblical drama. Continuous texture embodying arias, one ensemble; accompanied recitative; vocal line largely declamatory; few set numbers; familiar idiom overlaid with modern effects. Short introduction; short prelude to Act II. Three acts, sixteen scenes (ten essential sets, as simple as desired) (101 min).

ACT I i: House of the Holy Sages; ii: Courtyard between the palaces; iii: A Public Crier (blackout and spotlight, or before curtain); iv: Mordecai's house. ACT II v: Esther's room at the palace; vi: Same as iii; vii: Outside the palace gates; viii: Same as v. ACT III ix: Haman's house; x: The King's chamber; xi: Same as v; xii: Throne hall; xiii: Same, or same as x; xiv: Entrance to Esther's garden; xv: Esther's garden; xvi: Same as i.

Synopsis. After the Persian King Ahasuerus has his wife Vashti killed, he chooses as his queen, without knowing of her nationality, the Hebrew virgin Esther. On the advice of her uncle and guardian Mordecai, Esther keeps her secret until the evil and jealous Haman conceives a plot to destroy all the Jews in captivity throughout the kingdom. As a result of Esther's courageous plea to the king for her people, Ahasuerus has Haman hanged on the gallows which Haman had prepared for his enemy Mordecai. Esther thus becomes one of the great heroines of the Old Testament.

Major Roles. ESTHER (s); C3 to C5. AHASUERUS (bs-bar); C2 to F3. MORDECAI (t); E2 to B♭3. HAMAN (bar); A1 to F3.

Lesser Roles. THREE SAGES: DANIEL (bar), HISDA (t), and ELEAZAR (bs). BIGHAM (bar) and TERESH (bs), soldiers. CHAMBERLAIN (bs). VASHTI (m-s). CRIER (bar or bs). ZARESH, Haman's wife (m-s). ARIDATHA, Haman's eldest son (t). TWO ASTROLOGERS (med and low voices).

Chorus. SSATB. Maidens, soldiers, bystanders, crowd.

Orchestra. 2 fl, 2 ob, 2 cl, 2 bsn, 2 hrn, 2 trp, 2 trb, harp, perc (2 players), strings. *Reduced vers.* fl, 2 cl, bsn, 2 hrn, trp, trb, harp, perc (2 players), strings. *Stage:* 4 brass.

Material. FS-P: AMP (rent). VS: AMP (rent).

Photographs. Mus. Amer. Univ. of Illinois: 4.57 p. 8.

Performing Companies. 138 (3.17.57 − prem). 198A (5.58). Riverside Church, New York (2.60).

▶ Eugene Onegin

Music by Peter Ilytch Tchaikovsky (1840–1893). Libretto in Russian by the composer and K. S. Shilovsky, based on Pushkin's poem of the same name. Premiere: Moscow, March 29, 1879. Episodic lyrical romance. Melodic; set numbers; long accompanied recitatives. Setting: Russia about 1820. Three acts, seven scenes (137 min).

ACT I i: Garden of Madame Larina's country estate (31 min); ii: Tatyana's bedroom (24 min); iii: Another part of the garden (12 min). ACT II i: The ballroom of Madame Larina's house (22 min); ii: The bank of a nearby stream at dawn (14 min). ACT III i: Ballroom of Gremin's palace in St. Petersburg (21 min); ii: An anteroom in Gremin's palace (13 min).

59

Synopsis. The sensitive Tatyana, in love with her neighbor, Onegin, overcomes her natural shyness and sends him a letter asking him to marry her. His refusal humiliates her. At her birthday ball his attentions to her sister Olga infuriate his friend Lenski, Olga's fiancé, who challenges him to a duel. Onegin accepts, and kills his friend. After years of repentant wandering, he visits the court of his cousin, Prince Gremin, and is astounded to find that Tatyana is now Gremin's wife. Onegin, who now loves her desperately, asks her to run away with him. She wavers but in the end remains faithful, leaving him alone and remorseful.

Major Roles. TATYANA (lyr spin s); needs expressive warmth and decided character; C3 to B4. LENSKI (t); fine lyrical aria; D2 to A3. EUGENE ONEGIN (bar); strong acting part, dashing appearance desirable; high tessitura; G1 to G♭3 (G3 opt).

Lesser Roles. MADAME LARINA, Tatyana's mother (m-s). OLGA (c); G2 to F4. FILIPPEVNA, Madame Larina's old servant (m-s). PRINCE GREMIN (bs); one outstanding aria; G♭1 to E♭3. TRIQUET, a Frenchman (t). ZARETSKI, Lenski's duel second (bs). A CAPTAIN (bs). GILLOT, Onegin's duel second (mute).

Chorus. SSAATTBB. Peasants, ball guests, landowners, officers.

Ballet. Guests at country house ball in Act II; grand ball in Act III i.

Orchestra. 2 fl, picc, 2 ob, 2 cl, 2 bsn, 4 hrn, 2 trp, 3 trb, timp, harp, strings.

Material. FS-P: Map, Ka (rent). FS: Le $30. VS: AMP (BH − g) $6; Le (r) $18; G Sc (e − Reese) $5. CP: Map (i) (rent). Li: G Sc (e) 75¢. O Tr: Dent (Ox) $1.50; Goldovsky (T13); Mead (Ha).

Photographs. Moscow: 11.15.43 p. 6. Sadler's Wells: 10.13.52 p. 17; 12.3. 56 p. 25. Metropolitan: 12.2.57 pp. 8, 22–24, 26; 2.2.59 p. 15. Los Angeles: 3.10.52 p. 7. Wiesbaden: 4.5.54 p. 9. Bergen: 2.2.59 p. 24. Memphis: 3.9.59 p. 3. *Mus. Amer.* Metropolitan: 11.15.57 p. 3.

Performing Companies. 334 (46–48). 32 (1.52). 129A (2.15.52). 325A (2.24.52; 5.15.54). 327 (56–57). 329 (57–59). 328 (57–58).

🎝 Falstaff

Music by Giuseppe Verdi (1813–1901). Libretto in Italian by Arrigo Boito, based on Shakespeare's "The Merry Wives of Windsor" and parts of "Henry IV." Premiere: Milan, February 9, 1893. Comedy. Continuous texture; melodious vocal line over an accompaniment of great finesse; several very intricate and extended ensembles. Setting: Windsor, early 15th century. Three acts, six scenes (127 min).

ACT I i: Inside the Garter Inn (17 min); ii: Ford's garden (18 min). ACT II i: Inside the Garter Inn (25 min); ii: A room in Ford's house (20 min). ACT III i: In front of the Garter Inn (17 min); ii: Windsor Forest (30 min).

Synopsis. Sir John Falstaff, over the objections of his followers, Bardolph and Pistol, sends identical passionate love letters to the rich Mistresses Ford and Page, mainly with the aim of improving his impaired finances. The ladies, with the help of Dame Quickly, decide to play up to him and to teach him a lesson, subjecting him to several humiliating pranks. Mr. Ford also is taught a lesson: that he should not be jealous and distrustful of his wife. To atone, he gives his blessing to the marriage of his daughter, Anne, to young Fenton, although he had promised her to Dr. Caius. All agree in the end that only laughter is in order. The knight of the enormous girth is the first to admit it.

Major Roles. SIR JOHN FALSTAFF (bar); normal range, but requires flexibility and expert character acting. MR. FORD (high bar); difficult dramatic aria. MRS. FORD (lyr s). ANNE (NANETTA), their daughter (light lyr s). DAME QUICKLY (m-s or c). FENTON, Anne's suitor (lyr t).

Lesser Roles. MRS. PAGE (m-s). DR. CAIUS (t). BARDOLPH (t) and PISTOL (bs), followers of Falstaff. HOST of the Garter Inn (mute). ROBIN, a page (mute).

Chorus. SATB. Townspeople, disguised in Act III ii as woodsprites.

Ballet. Fairies' dance, Act III ii.

Orchestra. 3 fl (picc), 2 ob, Eng hrn, 2 cl, bs cl, 2 bsn, 4 hrn, 3 trp, 4 trb, timp, perc, harp, strings. *Stage:* guitar, chime, hrn.

Material. FS-P: Ri (rent). MS: Br (i) $17.50; Ri (i) $10.00. VS: Ri (i) $7. Li: Ri (i, e) 75¢; Ri (e — Kallman) 60¢. O Tr: Caldwell and Goldovsky (T13); Procter-Gregg (T2); Ducloux (T10).

Photographs. Metropolitan: 12.1.41 p. 8; 3.6.44 pp. 18–22. Edinburgh: 10.17.55 p. 21. *Mus. Amer.* Chicago Lyric Opera: 11.1.58 p. 3.

Performing Companies. 457A (4.53). 202 (3.1.53; 1.24.54). 254 (4.24. 53). 53 (5.28.53). 334 (1954). 215 (3.1.55). 321A (4.14.55). 80 (8.55). 180 (5.3.56). 32B (6.56). 72 (9.21.56). 148 (56–57). 48 (57–58; 4.18.59). 1957–58: 275, 358, 524.

⚱ La Fanciulla del west · The Girl of the Golden West

Music by Giacomo Puccini (1858–1924). Libretto by Guelfo Civinini and Carlo Zangarini, based on David Belasco's play of the same name. Premiere: New York, December 10, 1910. Melodrama of early American West. Set pieces woven into continuous flow of accompanied recitatives; vocal line frequently patterned after speech; whole-tone scales and nonharmonic progressions; syncopated Western dance motifs; extended and complicated ensembles. Brief prelude. Setting: California, during the Gold Rush, 1849–50. Three acts (127 min).

ACT I: The Polka Saloon (55 min). ACT II: Minnie's cabin (44 min). ACT III: A forest (28 min).

Synopsis. Sheriff Jack Rance, in common with most men near Cloudy Mountain, is in love with Minnie, the owner of the Polka Saloon. When Dick Johnson enters the saloon, neither Rance nor Ashby, the Wells Fargo agent, recognizes him as Ramerrez, the notorious outlaw they are both trailing. The men depart to continue their search. Johnson, now also smitten with Minnie, renounces his plan to rob her. She returns his love and hides him in her cabin; then, learning his true identity, she sends him away. As soon as he leaves the cabin he is shot, and Minnie once again conceals him. His hiding place in the loft is revealed to Rance by a falling drop of blood. Minnie plays cards with the sheriff with Johnson's life and her love as stakes; she cheats and wins. Nevertheless soon after Johnson's recovery he is captured. A lynching party is in progress when Minnie convinces the vigilantes that, for the sake of their love for her, Johnson should be freed. Minnie and Johnson ride off together to a new life.

Major Roles. MINNIE (lyr spin s); needs brilliant voice for lengthy role with consistently high tessitura; Bb2 to C5. DICK JOHNSON (RAMERREZ) (dram t); needs clarion quality, high range; C#2 to C4. JACK RANCE (bar); good actor; no excessive vocal demands; A1 to F#3.

Lesser Roles. NICK, bartender of the Polka (t). ASHBY, Wells Fargo agent (bs). SONORA (bar), TRIN (t), SID (bar), HANDSOME (bar), HARRY (t), JOE (t), HAPPY (bar), LARKENS (bs), miners. BILLY JACKRABBIT, Indian (bs). WOWKLE, Billy's squaw (m-s). JAKE WALLACE, traveling minstrel (bar). JOSE CASTRO, member of Ramerrez's gang (bs). A COURIER (t).

Chorus. TTBBB. Miners of the camp.

Orchestra. 3 fl, picc, 3 ob, Eng hrn, 3 cl, bs cl, 3 bsn, cont bsn, 4 hrn, 3 trp, 3 trb, tuba, timp, perc, 2 harp, glockenspiel, celeste, strings. *Reduced vers*: 2 fl, 2 ob, 2 cl, 2 bsn, 4 hrn, 3 trp, 3 trb, tuba, timp, perc, celeste, 2 harp, strings. *Stage:* Wind machine, tubular bells, fonica.

Material. FS-P: Ri (rent). VS: Ri (i) $12. Tr: Elkus (72).

Photographs. Florence: 10.18.54 p. 4. Chicago: 11.19.56 p. 6. Naples: 4.1. 57 p. 24.

Performing Companies. 130 (1956). 86 (1959). 329 (61–62).

✠ Faust

Music by Charles François Gounod (1818–1893). Libretto in French by Jules Barbier and Michel Carré, based on Goethe's "Faust," which contains a love story not in the medieval legend. Premiere (with dialogue): Paris (Théâtre Lyrique), March 9, 1859. Revised by Gounod for Christine Nilsson with accompanied recitatives and ballet; premiere: Paris (Opéra), March 3, 1869. Tragic romance. Set numbers with highly melodious vocal line. Prelude. Setting: Germany, 16th century. Five acts; or four, treating Act II as Act I ii (139 min without the frequently omitted Walpurgis Night).

ACT I: Dr. Faust's study (23 min). ACT II: A street fair — the Kermesse (25 min). ACT III: Marguerite's garden (48 min). ACT IV i (the original first scene in Marguerite's house is no longer performed): A church (9 min); ii: In front of Marguerite's house (18 min). ACT V i (often omitted): Walpurgis Night in the Hartz Mountains (20 min); ii: Marguerite's prison cell (16 min).

Synopsis. The old philosopher Faust sells his soul to Méphistophélès for the promise of youth and the possession of Marguerite. Rejuvenated, he is led to Marguerite by the devil. Marguerite quickly forgets a bouquet from the young Siébel (entrusted with her welfare by her soldier brother Valentin) in excitement over a casket of jewels placed on her doorstep by Méphistophélès. Encouraged by her neighbor Marthe, and bewitched by a spell wrought by Méphistophélès, she succumbs to Faust. Faust, challenged to a duel by Valentin, who has returned from war, kills him and flees, leaving Marguerite to her fate. She bears Faust's child and, in shame, kills it. Condemned to death, she languishes half-crazed in prison, from which the repentant Faust seeks to abduct her. But Marguerite recognizes the evil spirit that guides Faust and renounces her love. Commending her soul to heaven, she dies as a chorus of angels proclaims her salvation and Méphistophélès constrains Faust to keep his fatal bargain.

Major Roles. FAUST (lyr t); top C4. MEPHISTOPHELES (bs or bs-bar); great character role, demanding acting ability as well as flexible, strong voice; top E3 (opt F3). MARGUERITE (lyr s); coloratura passages; top B4 (C5 in Act III often cut). VALENTIN (bar); high tessitura, top G3. MARTHE (m-s or c). SIEBEL (m-s or s); top Bb4.

Lesser Role. WAGNER, a student (bar).

Chorus. SSAATTBB. Townspeople, students, soldiers, church choir, demons, angels.

Ballet. Waltzes in the Kermesse scene; large ballet in the Walpurgis Night scene.

Orchestra. 2 fl (picc), 2 ob (Eng hrn), 2 cl, 2 bsn, 4 hrn, 2 trp, 3 trb, bs tuba (in ballet, Act V i), timp, perc, 2 harp, strings. *Stage:* brass band; organ.

Production Problems. Quick transformation of old man to a youth. Sudden appearance of Méphistophélès. Apparition and apotheosis of Marguerite.

Material. FS-P: Map, Ri, Ka, TW (rent). MS: Br $17.50. CP: Ka, Map (f, e), TW (rent); G Sc (f, e) 85¢. VS: Map, TW (rent); G Sc (f, e) $5; Pet (f) $8.50; Ri (i) $5. O Tr: Blatt (215); Martin (T15); Mead (Ha); Bowe (T22); Morgan (T16); Redding (BMI); Vacano (148).

Photographs. Metropolitan: 3.11.40 pp. 16, 18, 19 (designs); 12.11.44 pp. 18–20; 12.30.46 p. 19; 12.26.49 p. 19; 12.18.50 pp. 18–21; 11.30.53 pp. 18–20 (Gérard designs); 4.26.54 p. 2 (III, ii); 2.14.55 pp. 18–21, 22 (Walpurgis). Walpurgis Night in French premiere: 3.11.40 p. 15. Riverside, Calif. (II): 3.17.41 p. 28. San Antonio (II): 4.21.47. Scranton (Kermesse): 2.23.48 p. 30. Alabama Polytech (Kermesse design): 4.25.49. Bob Jones Univ. (Kermesse): 2.12.51. Chautauqua (garden): 11.2.53 p. 14. Central City (church): 11.1.54 p. 9.

Performing Companies. Approx 57. 1956–57 only: 77B, 85, 109, 110, 125, 127, 176, 180, 229, 236, 278, 295, 311, 373, 391, 449, 456, 466, 513, 526.

🎭 La Favola d'Orfeo (Orfeo) · The Fable of Orpheus

Music by Claudio Monteverdi (1567–1643). Libretto in Italian by Alessandro Striggio. Premiere: Mantua, February 24, 1607. Classic drama. Vocal line often resembles chant or declamation; melody as such most frequently in chorus; occasional duets (the first used in opera); orchestra shows great variety in scoring; modal harmonies seem simple but reveal "modern" feeling and occasional dissonance. Overture; introductions and interludes (ritornelli). Numerous later versions exist. A Respighi orchestral "realization," adapted by Claudio Guastalla, reduces the original five acts to three, the third embodying the last three of the original (American premiere: Smith College, May 12, 1929). A version by Malipiero had its premiere at La Scala, Milan, March 16, 1935. Other versions are by Hindemith, Orff, and Wenzinger, and recently by Walter Rubsamen and Jan Popper of UCLA, with English translation by Ronald Farrar (premiere: May, 1945). Still more recently, Leopold Stokowski performed his own version at the New York City Opera on October 5, 1960. Setting: ancient Greece. Originally five acts and prologue (Popper vers, 121 min).

PROLOGUE: Delivered by La Musica, spirit of music (8 min). ACT I: A pastoral scene (18 min). ACT II: Another pastoral scene (28 min). ACT III: The bank of the River Styx (26 min). ACT IV: Hades (22 min). ACT V: The fields of Thrace (19 min).

Synopsis. The Spirit of Music vows to tell the story of Orfeo, and commands silence even from nature. In a pastoral scene, nymphs and shepherds celebrate the nuptials of Orfeo and Euridice. The joy is eclipsed when Sylvia, Euridice's messenger, brings Orfeo the news of Euridice's death by the sting of a serpent. Orfeo laments and vows to brave the underworld to recover his bride. At the edge of the River Styx Charon refuses passage to Orfeo until charmed by his song. In Hades, Pluto, persuaded by Persephone, releases Euridice on condition that Orfeo not look back on the journey homeward. Orfeo, fearful of the pursuing Furies, disobeys. Euridice disappears, and the infernal choir cries victory. Wandering in the fields of Thrace, Orfeo laments once more; his song is repeated offstage by Echo. (The story here departs from Greek legend, which claims that Orfeo was torn to pieces by Thracian women for lamenting Euridice too long.) Apollo, Orfeo's father, descends from a cloud and transports Orfeo to Olympus, to dwell in immortality. The chorus sings in praise of Apollo; general festivity prevails.

Roles. (Only Orfeo is "major," yet others have important scenes.) ORFEO (bar, occasionally t or m-s); requires sustained and florid singing; D2 to F3. EURIDICE (s); C3 to D4. LA MUSICA (m-s); sings entire prologue; F3 to D4. SYLVIA, a messenger (m-s); important long recitative; C3 to E4. HOPE (LA SPERANZA) (m-s); long recitative; C3 to E4. CHARON (CARONTE) (bs); F1 to A2. PERSEPHONE (c); D3 to F4. PLUTO (bs); G1 to A2. APOLLO (t); difficult florid passages; G2 to G3. ECHO (s or m-s); D3 to E4. SHEPHERD (t); D2 to F3. OTHER SHEPHERDS (s, m-s, c). SPIRITS (s, m-s, t, bs).

Chorus. SSATB. Two advisable: one onstage (shepherds, nymphs); one in auditorium for interludes.

Ballet. As elaborate as desired. Shepherds, dryads, bacchantes.

Orchestra. Original vers (Monteverdi asked for those indicated as well as the additions noted as "plus"): 2 harpsichords, double harp (plus 1), 2 large lutes (plus 1), 2 bass zithers, 3 bass gambas, 2 organs with wood pipes, organ with reed pipes, 2 small violins, 10 viole da braccio (4 violins, 4 violas, 2 violoncellos), 2 contrabass viols, 4 trb (plus 1), 2 cornets, 2 high recorders, high trp (clarino), 3 trp with mutes. Respighi vers: 4 fl, 3 ob, 3 cl, 2 bsn, 4 hrn, 3 trp, 3 trb, tuba, timp, 2 harp, organ, strings. *Stage:* 2 hrn, 3 trp, 2 trb, tuba, perc, harp. Malipiero vers: 2 fl, 2 ob, 2 cl, 2 bsn, 4 hrn, piano, celeste, harp, strings. Possible vers (suggested by Popper): 2 fl (picc), 3 ob, bsn, 3 trp, 5 trb, organ, harmonium, 1–2 harpsichord, strings. Stokowski vers: harpsichord, harp, organo di legno, regal, alto trb, vulgano trb, bs trb, trps, flautini, viola da gamba, chitarrone, lute, strings.

Material. Respighi vers: B & H (Ca). VS: B & H (Ca – i) $9.50. Malipiero vers: AMP (SZ – i). Orff vers: AMP (g) $5.

Photographs. Florence: 1.13.58 p. 11. Smith College: 12.1.58 p. 32.

Performing Companies. 47 (5.45). 336A (2.52 – conc). 187A (57–58). 104 (2.3.59). 334 (10.5.60).

🎵 Fidelio

Music by Ludwig Van Beethoven (1770–1827). Libretto in German by Joseph von Sonnleithner, based on the French play by Jean Nicolas Bouilly. Revised (3rd) version by Georg Friedrich Treitschke. Premiere: Vienna, November 20, 1805. Melodrama. Set numbers; considerable dialogue; vocal line melodious but also extremely demanding with difficult arias introduced by highly dramatic accompanied recitative. The music is exalted in spirit, endeavoring to embody the abstract ideas of good and evil. Overture. Setting: A state prison in Spain, 18th century. Two acts, including Leonore Overture, No. 3, before last scene (129 min).

ACT I i: The jailer's quarters (32 min); ii: The courtyard of the prison (36 min). ACT II i: A dark dungeon (34 min); ii: A bastion (27 min).

Synopsis: Don Pizarro has imprisoned his political enemy, Don Florestan, and plans to starve him to death. Leonore, Florestan's wife, disguised as Fidelio, works for the jailer, Rocco, hoping to find a way to free her husband. Embarrassingly, Marzelline, the jailer's daughter, is planning to marry Fidelio, spurning her former sweetheart, Jaquino. When Pizarro hears of an impending visit to the prison by his superior, Don Fernando, he attempts to murder Florestan, but his plan is frustrated by the heroic Leonore. The sympathetic Rocco informs Don Fernando of Pizarro's misdeeds, whereupon Pizarro is jailed and Florestan set free.

Major Roles. FLORESTAN, a Spanish nobleman (dram t); great power and flexibility; high tessitura; top B♭3. LEONORE (dram s); needs thrust and agility throughout wide range; difficult skips; top B4. DON PIZARRO (dram bs-bar); forceful personality; top F3. ROCCO (bs). MARZELLINE (lyr s); florid; top B♭4. JAQUINO, turnkey (lyr t). DON FERNANDO, prime minister (bs).

Chorus. SATTBB. Prisoners (2 solo, t and b), guards, soldiers, townspeople.

Orchestra. 2 fl, picc, 2 ob, 2 cl, 2 bsn, cont bsn, 4 hrn, 2 trp, 2 trb, timp, strings. *Stage:* trp. If Leonore Overture No. 3 is played, add trb in pit.

Material. FS-P: Map, Ri, TW (rent). MS: Pet (i, g; four overtures) $12, $15. CP: Map (g, e) (rent). VS: B & H (g, e – Dent) $5; Pet (g) $6.50; G Sc (g, e) $5; AMP (UE – g) $2.50. O Tr: Baker (329), Blatt (215), Dent (Ox), Lonner (T18), Reese (T31).

Photographs. San Francisco: 2.17.41 p. 17. Metropolitan: 2.17.41 pp. 18–

65

21; 3.12.45 pp. 20, 21; 3.5.51 p. 18. Munich: 12.1.52 p. 14. Vienna: 11.30.53 p. 31; 11.28.55 p. 4. Stuttgart: 10.31.55 p. 20.

Performing Companies. 460 (4.53; 56–57). 72 (1954). 518 (5.54). 215 (8.4.55). 70A (10.1.56). 297 (10.56). 1956–57: 310, 313, 460. 329 (1959–60). 333 (1959, 1961).

🦇 Die Fledermaus · The Bat

Music by Johann Strauss, Jr. (1825–1899). Libretto in German by Carl Haffner and Richard Genée after Meilhac and Halévy's "Le Reveillon" from Roderich Benedix's play "Das Gefaengnis." Premiere: Vienna, April 6, 1874. Comedy. Dialogue connects set numbers which, highly melodic, are essentially based on the dance tunes of the time. Overture. Setting, Bad Ischl, Austria, 1874. Three acts (161 min).

ACT I: A drawing room in Eisenstein's house (48 min). ACT II: The ballroom at Prince Orlofsky's (71 min). ACT III: At the local jail (42 min).

Synopsis. After a fancy-dress ball in which Dr. Falke was dressed as a bat, he was left asleep by his friend Eisenstein on a public bench to be awakened at broad daylight by a jeering crowd. Now Dr. Falke plots revenge. He takes Eisenstein — who should have reported to jail for a minor offense — to a ball given by Prince Orlofsky. There the unsuspecting victim meets his maid and his masked wife, Rosalinda, as well as the prison warden, who had in the meantime arrested a man he believed to be Eisenstein, as he had found him dining cozily with Rosalinda. This is Alfred, Rosalinda's former lover, a "typical" tenor. The complications come to a climax when all gather at the jail after the party breaks up early in the morning. There Dr. Falke discloses to the astonished Eisenstein that all the night's harassments had been merely the "bat's" revenge.

Major Roles. GABRIEL VON EISENSTEIN, a wealthy socialite (t); high tessitura; top A♭3; low tessitura in parlando. ROSALINDA (spin s); highly flexible; top D5. ADELE, their maid (col soubrette); top D5. ALFRED (lyr t); top B♭3.

Lesser Roles. DR. FALKE (bar). PRINCE ORLOFSKY (m-s; occasionally sung by a man). DR. BLIND, Eisenstein's lawyer (buf t). FRANK, jail warden (bar). FROSCH, jailer (speaking, comedian). IDA, Adele's sister (s or speaking).

Chorus. SSAATTBB. Guests of Prince Orlofsky, prisoners.

Orchestra. 2 fl (picc), 2 ob, 2 cl, 2 bsn, 4 hrn, 2 trp, 3 trb, timp, perc, chimes, harp, strings.

Material. FS-P: Map, G Sc, Ka, TW (rent). CP: G Sc 50¢. VS: G Sc (Martin) $4; B & H (g, e — Dietz and Kanin) $3.50; B & H ("Rosalinda" e — Kerby) $3.50. Li: B & H (Dietz and Kanin) 65¢; G Sc (Martin) 60¢. O Tr: Alden (Car); Bernauer and Melford (Wein); Bowe (T22); Hammond (T22); Warenskjold (38); Weiler (T22).

Photographs. Metropolitan: 1.15.51 pp. 18–20; 12.17.51 pp. 19, 20.

Performing Companies. Approx 81. 329 (50–56, 58–59 — Dietz vers). 1956–57 only: 57, 76, 78, 85, 106, 112, 137, 142, 189, 207, 216, 295, 334, 359, 385, 395, 410, 444, 455, 502, 522.

📖 Der Fliegende Holländer · The Flying Dutchman

Music by Richard Wagner (1813–1883). Libretto in German by the composer, based on Heine's adaptation of an old legend. Premiere: Dresden, January 2, 1843. Romantic drama with mystical and psychological overtones. Continuous texture, though several set pieces are separable; melodious vocal line. Overture. Setting: the coast of Norway, 18th century. Three acts (131 min).* ACT I: The shore (49 min). ACT II: A room in Daland's house (56 min). ACT III: The bay near Daland's house (26 min).

Synopsis. For blaspheming, the Flying Dutchman is doomed to sail the seas eternally; his only hope of redemption is to find a truly faithful love. In a storm he lands near Daland's ship. Daland, impressed by the Dutchman's wealth, offers his daughter Senta in marriage. Senta has already independently resolved to be the Dutchman's salvation if ever they meet. Finally face to face, the two exchange ecstatic pledges. Erik, Senta's sweetheart, vainly pleads with her to remember their own love. The Dutchman, overhearing, despairingly departs for his ship, which swiftly sets sail. Senta offers then the ultimate proof of devotion: she casts herself into the sea. The cursed ship sinks, and Senta and the Dutchman, transfigured, ascend to heaven.

Major Roles. SENTA (dram s); needs strong voice capable of sustaining high tessitura; Bb2 to B4. THE DUTCHMAN (bar); frequently high tessitura; dark, dramatic timbre desirable; G1 (F1 opt) to F3. DALAND, captain of a Norwegian vessel (bs); sustained; F1 to Eb3. ERIK, a huntsman (t); Db2 to Bb3.

Lesser Roles. A STEERSMAN (t). MARY, Senta's nurse (m-s).

Chorus. SSAATTBB (extended and difficult). Norwegian maidens, crew of Daland's vessel, crew of Flying Dutchman.

Orchestra. picc, 2 fl, 2 ob, Eng hrn, 2 cl, 2 bsn, 4 hrn, 2 trp, 4 trb, tuba, timp, tam-tam, harp, strings. *Stage:* 3 picc, tam-tam, wind machine, hrns.

Production Problems. Beaching, departure, and sinking of Dutchman's ship; apotheosis of Senta and Dutchman.

Material. FS-P: Map, Ri, TW (rent). VS: Map, TW (rent); Pet (g) $6.50; G Sc (g, e) $5. MS: Pet (Eul – g, e, i) $25. CP: Map (g) (rent).

Photographs. Metropolitan: 12.25.50 p. 8 (Elson), p. 18–20 (Acts I, II, and III), p. 7 (weather); 1.26.59 p. 5; 3.16.59 p. 5. Munich: 10.15.51 p. 21. Athens: 11.10.52 p. 3. San Francisco: 11.15.54 p. 5.

Performing Companies. 193 (3.11.49). 329 (50–51, 59–60). 72 (1954, 1956).

📖 La Forza del destino · The Force of Destiny

Music by Giuseppe Verdi (1813–1901). Libretto in Italian by Francesco Maria Piave, based on the play "Don Alvaro, o La Fuerza del sino" by Angel de Saavedra, the Duque de Rivas; later revised by Antonio Ghislanzoni. Premiere: St. Petersburg, November 10, 1862. Melodrama. Set numbers; melodious vocal line, many passages approximating speech; accompanied recitative;

large and extended ensembles. Overture. Setting: Spain and Italy; 18th century. Four acts, eight scenes (148 min).
ACT I: Palace of Marquis of Calatrava at Seville (28 min). ACT II i: An inn at Hornachuelos (18 min); ii: Monastery of Madonna degli Angeli (22 min). ACT III i: An Italian battlefield near Velletri (13 min); ii: Camp of the Spanish army (13 min); iii: The same (20 min). ACT IV i: Cloister of Madonna degli Angeli (19 min); ii: A hermitage near the monastery (15 min).

Synopsis. Don Alvaro, a nobleman of Spanish-Inca descent, is spurned as a suitor by Leonora's father, the Marquis of Calatrava. Discovered by the Marquis when he comes to elope with Leonora, Alvaro throws down his pistol in surrender. The gun accidentally fires, killing the old man. Alvaro flees, followed by the sworn vengeance of the Marquis' son, Don Carlo. Leonora, believing Alvaro dead, assumes a male disguise and begs a hermit's refuge from a monastery. In spite of her initial reception by the gruff Fra Melitone, her wish is granted by kindly Padre Guardiano. Meanwhile Carlo and Alvaro meet on a battlefield and, not recognizing each other, swear eternal friendship after Alvaro saves Carlo's life. While Alvaro recuperates from a battle injury, his identity is betrayed by a picture Carlo discovers among his effects. Upon his recovery he is challenged to a duel, which is prevented by the arrival of an armed patrol. Alvaro, seeking solace in a holy life, joins the brotherhood of Padre Guardiano; there, five years later, Carlo finds him and goads him into mortal combat. Their dueling takes them near Leonora's retreat; she goes to help her badly hurt brother, who stabs her just before he dies. Alvaro and Leonora bid each other farewell, as Guardiano reminds them of heavenly bliss.

Major Roles. LEONORA (dram s); long line, great dramatic intensity; wide dynamic range; Bb2 to B4. DON ALVARO (dram t); sustained; needs great stamina; Bb1 to B3. DON CARLO (bar); demands power; B1 to G3. PADRE GUARDIANO (bs); F1 to Fb3 (opt F♯3). PREZIOSILLA, a camp follower (m-s); considerable agility; A2 to C5.

Lesser Roles. CURRA, Leonora's maid (s). TRABUCCO, a pedlar (t). FRA MELITONE (buf bar). ALCLADE (bs). SURGEON (bar). MARQUIS DI CALATRAVA (bs).

Chorus. SSSATTTBBB. Peasants, beggars, muleteers, pilgrims, Spanish and Italian soldiers, vivandières, children.

Ballet. In Act III iii.

Orchestra. 2 fl (picc), 2 ob, 2 cl (bs cl), 2 bsn, 4 hrn, 2 trp, 3 trb, tuba, timp, perc, 2 harp, organ, strings. *Stage:* drums, 3 trp (usually doubled).

Material. FS-P: Ka, Map, Ri, TW (rent). CP: Map (i, e) (rent). VS: B & H (i, e – Martin) $4.50; Map, TW (rent); Pet (i, g) $6.50; Ri (i) $7.50.

Photographs. Metropolitan: 1.18.43 p. 11, 14; (Berman) 1.21.52 p. 15; 11.10.52 p. 15; 11.24.52 pp. 4, 5, 28; 3.2.53 p. 11; 3.12.56 pp. 10, 18–20. San Francisco: 10.2.44 p. 11.

Performing Companies. 295 (1954, 1955, 56–57). 303 (8.5.55). 321A (2.5.56). 92 (2.6.56). 1956–57: 130, 135, 189, 313. 329 (57–58, 59–60).

📧 Four Saints in Three Acts

Music by Virgil Thomson (1896–   ). Libretto in English by Gertrude Stein (1874–1946). Premiere: Hartford, Conn., February 8, 1934. Surrealistic mood piece. Often simple melodic line with shifting tonalities; set pieces, long accompanied recitative and short parlando sections. Setting: Spain, 16th century. Despite title, in four acts and a prelude. The Prelude, sung on stage, leads directly into Act I; and there is no intermission, only an intermezzo between Acts III and IV. The following description of the acts is quoted from Stein (90 min).

PRELUDE: A narrative of prepare for Saints. ACT I: Avila: St. Teresa half indoors and half out of doors (30 min). ACT II: Might it be mountains if it were not Barcelona (20 min). ACT III: Barcelona: St. Ignatius and one of two literally. ACT IV: The Sisters and Saints re-assembled and reenacting why they went away to stay (40 min).

Synopsis. The action is a series of highly stylized vignettes, most often with no concrete meaning but evocative nevertheless. Fictional but typical incidents from the lives of St. Teresa of Avila and St. Ignatius Loyola (two singers for St. Teresa) are intertwined kaleidoscopically with imaginary doings of imaginary characters like St. Settlement and St. Chavez. There are also a Commère and Compère. Staging invites imagination and great freedom by the very nature of the libretto: to a certain extent, the scenario can be made up, though one by Maurice Grosser is offered in the score.

Major Roles. ST. TERESA I (s); B♭2 to B4. ST. TERESA II (m-s); F2 to G4. ST. SETTLEMENT (s); C3 to A4. ST. CHAVEZ (t); C2 to C4. ST. IGNATIUS (bar); A1 to G3 (opt A3). COMMERE (m-s); C3 to E4. COMPERE (bs); E♭1 to F3.

Lesser Roles. ST. PLAN (bs). ST. STEPHEN (t). (Others from chorus.)

Chorus. SATB. Small chorus of named saints with solo lines. SATB. Large chorus of saints.

Ballet. Angels; sailors with Spanish girls (3 men, 3 women, sufficient for small or medium-size stage).

Orchestra. fl (picc), ob (Eng hrn), 2 cl, bsn, 2 hrn, trp, trb, accordion, harmonium, perc (1 or 2 players), bells, strings.

Material. All Pr (Mer). FS-P (rent). VS $9.50. Vocal material (rent).

Performing Companies. 92A (2.8.34 — prem). Empire Theatre, New York (2.34). Auditorium Theatre, Chicago (11.34). Broadway Theatre, New York (4.52).

📧 Lo Frate innamorato · The Brother in Love

Music by Giovanni Pergolesi (1710–1736). Libretto in Italian (Neapolitan dialect) by Gennaro A. Federico. Premiere: Naples, 1732. New version, musical adaptation by Richard Falk, with dialogue substituted for recitative, English translation by Edward Eager. Consists of 37 numbers, 31 of them arias. Chief difficulties are wide and unexpected skips. The time is early 18th century; the entire action in a street in Capodimonte, near Naples. Three acts (110 min).

Synopsis. A typical story of mistaken identity, with Carlo, a *nouveau riche*, trying to arrange a marriage between one of his two nieces and Don Pietro, supercilious son of the nobleman Marcaniello. For his part, Don Pietro wants his sister Lucrezia to marry Carlo. Carlo's maid, Vanella, is in love with Don Pietro; both of Carlo's nieces, Nina and Nena, as well as Lucrezia, are in love with Ascanio, Marcaniello's adopted son. Ascanio chooses Lucrezia. Don Pietro gives up his ideas of being a Don Juan and marries Vanella, while Cardella, Marcaniello's old maidservant, glad of anything, draws Carlo. In the end, Ascanio is revealed as Carlo's long-lost son.

Roles. MARCANIELLO, a nobleman (buf bs); considerable agility; occasional high tessitura; top G3. DON PIETRO (bs-bar); frequently high tessitura; often florid; top G3. LUCREZIA (m-s). CARDELLA (s). ASCANIO (light or lyr t). CARLO (lyr t); top A3. NINA (m-s) NENA (col s); high tessitura; top B♭4. VANELLA (s).

Orchestra. Strings with occasional fl or ob obbligato. Second vers: fl, ob, 2 hrn, strings. Harpsichord or piano optional.

Material. Estate of Dr. Richard Falk. Li: Edward Eager (T33).

◢ Die Frau ohne Schatten · The Woman without a Shadow

Music by Richard Strauss (1864–1949). Libretto in German by Hugo von Hofmannsthal. Premiere: Vienna, October 10, 1919. Legend with supernatural and philosophical overtones. Monumental musical and dramatic demands; melodious but difficult vocal line over heavy orchestra of continuous texture; occasional dissonance in diatonic harmony. A few set pieces: extended scenas, ensembles, speech over music. No overture; orchestral interludes between scenes. The setting is the South Eastern Islands in legendary times. Three acts, ten scenes (188 min).

ACT I i: A roof above the palace gardens; ii: The dyer's hut (64 min). ACT II i: The dyer's hut; ii: The Emperor's falcon house; iii: The dyer's hut; iv: The empress's bedroom in the falcon house; v: The dyer's hut (64 min). ACT III i: A subterranean vault; ii: Judgment hall of the spirits; iii: Landscape with waterfall on upper level, lower level a chasm (60 min).

Synopsis. The theme of redemption through love and suffering is mingled with Oriental fancies and superstitions. One couple (the dyer Barak and his wife) is too earthbound; the other (the Emperor and his half-supernatural Empress) too proud and remote. Both couples must be cleansed. Because of her supernatural ancestry, the Empress cannot bear mortal children; as a symbol, she casts no shadow. The dyer's wife, vain and selfish, wants no children and is willing to sell her shadow to the Empress. Barak, a man of great character and integrity, gradually influences the Empress to believe in the dignity of humanity; when her ultimate challenge arrives, she resists the temptation to gain humanity by usurping the other woman's birthright (her shadow) even though her Emperor must be turned to stone. Her steadfastness is rewarded: the Emperor is restored to life and their unborn children hail them. Barak and his wife too are reunited after long trials.

Major Roles. THE EMPEROR (dram t); high tessitura, same demands as Bacchus in "Ariadne" except more extended, although less exposed; B1 to B3 (one C4 at finale). THE EMPRESS (spin s); constant high tessitura; needs great sustaining power; B2 to D5. THE EMPRESS'S NURSE (c); extremely dramatic; very difficult intervals; E♭2 to B♭4. BARAK (bar); voice should be dark, though range is high; F♯1 to G3. HIS WIFE (dram s); requires great stamina over extended range; F2 to C♯5.

Lesser Roles. SPIRIT MESSENGER (bar); difficult intervals; G1 to F♯3. FALCON (s); birdlike appoggiaturas. BARAK'S THREE BROTHERS: HUNCHBACK (t); top C♭4; ONE-EYE (bs); top F♯3; ONE-ARM (bs); top G♭3. APPARITION OF YOUTH (t); can be dancer, with voice from prompter's box, pit, or wings; top A3. KEEPER OF TEMPLE (col s, or specially talented falsetto t); florid; C♯2 to A3.

Chorus. SSAATTBB, in various combinations, as many as six solo voices; unborn children (SS) effective if from pit. Children (boys' choir backstage).

Orchestra. 4 fl, 3 ob, Eng hrn, 5 cl (bs cl), basset hrn, 4 bsn (cont bsn), 8 hrn (4 ten tuba), 3 trp, 4 trb, bs tuba, timp, perc (6 gongs, 4 tam-tams, etc.) 2 harp, 2 celeste (glass harmonica), organ, strings.

Production Problems. In addition to the inordinate length, difficulty in casting, and the size of the orchestra, problems are almost insurmountable except for large and well-equipped houses. Short intervals between the many scenes, predetermined by musical interludes, demand the utmost in dexterity, even with a revolving stage. The two-level stage at the finale, the earth's opening, the disappearance of a subterranean vault, and the effect of a chasm across which a shadow bridge is cast are among the larger difficulties. Lesser ones include a sword flying into Barak's hand and the effect of the Emperor's turning to stone. A special lighting problem is the Empress's lack of a shadow.

Material. FS-P: B & H (rent). VS: B & H (g) $20.

Photographs. Munich: 10.18.54 p. 13; 2.21.55 p. 13; 2.4.57 p. 24; 2.2.59 p. 7.

Performing Companies. 72 (9.18.59 — Amer prem).

✠ Der Freischütz · The Free-Shooter

Music by Carl Maria von Weber (1786–1826). Libretto in German by Friedrich Kind. Premiere: Berlin, June 18, 1821. Gothic legend, in German Romantic setting. Very melodious; occasional atmospheric music and folk elements; set numbers; dialogue. Overture. Setting: Bohemia, shortly after the Seven Years' War. Three acts, five scenes.

ACT I: A forest shooting range. ACT II i: Agathe's house; ii: The Wolf's Glen. ACT III i: Agathe's room; ii: The shooting range.

Synopsis. Max, a huntsman for Prince Ottokar, is in love with Agathe, whose hand will be his if he wins a sharpshooting contest. He loses a preliminary trial, however, and in his despondency he agrees to join his fellow huntsman Caspar in bondage to Zamiel, the demon hunter, in return for magic bullets that never miss. Agathe, meanwhile, after dismissing her cousin Ännchen, prays for help in her love. She unsuccessfully tries to dissuade Max from going to Zamiel's haunted glen; Max and Caspar, with the evil one's help, cast the magic bullets. At the contest Max is unbeatable. With his last bullet he shoots at a white dove, despite Agathe's assertions that she is the dove. She faints and Caspar, who had planned to buy time from Zamiel with her life, is killed by the shot. The Demon appears to claim Max and tells of the magic bullets. Ottokar is about to banish Max for his duplicity when a strange hermit appears, revives Agathe and defends Max, saying that divine mercy has answered Agathe's prayer.

Major Roles. AGATHE (dram s); several florid passages; B2 to B4. ANNCHEN (lyr s); needs trill, coloratura; B2 to B♭4 (opt B4). MAX (t); C2 to A3. CASPAR (bs); occasional florid singing; F♯1 to F♯3.

Lesser Roles. KILIAN, a peasant (bs); D2 to E3. KUNO, head of Ottokar's forest service and Agathe's father (bs); F1 to E3. PRINCE OTTOKAR of Bohemia (bar). HERMIT (bs).

Bit Parts. BRIDESMAID (s). ZAMIEL (speaking).

Chorus. SATTTBB. Huntsmen, peasants, bridesmaids, invisible spirits.

Orchestra. 2 fl (picc), 2 ob, 2 cl, 2 bsn, 4 hrn, 2 trp, 3 trb, timp, strings. *Stage:* cl, 2 hrn, trp, 2 vln, vlc.

Production Problem. Manifestation of Zamiel in Wolf Glen scene.

Material. FS-P: Map, TW (rent). FS: Br (g) $17.50; Pet (g) $80. CP: Map (g) (rent). VS: Map, TW (rent); Pet (g) $3.50; G Sc (g, e) $5. Tr: Dent (Ox); Martin (B & H); Mead (Ha).

Photographs. Dresden: 11.20.50 p. 27. Rome: 3.24.52 p. 13. Edinburgh: 10.13.52 p. 29. Munich: 12.21.52 p. 12. Univ. of Oklahoma: 11.15.54 p. 15. *Mus. Amer.* Florence, Act II: 3.57 p. 5.

Performing Companies. 182 (4.6.48). 306A (1.18.52). 351A (1.19.52). 424 (4.54). 71A (1956). 407 (56–57).

⚜ Il Geloso Schernito · The Jealous Husband

Music by Giovanni Battista Pergolesi (1710–1736). Anonymous libretto in Italian. Premiere: Naples, 1731. Farce. Set numbers, arias, duets; recitative; dialogue. Overture. Setting: a garden in front of the home of Dorina and Masacco, about 1730. Three acts (100 min).

Synopsis. Dorina, married to the jealous Masacco, wants only to be ruled by him and deplores the plots of the more dominating Lucrezia to teach him a lesson. Still she agrees to dupe him if it will cure his jealousy. Pietro, a clever fop, suggests that Masacco pretend to go away and return unexpectedly. In disguise, Masacco makes advances to Dorina, who flirts outrageously with him and with a postman (Pietro). Then she dresses as a gallant, presumably another suitor, and provokes a duel with her husband, trouncing him badly. His amour-propre is badly wounded, his jealousy deflated by the truth as finally revealed. Meanwhile, Pietro and Lucrezia have also decided on married bliss.

72

Roles. DORINA (s); needs trill; C3 to B4. MASACCO (buf bs); florid; Bb1 to G3. DON PIETRO (t) and LUCREZIA (m-s) (only in Falk vers).
Chorus. SATB. In finale only.
Orchestra. fl, ob, cl, 2 hrn, piano.
Material. Adaptation by Dr. Richard Falk. Available through Dr. Falk's estate. Li: Edward Eager (T33).

✹ Giants in the Earth

Music by Douglas Moore (1893–   ). Libretto in English by Arnold Sundgaard and Douglas Moore, based on the novel by O. E. Rölvaag. Premiere: New York, March 28, 1951. Pulitzer Prize in Music, 1951. Tragic romance of American pioneer life. Continuous texture with vocal line patterned on rhythms of speech. No overture. Setting: the Dakota Territory, in 1873. Three acts, four scenes (150 min).

ACT I: The crest of a low hill. ACT II: Interior of Per Hansa's hut. ACT III i: Outside Per Hansa's hut; ii: Interior of Per Hansa's hut.

Synopsis. Per Hansa and his wife Beret arrive from Norway to join their friends in settling the Dakota Territory. They are met by Hans Olsa and his wife Sorrine, Syvert and his wife Kjersti, and Henry, who is disappointed that his old sweetheart did not come with them. Per is a natural-born pioneer, but Beret is frail and afraid. Her fears that they will become godless and savage seem justified when she finds some stakes hidden in a chest which indicate that Per had no right to the land on which they have settled; his assurances that the stakes were planted illegally and that the land really is his fail to convince her. Henry weds Dagmar, a Norwegian girl, and after the ceremony, Per brings his infant boy to the preacher to be baptized. But Beret refuses permission to name the child Victorious because of her firm belief that God disapproves of their life. Her mind finally unhinged by the rigors of pioneer life, Beret sends Per out into a raging storm to find a preacher to baptize her dying boy, then realizes too late that she has sent her husband to his death.

Major Roles. PER HANSA (bar); high tessitura; A♯1 to G♭3. BERET (s); C3 to C5. HANS OLSA (bs-bar); B♭1 to E♭3. SORRINE (c); C3 to E♭4. SYVERT (t); E♭2 to A♭3. KJERSTI (s); D3 to G4. HENRY (t); F2 to A3.
Lesser Roles. DAGMAR (s). A PREACHER (bar). O'HARA (bs). SULLIVAN (mute). OLA and ANNA, children of Per and Beret (speaking).
Ballet. Folk dancers at the wedding.
Orchestra. 2 fl, ob, 2 cl, bsn, 2 hrn, 2 trp, 2 trb, timp, perc, strings.
Material. FS-P: Fi (rent). VS: Fi (rent).
Performing Companies. 302 (3.28.51 – prem). 113 (5.52).

✹ La Gioconda

Music by Amilcare Ponchielli (1834–1886). Libretto in Italian by Tobia Gorrio (Arrigo Boito) based on Victor Hugo's play "Angelo, tyran de

73

Padoue." Premiere: Milan, April 8, 1876. Romantic melodrama. Abundant melodies; simple harmonic structure; set numbers; accompanied recitatives. Prelude. Setting: Venice; 17th century. Four acts, five scenes (156 min).

ACT I: The ducal palace (51 min). ACT II: On the Fusina Lagoon (36 min). ACT III i: A room in the Cà d'Oro, Alvise's palace (15 min); ii: Grand hall in the Cà d'Oro (23 min). ACT IV: A ruined palace on the island of Giudecca (31 min).

Synopsis. Barnaba, a spy for the Inquisition, lusts after La Gioconda, a beautiful streetsinger, who detests him and loves Enzo Grimaldo, an exiled Genoese nobleman disguised as a sea captain. Barnaba turns the crowd against Gioconda's mother, La Cieca, by accusing her of witchcraft; only the arrival of Alvise Badoero, an official of the Inquisition, and his wife, Laura Adorno (who was once betrothed to Enzo), saves the blind old woman. In gratitude, La Cieca gives Laura her rosary. Barnaba arranges a tryst between Enzo and Laura, then informs Alvise. Gioconda overhears. That night Laura and Enzo reaffirm their passion on Enzo's ship. Gioconda comes to kill her rival, but catches sight of the rosary and sends Laura to safety. Enzo, about to be captured by Alvise, sets fire to his ship. Convinced of Laura's infidelity, Alvise insists that she drink poison. Gioconda, who has hidden nearby, substitutes a sleeping potion. Enzo, again disguised, is horrified at Laura's supposed death and, ripping off his mask, tries to stab Alvise, but is arrested. Gioconda offers herself to Barnaba if he will save Enzo and bring Laura safely to the island of Giudecca. He agrees, but holds La Cieca as hostage. Enzo tries to kill Gioconda for refusing to reveal the whereabouts of Laura's body, but the sound of Laura's voice stops him. The lovers express their gratitude to Gioconda and bid her farewell. Barnaba comes to claim Gioconda, but she stabs herself, dying before he can reveal that he has strangled La Cieca.

Major Roles. LA GIOCONDA (dram s); demands great strength throughout range; many recurring high tones; B♭2 to C5; LAURA (m-s); high tessitura; A♯2 to B♭4. LA CIECA (c); A2 to A4. ENZO (dram t); C2 to B♭3. BARNABA (bar); B1 to G3. ALVISE (bs); G1 to F3.

Lesser Roles. ZUANE, boatman (bs). ISEPO, public letter-writer (t). PILOT (bs). A MONK (bs). TWO STREETSINGERS (2 bar). TWO VOICES in the distance (t, bs).

Chorus. SSATTBB. Monks, senators, sailors, shipwrights, ladies, gentlemen, populace, masquers, boys' chorus (SS).

Ballet. Furlana (Act I); Dance of the Hours (Act III).

Orchestra. picc, 2 fl, 2 ob (Eng hrn), 2 cl, 2 bsn, 4 hrn, 4 trp, 4 trb, tuba, timp, perc, 2 harp, strings. *Stage:* bells, organ, harp, 2 cl, 2 bsn, 3 hrn; military band in opening chorus (should play with pit orchestra in Furlana, but never done because of difficulty in keeping together). Necessary in any case: 2 cl, 2 bsn, 2 hrn, harp.

Production Problem. Burning of Enzo's ship.

Material. FS-P: Ri, Ka, TW (rent). CP: Map (rent). VS: Ri (i) $7; G Sc (i) $5. Li: Ri (e) 50¢.

Photographs. La Scala: 12.25.39 pp. 19, 20. Metropolitan: 2.26.45 pp. 12,

18; 3.28.55 pp. 18–22. Kansas State College: 11.5.45 p. 10. Caracalla: 10.
6.47 p. 15. Naples: 10.14.57 p. 13 (ballet).
Performing Companies. 329 (47–48; 52–53; 56–57; 60–61). 443B (56–
57). 130 (57–58, 1959).

🎭 Giulio Cesare in Egitto · Julius Caesar in Egypt

Music by George Frideric Handel (1685–1759). Libretto in Italian by Niccolo
Haym. Premiere: London, February 20, 1724. Historical drama. Simple harmonic structure in stately classical form; set numbers with accompanied recitative; vocal line difficult, both sustained and florid. Overture. Setting: Egypt,
48 B.C. Three acts, nine scenes (135 min — by omitting *da capos*).
ACT I i: A spacious plain on the Nile; ii: A hall in Ptolemy's palace; iii:
Pompey's tomb in Caesar's camp; iv: Banquet hall in Ptolemy's palace. ACT
II i: Cleopatra's terrace adjoining the banquet hall; ii: Room in Ptolemy's ha-
rem. ACT III i: A plain by the sea near Alexandria; ii: Interior of Ptolemy's
tent in his camp; iii: Same as I i.

Synopsis. The scene is Egypt just after Caesar has conquered Pompey, who
had fled Rome after starting civil war. Caesar promises Pompey's wife, Cornelia, pardon for her husband and family as Achillas, an Egyptian lord, arrives. Achillas brings Pompey's head, which Ptolemy has had cut off. Pompey's
son, Sextus, vows revenge. Cleopatra prepares to meet Caesar, whom she hopes
to persuade to debar her brother Ptolemy from Egypt's throne. Caesar agrees.
Cleopatra offers to help Sextus in his revenge. Ptolemy entertains Caesar in
his palace. Sextus enters and challenges Ptolemy to a duel, but is taken prisoner with his mother. The second and third acts deal with a maze of plots to
assassinate Caesar and Ptolemy, a battle between Ptolemy and Cleopatra in
which Cleopatra is taken prisoner, and the eventual death of Ptolemy by
Sextus's hand, followed by general rejoicing.

Major Roles. CAESAR (bs-bar); extremely difficult, highly ornamented and
taxing role; A1 to F3. CORNELIA (c); B2 to D4. SEXTUS (t); several florid
passages requiring technique and agility; C2 to B♭3. PTOLEMY (bs); B♭1 to
F3. CLEOPATRA (dram or col s); very taxing role, needs expert technique and
flexibility; D3 to B♭4 (opt C5).

Lesser Roles. CURIO, a Roman tribune (bs). ACHILLAS (bs-bar). NIRENUS,
a confidant of Cleopatra (bs).

Chorus. SATB. Romans, Egyptians, slaves, attendants of Cleopatra.

Ballet. Short. Romans and Egyptians.

Orchestra. 2 fl, 2 ob, 2 hrn, 2 trp, 2 harp, harpsichord, strings. *Stage:* ob,
bsn, 2 vln, vla, vcl.

Material. FS-P: Map, Pr (Gebert) (rent). VS: Map, Pr (rent); Pet (i, g)
$5; Pr (e) (rent).

Photographs. Wiesbaden: 10.18.54 p. 5. Rome: 3.11.57 p. 12. Univ. of
California at Los Angeles: 11.10.58 p. 16. Vienna: 4.6.59 p. 14.

Performing Companies. 297 (10.9.56; 57–58). 47 (57–58). 518 (6.2.58).

◢ The Good Soldier Schweik

Music by Robert Kurka (1923–1958). Libretto in English by Lewis Allan, based on Jaroslav Hasek's novel. Premiere: New York, April 23, 1958. Satire. Episodic; astringent; a few simple set pieces; occasional parody of dance forms; vocal line not melodious and often exacting, with difficult intervals; highly rhythmic. Orchestration completed by Hershey Kay. Setting: Bohemia, before and during World War I. Spoken prologue and epilogue; two acts, nineteen scenes, many of which may be suggested rather than fully set (103 min).

ACT I i: Schweik's flat in Prague; ii: A tavern; iii: Police headquarters; iv: A prison cell; v: Another room in Police headquarters; vi: Insane asylum; vii a: Schweik's flat; vii b: A street (45 min). ACT II i: An infirmary; ii a: Guardhouse; ii b: A pulpit; iii: Lt. Lukash's flat; iv: Interior of Prague-Budejovice Express; v: A private room in a café; vi a: A street; vi b: A tavern; vi c: A street; vii a: A dugout at the front; vii b: The devastated front (58 min).

Synopsis. Schweik is arrested for harmless political remarks and because of his bland good nature is deemed an idiot by psychiatrists and committed to an insane asylum. Thoroughly happy there, he is accused of malingering and thrown out. Suffering an attack of rheumatism, he nevertheless reports for army duty. In the infirmary an army doctor attempts to convert him and other suspected malingerers to patriotism by prescribing an enema three times a day. The Baroness von Botzenheim comes to see Schweik, whose gesture in reporting for the draft in a wheelchair has aroused wide acclaim. The doctor throws Schweik in the guardhouse, where the chaplain picks him as orderly, soon losing him to Lt. Lukash in a poker game. Schweik complicates his master's life with a dog, and by arranging an embarrassing meeting between the lieutenant, his mistress, and her husband. The lieutenant is ordered to the front. Schweik is taken off the train for pulling the emergency cord, but the lieutenant's relief is shortlived: his faithful servant cheerfully returns. They finally reach the front. Schweik goes out on patrol, loses himself, and wanders off, following his inclination.

Major Role. JOSEPH SCHWEIK (buf t); long and arduous role; difficult at both extremes of range; acting ability necessary; A1 to B3.

Lesser Roles. (Doubling possibilities are shown. Each role may be taken by separate singer or actor). BRETSCHNEIDER, secret policeman; FIRST PSYCHIATRIST, FIRST DOCTOR (t). A GUARD, A SERGEANT, MR. WENDLER (t). PALIVEC, GENERAL VON SCHWARZBURG, MR. KAKONYI (bar). SECOND PSYCHIATRIST, SECOND DOCTOR, ARMY DOCTOR, LT. LUKASH (bar). POLICE OFFICER, THIRD PSYCHIATRIST, COL. KRAUS VON ZILLERGUT (bs). MRS. MULLER, KATY, MRS. KAKONYI (s). BARONESS VON BOTZENHEIM (c). PROLOGUE, THE DOG, VODITCHKA, SERGEANT VANEK (speaking).

Chorus. TB. Prisoners, malingerers, wounded soldiers. SATB. The Baroness's retinue, tavern patrons.

Ballet (or pantomimists). Guards, suspects at police headquarters, attendants and inmates at insane asylum, tavern patrons, civilians, soldiers, police.

Orchestra. picc, fl, ob, Eng hrn, cl, bs cl, bsn, cont bsn, 3 hrn, 2 trp, trb, sn drum, timp (no strings).

Material. All We: FS-P, VS, CP (rent), CP 50¢. Polka and waltz: FS $3; P $6. Suite: MS $3.50. Li $1.

Photographs. Mus. Amer. N.Y. City Opera: 5.58 p. 7.

Performing Companies. 334 (4.23.58 – prem).

La Grande Duchesse de Gérolstein · The Grand Duchess of Gerolstein

Music by Jacques Offenbach (1819–1880). Libretto by Henri Meilhac and Ludovic Halévy. Premiere: Paris, April 12, 1867. Comedy. Set numbers and dialogue. Short introduction. Setting: the fictitious German Duchy of Gerolstein, 1720. Three acts, four scenes.

ACT I: An encampment. ACT II: A drawingroom in the palace. ACT III i: The Red Room; ii: The camp.

Synopsis. Baron Puck and General Boum have been managing the affairs of Gerolstein for the early-orphaned Duchess. To occupy her mind until her marriage to Prince Paul, a weakling whom they would welcome, Puck and Boum arrange a big parade. But the Duchess takes a fancy to the common soldier, Fritz, and keeps postponing her wedding. Ignoring Fritz's confessed attachment to the peasant girl Wanda, the Duchess creates him Baron of Vermout-von-bock-bier, Count of Avall-vintt-katt-schopp-vergiss-mein-nicht, and makes him commanding general of the army for the imminent war against her neighbors. The victorious general returns and marries his Wanda. Then he retires with her to the Red Room, assigned to him by the Duchess because a secret passage connects it with her own apartments. The Duchess, outraged, joins a plot by Puck, Boum, and Prince Paul. The bridal night is successfully ruined, the groom thoroughly beaten up and returned to his former grade of private and his former status of commoner. The Duchess, after another short flirtation – with Ambassador von Grog, who turns out to be married and the father of four children – restores Puck and Boum to their former positions and resignedly settles down to married life with Prince Paul.

Major Roles. LA GRANDE DUCHESSE (m-s); A2 to B♭4 or at least A4. FRITZ (t); high tessitura, strong and flexible; C2 to B3. WANDA (lyr col s); D3 to C5. GENERAL BOUM (buf bs or buf bar); unexacting vocal requirements; A1 to F3 (G3 opt).

Lesser Roles. BARON PUCK (t); A1 or at least D2 to A3 or at least G3. PRINCE PAUL (buf t or bar); A1 or at least D2 to G3. (Alternate notes indicate possible transpositions.) IZA, OLGA, AMELIE, CHARLOTTE, maids of honor (2 s to G♯4; 2 m-s); often reduced to bit parts by cutting the Letter Couplets at the opening of Act II.

Bit Parts. BARON GROG, ambassador from Prince Paul's electorate. NEPO-MUC, aide-de-camp of the Grand Duchess.

Chorus. SATTBB. Lords and ladies of the court, maids of honor, pages, soldiers, country girls, etc.

77

Orchestra. 2 fl, 2 ob, 2 cl, bsn, 2 hrn, 2 trp, 2 trb, perc, timp, strings. *Stage:* Chimes BCDE, sn drum, trp.
Material. FS-P: Map, TW (rent). VS: B & H (f, e — Baynes-Robinson) (rent); Map (f) (rent); TW (e — Martin) (rent).
Performing Companies. 97E (8.21.54). 297 (57–58, 59–60).

🎵 Hänsel und Gretel · Hansel and Gretel

Music by Engelbert Humperdinck (1854–1921). Libretto in German by Adelheid Wette based on the fairy tale by Ludwig Grimm. Premiere: Weimar, December 23, 1893. Fairy tale. Set numbers; accompanied recitative woven into continuous texture; folk-like melodies with vocal line patterned on the inflections of speech. Overture. Setting: the Hartz Mountains in Germany; once upon a time. Three acts (91 min).

ACT I: Peter's house (30 min). ACT II: The forest (24 min). ACT III: The Witch's house (37 min).

Synopsis. Hänsel and Gretel are sent by their mother, Gertrude, into the woods to pick berries for supper. Later, when their father, Peter, returns with food and finds the children still gone, he apprehensively leads his wife out to search. Hänsel and Gretel have meanwhile wandered deep into the forest, where night overtakes them. Thoroughly lost, they eat the berries they have picked and say their prayers. The Sandman puts them to sleep as angels descend to guard them. The next morning, awakened by the Dewman, the children discover a gingerbread house which they proceed to nibble. The Witch appears from the house, captures them, sets Gretel to work, and puts Hänsel in a cage preparatory to eating him. Gretel soon frees her brother, and when the Witch demonstrates to Gretel how to examine a hot oven, the children push her in and slam the door. The explosion of the oven breaks the Witch's spell and children she had transformed into gingerbread return to life. Peter and Gertrude rush in for a joyous reunion.

Major Roles. GRETEL (lyr s); should have trill, girlish appearance; C3 to Bb4 (opt D5). HANSEL (m-s); should look boyish; voice must blend well with Gretel's; A2 to Ab4 (opt A4). GERTRUDE (m-s); B2 to B4. PETER (bar), Bb1 to F♯3 (opt A3 laugh). WITCH (m-s); need not have pleasing quality; can sound harsh, rasping, and evil; Bb2 to A4 (opt B4).

Lesser Roles. SANDMAN (s); C♯3 to F♯4. DEWMAN (s); E3 to A4.
Chorus. SA. Children.
Ballet. Fourteen angels.
Orchestra. 2 fl, picc, 2 ob (2 Eng hrn), 2 cl (bs cl), 2 bsn, 4 hrn, 2 trp, 3 trb, bs tuba, timp, perc, harp, strings. *Stage:* cuckoo instrument.
Production Problems. Descent of the angels; explosion of the oven; revitalization of the gingerbread children; mist parting to reveal witch's house.
Material. FS-P: G Sc, Ka, Map, TW (rent). FS: Br (g) $17.50. MS: Pet (Eul — g) $15. CP: Map (rent); G Sc 50¢. VS: Map, TW (rent); AMP (Sch — g) $9, (e) $7.50, School (e) $3; G Sc (e — Bache) $4. O Tr: Sour (BMI); Longstreth (B & H).

78

Photographs. Philadelphia Academy of Vocal Arts: 11.6.44 p. 12. Metropolitan: 1.6.47 p. 19. Scranton: 2.23.48 p. 30. Passaic: 3.22.48 p. 23. Texas Christian Univ.: 12.7.53 p. 28. Hartt College: 1.18.54 p. 3.
Performing Companies. Approx 72. 1956–57 only: 64, 69, 88, 109, 215, 247, 304, 321A, 346, 359, 420, 448, 512, 526.

🎭 He Who Gets Slapped, formerly Pantaloon

Music by Robert Ward (1917–   ). Libretto in English by Bernard Stambler, based on Andreyev's play by the same name. Premiere: New York, May 17, 1956. Drama; the original tragedy has been mellowed in the libretto to resignation, even with a suggestion of happiness to come. Highly melodic, in several styles; arias and recitative; conservatively harmonized. No overture. Short preludes to Acts II and III. The set for all three acts is the combined office, rehearsal room, and lounging room of a small circus in a French city, around 1910 (150 min).

Synopsis. Into the world of a small, provincial circus enters a stranger who begs to be taken on as a clown. He is obviously a gentleman — in fact, he has tried many careers but has always failed and been slapped down by fate. Now he wants to be Pantaloon, "he who gets slapped." Briquet, the owner of the circus, consents. Immediately Pantaloon becomes a catalyst in the lives of those about him. The bogus Count Mancini is scheming to marry his lovely daughter, Consuelo, to a dissolute old nobleman, Baron Regnard. Consuelo, however, is strongly attracted to her partner, Bezano, the stalwart bareback rider who has also caught the fancy of Zinida, the lion-tamer. Zinida is restrained only by the watchful eye of her husband, Briquet. To save Consuelo, whom he deeply cherishes, from a loveless marriage, Pantaloon stages a mock ceremony, in which the true characters of the Baron and Mancini are brought out. He himself is exposed as a failure by Zinida, who knows his past life. He quits the circus in sorrow, leaving behind him the shattered plans of the schemers and the beginning of hope for the young lovers.

Major Roles. COUNT MANCINI, a shopworn aristocrat (t); C♯2 to B♭3. BRIQUET, owner and ringmaster (bs-bar); F1 to F3. ZINIDA (dram s); high tessitura; C3 to G5. PANTALOON (bar); G1 to G3. CONSUELO, Bareback Tango Queen (s); C♯3 to B4. BEZANO (t); C♯2 to B3. BARON REGNARD, a stolid aristocrat from commerce (bs-bar); B♭1 to E3.

Lesser Roles. TILLY and POLLY, clowns (mute). CLOWN MAESTRO (mute).

Chorus. SSAATTB. Clowns, barker, tall man, small man, fat lady, acrobats, dancers, other circus personnel.

Orchestra. 2 fl (picc), 2 ob (Eng hrn), 2 cl (bs cl), 2 bsn (cont bsn), 4 hrn, 3 trp, 3 trb, timp, perc, xyl, maracas (2), harp, strings. P-Yes.

Material. FS-P: Ga (Hi) (rent). VS: Ga (Hi — e, g) (rent).

Photographs. Columbia Univ.: 11.19.56 p. 21. *Mus. Amer.* N.Y. City Opera: 5.59 p. 7.
Performing Companies. 302 (5.17.56 — prem). 334 (4.12.59).

⍚ Idomeneo

Music by Wolfgang Amadeus Mozart (1756–1791). Libretto in Italian by Abbé Giambattista Varesco, based on Danchet's libretto for "Idoménée" by André Campra. Premiere: Munich, January 29, 1781. Stately classical drama. Set numbers, several of them display pieces; expressive, often exalted, melody; recitative. Overture. Setting: Crete in mythological times. Three acts, four scenes (approx 140 min).

ACT I: Outside Idomeneo's castle (40 min). ACT II: The castle (36 min). ACT III i: The castle (24 min); ii: The Temple of Neptune (32 min).

Synopsis. Idomeneo, King of Crete, is beset by storms as he returns from the Trojan wars, and, in return for safe passage, vows to sacrifice to Neptune the first person he meets on his return home. Tragically, the person is his son Idamante. To avert the consequences of his oath he sends his son to Greece with Electra, who loves him, but their departure is prevented by a wild tempest. Idomeneo, realizing the gods' wrath at his duplicity, confesses all to the High Priest. Meanwhile, Idamante and Ilia, a captured Trojan princess, express their love. Idamante departs to fight an evil monster sent by Neptune. He kills the beast; then, learning of his father's vow, offers his life to the gods. Ilia begs to be sacrificed in his place, but Neptune himself intercedes: if Idomeneo abdicates, and Idamante and Ilia are proclaimed rulers of Crete, all will be forgiven. Everyone rejoices except the spurned Electra.

Major Roles. (All demand classical, florid style.) ILIA (lyr s); needs trill; long sustained line; D3 to C♯5. ELECTRA (dram s); strong penetrating quality desirable; B2 to C5. IDAMANTE (s – usually sung by t); trill and coloratura technique necessary; C3 to B♭4 (C2 to B♭3 for t). IDOMENEO (t); demands great technical facility; C2 to A3.

Lesser Roles. ARBACE, confidant of Idomeneo (bar). HIGH PRIEST (t). VOICE OF NEPTUNE (bs).

Chorus. SSAATB (SATB solos). People of Crete, Trojan prisoners, sailors, soldiers, priests of Neptune, dancers.

Orchestra. 2 fl, picc, 2 ob, 2 cl, 2 bsn, 4 hrn, 2 trp, 3 trb, timp, strings.

Material. VS: AMP (SZ – i) $6; Ri (i) $7. Tr: Caldwell and Goldovsky (T13); Radford (T14); Mangan (321).

Photographs. Glyndebourne: 10.15.51 p. 9. Munich: 2.27.56 p. 30. Berlin: 11.2.56 p. 12.

Performing Companies. 323 (1952). 202 (1.11.53). 321 (1.27.55). 53 (3.7.55). 479A (11.56). 104 (2.9.61).

⍚ L'Incoronazione di Poppea · The Coronation of Poppea

Music by Claudio Monteverdi (1567–1643). Libretto in Italian by Giovan Francesco Busenello. Premiere: Venice, 1642. Historical drama, set in Rome at the apex of Nero's rule, A.D. 62. Intensely dramatic recitatives, expressive ariosos, arias, and duets mostly consisting of short sections connected by orchestral interludes (ritornellos), and occasional choral numbers. The original libretto gives five settings: At Poppea's palace; Garden at Poppea's palace; Nero's palace; Seneca's country house; In the city of Rome (any neutral location or interior in the palace is adequate). Several modern versions exist: Giacomo Benvenuti, prologue and 3 acts; premiere: Florence, June 3, 1937. G. F. Ghedini, 3 acts, 4 parts, 13 scenes; premiere: Milan, January 6, 1953. Ernst Krenek, 2 acts, 7 scenes. G. F. Malipiero, 3 acts. (Approx 150 min — American Opera Society vers approx 90 min.)

Synopsis. Ottone, Nero's general, cannot forget his love for his wife Poppea, who has given herself to Nero. His efforts to return Drusilla's love are vain. Nero, overriding Seneca's opposition, decides to divorce Ottavia and marry Poppea. Ordered by Ottavia to kill Poppea, Ottone dresses in Drusilla's clothes and bungles his half-hearted effort. His confession saves the accused Drusilla; both are sent into exile. Ottavia also is banished, Seneca is condemned to death, and Poppea is crowned empress.

Major Roles. (Florid singing required from all.) POPPEA (m-s); C3 to G4. NERO (lyr t); needs strong low tessitura; D2 to A3. OTTAVIA (m-s or s); low tessitura; C3 to A4. OTTONE (bar); A1 to Eb3.

Lesser Roles. SENECA (bs); G1 to E3. DRUSILLA (light s); C3 to G4. ARNALTA, companion of Poppea (c); A2 to D4. VALETTO, page (s); D3 to B4. DAMIGELLA, lady of the court (s); D#3 to F4. TWO SOLDIERS (both t); top G3. PALLAS (s). MERCURY (t). NUTRICE (NURSE) of Ottavia (c). AMORE (s).

Bit Parts. LIBERTO, captain of the palace guard (t). LICTOR (bs). (Except for Seneca and the soldiers all male roles were originally sung by women.)

Chorus. SATTBB (small part). Consuls, friends of Seneca, Tribunes, Romans.

Ballet. Opt.

Orchestra. Original: strings (viole da braccio and da gamba), 2 organs, chitarrone, harpsichord. Benvenuti: 3 fl, 2 ob, 2 cl, 2 bsn, 4 hrn, 2 trp, 3 trb, tuba, 2 harp, strings. *Stage:* 2 bands. Ghedini: 3 fl, 4 ob, 4 cl, 4 bsn, 3 trp, 3 trb, organ, clavichord or piano, harp, strings. Krenek: fl, ob, cl, bsn, 2 hrn, trp, trb, harp, harmonium, piano, or cembalo. Malipiero: 2 fl, 2 ob, 2 cl, 2 bsn, 2 hrn, trp, harp, piano. American Opera Society: strings, harp, piano.

Material. FS-P: AMP (SZ — Benvenuti; UE — Krenek) (rent); Pr (Mer — Malipiero) (rent); Ri (Ghedini) (rent). VS: AMP (SZ — Benvenuti — i) $8.25; (UE — Krenek — i, g) $6; Pr (Mer — Malipiero — i, f) $5; Ri (Ghedini) $10. O Tr: Kallman (297); Stuart (T6).

Performing Companies. 198A (5.12.50). 297 (2.8.53; 55–56; 2.2.58). 176 (4.29.55). 133 (5.23.56). 358 (57–58).

⚜ Iphigénie en Aulide · Iphigenia in Aulis

Music by Christoph Willibald von Gluck (1714–1787). Libretto in French by Bailli du Roullet based on a drama by Racine, originally from Euripides, after the myth. Premiere: Paris, April 19, 1774 (later edition by Richard Wagner). Accompanied recitatives and set numbers in expressive classic style.

Simple harmonic structure. Overture. Setting: Aulis, before the Trojan War. Three acts, four scenes.

ACT I: Agamemnon's camp. ACT II: Agamemnon's palace. ACT III i: Agamemnon's tent; ii: Altar of Artemis.

Synopsis. Agamemnon, King of Greece, has incurred the wrath of the goddess Artemis (Diana), who takes revenge by becalming the Greek ships in Aulis bound for the Trojan War. To propitiate her, Agamemnon reluctantly agrees to sacrifice his daughter, Iphigenia, but secretly sends a message warning her not to come to Aulis. The girl and her mother Clytemnestra arrive unexpectedly to join Iphigenia's betrothed, Achilles. Agamemnon, though reassuring the High Priest Calchas that he will allow the sacrifice, tries another ruse, informing Iphigenia that Achilles has been unfaithful to her and urging her to depart. The hero himself clears up this misunderstanding, and all is in readiness for the wedding ceremony. The vacillating Agamemnon can no longer appease the Greeks, who demand the sacrifice. In spite of Clytemnestra's anguished protests and Achilles' resort to armed intervention, the High Priest's knife is lifted over the victim, when the goddess herself relents. Iphigenia is saved — not for marriage with Achilles, as the triumphant celebrational ending of the opera might indicate, but as a potential priestess for Diana, as she appears in the original myth and in Gluck's own sequel, "Iphigenia in Tauris."

Major Roles. IPHIGENIA (s); florid style, long sustained line; B♭2 to A4. CLYTEMNESTRA (m-s); C♯3 to A4. ACHILLES (t); extremely high tessitura; dramatic, lengthy role; F♯2 to B3. AGAMEMNON (bar). Understanding of classic style necessary for all roles.

Lesser Roles. PATROCLAS, Achilles' friend (bs). CALCHAS, High Priest (bs). ARKAS, captain of the guard (bs). ARTEMIS (DIANA), a goddess (s).

Chorus. SATTBB. Greeks.

Ballet. Several important dances.

Orchestra. 2 fl, 2 ob, 2 cl, 2 bsn, 2 hrn, 2 trp, 3 trb, timp, strings.

Material. FS-P: Ka, TW (rent). VS: TW (rent); AMP (BH — g) $1.80; Pet (f) $8; (f, g) $6.

Photographs. Boboli Gardens: 10.16.50 p. 7. Berlin: 10.31.55 p. 21.

Performing Companies. None recently.

◪ Iphigénie en Tauride · Iphigenia in Tauris

Music by Christoph Willibald von Gluck (1714–1787). Libretto in French by François Guillard, based on Euripides' drama. Premiere: Paris, May 18, 1779. Classic drama. Accompanied recitatives and set numbers; simple harmonic structure; less florid and more directly dramatic than earlier Gluck works; highly expressive; prominent chorus. Overture. Setting: Tauris, after the Trojan War. Four acts.

ACT I: Entrance to the Temple of Diana. ACT II: A subterranean chamber in the Temple of Diana. ACT III: Iphigenia's apartment in the temple. ACT IV: Interior of the temple.

82

Synopsis. Iphigenia has become a priestess in the Temple of Diana on Tauris, and is ignorant of the death of her father Agamemnon at the hands of her mother Clytemnestra, and the subsequent slaying of Clytemnestra by Orestes, Iphigenia's brother. However, she dreams that an evil fate has overtaken her family, and is unresponsive when Thoas, King of Scythia, demands a human sacrifice. He has been told by the oracle that any stranger who appears on the island must be killed. Providentially two shipwrecked Greeks appear: they are Orestes and his friend Pylades. Without revealing his identity, Orestes tells Iphigenia of their parents' fate, saying that Orestes is also dead. Iphigenia senses a resemblance between the stranger and her brother and tries to save him by sending him with a letter to her sister Electra, but Orestes refuses, threatening to kill himself unless she sends his friend. Pylades takes the letter, hoping to rescue Orestes. At the moment of sacrifice, Iphigenia cannot strike, and discovers Orestes' identity. As Thoas threatens both, Pylades rushes in and stabs the king; Greek warriors overcome the Scythians. Diana appears and pardons Orestes.

Major Roles. IPHIGENIA (s); long line, must give impression of strength; B2 to A4. PYLADES (t); F2 to A3. ORESTES (bar); high tessitura; D2 to F♯3. THOAS (bs or bar); high tessitura; E♯2 to G3.

Lesser Roles. DIANA (s). A GREEK WOMAN (s). TWO PRIESTESSES (s, s). MINISTER OF THE SANCTUARY (bs). A SCYTH (bar).

Chorus. SATTB. Scythians, priestesses, Greeks, furies.

Ballet. One of importance, others sometimes interpolated.

Orchestra. 3 fl (bs fl), 2 ob, 2 cl, 2 bsn, 2 hrn, 2 trp, 3 trb, timp, perc, strings. Strauss vers: 2 fl, 2 ob, 2 cl, 2 bsn, 2 hrn, 2 trp, 3 trb, timp, strings.

Material. FS-P: B & H (Strauss) (rent). MS: Pet (Eu—f, g) $6. VS: Pet (f) $8. Tr: Goldovsky and Caldwell (T13).

Photographs. Berkshires: 10.10.49 p. 28. Pittsburgh: 10.31.49 p. 20. Aix: 11.10.52 p. 14. Munich: 1.5.59 p. 26.

Performing Companies. 297 (2.12.55). 323 (1.19.59—conc).

⚜ L'Italiana in Algeri · The Italian Woman in Algiers

Music by Gioacchino Rossini (1792–1868). Libretto in Italian by Angelo Anelli. Premiere: Venice, May 22, 1813. Comedy in tradition of commedia dell' arte. Very melodious; set numbers with accompanied recitatives. Overture ("Sinfonia"). Setting: Algiers, 18th century. Two acts, eight scenes (120 min).

ACT I i: Little apartment in the Bey's palace; ii: Near the seashore; iii: Same as I i; iv: Grand hall in the palace. ACT II i: Same as I i; ii: Large apartment in the palace; iii: Same as I i; iv: Same as I iv.

Synopsis. Mustapha, the Bey of Algeria, has grown tired of his wife Elvira and sends Haly, the captain of his guard, to find an Italian wife for him. Lindoro, an Italian slave at the Bey's court, bemoans the absence of Isabella, his Italian fiancée. Isabella is conveniently shipwrecked on the shores of Algeria while roaming the seas searching for Lindoro. Her traveling companion is the foolish old Taddeo, who loves her. Haly brings his captives to the Bey, and Isabella is reunited with Lindoro. The Bey, however, insists that Lindoro marry Elvira to take her off his hands and free him to marry Isabella. Isabella manages to avoid being alone with Mustapha, declaring that she will marry him only on condition that he go through an ancient and noble ceremony of proving that he will make a completely docile husband. At the end of the ridiculous initiation ceremony, a boat which Isabella has ordered appears; she and Lindoro embark with the rest of the Italian colony in Algiers. Realizing that he has been hoodwinked, Mustapha perforce forgives his departing captives and returns to Elvira.

Major Roles. MUSTAPHA (bs); florid, requires agility; B♭1 to G3. ELVIRA (s); E3 to C5. LINDORO (lyr t); difficult coloratura; consistently high tessitura; demands extraordinary technique; F2 to C4. ISABELLA (c); extreme facility required; considerable coloratura; A2 to B4. TADDEO (buf bs); C2 to G3.

Lesser Roles. ZULMA, Elvira's companion (m-s). HALY (bs).

Chorus. TTBB. Eunuchs of the seraglio, guards, sailors. Women of the seraglio (mute).

Orchestra. 2 fl, 2 ob, 2 cl, 2 bsn, 2 hrn, 2 trp, trb, timp, perc, piano for recitatives, strings.

Material. FS-P: Map, TW (rent). CP: Map (i) (rent). VS: Ri (i) $10; Map (rent).

Performing Companies. 474C (1957, 1958).

🞏 Die Königskinder · The King's Children

Music by Engelbert Humperdinck (1854–1921). Libretto in German by Ernst Rosmer (Mrs. Max Bernstein). Premiere: New York, December 28, 1910. Morality play in form of a fairy tale. The post-Wagnerian music of continuous texture is, nevertheless, basically simple, tuneful, and often folklike. Setting: Hellabrunn, Germany, and surroundings; Middle Ages. Three acts (160 min).

ACT I: Woods in front of the witch's hut (60 min). ACT II: At the city gates of Hellabrunn (40 min). ACT III: In front of the witch's hut (60 min).

Synopsis. A king's daughter has been put under a witch's spell and lives in a forest as a goose girl. She is discovered by a king's son who has hired out as a swineherd to gain experience. They love each other, but the Princess cannot break the spell. The Prince continues his wanderings. A broommaker and a minstrel, ambassadors from a city that has long been without a ruler, ask advice of the witch, who says the proper ruler will be the first person to enter the city gates after noon the next day. The minstrel recognizes the Princess, breaks the spell, and takes the girl with him. She is first through the gate and meets the Prince, who embraces her. The couple are not recognized as royalty by the populace, who ridicule and chase them out of town. Eventually, driven by hunger, they are forced to give their royal crown to greedy merchants, in exchange for a loaf of bread. But the bread has been poisoned by the

84

witch. The lovers die in each other's arms and are buried by the snow. The children — the only ones to recognize the royal pair for what they are — find them buried under the tree where they first met.

Major Roles. KING'S SON (lyr t); C2 to B♭3. GOOSE GIRL (lyr s); D♭3 (one B2) to A4 (B4 opt) — one shout written as C♯5. FIDDLER (high lyr bar); D2 to G♭3 (G3 opt) — one A♭3. WITCH (dram c); a character role; A♭2 to F♯4.

Lesser Roles. WOODCUTTER (bs); B♭1 to F3. BROOMMAKER (buf t); top G3. INNKEEPER'S DAUGHTER (s); C3 to G4. INNKEEPER (bs), top F♯3. STABLE MAID (m-s); G2 to F♯4. BROOMMAKER'S DAUGHTER (child); D3 to D4.

Bit Parts. TAILOR (t). SENIOR COUNCILLOR (bs). TWO GATEKEEPERS (both bar).

Chorus. SAATTTBBBB and 3-part children's chorus or additional SAA. Townsfolk, burghers, tradespeople, youths, the village band, children.

Orchestra. 2 fl, picc, 2 ob, Eng hrn, 2 cl, bs cl, 2 bsn, cont bsn, 4 hrn, 3 trp, 3 trb, bs tuba, timp, perc, harp, celeste, strings. *Stage:* 2 vln, vla, vcl, chimes, tam-tam (piano).

Production Problem. Geese, live or mechanical, must move.

Material. Not in U.S.

𝕸 Lakmé

Music by Léo Delibes (1836–1891). Libretto by Edmond Gondinet and Phillipe Gille, based on Gondinet's play "Le Mariage de Loti." Premiere: Paris, April 14, 1883. Oriental romance. Simple melodies with many coloratura passages; set numbers; accompanied recitatives; dialogue, sometimes over music. Music often has pseudo-Oriental flavor. Prelude. Setting: India, 19th century. Three acts (133 min).

ACT I: A temple garden (49 min). ACT II: A public square (55 min). ACT III: A forest (29 min).

Synopsis. Gerald, a British soldier, trespasses in a forbidden Hindu garden, discovering Lakmé, daughter of the priest Nilakantha. They are immediately drawn to each other. She begs him to leave before her father finds him, but he delays too long. Nilakantha vows death to the desecrator of holy ground. To discover the trespasser's identity he forces the disguised Lakmé to sing in the public square, where Gerald rushes to her. Nilakantha stabs the young man, leaving him for dead, but Lakmé nurses him back to health. Their idyll ends when Gerald, hearing martial music in the distance and heeding the advice of his comrade Frederic, feels the call to duty. Divining his intentions, Lakmé eats a poisonous flower and dies, proclaiming her love. Her father, who has returned to kill Gerald, sets him free.

Major Roles. LAKME (col s); needs high, accurate voice with great agility and good trill; small, lithe figure preferable; D3 to D♯5 (opt E5). GERALD (lyr t); requires facility in high range; E2 to B3. NILAKANTHA (bs); G1 to F♯3.

Lesser Roles. FREDERIC, a British soldier (bar). HADJI, a Hindu slave (t). ELLEN, daughter of the governor (s). ROSE, Ellen's friend (s). MRS. BENSON, governess of the young ladies (m-s). MALLIKA, Lakmé's slave (m-s).

Chorus. SSTTBB. Hindu men and women, English officers and ladies, sailors, Chinese, musicians, Brahmins.

Orchestra. 2 fl, 2 ob, 2 cl, 2 bsn, 4 hrn, 2 trp, 3 trb, timp, perc, harp, strings. *Stage:* fl, 2 picc, ob, cl, 2 hrn, side drum, triangle, cymbal, tambourine.

Material. FS-P: Pr, Ka, Map, TW (rent). CP: Map (f, i) (rent). VS: Map (rent); Pr (f) $12; Pr (Mer − f) $12. Tr: Carpenter and Norton (Univ. of Oklahoma Press).

Photographs. Metropolitan: 1.1.40 p. 16; 12.22.41 pp. 17, 18, 20; 1.4.43 pp. 12, 16. San Francisco: 10.7.40 cover.

Performing Companies. 397 (10.52). 180 (12.2.54; 10.22.59). 495 (3.6. 54). 33 (5.17.55). 391 (7.55). 38 (56–57). 443B (3.4.60).

⚜ Lohengrin

Music by Richard Wagner (1813–1883). Libretto in German by the composer, based on a medieval legend. Premiere: Weimar, August 28, 1850. Romantic drama with some religious symbolism. Heavily orchestrated, moderate use of leitmotifs; prominent chorus; continuous texture with several formal numbers. Preludes to Acts I and III. Setting: in and around Antwerp, early 10th century. Three acts, four scenes (185 min).

ACT I: The banks of the River Scheldt (58 min). ACT II: Courtyard of King Henry's castle at Antwerp (71 min). ACT III i: The bridal chamber (27 min); ii: Same as Act I (29 min).

Synopsis. Elsa of Brabant is accused by Count Telramund of murdering her young brother Gottfried. In trial by combat she is successfully defended by a mysterious knight who appears in answer to her prayer in a swan-drawn boat. He offers her his hand on condition that she never ask his name or origin. She accepts and they are married. Telramund's wife Ortrud has meanwhile convinced Elsa she must ask the forbidden question, and, in the bridal chamber, she does. The knight assembles the court and tells his story: he is Lohengrin, a servant of the Holy Grail. Before he leaves he transforms his swan into the missing Gottfried, who had been put under a spell by Ortrud. Sadly Lohengrin bids Elsa farewell and sails away, his boat now drawn by the dove of the Holy Grail. Elsa falls lifeless in Gottfried's arms.

Major Roles. LOHENGRIN (dram t); fine-spun singing necessary for many passages; Db1 to A3. HENRY I (HENRY THE FOWLER) (bs); high tessitura; E1 to F3. FREDERICK, COUNT TELRAMUND (bar); sustained high singing; B1 to G3. ELSA (spin s, often dram s); needs strong, clear voice for ensembles, good high pianissimo; C3 to B4. ORTRUD (m-s, frequently sung by dram s); requires large voice with strong top; keen dramatic sense; Bb2 to Bb4.

Lesser Role. ROYAL HERALD (bar).

Bit Parts. GOTTFRIED (mute). FOUR NOBLES OF BRABANT (TTBB). FOUR PAGES (SSAA). EIGHT LADIES (SSAA).

Chorus. SSAATTBB (as large as possible; frequently divided into two separate choruses). Saxon and Brabantian nobles, ladies, and pages.

Orchestra. 3 fl, 3 ob (Eng hrn), 3 cl (bs cl), 3 bsn, 4 hrn, 3 trp, 3 trb, tuba, timp, perc, harp, strings. *Stage:* picc, 2 fl, 3 ob, 3 cl, 2 bsn, 4 hrn, 3 trb, 12 trp (can be fewer), side drum, harp.

Production Problems. Swan boat entrance and exit; transformation of swan to human form; appearance of dove.

Material. FS-P: Map, Ka, Ri, TW (rent). CP: Map (g) (e) (rent). VS: G Sc (g, e) $5; Map, TW (rent). Tr: Spaeth and Cowdrey (T22).

Photographs. Metropolitan: ACT I: 12.28.42 p. 16, 17; 12.17.45 p. 5; 4.3.50 p. 12; 4.6.53 p. 18; 12.21.53 p. 7. ACT II: 4.6.53 p. 19; 12.19.55 p. 20. ACT III i: 12.28.42 p. 20; 12.17.45 p. 20; 1.26.59 p. 20. ACT III ii: 4.6.53 p. 18; 1.26.59 p. 21. Munich: ACTS I, II: 1.20.47 p. 4; 3.14.55 p. 28. Antwerp: ACT II: 1.2. 50 p. 30. Brussels: 4.17.50 p. 28 (sketch). Vienna: 2.4.52 p. 32. Bayreuth: 10.19.53 p. 8 (Act I); 9.29.58 p. 7 (Act II). *Mus. Amer.* Bayreuth, ACT II ii: 9.58 p. 5.

Performing Companies. 449 (2.25.54; 59–60). 443B (3.19.54). 72 (10. 20.55). 329 (55–56, 58–59). 463 (2.16.56). 308 (56–57).

🎭 Louise

Music by Gustave Charpentier (1860–1956). Libretto in French by the composer. Premiere: Paris, February 2, 1900. Naturalistic romance. Some mild dissonance; readily singable melodies. Set numbers separated by lengthy accompanied recitative. Prelude. Setting, Paris, about 1900. Four acts, five scenes (158 min).

ACT I: A room in a tenement (38 min). ACT II i: A street in Montmartre (29 min); ii: A dressmaking factory (16 min). ACT III: A small garden in Montmartre (45 min). ACT IV: Same as Act I (30 min).

Synopsis. It has been said that Paris is the heroine of this opera, and certainly the city's effect on the characters is an important element. Louise, the daughter of a working man, is in love with the artist Julien. He writes to her father asking formal permission to marry her, but the absolute opposition of her mother makes denial certain. At Julien's insistence, Louise runs away from home and from her job as a seamstress and goes to live with him. They are blissfully happy, surrounded by the life of a city they both adore; but their idyll is interrupted when Louise's mother brings the news that her father is desperately ill and longs to see her again. Despite Julien's suspicions, Louise returns home upon the promise that she may rejoin her lover whenever she desires. Under her care her father returns to health, but his self-pity does not keep Louise from pining for Julien and Paris, both now denied her by her parents despite their promise. After a violent argument, the girl rushes back to freedom as her father curses the city.

Major Roles. LOUISE (lyr s); should have sustained high pianissimo, stamina; C3 to B4. JULIEN (lyr t); opportunity for light, lyrical singing; D♯2 to B3. THE MOTHER (m-s); should give vocal impression of older woman; A♯2 to G♯4. THE FATHER (bar); also elderly type, good character actor desirable; comfortable tessitura; A1 to G♭3.

Bit Parts. IRMA (s). CAMILLE (s). GERTRUDE (m-s). AN ERRAND GIRL (s).

ELISE (s). BLANCHE (s). SUZANNE (m-s). A STREETSWEEPER (m-s). A YOUNG
RAGPICKER (m-s). A FOREWOMAN (m-s). A MILK WOMAN (s). A NEWSPAPER
GIRL (s). A COAL GATHERER (m-s). MARGUERITE (s). MADELEINE (m-s). A
DANCER (mute). A NOCTAMBULIST (t). A RAGMAN (bs). AN OLD BOHEMIAN
(bar). A SONG WRITER (bar). A JUNKMAN (bs). A PAINTER (bs). TWO PHILOSO-
PHERS (t, bs). A YOUNG POET (bar). A STUDENT (t). TWO POLICEMEN (bar).
A STREET ARAB (s). A SCULPTOR (bar). AN OLD CLOTHES MAN (t). AN APPREN-
TICE (bar). THE KING OF FOOLS (t). (Many may be doubled.)

Chorus. SATB. Street peddlers, working men and women, voices of the
town, etc.

Orchestra. 3 fl (picc), 2 ob (Eng hrn), 3 cl (bs cl), 2 bsn, 4 hrn, 3 trp,
3 trb, bs tuba, timp, perc, 2 harp, celeste, strings.

Material. FS-P: Pr (rent). VS: Pr (Mer — f, e, g, i) $13.50; G Sc (f, e)
$7.50. VS: Pr (Mer — f, e, g, i) $13.50.

Photographs. Metropolitan: 1.16.39 p. 3; 2.15.43 p. 12; 1.4.48 pp. 18,
19. Paris Opéra Comique: 2.15.43 p. 18.

Performing Companies. 329 (47–49). 32B (54–55). 55A (1.55). 72 (10.
25.55). 514 (56–57).

☙ The Love for Three Oranges

Music by Serge Prokofiev (1891–1953). Libretto in Russian by the composer,
based on the comedy by Carlo Gozzi. Premiere: Chicago, December 30, 1921.
Highly complicated, fantastical farce. Continuous texture; melodic and harmonic modernism. Setting: a theater; on its stage a playing-card kingdom,
once upon a time. Prologue, four acts, ten scenes — two acts in N.Y. City
Opera version which is used below (85 min).

PROLOGUE: The theater. ACT I i: The Prince's room; ii: The great hall of
the palace (40 min). ACT II i: The desert; ii: Outside Cleonte's kitchen; iii:
Another part of the desert; iv: The royal kitchen (40 min).

Synopsis. An active and noisy audience watches, even takes part in, the
performance of a play from stage boxes. A Prince is dying of gloom despite
the efforts of the jester Truffaldino, the King's adviser Pantalon, and the
King's magician Celio. Laughter, the only cure, is successfully prevented by
the sorceress Fata Morgana (who is in league with the wicked prime minister
Leandro and the even wickeder niece of the King, Princess Clarissa) until the
sorceress herself is accidentally turned topsy-turvy by the palace guards. Her
ridiculous somersault breaks the Prince's solemnity and cures him. The joy
of the court is shortlived, however; Fata Morgana places a curse on the
Prince. He must find and fall in love with three oranges. After a hazardous
journey, he steals the oranges from Cleonte, the cook, and discovers that
each contains a lovely princess. Two immediately die of thirst, but the third,
Ninetta, is saved by a bucket of water conveyed from a stage box. After trials
that would dishearten lesser folk, the Prince and Princess are joined forever;
the evil-doers, sentenced to hang, are saved at the last minute by the redoubt-
able Fata Morgana.

Major Roles. FATA MORGANA (s); must convey characterization in voice; needs trill; B♭2 to B4. THE PRINCE (t); florid, lyrical singing; C2 to B3. TRUFFALDINO (t); needs trill; C2 to A♯3. LEANDRO (bar); A1 to F3. KING OF CLUBS (bs); impressive, weighty tones; G1 to E♭3.

Lesser Roles. PRINCESS CLARISSA (c); dark tones conveying evil; A2 to G4. PANTALON (bar); high tessitura; C2 to G3. CELIO (bs); B♭1 to E3. NINETTA (lyr s); C3 to A♯4. SMERALDINA, Fata Morgana's negro servant (m-s); D3 to G4. CLEONTE (bs).

Bit Parts. LINETTA, Princess in first orange (c). NICOLETTA, Princess in second orange (m-s). FARFARELLO, a devil (bs). MASTER OF CEREMONIES (t). HERALD (bs). TEN REASONABLE SPECTATORS (5 t, 5 bs).

Chorus. SSAATTTTTBBBBBB. Joys, Glooms, Emptyheads, Doctors, Jesters, Courtiers, Monsters, Drunkards, Gluttons, Guards, Servants, Soldiers.

Ballet. As large as desired.

Orchestra. 3 fl (picc), 3 ob, Eng hrn, 3 cl (E♭ cl, bs cl), 3 bsn (cont bsn), 6 hrn, 3 trp, 3 trb, bs tuba, timp, perc (3 players), 2 harp, strings.

Material. FS-P: B & H (rent). VS: B & H (r, f) $15. Li (e – Seroff) B & H 50¢.

Photographs. Iowa State Univ.: 11.15.54 p. 15. N.Y. City Opera: 4.11. 55 p. 13.

Performing Companies. 53 (5.52). 334 (1949, 1950, 1952, 1955). 156 (4.17.52). 161 (7.27.54). 94 (4.56). 489 (5.56). 148 (5.15.58).

✄ Lucia di Lammermoor · Lucia of Lammermoor

Music by Gaetano Donizetti (1797–1848). Libretto in Italian by Salvatore Cammarano, based on Sir Walter Scott's novel "The Bride of Lammermoor." Premiere: Naples, September 26, 1835. Tragic romance. Set numbers; accompanied recitative; highly melodious, often florid, vocal line. Setting: Scotland, end of the 17th century. Short prelude. Three acts, five scenes (109 min). ACT I i: Outside Ravenswood Castle (12 min); ii: Garden of the castle (26 min). ACT II: Apartment in Lammermoor Castle (32 min). ACT III i: Great hall of Lammermoor Castle (22 min); ii: Crypt of Ravenswood Castle (17 min).

Synopsis. Although their families are locked in a feud, Lucia of Lammermoor and Edgardo of Ravenswood exchange vows of love before he leaves Scotland on a diplomatic mission. Lucia's brother Enrico, using a forged letter, persuades her that her lover is untrue; she agrees to marry Enrico's friend Arturo Bucklaw. The wedding is interrupted by the return of Edgardo, who, believing himself betrayed, flings the ring Lucia had given him at her feet and curses her. Her mind broken by her unhappiness, Lucia kills Arturo in the marriage chamber, then horrifies the lingering guests by a display of madness. At the cemetery of his family, Edgardo is informed of Lucia's tragic end, and stabs himself.

Major Roles. LUCIA (col s); needs extreme facility, stamina; Mad Scene B♭2 to B♭4 (opt C5); (interpolated high ending, E♭5, not in score); remain-

89

der of role C3 to C5. EDGARDO (lyr t); considerable florid singing, high tessitura; D2 to B♭3 (opt E♭3). ENRICO ASHTON (bar); requires agility; B♭1 to
F♯3 (opt G3).

Lesser Roles. ALISA, Lucia's companion (m-s). NORMANNO, Captain of the
Guard of Lammermoor (t). ARTURO BUCKLAW (t). RAIMONDO BIDEBENT,
Lucia's teacher and confidant (bs).

Chorus. SSTTBB. Ladies and knights, inhabitants of Lammermoor, pages,
soldiers, domestics in Ashton family.

Ballet. Optional, Act III i.

Orchestra. 2 fl, picc, 2 ob, 2 cl, 2 bsn, 4 hrn, 2 trp, 3 trb (tuba, not in
score but published, duplicates 3rd trb), timp, perc, harp, strings. *Stage:* band
(4 hrn adequate, or 3 hrn, trb).

Material. FS-P: Ka, Map, Ri, TW (rent). CP: Map (i, e) (rent). VS:
Map, TW (rent); Ri (i) $5; G Sc (i, e) $4.

Photographs. Metropolitan: 1.29.40 p. 21; 11.23.42 p. 14 (design); 1.3.44
pp. 18–21; 12.27.48 p. 19. San Francisco: 11.4.40 p. 15. Mexico City: 10.25.
52 p. 4. San Antonio: 3.28.55 p. 14.

Performing Companies. Approx 33; 1956–57 only 283, 295, 329, 391, 463.

⚑ Die Lustigen Weiber von Windsor · The Merry Wives of Windsor

Music by Otto Nicolai (1810–1849). Libretto in German by Salomon Hermann Mosenthal, based on Shakespeare's "The Merry Wives of Windsor."
Premiere: Berlin, March 9, 1849. Sophisticated comedy. Set numbers, ensembles, recitatives; tuneful, light, and delicate effects. Overture. Setting:
Windsor, England, 15th century. Three acts, seven scenes.

ACT I i: A courtyard between the Ford and Page homes; ii: Room in Ford's
house. ACT II i: The Garter Inn; ii: Garden of Page's home; iii: Same as I ii.
ACT III i: Room in Page's house; ii: Windsor Forest.

Synopsis. The story is substantially the same as Verdi's "Falstaff." Sir John
Falstaff, the middle-aged knight, is courting Mistress Ford and Mistress Page,
to the fury of their husbands; but the ladies enjoy the proceedings and decide
to teach old John a lesson. Falstaff is mocked and humiliated, first by the
ladies, and then by the whole town, till he swears never again to indulge in
amorous pursuits.

Major Roles. SIR JOHN FALSTAFF (bs); wide range; flexibility; low E1. MR.
FORD (HERR FLUTH) (bar). MR. PAGE (HERR REICH) (bs). FENTON (lyr t).
MISTRESS FORD (lyr or dram s); exacting coloratura aria; top B♭4. MISTRESS
PAGE (m-s). ANNE PAGE (lyr s); considerable florid singing.

Lesser Roles. SLENDER, one of Anne's suitors (t). DR. CAIUS, another suitor
(bs).

Chorus. SATB. Townspeople.

Ballet. Dances in the Windsor Forest scene.

Orchestra. 2 fl, 2 ob, 2 cl, 2 bsn, 4 hrn, 2 trp, 3 trb, timp, perc, bells, harp,
strings.

Material. FS-P: Ri, Map, Ka, TW (rent). CP: Map (rent). VS: Map, TW (rent); Pet (g) $5; G Sc (g, e — Blatt) $5. O Tr: Urbach (T3); Fleischer and Burt (T22); Ryan and Goldovsky (T13).
Photographs. Hollywood Bowl: 3.16.42 p. 24. Tanglewood: 10.5.42 p. 27. Haverford, Pa.: 10.5.42 p. 28. Central City: 11.2.53 p. 13. Univ. of Michigan: 11.2.53 p. 21. N.Y. City Opera: 4.11.55 p. 14. Indiana Univ.: 11.10.58 cover (sketch).
Performing Companies. 82 (1953). 235 (1.14.54). 48 (3.54). 480 (10.26. 54). 273 (1.12.55). 479 (3.28.55). 334 (3.31.55; 55–56). 283 (8.5.55). 176 (2.23.56). 177 (3.1.56). 1956–57: 241, 372, 506. 148 (58–59). 178 (58–59). 187 (58–59).

🖾 Macbeth

Music by Giuseppe Verdi (1813–1901). Libretto in Italian by Francesco Piave, additional verses by Andrea Maffei, based on Shakespeare's play. Premiere: Florence, March 14, 1847. Tragedy. Tightly knit set numbers with several extremely dramatic scenes; accompanied recitative; highly melodious but exacting vocal line; extended ensembles. Prelude. Setting: medieval Scotland. Four acts, ten scenes (127 min).
ACT I i: A lonely heath (16 min); ii and iii: Macbeth's castle (30 min). ACT II i: The castle (6 min); ii: A wood near the castle (8 min); iii: Banquet hall of the castle (13 min). ACT III: The witches' cavern (18 min). ACT IV i: Near the English border (11 min); ii: Macbeth's castle (12 min); iii: The castle (13 min).

Synopsis. On a barren heath a group of witches hail Macbeth as thane of Cawdor and King of Scotland, and Banquo as father of kings to come. Immediately a messenger arrives to tell of the execution of the former thane of Cawdor and the elevation of Macbeth to that title. Lady Macbeth persuades her husband to kill King Duncan and fulfill the second part of the witches' prophecy. After the bloody deed is done, Macduff and Banquo arrive at the castle, discover the murder, and rouse the court. To circumvent discovery and a prophesied rival, Macbeth has Banquo assassinated, but Fleance, Banquo's son, escapes. At a feast that night Banquo's ghost appears to Macbeth. In time, Lady Macbeth cracks under the strain of her guilt and dies. Macbeth's tyranny is overwhelmed by an uprising led by Duncan's son Malcolm and Macduff, whose family Macbeth has murdered. The bloody King of Scotland himself is killed in single combat with Macduff.
Major Roles. LADY MACBETH (dram col s); demands great power and agility throughout range; must give off evil aura; B♭2 to D♭5. MACBETH (bar); high tessitura; must convey great virility; B1 to G3.
Lesser Roles. MACDUFF (t); B1 to B♭3. BANQUO (bs); A♭1 (opt F1) to F♭3. LADY-IN-WAITING to Lady Macbeth (m-s). MALCOLM (t).
Bit Parts. DOCTOR (bs). SERVANT to Macbeth (bs). MURDERER (bs). HERALD (bs). APPARITIONS (s, s, bs). HECATE (dancer). DUNCAN (mute). FLEANCE (mute).

Chorus. SSAATTBB. Witches, messengers of the king, Scottish noblemen and noblewomen, Scottish exiles, murderers, soldiers, spirits, etc.

Orchestra. 2 fl, 2 ob (Eng hrn), 2 cl (bs cl), 2 bsn, 4 hrn, 2 trp, 3 trb, tuba, timp, perc, harp, strings. *Stage:* military band Act I; 4 trp Act IV; wind ensemble Act III — 1 or 2 ob, 3 or 6 cl, 2 bsn, cont bsn.

Production Problems. Witches' scenes. Appearance of Banquo's ghost. Birnam Wood disguise and final battle.

Material. FS-P: Map, Ri (rent). VS: Map (rent); Ri (i) $12. Tr: Cardelli (333); Williams (33); Zytowski (30).

Photographs. Edinburgh: 10.6.47 p. 22. Munich: 1.26.53 p. 12. Hamburg: 3.2.53 p. 15. Hartt College: 3.9.53 p. 5. San Francisco: 10.31.55 p. 7. Entire issue 2.16.59.

Performing Companies. 94 (52–53). 72 (11.1.55). 33 (1955). 397 (56–57). 334 (1957). 329 (57–60).

🦋 Madama Butterfly · Madame Butterfly

Music by Giacomo Puccini (1858–1924). Libretto by Luigi Illica and Giuseppe Giacosa, based on a play by David Belasco in turn based on a short story by John Luther Long. Premiere: Milan, February 17, 1904. Lyric tragedy. Continuous texture of quasi-recitative connected by more or less self-contained numbers. Highly melodious vocal line over consonant accompaniment, containing occasional references to Oriental material. No overture. Setting: near Nagasaki, Japan, about 1900. Three acts (129 min).

ACT I: The garden of Cio-Cio-San's house near Nagasaki (48 min). ACT II: Inside the house (49 min). ACT III: The same (32 min).

Synopsis. Lieutenant Pinkerton, an American naval officer on duty in Japan, marries Cio-Cio-San, called Madame Butterfly, despite the misgivings of the American consul, Sharpless. Even Butterfly's loving relatives are shocked, and desert her when she exchanges her religion for Pinkerton's. Soon Pinkerton's duty calls him away, but Butterfly, with their child, faithfully waits. After three years he returns, but with an American wife, Kate. Kate asks Cio-Cio-San to give up her child to be raised in America, and tearfully Cio-Cio-San agrees, if his father will come to take him. Before Pinkerton arrives, the hapless Butterfly kills herself.

Major Roles. CIO-CIO-SAN (lyr spin s); needs high pianissimo; should convey dramatic intensity and create Oriental image; B♭2 to D♭5 (opt B♭4). LT. B. F. PINKERTON (t); straightforward lyrical role; D2 to C4. SHARPLESS (bar); B♭1 to G3.

Lesser Roles. SUZUKI, Cio-Cio-San's servant (m-s). KATE PINKERTON (m-s). GORO, a marriage broker (t). PRINCE YAMADORI, Cio-Cio-San's wealthy suitor (bar). THE BONZE, Cio-Cio-San's uncle (bs).

Bit Parts. THE IMPERIAL COMMISSIONER (bs). THE OFFICIAL REGISTRAR (bar). YAKUSIDE (bar). Cio-Cio-San's MOTHER (m-s), AUNT (m-s), COUSIN (s), solo roles from chorus. TROUBLE, Cio-Cio-San's child (mute).

Chorus. SSATT. Friends, relatives, wedding guests; sailors; humming chorus.

Orchestra. 3 fl (picc), 2 ob, Eng hrn, 2 cl, bs cl, 2 bsn, 4 hrn, 3 trp, 3 trb, bs tuba, timp, perc, bells, small bells, harp, strings. *Stage:* vla.

Material. FS-P: Ri (rent). VS: Ri (i, e – Martin) $12, $9; (i) $12; G Sc (e – Gutman) in preparation. O Tr: Blatt (215); Treash (358).

Photographs. Metropolitan: 1.20.41 p. 15; 2.3.47 pp. 18–22; 3.24.47 p. 16; 1.28.52 pp. 14, 19; 3.24.58 pp. 19–24, cover (Nagasaki production). Fisk College: 11.17.47 p. 10. Hollywood Bowl: 11.8.48 p. 26. Stephens College: 1.23.50 p. 13; 12.22.52 p. 3. Scranton: 2.13.50 p. 31. Caracalla: 10.13.52 p. 13. Santa Barbara: 11.15.54 p. 18. New Haven (design): 3.21.55 p. 31. Baylor Univ.: 11.14.55 p. 18. Houston: 3.26.56 p. 32.

Performing Companies. Approx 85; 1956–57 only 34, 37, 58, 64, 72, 111, 133, 180, 185, 197, 230, 258, 275, 285, 304, 324, 329, 332, 363, 391, 411, 446, 494.

🎭 Il Maestro di musica · The Music Master

Music (probably only partly) by Giovanni Battista Pergolesi (1710–1736). Anonymous libretto in Italian. Premiere: Naples, probably 1731. Comedy. Melodious; conventional harmonies; set numbers; arias, ensembles, recitative, dialogue. Setting: Naples, about 1730. Two acts (105 min).

ACT I: A room in Lamberto's house. ACT II: The same, with one interlude before curtain, in an anteroom or anywhere out of sight of Lamberto's room.

Synopsis. Lamberto refuses to let his prize pupil Lauretta sing in public because, although she is ready, he secretly wants to keep her with him. She foils him by signing a contract with the impresario Colagiani, who expects her love along with the business arrangements. But the clever girl induces Lamberto to reveal his affection for her, then tells Colagiani that all three of them must go on tour: she to sing, Lamberto to accompany her on the harpsichord, and Colagiani to collect the money.

Major Roles. LAMBERTO (t); florid; A1 to Bb3. LAURETTA (s); coloratura passages, trill necessary; D2 to B4. COLAGIANI (buf bs); G1 to Gb3 (one G3).

Lesser Role. DORINA, a pupil (m-s).

Bit Parts (in Eager vers). BEPPO, a servant (mute). MAJORDOMO (mute).

Chorus. SAB. Pupils.

Orchestra. Strings.

Material. Available from estate of Dr. Richard Falk. Li: Eager (T33).

Performing Companies. 390 (7.14.53). 491 (57–58). 482 (4.2.59).

🎭 Manon

Music by Jules Massenet (1842–1912). Libretto in French by Henri Meilhac and Philippe Gille, based on Abbé Prévost's novel "Les Aventures du Chevalier des Grieux et de Manon Lescaut." Premiere: Paris, January 19, 1884.

Tragic romance. Continuous texture containing set numbers; accompanied recitative; melodious vocal line; occasional dialogue. Prelude. Setting: France; early 18th century. Five acts, six scenes (139 min).

ACT I: Inn courtyard at Amiens (34 min). ACT II: Manon's apartment in Paris (25 min). ACT III i: Cours la Reine, Paris (occasionally omitted) (30 min); ii: Antechapel of St. Sulpice (20 min). ACT IV: Hotel Transylvanie (17 min). ACT V: The road to Le Havre (13 min).

Synopsis. Manon Lescaut, pausing at Amiens on her way to a convent, falls in love with the young Chevalier Des Grieux and elopes with him to Paris. Manon's cousin Lescaut arranges for Des Grieux to be kidnapped, thus freeing the flighty Manon for a new adventure with De Brétigny. Learning from Des Grieux's father that his son intends to take holy orders, Manon determines to see him again. With impassioned words she persuades him to renounce his vows and rejoin her in a life of pleasure. His money soon gone, Des Grieux gambles and wins, but is accused of cheating by a rival for Manon and is arrested, though later freed by his father. Manon is not so fortunate; arrested and condemned to be deported to Louisiana, she is rescued by Des Grieux in vain — her life is over.

Major Roles. MANON LESCAUT (s); lyric; frequent florid and several dramatic passages; top D5 (opt E5). DES GRIEUX (t); lyric; needs sustained legato; top B♭3. LESCAUT (bar).

Lesser Roles. COUNT DES GRIEUX (bs). GUILLOT DE MORFONTAINE, an old admirer of Manon (t). DE BRETIGNY (bar). POUSETTE (s), JAVOTTE (s or m-s), and ROSETTE (s or m-s), actresses.

Chorus. SATB. Soldiers, citizens.

Ballet. A full ballet in the Cours la Reine scene.

Orchestra. 2 fl, 2 ob (Eng hrn), 2 cl, 2 bsn, 4 hrn, 2 trp, 3 trb, timp, perc, harp, strings. In Cours la Reine scene: 2 vln, cl, bsn.

Material. FS-P: Map, Ka, TW (rent). CP: Map (f, e) (rent). VS: Map, TW (rent); G Sc (f, e) $5; Pr (Mer — f, i) $13.50. Tr: Steiner (BMI); Morgan (T16).

Photographs. Paris Opéra Comique: 1.8.40 p. 15; 12.26.49 p. 31. Metropolitan: 1.8.40 p. 17; 12.15.47 pp. 18, 20, 22, 23; 12.10.51 pp. 18–20; 12.13. 54 pp. 19, 20 (sketches). Covent Garden: 11.14.49 p. 14 (sketches).

Performing Companies. 178 (3.16.50). 449 (11.20.52). 189 (4.17.53). 72 (1954). 443B (1.14.54). 329 (54–55). 76 (54–55). 55A (2.55). 487 (2. 12.55). 64 (2.15.55; 56–57). 391 (7.55). 180 (10.27.55). 1956–57: 295, 313.

🖾 Manon Lescaut

Music by Giacomo Puccini (1858–1924). Libretto in Italian by Ruggiero Leoncavallo, Marco Praga, Domenico Oliva, Giuseppe Giacosa, Giulio Ricordi, and Luigi Illica. Based on "Les Aventures du Chevalier des Grieux et de Manon Lescaut" by the Abbé Prévost. Premiere: Turin, February 1, 1893. Romantic melodrama. Continuous texture with separable arias; passionate emotional atmosphere sustained over long periods; highly melodious. Brief

94

prelude. Setting: France and Louisiana; early 18th century. Four acts (108 min).

ACT I: Courtyard of an inn at Amiens (33 min). ACT II: Manon's dressing-room in Geronte's house (37 min). ACT III: The harbor of Le Havre (21 min). ACT IV: A plain in Louisiana (17 min).

Synopsis. The story is substantially the same as Massenet's "Manon," although the action in Puccini's opera, with the exception of the similar first act, takes place in the interim between the acts of Massenet's work. Manon, having eloped with Des Grieux, quickly tires of him, takes old Geronte as a protector, and tires as quickly of him, although she loves the luxury he provides for her. She infuriates the old man by telling him she has decided to return to Des Grieux. Lescaut (her brother in this version) urges her to escape, but she is too slow, and is arrested and deported to Louisiana, where Des Grieux is permitted to go with her. She is already fatally ill, however, and dies in the arms of her lover.

Major Roles. MANON LESCAUT (lyr or dram s); requires warmth of expression, volatile characterization; high tessitura; top C5. LESCAUT (bar). CHEVALIER DES GRIEUX (t); lyric; considerable sustained singing; several dramatic passages; top B3.

Lesser Roles. GERONTE DI RAVOIR, treasurer-general (bar). EDMONDO, a student (t). SINGER (s or m-s). MUSIC MASTER (t). NAVAL CAPTAIN (bs). SERGEANT (bs). LAMPLIGHTER (t).

Chorus. SATTBB. Students, girls, citizens, old beaux, courtesans, archers, sailors.

Orchestra. 3 fl (picc), 2 ob, Eng hrn, 2 cl, bs cl, 2 bsn, 4 hrn, 3 trp, 3 trb, tuba, timp, perc, bells, celeste, harp, strings. *Stage:* side drum, trp.

Material. Map, Ri (rent). VS: Map (rent); Ri (i) $10. Tr: Matz (T21); Ducloux (T10).

Photographs. Metropolitan: 12.5.49 pp. 19, 20 (sketches); 11.13.50 pp. 18, 20, 21.

Performing Companies. 329 (49–51, 55–56, 58–59, 60–61). 72 (9.13.56). 130 (1957). 48 (11.21.58). 92 (1959).

▰ Maria Golovin

Music and libretto in English by Gian-Carlo Menotti (1911–   ). Commissioned by the National Broadcasting Company. Premiere: Brussels, August 20, 1958. Romantic tragedy. Vocal line patterned largely after speech; continuous texture with set numbers interwoven. Since theatrical values are high, considerable acting ability is required of the principals. Setting: a villa near a frontier in a European country; time, the present. Three acts, seven scenes, two sets (112 min).

ACT I i ii: Livingroom (42 min). ACT II i ii: Terrace (34 min). ACT III i ii iii: Livingroom (36 min).

Synopsis. Maria Golovin comes with her young son to spend the summer in a villa in which she has rented an apartment, because it is near the camp where her husband is a prisoner of war. She soon falls in love with blind Donato, whose mother owns the house. Donato's possessiveness and jealousy create a tension that affects the whole household. A prisoner escapes and finds Donato alone, the others having gone to a fireworks display. Donato hides the fugitive, who leaves his gun, telling Donato he may need it. Maria's husband returns, but she still attempts to meet Donato clandestinely. When she is late, Donato determines to kill her. At her entrance, he desperately tries to shoot, but cannot find her. His mother enters and immediately grasps the situation. Helping him to point the gun at empty space, she motions Maria aside and tells Donato to fire. Maria creeps from the room while Donato, grieving yet glorying in his deed, is persuaded by his mother not to go near the place where he believes the body to lie but to go with her into temporary hiding. He drops a rose as a last tribute and allows his mother to lead him away.

Major Roles. MARIA GOLOVIN (s); occasional high tessitura. DONATO (bar). Both need great dramatic intensity. AGATA, the maid of all work (m-s); character role. THE MOTHER (s). DR. ZUCKERTANZ (high buf t).

Lesser Roles. THE PRISONER (bar). TROTTOLO, Maria's son (mute); a young boy.

Chorus. TB. Prisoners, offstage.

Orchestra. 2 fl (picc), 2 ob (Eng hrn), 2 cl (bs cl), 2 bsn, 4 hrn, 3 trp, 3 trb, tuba, timp, harp, xyl, perc (2 players), strings. *Reduced vers:* fl (picc), ob (Eng hrn), 2 cl, bsn, 2 hrn, trp, trb, timp, perc, harp, strings. *Stage:* piano, jazz band (piano, cl, vln).

Production Problems. Fireworks in distance if possible. Gun shot.

Material. FS-P: Ri (rent). VS: Ri (in prep).

Photographs. Mus. Amer. Brussels: 10.58 p. 17.

Performing Companies. 333 (3.8.59). 334 (3.30.59).

✄ Martha

Music by Friedrich von Flotow (1812–1883). Libretto in German by W. Friedrich, based on a ballet by Vernoy de Saint-Georges, for which Flotow wrote part of the music. Premiere: Vienna, November 25, 1847. Romantic comedy of 18th-century England. Set numbers, accompanied recitative; light, graceful melody; several quartets for the principals. The aria "M'Appari" (from Flotow's earlier "L'Ame en Peine") was interpolated in Paris in 1865. "The Last Rose of Summer" is also an interpolation. Setting: Richmond during the reign of Queen Anne, about 1710. Four acts, six scenes.

ACT I i: Boudoir of Lady Harriet; ii: Fairground at Richmond. ACT II: Room in Plunkett's farmhouse. ACT III: Forest near Richmond. ACT IV i: The farmhouse; ii: Lady Harriet's park.

Synopsis. Lady Harriet Durham, maid of honor to the queen, is bored with court life and with her many suitors. At the suggestion of her gay young maid, Nancy, the two girls go to the Richmond fair in disguise, offering themselves as servants to farmers. They are quickly bound over by Plunkett, a young farmer, and his foster-brother, Lionel (whose background and antecedents are a mystery). The two "maids" thoroughly upset the household — and the hearts — of their masters before they escape to return to court. Nancy and Plunkett soon meet and come to an understanding, but only after Lionel is revealed to be the Earl of Derby do the highborn lovers also find happiness.

Major Roles. LADY HARRIET, posing as Martha (lyr s); needs considerable flexibility; C3 to D5. NANCY, posing as Julia (m-s); requires agility throughout a wide range; G2 to G4. LIONEL (lyr t); considerable high tessitura; C2 to B♭3. PLUNKETT (bar or bs); should possess well-developed high range and facile articulation; F1 to F3.

Lesser Roles. LORD TRISTAN OF MICKLEFORD, Lady Harriet's old cousin and suitor (bs). A SHERIFF (bs).

Chorus. SATB. Villagers, ladies-in-waiting.

Orchestra. 2 fl, 2 ob, 2 cl, 2 bsn, 4 hrn, 2 trp, 3 trb, tuba, timp, perc, bells, harp, strings. *Stage:* band.

Material. FS-P: Ka, Map, Ri, TW (rent). VS: Map, TW (rent); G Sc (g, e — Baum and Ronell) $5. Tr: Dent (Ox) $1.50; Lucas (407); Warenskjold (38).

Photographs. Univ. of Oregon: 10.30.50 p. 22. Catholic Univ., Washington, D.C.: 10.27.52 p. 21. Metropolitan: 2.25.61 pp. 12, 13, 16, 24, 25, 26 (sketches).

Performing Companies. Approx 47; 1956–57 only: 17, 113, 226, 359, 361, 382, 487. 329 (60–61).

🎭 Mathis der Maler · Mathias the Painter

Music by Paul Hindemith (1895–   ). Libretto in German by the composer, based on the life of the 16th-century painter, Mathias Grünewald. Premiere: Zurich, May 28, 1938. Political drama with religious implications. Often given as oratorio. Great variety of musical styles with suggestions of medieval modality; contrapuntal texture; vocal line difficult. Several important ensembles. Prelude (subtitled "Concert of Angels") inspired by part of the Isenheim "polyptych," used as first movement of symphony arranged by the composer from music of the opera. An interlude in scene vii forms slow movement of the symphony. Setting: in and near Mainz; time, the Peasants' War, about 1525. Seven scenes, interval customary after fourth (approx 4 hours).

Scene i: Courtyard of St. Anthony's monastery at Mainz; ii: Hall in the Martinsburg, the Archbishop's palace; iii: Room in Riedinger's house; iv: A war-ravaged village; v: Cardinal's study; vi: In the Odenwald; vii: Mathis' studio in Mainz.

Synopsis. Mathis, a painter in the employ of Cardinal Albrecht, Archbishop of Mainz, is persuaded to take an interest in the peasants' struggle for freedom by Schwalb, leader of the peasants' army, and his daughter Regina, whom the painter helps to escape. There is also dissension between the papists, represented by Pommersfelden, Dean of Mainz, and Lutherans, among whom are Capito, the cardinal's counselor; Riedinger, a rich citizen; and his daugh-

97

ter Ursula. An order from Rome to burn the Lutherans' books is reluctantly carried out by the cardinal, in spite of Riedinger's efforts. Sylvester, an officer in the Swabian Army under von Waldburg, accuses Mathis of helping Schwalb escape; Mathis defies the cardinal, who tells him not to interfere in what he does not understand, and allows him to withdraw from his post. After a year's absence, Mathis finds Ursula, whom he loves, promised to the cardinal in order to bring him a fortune. The lovers resign themselves to their fate.

Mathis devotes himself to the struggle for freedom, but is horrified when the peasants kill a local noble and threaten his wife, Countess von Helfenstein. In the fight between the trained Swabian Army and the peasants, Schwalb is killed, and Mathis is saved only by the Countess's intervention. He is a complete failure as a man of action. Meanwhile, Capito tries to persuade the cardinal to renounce celibacy and marry Ursula for her fortune. His own nature rebels, and he is strengthened in his resolve by Ursula's noble sacrifice, promising to allow the Lutherans to declare themselves openly. Mathis has rescued Regina from the battle, and now she lies in a fever in the Odenwald, beset by hallucinations. To calm her, the painter describes the vision that inspired his painting of the great altarpiece at Isenheim. In his despair he experiences a further vision — in turn luxury, a beggar, a courtesan, a martyr, a scholar, and a knight appear before him. At the climax, demons tempt St. Anthony (Mathis); the cardinal in the guise of St. Paul gives comfort. The artist, who has betrayed himself, will return to his art, putting all else out of his life.

Major Roles. MATHIS (ST. ANTHONY) (bar); demanding, long, and sustained; some high tessitura; A1 to G3. ALBRECHT VON BRANDENBURG (ST. PAUL), Cardinal (t); D2 to A3 (one B3). LORENZ VON POMMERSFELDEN (WEALTH) (bs); F#1 to E3. WOLFGANG CAPITO (SCHOLAR) (t); B2 to Ab3 (one A3). URSULA (MARTYR) (s); sustained, forceful; some high tessitura; C3 (one B2) to B4 (one C5). REGINA (s); E3 to B4.

Lesser Roles. RIEDINGER (bs); G#1 to Eb3. HANS SCHWALB (KNIGHT) (t); Eb2 to B3 (one C4). COUNTESS VON HELFENSTEIN (LUXURY) (c); G2 to A4. TRUCHSESS VON WALDBURG (bs); E2 to Fb3. SYLVESTER VON SCHAUMBERG (t); D2 to G3.

Bit Parts. PIPER (t). COUNT VON HELFENSTEIN (mute).

Chorus. SSAATTTBB. Monks, papists, Lutherans, women, students, peasants, demons.

Orchestra. 2 fl, 2 ob, 2 cl, 2 bsn, 4 hrn, 2 trp, 3 trb, tuba, timp, perc (2 players), strings. *Stage:* 3 trp.

Material. FS-P: AMP (rent). VS: AMP (Sch — g) $12.50. Tr: (197).

Photographs. Hamburg (Scene i): 10.13.52 p. 28. Stuttgart: 12.6.54 p. 31. Graz (Scene vii): 1.2.56 p. 30. Boston Univ.: 3.19.56 p. 11.

Performing Companies. 197 (2.17.56 — Amer prem).

▨ Il Matrimonio segreto · The Secret Marriage

Music by Domenico Cimarosa (1749–1801). Libretto in Italian by Giovanni Bertati, after the play "The Clandestine Marriage" by George Colman the elder and David Garrick. Premiere: Vienna, February 7, 1792. Comedy. Simple harmonic structure; melodic; set numbers, accompanied recitative. Overture ("Sinfonia"). Setting: Bologna, 18th century. Two acts: various rooms in Geronimo's house, including reception room and hallway (approx 120 min).

Synopsis. Geronimo, a wealthy citizen of Bologna, has two daughters, Elisetta and the more attractive Carolina. His sister Fidalma keeps house for them. Carolina is secretly married to her father's bookkeeper, Paolino, whose former employer, Count Robinson, arrives from England with the intention of marrying Elisetta. When he sees Carolina, however, he changes his mind and decides that he will marry her instead. Elisetta and Fidalma decide to send Carolina to a convent so that Elisetta can marry Robinson and her aunt can marry Paolino. The misunderstandings which develop are cleared up when Carolina and Paolino finally reveal their marriage. All is forgiven, and the count agrees to marry Elisetta.

Roles. GERONIMO (bs); A1 to E3. ELISETTA (high m-s or s); B2 to B4. CAROLINA (s); D♭3 to C5. FIDALMA (c); B2 to A4. COUNT ROBINSON (bs or bar); A1 to F3. PAOLINO (t); E2 to C4. All roles have florid passages and require agility.

Orchestra. 2 fl, 2 ob, 2 cl, 2 bsn, 2 hrn, 2 trp, timp, perc, strings.

Material. FS-P: Ri, Ka, TW (rent). VS: Ri (i) $10. Tr: Arundel (T1); Gatty (32B); Goldovsky and Caldwell (T13); Bird and Witherspoon (378); Rosinbum (518).

Photographs. Mus. Amer. Piccola Scala, Edinburgh: 10.57 p. 9.

Performing Companies. 290 (10.5.50). 137A (5.24.51). 32B (2.53). 518 (5.54). 451A (8.22.54). 31A (1.16.55). 202 (9.15.56). 378 (55–56). 475 (10.56). 47 (12.57). 24 (10.59).

🎬 Le Médecin malgré lui · The Doctor in Spite of Himself

Music by Charles Gounod (1818–1893). Libretto in French by Barbier and Carré based on a play by Molière. Premiere: Paris, January 15, 1858. Farce. Set numbers, dialogue; simple and melodious. English version: music arranged by Marshall Bartholomew; libretto and adaptation by Alexander Dean (condensed and simplified). Several lyrics adapted from Henry Fielding's translation, "The Mock Doctor." Others revised by Phyllis McGinley, Richard Corbin, and Mr. Dean. Setting: the great audience hall of the Louvre in Paris, August 6, 1666. In the center, a stage is placed for a play with two acts: ACT I, a cleared place in a wood; ACT II, a room in Geronte's house (approx 150 min).

Synopsis. At a soirée, King Louis XIV and his court dance and watch a play by Molière. The plot concerns three couples who are in difficulties. Sganarelle, a lazy woodcutter, beats his wife, Martine. Lucinda, daughter of the rich Geronte, is supposed to marry a wealthy old man but loves Leander. Jacqueline, Lucinda's flighty governess and wife of Lucas, is inclined to

99

philander. Lucinda pretends to be dumb in order not to marry. In search for a physician, Geronte's servants are persuaded by Martine that Sganarelle can cure Lucinda — but only if they beat him to make him acknowledge that he is a doctor. The roguish woodcutter agrees to obtain a cure, advising Lucinda to elope. When Leander's rich uncle dies, all is forgiven. The other two couples are reconciled and all are happy, cured by the three drams of matrimonium prescribed by the false physician.

Roles. LOUIS XIV, King of France (bar); age 28 at time of play; should dance well. SGANARELLE (buf bar); needs comedy sense and acting ability. MARTINE (m-s). LEANDER, a young gallant (t). LUCINDA, Geronte's daughter, in love with Leander (s). VALERE, Geronte's servant (bs-bar); physical size more important than vocal equipment. LUCAS, Geronte's steward (buf t). JACQUELINE, Lucinda's governess, Lucas' wife (c). GERONTE, a rich country gentleman (bs); acting ability more important than voice.

Chorus. SSAATTBB. Lords and ladies of the court of France.
Ballet. The king and his court.
Orchestra. picc, fl, 2 ob, 2 cl, bsn, 4 hrn, 2 trp, 3 trb, timp, drums, strings.
Stage: trp.
Production Note. The Dean version may be given without chorus and ballet, omitting scenes with king and court.
Material. FS-P: Ka, Si (Dean vers) (rent). VS: Si (Dean vers with introd notes, complete director's book, costume and set sketches, etc.) $4.50.
Photographs. Hartt College: 12.18.44 p. 5.
Performing Companies. 387 (3.10.50). 343A (4.14.50). 154 (2.51). 404A (5.9.51). 321 (51–52). 16 (7.27.55).

▶ Médée · Medea

Music by Luigi Cherubini (1760–1842). Libretto in French by François Benoît Hoffmann, based on Euripides' drama. (Score available in America only in Italian translation by Carlo Zangarini.) Premiere: Paris, March 13, 1797. Tragedy in florid style; bridge between classic and romantic grand opera tradition. Simple harmonic structure; dramatic orchestration. Recitatives, set arias and numbers. (Originally with dialogue; recitatives added in 1854 by Franz Lachner.) Overture and introduction to Acts II and III. Setting is Corinth, in antiquity. Three acts (109 min).

ACT I: Royal court in Creon's palace (42 min). ACT II: Wing of Creon's palace (41 min). ACT III: Hilly area outside the temple (26 min).

Synopsis. Before the opera begins, Medea, a sorceress, has helped Jason steal the Golden Fleece, killing her brother who pursues them, and alienating herself from her native land. Her cruelty eventually repels Jason, who abandons her, taking their two sons with him to Corinth. Here he is about to marry Glauce, daughter of King Creon, when the opera opens. Medea arrives in Corinth determined to prevent the wedding. She pleads vainly with Jason to return to her. Although the Corinthians want to kill her, Creon decrees that she be banished from his kingdom before the following dawn. She begs one

100

more day to say farewell to her children; reluctantly he grants it. When she realizes Jason still loves his sons, she determines to kill them. Her maid Neris gives the children a poisoned diadem and mantle to take to Glauce as a wedding present — they will cause the flesh to fall from Glauce's bones. The wedding takes place in the palace as Medea lurks outside. She attempts to kill her children, but cannot bring herself to do it. Neris describes Glauce's death to Medea, and takes the children into the temple to protect them from Medea. Hearing Jason mourn Glauce's death, Medea rushes into the temple, emerging with a bloody knife to confront the horrified Jason. As he begs to see the sons she has murdered, Medea sets fire to the temple, which crashes down before the terrified throng.

Major Roles. MEDEA (dram s); high tessitura; great dramatic power, extremely taxing, lengthy role; Bb2 to B4. GLAUCE (lyr s); high tessitura; C3 to C5. NERIS (m-s); A2 to A4. JASON (t); C#2 to Bb3. CREON (bs); A1 to F#3. (All roles demand long, sustained line and extremely florid style.)

Lesser Roles. Two MAIDSERVANTS of Glauce (s, s). CAPTAIN OF THE GUARD (bar). Two CHILDREN of Medea and Jason (mute).

Chorus. SSTTB. Servants of Glauce, Argonauts, priests, warriors, people of Corinth.

Ballet. Can be as elaborate as desired .

Orchestra. 2 fl, 2 ob, 2 cl, 2 bsn, 4 hrn, timp, perc, strings. *Stage:* band (2 fl, 2 ob, 2 cl, 2 bsn, 2 hrn, trb.)

Material. All Ri. FS-P (rent). VS (i) $15. Tr: Anstruther.

Photographs. La Scala: 3.1.54 p. 7. *Mus. Amer.* San Francisco, Act II: 10.58 p. 3.

Performing Companies. 297 (11.5.55 — Amer prem; 56–57; 3.10.59). 367A (6.23.56). 72 (9.12.58 — Amer stage prem). 474C (1958, 1959).

✴ Die Meistersinger von Nürnberg · The Mastersingers of Nuremberg

Music by Richard Wagner (1813–1883). Libretto in German by the composer, using historical personages. Premiere: Munich, June 21, 1868. Comedy with satirical and patriotic substrata. Solo voices subordinated to orchestral and vocal choirs: continuous texture in fullest Wagnerian sense. Prelude. Setting: Nuremberg, 16th century. Three acts, four scenes (221 min).
ACT I: St. Katherine's Church (74 min). ACT II: The street outside Sachs' shop (50 min). ACT III i: Inside Sachs' shop (64 min); ii: An open field near Nuremberg.

Synopsis. In Nuremberg a song contest is to be held by the Mastersingers, the prize being the hand of Pogner's lovely daughter Eva. Walther von Stolzing, a visiting knight, has met and fallen in love with Eva at church and determines to enter the contest. In spite of help from the apprentice David, his first attempt, free and spontaneous, fails to please the Mastersingers, who are swayed by the jealous and reactionary Beckmesser. Only the wise cobbler Sachs senses Walther's talent; he becomes the young man's mentor, even though he himself cherishes an affection for Eva. Sachs, the pivotal character, shows the greatness to acknowledge progress while retaining the virtues of tradition. His advice guides the young couple through the vicissitudes of their courtship. Walther finally completes his Prize Song, and Sachs, impressed, urges him to write down his poem. Beckmesser later finds the manuscript, which Sachs presents to him, and, at the song contest, makes a fool of himself by trying to fit the purloined verses to his own tune. Walther sings his Prize Song and is chosen the victor. He and Eva celebrate their betrothal as the assembled crowd acclaims the beloved Hans Sachs.

Major Roles. EVA (lyr s); clear, cool, sustained voice; C3 to B♭4. WALTHER (t); fresh, virile voice; D2 to B♭3 (C4 opt). HANS SACHS (bs; can be sung by bs-bar); warm, mature, sympathetic role; A1 to G3.

Lesser Roles. MAGDELENA, Eva's attendant (s, often sung by m-s); C3 to A4 (C5 opt). DAVID, Sachs' apprentice (lyr t); requires high, florid singing; C♯2 to B3. BECKMESSER (bs); consistently high tessitura in buffo style; B1 to A3. POGNER (bs); A1 to F3. KOTHNER, a Mastersinger (bs); B1 to F3. *Note.* Trills are indicated for the following roles: Eva, Walther, Sachs, Magdelena, David, Beckmesser, Kothner.

Bit Parts. VOGELGESANG (t), NACHTIGALL (bs), ZORN (t), EISSLINGER (t), MOSER (t), ORTEL (bs), SCHWARZ (bs), FOLTZ (bs), Mastersingers. A NIGHT-WATCHMAN (bs).

Chorus. SSSSAAATTTTTTBBBB. Men and women of all guilds, journeymen, apprentices, townspeople. Extremely complicated and difficult.

Orchestra. 2 fl, picc, 2 ob, 2 cl, 2 bsn, 4 hrn, 3 trp, 3 trb, tuba, timp, cymbals, triangle, glockenspiel, harp, lute (simulated by special harp with steel strings), strings. *Stage:* side drums, watchman's horn (usually trb, hrn, or both), organ, several hrn, 6 or more trp.

Material. FS-P: Ri, TW (rent). MS: AMP (Sch − g, e, f) 2 vols $23.50; Pet (Eu) $25. VS: Pet (g) $6.50; G Sc (g, e) $10; TW (rent). Tr: Gutman (329).

Photographs. Metropolitan: ACT I: 2.5.45 p. 19; 12.10.45 pp. 6, 18; 11.24. 47 p. 18; 1.5.53 p. 18; 12.6.54 p. 18. ACT II i: 2.5.45 p. 21; 1.5.53 p. 18. ACT II ii: 2.5.45 p. 20; 12.6.54 p. 19. ACT III i: 12.10.45 p. 20; 11.24.47 p. 20. ACT III ii: 2.5.45 p. 22; 12.10.45 p. 21; 1.5.53 p. 19. Prize Song: 2.5.45 (cover); 3.17.52 p. 19; 1.5.53 p. 20; 12.6.54 p. 20. Salzburg: 1.26.42 p. 30 (sketch). Bayreuth: 12.10.45 p. 8; 12.31.51 p. 8; 10.22.56 p. 23; 3.2.59 p. 13. Vienna: 1.16.50 p. 30; 12.19.55 p. 12. Munich: 10.16.50 p. 13. Hamburg: 1.21.52 p. 14. Berlin: 2.22.54 p. 14. Mainz: 10.19.53 p. 28.

Performing Companies. 334 (1950, 1951). 329 (56–57; 58–59).

⚘ Mignon

Music by Ambroise Thomas (1811–1896). Libretto in French by Michel Carré and Jules Barbier, based on Goethe's novel "Wilhelm Meister." Premiere (with dialogue): Paris, November 17, 1866. Revised in Italian with accompanied recitatives; premiere: London, July 5, 1870. Thomas also revised the title role originally for mezzo-soprano, in honor of Christine Nilsson. Ro-

102

mance. Uncomplicated, bright, sentimental melodies. Overture. Setting: Germany and Italy; 18th century. Three acts, four scenes (141 min).
ACT I: Courtyard of an inn in Germany (55 min). ACT II i: Boudoir in the castle of Baron Frédéric (30 min); ii: Garden of the castle (22 min). ACT III: A castle in Italy (34 min).

Synopsis. Lothario, an old wandering minstrel, has long been searching for his lost daughter. He comes across Mignon, who has been adopted by a gypsy band and is mistreated by their leader. Lothario and Wilhelm Meister, a young student, rescue her. Laerte and Philine, actors engaged to appear in Frédéric's castle nearby, observe the scene. Mignon becomes passionately attached to her new mentor, but Wilhelm has eyes only for Philine. Scenes which only emphasize the gulf between the young girl, dressed in boy's clothes, and the sophisticated actress, inflame Mignon further, until she violently wishes that Philine be burned alive. Lothario takes her at her word and fires the building where Philine is playing, but it is Mignon who is trapped. Wilhelm saves her and takes her to an Italian castle which, he tells Lothario, he intends to buy for Mignon. Here Lothario recovers his memory – it is his castle, and Mignon is his noble daughter.

Major Roles. MIGNON (m-s or s); sustained lyrical role with dramatic passages; contradictory character, naive, volatile, sensitive; requires subtle acting; Bb2 to A4 (Bb4 for s). PHILINE (col s); florid; C3 to E5 (opt C5). WILHELM MEISTER (lyr t); occasional high tessitura; moments of dramatic intensity; E2 to C4. LOTHARIO (bs); B1 to E3.
Lesser Roles. FREDERIC (buf t or c). LAERTE (t). GIARNO, leader of the gypsies (bs).
Chorus. SATB. Gypsies, actors, peasants, servants, guests at the castle.
Orchestra. 2 fl, 2 ob, 2 cl, 2 bsn, 4 hrn, 2 trp, 3 trb, timp, perc, harp, strings. *Stage:* harp.
Material. FS-P: Map, Ka, TW (rent). CP: Map (f), TW (rent). VS: Map (rent); Pr (f, e, g, i) $13.50; G Sc (f, e) $5.
Photographs. Metropolitan: 12.20.43 pp. 18–22; 11.29.48 pp. 18, 20.
Performing Companies. 339 (48–49). 182 (1951). 216 (56–57). 334 (56–57).

✄ Il Mondo della luna · The Man in the Moon

Music by Franz Joseph Haydn (1732–1809). Libretto in Italian by Goldoni. Premiere: 1777. Comedy. Melodious; simple harmonic structure; set numbers with accompanied recitative. Overture. Setting: Venice, 1750. Prologue and two acts (120 min).
PROLOGUE: A square in Venice with a puppet show. ACT I: Before a little gate and balcony. ACT II: The garden of Buonafede's house.

Synopsis. Buonafede, a rich merchant of Venice, stubbornly refuses to allow his daughter Clarissa to marry the impecunious poet Leandro. Through a complicated ruse, a doctor from Bologna and Leandro's servant Cecco trick the intractable Buonafede into believing that he has been transported to the moon.

103

While there, the gullible old man is terrified into seeing matters in a somewhat different light. He finally agrees to allow Clarissa to marry Leandro.

Major Roles. BUONAFEDE (bs); F1 to F♯3. THE DOCTOR (bar); A1 to F3. CECCO (buf t); C2 to G3. LEANDRO (t); florid, ornamented passages requiring flexibility; D2 to A3. CLARISSA (s); several coloratura passages requiring agility; D3 to C5. LISETTA, Clarissa's maid (m-s); A2 to G4.

Lesser Roles. FOUR ZANIES (2 t, 2 bar). FOUR MARIONETTES (2 s, 2 bar). *Chorus.* SATB. Zanies and marionettes.

Ballet. Minuet and gavotte.

Orchestra. 2 fl, 2 ob, 2 Eng hrn, 2 cl, 2 bsn, 2 hrn, 2 trp, timp, strings.

Material. P: Se (rent). VS: Se (g) (rent). Tr: Gutman (Se); Craig and Urbach (T3); Ornest (293).

Photographs. Holland Festival: 10.3.59 p. 3. Salzburg: 10.3.59 p. 4.

Performing Companies. 321C (1949). 46A (57–58).

⚜ The Mother of Us All

Music by Virgil Thomson (1896–   ). Libretto in English by Gertrude Stein, based on historical and imaginary characters. Premiere: New York City, May 7, 1947. Free-form drama; vocal line patterned somewhat after speech; continuous texture, in modern idiom. Preludes to scenes. Setting: in and around Susan B. Anthony's house and at public political gatherings; late 19th century. Two acts, eight scenes, five sets (104 min).

ACT I i (prologue): Room in the house of Susan B. Anthony; ii: Political meeting in a tent; iii: Village green before Susan B. Anthony's house; iv: The same; v: The same (63 min). ACT II i: Drawingroom in Susan B. Anthony's house; ii: The same; iii (epilogue): Halls of Congress, some years later (41 min).

Synopsis. This is virtually a pageant, capable of variation in details of production, centering on the life and political ideals of Susan B. Anthony. The characters are drawn from a century of American history and from imagination, and are all treated as contemporary acquaintances and political associates. There is no objective plot; Susan B. Anthony is shown in private and public life crusading for women's rights. The action is a series of vignettes; the text is semi-surrealistic.

Major Roles. SUSAN B. ANTHONY (dram s); must convey great strength and determination; lengthy role; C3 to B♭4. ANNE, Susan B.'s confidante (c); A2 to E4. DANIEL WEBSTER (bs); G1 to E3. CONSTANCE FLETCHER, gracious, beautiful lady (m-s). JOHN ADAMS, presumably John Quincy Adams (lyr t). JO THE LOITERER, former Civil War soldier (t); C2 to A3.

Lesser Roles. GERTRUDE S., narrator (s); middle-aged, stocky woman; B♭2 to A4. VIRGIL T., master of ceremonies (bar); C2 to G3. INDIANA ELLIOT, a young provincial girl (c); B♭2 to F4. ANGEL MORE, part angel, part ghost, part ingénue (lyr s). CHRIS THE CITIZEN, former Civil War soldier (bar). ANDREW JOHNSON (t); B1 to A3. THADDEUS STEVENS (t); C2 to G3. LILLIAN RUSSELL, actress (lyr s). ULYSSES S. GRANT (bs-bar). ANTHONY COMSTOCK (bs). JENNY

REEFER, comical, outspoken feminist (m-s). ANNA HOPE, feminist (c). HER-
MAN ATLAN, elegant young French painter (high bar). DONALD GALLUP, tweedy
young college professor (bar). GLOSTER HEMING (bar) and ISABELLA WENT-
WORTH (m-s), intellectuals in knickerbockers. HENRIETTA M., mannish femi-
nist (s). HENRY B., poetic gentleman (bs-bar). INDIANA ELLIOT'S BROTHER,
Midwestern farmer (bs-bar). TTAA (may be any number and, if desired,
may constitute a corps de ballet), pageboys or postillions. NEGRO MAN and
WOMAN, rural laborers (speaking).

Chorus. SATB. Observers of public life (the entire cast; members may
be added in public life scenes).

Orchestra. fl (picc), ob (Eng hrn), 2 cl (bs cl), bsn, 2 hrn, 2 trp, trb, harp,
celeste, xyl, bells, perc (2 players), piano, strings.

Material. All Pr (Mer). FS-P (rent). VS $10. Voc material (rent).

Photographs. Univ. of Denver: 10.25.48 p. 13.

Performing Companies. 302 (5.7.47 — Amer prem). 357 (3.54). Phoenix
Theatre, New York (4.16.56). Harvard Univ. (3.3.56).

☙ Norma

Music by Vincenzo Bellini (1801–1835). Libretto in Italian by F. Romani,
based on the tragedy of the same title by L. A. Soumet. Premiere: Milan,
December 26, 1831. Romantic tragedy. Set numbers; accompanied recitative;
highly melodious, often florid vocal line. Overture. Setting: Gaul during the
Roman occupation; about 50 B.C. Four acts, five scenes (143 min).
ACT I: The sacred grove of the Druids (55 min). ACT II: Norma's dwelling
(26 min). ACT III: Bedroom in Norma's dwelling (22 min). ACT IV i: A rocky
cavern near the sacred grove (9 min); ii: The temple of Irminsul (31 min).

Synopsis. Norma, the high priestess of the Druids, a religious sect who
worship the god Irminsul, has secretly violated her vow of virginity and
married Pollione, the proconsul of the occupying Romans. To him she has
borne two children. Pollione, however, now loves Adalgisa, a virgin of the
temple, and begs her to flee with him to Rome. Distraught, Adalgisa confides
in Norma and asks to be released from her vows. Norma agrees. Then she
learns that Adalgisa's lover is her own husband. Norma's brief rage of jealousy
gives way to remorse; summoning the Druids and warriors to arise against
their oppressors, she offers herself as the necessary sacrifice. Overcome by
Norma's magnanimity, Pollione feels his love for her returning and mounts
the sacrificial pyre with her.

Major Roles. NORMA (dram s); one of the most difficult of all operatic
roles; requires a combination of strength for the sustained line and extreme
agility for the florid dramatic coloratura; trill; Bb2 to C5. ADALGISA (m-s or
s); considerable fioriture; C3 to C5. POLLIONE (lyr dram t); agility required;
some high tessitura; D2 to C4. OROVESO, Norma's father, the archdruid (bs);
stately, legato singing; B1 to E3.

Lesser Roles. FLAVIO, Pollione's friend (lyr t). CLOTILDE, Norma's nurse
(m-s).

105

Chorus. SSTTBB. Druid priests and priestesses, temple virgins, Gallic soldiers and attendants.

Orchestra. 2 fl (picc), 2 ob, 2 cl, 2 bsn, 4 hrn, 2 trp, 3 trb, tuba, timp, perc, harp, strings. *Stage:* military band.

Material. FS-P: Map, Ka, Ri, TW (rent). VS: AMP (UE—i, g) $3.50; B & H (i, e) $3.50; Pet (i, g) $6.50; Ri (i) $6; G Sc (i) $5.

Photographs. Metropolitan: 2.7.44 pp. 18–21, 24; 3.22.54 pp. 19, 20. Bob Jones Univ.: 2.25.52 p. 15. La Scala: 1.9.56 p. 10.

Performing Companies. 456 (12.51). 329 (53–54; 56–57). 354 (2.28.54). 130 (11.1.54). 340 (12.5.54; 56–57). 33 (56–57). 443B (10.31.57). 180 (2.26.59).

✠ Le Nozze di Figaro · The Marriage of Figaro

Music by Wolfgang Amadeus Mozart (1756–1791). Libretto in Italian by Lorenzo da Ponte, based on the French comedy by Beaumarchais. Premiere: Vienna, May 1, 1786. Comedy, embodying social satire that proved revolutionary at the time of the play's premiere. Set numbers, several impressive ensembles; highly melodious vocal line; intricate patter recitative and accompanied recitative. Overture. Setting: Count Almaviva's chateau of Aguas Frescas near Seville; 18th century. Four acts (160 min).

ACT I: Figaro's room in the Count's castle (43 min). ACT II: The Countess's room (45 min). ACT III: Audience room of the Count (41 min). ACT IV: Garden of the castle (31 min).

Synopsis. Figaro, the Count Almaviva's valet, and Susanna, the Countess's maid, are about to be married when Figaro discovers that the Count is determined to revive an old custom—the seignorial right to anticipate the bridegroom on a servant's wedding night. He vows to outwit his master. His own troubles multiply as the aging Marcellina attempts, with the assistance of the lawyer Dr. Bartolo, to hold Figaro to a marriage contract he has signed as a promissory note for a loan. (Old enough to be his mother, in reality she is—and Bartolo is his father, as is revealed later.) The young page Cherubino, in love with love and every woman he sees, complicates the situation by overhearing the Count making advances to Susanna. The Countess and Susanna plot against the Count, first dressing Cherubino as a girl to lure the Count, then, when this scheme goes awry, exchanging costumes so that the Count believes he is meeting Susanna in the garden, whereas his own wife confronts him. Outwitted at every turn, the selfish, vengeful Count is forced to apologize. Figaro, too, apologizes to Susanna for his suspicions of trickery and unfaithfulness.

Major Roles. FIGARO (bar); needs vitality, facile articulation; also a good firm vocal line, spirited acting ability; G1 to F3. COUNT ALMAVIVA (bar); dramatic voice, sustained passages; A1 to F3. COUNTESS (s); sustained, lyrical, also dramatic moments; C3 to A4. SUSANNA (s); wide range, both light and flexible; D3 to B4. CHERUBINO (s, often m-s); needs agility, boyish appearance; C3 to G4.

106

Lesser Roles. MARCELLINA (s, often m-s); D♯3 to B♯4. DR. BARTOLO (buf bs); needs rapid articulation; G1 to E3. DON BASILIO, music master (t); E2 to A3. DON CURZIO, notary (t). ANTONIO, gardener (bs). BARBARINA, his niece (s).

Chorus. SATB.

Ballet. In wedding scene, Act III.

Orchestra. 2 fl, 2 ob, 2 cl, 2 bsn, 2 hrn, 2 trp, timp, strings.

Material. FS-P: Ka, Map, Ri, G Sc, TW (rent). FS: Br (g, i) $17.50. MS: Pet (Eu − i, g) $10, $15. CP: Map (i, e − rent); G Sc (i, e) 50¢. VS: AMP (BH − i, g) $4.75; B & H (i, e − Dent) $4, $5; Pet (i, g) $5; Ri (i) $7.50; G Sc (i, e − Martin) $6. Li: Ox (e − Dent) $1.50. O Tr: Eager (333); Levin (T26); Sternberg (491).

Photographs. Florence: 1.29.30 pp. 2–4. Prague: 2.5.40 p. 17 (orig design). Metropolitan: 3.4.40 pp. 17, 18. Glyndebourne: 10.6.47 p. 23. Pittsburgh: 2.9.48 p. 20. Brno: 2.14.49 p. 8. Covent Garden: 10.31.49. p. 11. Univ. of Wichita: 1.23.50 p. 12. Design: 12.21.53 p. 18. *Mus. Amer.* Salzburg, Act I: 10.52 p. 6.

Performing Companies. Approx 100. 1956–57 only: 4, 43, 209, 228, 235, 259, 293, 329, 332, 391, 395, 435, 523, 525.

▰ Orfeo ed Euridice · Orpheus and Eurydice

Music by Christoph Willibald Von Gluck (1714–1787). Libretto in Italian by Raniero da Calzabigi. Premiere: Vienna, October 5, 1762. Classic drama. Vocal line patterned after declamation; except for a few set pieces, arioso form prevails; recitative accompanied by strings; chorus vitally important. Overture. Setting: ancient Greece. Three acts, five scenes (110 min).

ACT I i: Euridice's tomb (31 min); ii: Descent to Hades (15 min). ACT II: Elysian Fields (25 min). ACT III i: On the way back to earth (26 min); ii: Temple of Love (13 min).

Synopsis. Orfeo laments the death of his wife Euridice. The god of love, Amore, informs him that the gods have taken pity on him and will allow him to go to the underworld to plead for the return of Euridice. One condition is imposed: if Orfeo succeeds, he shall not look upon the face of Euridice until they have returned to earth. His prayers are granted after he has charmed the Furies with his song. On the way back to earth Euridice cannot understand his apparent coldness and indifference, and begs him to look at her. Finally he yields, whereupon Euridice falls dead. Orfeo is about to kill himself when Amore reappears and tells him that his great love has moved the hearts of the gods. Euridice is restored to him once more. The opera ends with a chorus of thanks to the gods and a trio in praise of love.

Roles. ORFEO (m-s); sustained, dramatic; G2 to G4. EURIDICE (s); D3 to A4. AMORE (s); D3 to A4. OMBRA FELICE (HAPPY SPIRIT), E3 to A4 (sometimes sung by Euridice).

Chorus. SATB.

Ballet. Plays important role, as Furies and blessed spirits. Solo dancer often used.

Orchestra. 2 fl, 2 ob, 2 cl, 2 bsn, 2 hrn, 2 trp, cornetto, 3 trb, timp, strings.

Stage: strings, harp, ob (sometimes Eng hrn, sometimes tarogato).

Material. FS-P: Ri, Ka, Map, G Sc, TW (rent). MS: Br (f, g, e) $17.50. CP: Map (i, e) (rent). VS: AMP (BH—i, g) $3.60; Novello $3.25; Pr (f) $7.50; Ri (i) $7.50; G Sc (e—Ducloux) $5. Li: G Sc (i, e—Ducloux) 60¢. O Tr: Dent (Ox) $1.50.

Photographs. Salzburg: 1.9.39 p. 5. Metropolitan: 1.9.39 pp. 6, 7 (sketch); 1.15.40 pp. 21, 23; 4.4.55 pp. 5, 17–20; 1.13.58 pp. 18–20. Music Club of Greensboro, N.C.: 11.8.48 p. 10. Fenice, Venice: 11.22.48 p. 7. Hamburg: 12.7.53 p. 12. Holy Name College, Spokane: 12.7.53 p. 29. Wiesbaden: 1.24.55 p. 10; 4.4.55 pp. 17–20.

Performing Companies. 371 (4.1.50). 249A (2.29.52). 518A (4.53). 196A (12.18.53). 329 (54–55, 57–58). 389 (4.27.54). 283 (8.13.54). 518 (2.8.55). 451A (8.20.55). 57 (11.22.55). 182 (11.27.55). 241 (4.10.56). 78 (4.13.56). 1956–57: 131, 316, 323, 445. 72 (1959).

◪ Orphée aux enfers · Orpheus in the Underworld

Music by Jacques Offenbach (1819–1880). Libretto in French by Hector Crémieux and Ludovic Halévy. Premiere: Paris, October 21, 1858. Comic parody of the Orpheus legend. Simple harmonic structure; set numbers; light and melodious; dialogue. Overture. Setting: Greece in the classical past. Two acts, four scenes (180 min).

ACT I: A field of Thebes and Mount Olympus. ACT II: The underworld.

Synopsis. Public Opinion introduces the characters. Eurydice sings of her extramarital affair with Pluto, who appears on earth as the shepherd Aristée. Her husband, Orpheus, bores her with his violin playing; they quarrel, and she leaves for the underworld with Pluto. Public Opinion threatens a scandal if Orpheus does not follow her to Hades, and he reluctantly agrees. On Mount Olympus the gods complain of Jupiter's domination and the monotony of their nectar and ambrosia diet. When Eurydice arrives with Pluto, Jupiter displays obvious interest in her. Orpheus and Public Opinion also arrive and, to Orpheus's dismay, Jupiter orders Pluto to return Eurydice to her husband. In Hades Eurydice is attended by John Styx, a fool on earth, now charged with prison duties. Jupiter comes looking for her, disguised as a fly. Eurydice is intrigued, and they sing a happy duet. Jupiter turns her into a bacchante. Orpheus, distracted by a thunderbolt hurled by Jupiter, looks back on his wife and is delighted to learn that he has lost his right to her. The opera concludes with general rejoicing and a can-can.

Major Roles. EURYDICE (s); florid passages, trill; C3 to B4. ORPHEUS (t); E2 to B♭3. ARISTEE (PLUTO) (t); D2 to A3.

Lesser Roles. JUPITER (t). PUBLIC OPINION (s or m-s). CUPIDON (s or m-s). MERCURY (t). JOHN STYX (t). VENUS (s or m-s). DIANA (s); florid. MARS (bar). JUNO (m-s).

Bit Parts. MORPHEUS, MINERVA, CYBELE, POMONE, FLORE, CERES, MINOS, BAQUE, RADAMANTE (appear mostly ensemble).
Chorus. SSATTBB. Shepherds, gods, goddesses, infernal spirits, policemen.
Ballet. Many dances, including can-can.
Orchestra. 2 fl, 1 or 2 ob, 2 cl, 1 or 2 bsn, 2 hrn, 2 trp, 1 or 3 trb, timp, perc, strings.
Material. FS-P: Map (rent). VS: AMP (BB – g) $13.50; Pr (Mer – Heu – f) $13.50. Tr: Bentley (334); Kahn (T22); Glowacki (TW); Weiler (T22).
Photographs. N.Y. City Opera: 11.5.56 p. 10.
Performing Companies. 400 (5.18.55). 334 (1956). 533 (1959).

📖 Otello

Music by Giuseppe Verdi (1813–1901). Libretto in Italian by Arrigo Boito, based on Shakespeare's tragedy. Premiere: Milan, February 5, 1887. Tragic romance. Continuous texture embodies scenes of uninterrupted action; set numbers and accompanied recitative; long-spun melodious vocal line, often reaches strenuous dramatic intensity. No overture. Setting: the island of Cyprus, late 15th century. Four acts (135 min).

ACT I: Open square on the shore of the island (33 min). ACT II: A pavilion of the palace (36 min). ACT III: The great hall of the palace (37 min). ACT IV: Desdemona's bedchamber (30 min).

Synopsis. Otello, the Moor, governor of Cyprus, is welcomed back from war with the Turks by his bride, Desdemona, and the populace. Iago, his ensign, is jealous and bitterly angry that Otello has promoted another officer, Cassio. Iago proceeds to arouse Otello's jealousy by making him suspicious of his wife and Cassio, who he says has dreamed about Desdemona. Further, he claims to have seen Desdemona's wedding handkerchief in Cassio's hands. Otello falls prey to Iago's maneuvering and is convinced of his wife's guilt. He insults her in front of the visiting ambassador from Venice. Later he strangles her in her bed, only to learn from the horrified Emilia that his wife is innocent. He stabs himself, dying at her side.

Major Roles. OTELLO (dram t); demands dramatic power for sustained high tessitura; forceful acting ability required; ringing A3's and Bb3's; touches C4. IAGO (bar); subtle characterization essential; vocal coloration important; needs F♯3 for dramatic, declamatory scena. DESDEMONA (dram or lyr s); several dramatic passages; requires command of high pianissimo in last act, with firm Ab4 and A♯4; top B4.

Lesser Roles. CASSIO (t). EMILIA, Iago's wife and Desdemona's lady-in-waiting (m-s). RODERIGO, a Venetian gentleman (t). LODOVICO, Ambassador of Venice (bs). MONTANO, former Governor of Cyprus (bs). A HERALD (bs).

Chorus. SSATB. People of Venice and Cyprus, soldiers, ladies-in-waiting, children.

Orchestra. 3 fl (picc), 2 ob (Eng hrn), 2 cl (bs cl), 4 bsn, 4 hrn, 4 trp, 4 trb, timp, perc, harp, strings. *Stage:* band; mandolins, guitars, cornemuse (usually played by Eng hrn); trp (minimum 6), 3–4 trb.

109

Material. FS-P: Map, Ri, TW (rent). MS: Br (i) $20. CP: Map (i, e) (rent). VS: Map, TW (rent); Ri (i, e) $5, Ri (i) $7.50; G Sc (i, e) $6. Tr: Procter-Gregg (T2); Ducloux (T10).

Photographs. Metropolitan: ACT I: 2.18.46 p. 18 (sketch); ACT II: 2.19.40 p. 17; ACT III: 2.19.40 p. 16; ACT IV: 2.18.46 p. 21; (Meyer) 3.7.55 pp. 18–20. La Scala at Covent Garden: 11.13.50 p. 27. San Antonio: 4.5.54 p. 27.

Performing Companies. 478 (11.51). 449 (3.19.53; 2.1.55). 443B (11.10. 53; 56–57). 329 (48–49; 51–52; 54–55; 58–60). 487 (2.54). 180 (10.21. 54). 321A (10.31.54; 11.27.55). 245 (2.7.57). 33 (56–57). 515 (56–57). 491 (56–57). 339 (57–58). 72 (1959).

🎵 Parsifal

Music by Richard Wagner (1813–1883). Libretto in German by the composer, based on medieval legend and a poem by Wolfram von Eschenbach. Called a consecrational festival play (Bühnenweihfestspiel). Premiere: Bayreuth, July 26, 1882. Religious drama, laden with mystic symbolism. Orchestra predominates; continuous texture; complex chromatic harmonies, unified construction. Preludes to Acts I, II, III; Good Friday music between III i and ii. Setting: in and near Monsalvat in the Spanish Pyrenees; Middle Ages. Three acts, six scenes (222 min).

ACT I i: A forest near Monsalvat (62 min); ii: The Hall of the Holy Grail (36 min). ACT II i: Klingsor's castle (15 min); ii: Klingsor's magic garden (42 min). ACT III i: Gurnemanz's hut near Monsalvat (48 min); ii: The Hall of the Holy Grail (19 min).

Synopsis. Klingsor, an evil magician, had been denied entrance into the brotherhood of Knights of the Holy Grail. Enraged, he built a magic garden and thence, with his slave Kundry as temptress, he lured Amfortas, son of Titurel and King of the Knights of the Grail. Klingsor seized from him the Holy Spear and wounded him. The wound can now be healed only by being touched with the Spear held by a Guileless Fool able to withstand all temptation. Into this situation blunders young Parsifal. His total innocence enables him to resist the blandishments of Kundry and the Flower Maidens in Klingsor's garden. He magically grasps the Spear hurled at him by the sorcerer and with it makes the sign of the cross, thereby destroying Klingsor and his castle. For years Parsifal wanders the earth, returning to Monsalvat on a Good Friday. The knight Gurnemanz, now a hermit, and the repentant Kundry lead him to the gloomy Hall of the Grail, unhallowed since Amfortas' unredeemed transgression. Parsifal restores the erstwhile king of the brotherhood to health and causes the Holy Grail once again to assume its consecrational powers as the transfigured Kundry dies.

Major Roles. KUNDRY (dram s); needs particularly strong low and middle range, great stamina; G2 to B4. PARSIFAL (dram t); true Heldentenor able to be heard above full orchestra; Db2 to A3. AMFORTAS (bar); demands powerful actor as well as singer; Ab1 to G3. GURNEMANZ (bs); regal bearing; Gb1

110

to F3. KLINGSOR (bs); requires dark tone and appearance suggestive of malevolence; A♯1 to F♯3.

Lesser Roles. TITUREL, former King of Knights of the Grail (bs). FIRST AND SECOND KNIGHTS OF THE GRAIL (t and bs). FOUR ESQUIRES (s, a, t, t). Klingsor's FLOWER MAIDENS (6 s).

Chorus. SSSAAATTTTBBBB. Flower Maidens, Grail knights, youths, and boys.

Orchestra. 3 fl, 3 ob, Eng hrn, 3 cl, bs cl, 3 bsn, cont bsn, 4 hrn, 3 trp, 3 trb, bs tuba, timp, 4 bells, 2 harp, strings. *Stage:* 2 trp, 4 trb, side drum.

Production Problems. Disappearance of Klingsor's garden; throwing and catching of spear.

Material. FS-P: Map, Ri, TW (rent). FS: Br $25. VS: Map, TW (rent); B & H (g, e – Teschemacher) $6; Ri (e) $12; G Sc (g, i) $5. CP: Map (g, e) (rent). Tr: Hoffmann (148).

Photographs. Metropolitan: ACT I: 4.12.43 p. 11; 4.22.46 p. 18; 4.7.52 p. 19; 4.12.54 p. 18. ACT II: 4.12.43 cover; 4.7.52 p. 19; 4.12.54 p. 19. ACT III: 4.12.43 p. 12; 4.7.52 p. 19; 4.12.54 p. 20. Bayreuth: ACT I: 4.7.52 p. 4; 4.12.54 p. 9; ACT III: 2.26.59 p. 7. Indiana Univ.: 4.7.52 p. 7; 4.11.57 p. 18.

Performing Companies. 148 (4.3.55; 56–57). 329 (56–58; 59–61).

🎭 Pelléas et Mélisande · Pelléas and Mélisande

Music by Claude Debussy (1862–1918). Libretto in French, using the play by Maurice Maeterlinck. Premiere: Paris, April 30, 1902. Poetic legend of tragic love, set in a legendary kingdom, Allemonde, in the Middle Ages. Orchestrally important; continuous texture, using whole-tone scales and nonharmonic progressions; difficult vocal line basically an idealized inflection of speech. No overture; orchestral interludes connect the scenes. Five acts, thirteen scenes (131 min).

ACT I i: In a forest (10 min); ii: Castle of King Arkel (9 min); iii: Garden of the castle by the sea (6 min). ACT II i: A fountain in the park (6 min); ii: Golaud's room in the castle (11 min); iii: A cavern by the sea (4 min). ACT III i: Outside Mélisande's room in a tower (13 min); ii: The underground vaults of the castle (3 min); iii: Terrace at entrance to vaults (3 min); iv: Before the castle (10 min). ACT IV i: A room in the castle (16 min); ii: The fountain (14 min). ACT V: Mélisande's bedroom (26 min).

Synopsis. Prince Golaud finds Mélisande, a young princess, lost in the forest, brings her to his castle and marries her. Pelléas, his younger brother, and Mélisande fall in love and arouse Golaud's suspicion. His jealousy grows, and when he finds the two together at the fountain late at night, he kills his brother. Mélisande dies after giving birth to a daughter, and Golaud, still not certain of her guilt or innocence, bows his head in grief and remorse.

Major Roles. MELISANDE (lyr s); one of the most difficult of operatic roles because of its ethereal, other-worldly quality; requires subtle acting; not too demanding in range or strength; taste, phrasing, and coloration are paramount; C3 to A♭4. PELLEAS (lyr t or high bar); youthful appearance and ardent bearing are important; C2 to A3. GOLAUD (bar); difficult acting role calling for strength, passion, and sudden changes of mood; A1 to F♯3.

Lesser Roles. ARKEL, the old king (bs); F1 to D♯3. GENEVIEVE, his daughter, mother of Pelléas and Golaud (m-s); A2 to F♯4. YNIOLD, Golaud's son (s); must be short; C3 to A♭4. PHYSICIAN (bs); B♭1 to D3. SHEPHERD'S VOICE (bar). SERVING WOMEN (mute).

Chorus. AATBB. Behind scene, Act I iii.

Orchestra. 3 fl, 2 ob, Eng hrn, 2 cl, 3 bsn, 4 hrn, 3 trp, 3 trb, tuba, timp, perc, 2 harp, strings. *Stage:* bell.

Material. FS-P: El-V (rent). VS: El-V. MS: Pet $24. Tr: Goldovsky and Caldwell (T13); Levin (T26); NBC-TV (333); Treash (358).

Photographs. Metropolitan: 1.8.45 pp. 18–20; 12.28.53 pp. 19, 20.

Performing Companies. 334 (47–48). 202 (12.5.53). 329 (48–49, 53–54, 59–60). 333 (4.10.54). 148 (3.4.61).

🎭 La Périchole

Music by Jacques Offenbach (1819–1880). Libretto in French by Henri Meilhac and Ludovic Halévy. Premiere: Paris, October 6, 1868. Satirical comedy with overtones of farce. Highly melodious; set numbers, spirited ensembles. Overture. Adaptation in English by Maurice Valency, new musical version by Jean Morel and Ignace Strasfogel, performed at the Metropolitan in 1956–57. Setting: Lima, Peru; mid-19th century. Three acts, four scenes (128 min).

ACT I: Public square in Lima (49 min). ACT II: Viceroy's palace (39 min). ACT III i: Dungeon of Recalcitrant Husbands (28 min); ii: Public square (12 min).

Synopsis. Paquillo and La Périchole, two streetsingers, arrive in Lima on the Viceroy's birthday, which is being celebrated by his own order. Paquillo's jealousy will not permit La Périchole to accept pay from other men, so the two are perilously near starvation. A dinner from the smitten Viceroy tempts La Périchole, as does his invitation to the palace. By law, no unmarried woman may enter the royal household, so a husband must be found for the new favorite. Conveniently, Paquillo, made drunk by the Viceroy's henchmen, is pressed into service; neither he nor the tipsy bride recognizes the other. He is furious when he discovers the deception and is imprisoned by the Viceroy. La Périchole tricks the Viceroy; the pair escapes with the aid of a long-incarcerated political prisoner. When the Viceroy realizes the lovers' true devotion, he forgives them.

Major Roles. DON ANDRES, Viceroy of Peru (bar); a part with great comic possibilities. LA PERICHOLE (s or m-s). PAQUILLO (t or high bar).

Lesser Roles. DON PEDRO, governor of Peru (bar). COUNT OF PANATELLAS (t). MARQUIS OF TARAPOTE (speaking). GUADELENA and ESTRELLA, cousins (both s). VIRGINELLA, a third cousin (m-s). AN OLD PRISONER (t). FIRST and SECOND NOTARY (both t). FOUR LADIES-IN-WAITING (s and m-s).

Chorus. SATTB. Townspeople, soldiers, courtiers, circus performers, Indians.
Ballet. As large and elaborate as desired, in Act II.
Orchestra. Met vers: picc, 2 fl, 2 ob, 2 cl, 2 bsn, 4 hrn, 2 trp, 3 trb, timp, perc, harp, strings. *Stage:* band. Orig vers: 2 fl, ob, 2 cl, bsn, 2 hrn, 2 trp, trb, perc, strings.
Material. FS-P: Map (rent). VS: B & H (e − Valency) $6.
Photographs. Metropolitan: 1.14.57 pp. 16, 18–20. *Mus. Amer.* Central City: 9.58 p. 16.
Performing Companies. 329 (56–58). 297 (2.14.56). 82 (1958). 35 (1958).

♬ Peter Grimes

Music by Benjamin Britten (1913–   ). Libretto in English by Montagu Salter after the poem, "The Borough," by George Crabbe. Commissioned by the Koussevitzky Music Foundation. Premiere: London, June 7, 1945. Tragedy in a seacoast village. A taxing vocal line over continuous texture of rhythmically intricate orchestra, embodying set pieces, recitatives, and ensembles. Several elaborate choruses and ensembles; one extremely difficult contrapuntal sextet and chorus. Six orchestral interludes, highly expressive of the moods of the sea and the emotions of the characters. Setting: the Borough, a small fishing town on the east coast of England, about 1830. Prologue and three acts, six scenes (118 min).

PROLOGUE: A room in the moot hall (9 min). ACT I i: The beach and street (21 min); ii: Inside the Boar Inn (14 min). ACT II i: Same as I i (29 min); ii: Peter Grimes's hut (12 min). ACT III i: Same as I i (22 min); ii: The same (11 min).

Synopsis. The fisherman Peter Grimes, a self-tortured, ambivalent soul, is unpopular in the Borough, friendless except for Ellen Orford, the schoolmistress. His treatment of a succession of young apprentices invokes the village's disapproval, although he is acquitted of the charge of murdering one. The latest, a lad from the workhouse, meets with a fatal accident, and this time the temper of the village is implacably menacing. Captain Balstrode, the only cool head among them, remonstrates in vain, and the entire population sets out to bring Grimes to justice. Half demented, the unfortunate man soliloquizes about his hard fate, his dreams of marrying Ellen and finding peace now shattered. Following Balstrode's counsel of desperation, he puts his boat out to sea and sinks it. The village resumes its normal life, outwardly respectable, underneath ridden by hypocrisy, hate, and lechery, dominated always by the sea.

Major Roles. PETER GRIMES (t); needs dramatic intensity, sustained power; high tessitura with wide skips and considerable floridity; C2 to B3. ELLEN ORFORD (s); difficult intervals, often high tessitura; A♯2 to C5. CAPTAIN BALSTRODE, retired merchant skipper (bar); tessitura often high; A1 to G♭3 (opt G♯3 in ensemble).

Lesser Roles. AUNTIE, landlady of the Boar Inn (c); G2 to F♯4 (opt A4 and

113

G♯4 in ensembles). NIECE I (B2 to C♭4); NIECE II (B2 to B4) (both s); chief attractions of the Boar, they sing mostly in unison. BOB BOLES, fisherman and Methodist (t); many florid passages in high tessitura; B♭1 to C♭4. SWALLOW, lawyer, mayor, coroner (bs); F1 to F♯3. MRS. (NABOB) SEDLEY, rentier widow of an East India Company factor (m-s); considerable singing at low extreme of register; G2 to G4 (opt G♯4 in ensemble). REV. HORACE ADAMS, the rector (t); B1 to A3. NED KEENE, apothecary and quack (bar); often high tessitura; G♯1 to G3 (opt G♯3 and A♭3 in ensembles). HOBSON, a carrier (bs); F♯1 to F3. DR. THORP (mute). BOY, apprentice (mute).

Chorus. SSAATTBB. Townspeople and fisherfolk.

Orchestra. 2 fl (2 picc), 2 ob (Eng hrn), 2 cl (E♭ cl), 2 bsn, cont bsn, 4 hrn, 3 trp, 3 trb, tuba, timp, perc (2 players), celeste, harp, strings. *Stage:* organ, dance band (2 cl, perc, solo vln, solo cb, piano).

Material. All B & H. FS-P (rent). VS $15. Li $1. Analytical bklt $1.

Photographs. Sadler's Wells: 11.19.45 p. 22. Tanglewood: 10.7.46 pp. 20, 21. Berlin: 2.2.48 p. 4. Zurich: 2.2.48 p. 4. Metropolitan: 3.8.48 pp. 18–21. Hamburg: 12.10.51 p. 13.

Performing Companies. 205 (1946 — Amer prem). 329 (47–49).

🖾 Pique Dame · The Queen of Spades

Music by Peter Ilytch Tchaikovsky (1840–1893). Libretto in Russian by Modest Tchaikovsky, revised by the composer, based on a story by Pushkin. Premiere: St. Petersburg, December 19, 1890. Fantastic tragedy. Set numbers with accompanied recitative; conventional harmonic structure. Prelude. Setting: St. Petersburg, near the end of the 18th century. Three acts, seven scenes.

ACT I i: A summer garden in St. Petersburg; ii: Lisa's room with veranda. ACT II i: A large ballroom; ii: The Countess's bedroom. ACT III i: Herman's room; ii: Lisa's room; iii: Gambling room.

Synopsis. The young officer Herman is in love with Lisa, granddaughter of a countess called the Queen of Spades, who was once an expert cardplayer and the belle of St. Petersburg. Herman determines to learn the combination of three cards which is the secret of the Countess's gambling success, in order to get enough money to marry Lisa. Lisa gives Herman a key at a masked ball; he later surprises the Countess in her bedroom. She dies of fright without telling the secret. Her ghost returns and reveals the three cards. Lisa betroths herself to Prince Yeletsky to prevent Herman from using the ghostly knowledge. He disregards her pleas and she drowns herself. Herman gambles with Prince Yeletsky and wins the first two times. The third time he turns up the queen of spades instead of the expected card. Faced with the smiling ghost, he commits suicide.

Major Roles. LISA (lyr s); comfortable tessitura; C3 to B4. COUNTESS (m-s); extremely low tessitura; A2 to E4. HERMAN (t); frequent use of entire range; D2 to B3.

Lesser Roles. COUNT TOMSKY, Herman's friend (bar). PRINCE YELETSKY (bs). PAULINE, Lisa's friend (m-s). GOVERNESS (m-s). MASCHA, a chamber-maid (s). TCHEKALINSKY (t), SOURIN (bs), TCHAPLITSKY (t), NARUMOV (bs), Russian officers and noblemen. MASTER OF CEREMONIES (t). Characters in interlude at masked ball: CHLOE (s); DAPHNIS (PAULINE); PLUTUS (TOMSKY). *Chorus.* SSSAATTBB. Guests, children, soldiers, promenaders, masquer-aders, etc.

Ballet. Masked ball and interlude in II i.

Orchestra. picc, 2 fl, 2 ob, Eng hrn, 2 cl, bs cl, 2 bsn, 4 hrn, 2 trp, 3 trb, tuba, harp, timp, perc, strings.

Materials. FS-P: Ka, Map (rent). FS: Le $50. VS: Map (rent); Le $18; G Sc (e) $5. CP: Map (i) (rent). Tr: Austin (T1). Goldovsky and Caldwell (T13).

Photographs. Stockholm: 12.26.49 p. 10. Teatro Communale, Florence: 2.2.53 p. 30. Rome: 4.9.56 p. 12.

Performing Companies. 202 (12.2.51). 333 (1.3.52). 325A (4.25.52). 491 (4.22.54). 104 (1960).

𝄢 The Poisoned Kiss

Music by Ralph Vaughan Williams (1872–1958). Libretto in English by Evelyn Sharp, after incidents from "The Poisoned Maid" by Richard Garnett and from "Rapaccini's Daughter" by Nathaniel Hawthorne. Premiere: Cam-bridge, 1936. Satire, fantasy. Melodic, humorous; set numbers, dialogue. Brief overture. Setting: a mythical kingdom. Three acts (120 min).

ACT I: The magician's hut in the forest. ACT II: Tormentilla's apartment in Golden Town. ACT III: A room in the Empress's palace.

Synopsis. Dipsacus, a professional magician, has feuded for years with the Empress Persicaria of Golden Town, a mere amateur. He feeds his daugh-ter Tormentilla poison from birth so that whoever kisses her will die. His object is to get at the Empress's son, Prince Amaryllus. Sure enough, the Prince falls in love with Tormentilla and finally, overriding her objections, kisses her. Nothing happens, except that the two become more deeply enam-ored. The Empress, for all her amateur standing, has been clever enough to feed her son antidotes.

Major Roles. DIPSACUS (bs). TORMENTILLA (s). EMPRESS PERSICARIA (c). AMARYLLUS (t). GALLANTHUS, the Prince's attendant (bar). ANGELICA, Tor-mentilla's companion (m-s).

Lesser Roles. HOB (t), GOB (bar), LOB (bs), the magician's hobgoblins. FIRST MEDIUM (s), SECOND MEDIUM (m-s), THIRD MEDIUM (c), the Empress's assistants. ATTENDANT, PHYSICIAN (speaking).

Chorus. SATB. Day and night voices, hobgoblins, witches and forest crea-tures, messenger boys, milliners, flowergirls, lovers, etc.

Orchestra. 2 fl (picc), ob (Eng hrn), 2 cl, bsn, 2 hrn, 2 trp, t trb, timp, perc (2 players), harp (or piano), strings.

Material. FS-P: Ox (rent). VS: Ox (rent).

Performing Companies. 279 (1959). 364 (1959).

115

ᴍ Porgy and Bess

Music by George Gershwin (1898–1937). Libretto by Du Bose Heyward, based on Du Bose and Dorothy Heyward's play "Porgy," with lyrics by Ira Gershwin. Premiere: New York, October 10, 1935 (previous Boston tryout). Melodrama of American negro life. Set numbers with recitative and dialogue on musical pitch; highly melodious, conventional vocal lines alternating with lively, syncopated songs in contemporary idiom, also spirituals and hymns; several vigorous ensembles. Short prelude. The setting is Charleston, South Carolina, in the recent past. Three acts (often given in two), nine scenes (approx 150 min).

ACT I i: Catfish Row; ii: Serena's room. ACT II i: Catfish Row; ii: Kittiwah Island; iii: Catfish Row; iv: Serena's room. ACT III i: Catfish Row; ii: Catfish Row; iii: Catfish Row.

Synopsis. Catfish Row, once the site of aristocratic mansions, is now a negro tenement district. Porgy, a crippled beggar, loves Bess, who is scorned by the community because she is the mistress of Crown, a tough stevedore. In a drunken quarrel during a crap game, Crown kills Robbins and escapes to Kittiwah Island. Bess turns to Porgy for protection. Sportin' Life, in an attempt to seduce Bess, tries to sell her dope, but Porgy drives him away. During a picnic on Kittiwah, Crown appears from hiding and prevents Bess from leaving with the others. She reluctantly yields to him. A storm at sea kills several of the fishermen. Bess returns contritely to Porgy, who forgives her gladly. Crown stealthily enters, seeking Bess, and is surprised by Porgy, who strangles him. The police take Porgy, but only as an identifying witness. While he is gone, Bess succumbs to Sportin' Life's "happy dust" and elopes with him to New York. When Porgy returns from jail, bearing gifts for everyone as the result of a run of luck at crapshooting, he finds Bess gone. Maria and Serena explain her flight, but in spite of their condemnation, Porgy sets off for New York in his goatcart to find Bess, wherever she may be.

Major Roles. PORGY (bs-bar); needs great physical stamina to simulate cripple; entire role played on knees on little cart; B1 to F3 (opt G3); BESS (s); Bb2 to C5. SPORTIN' LIFE (t); D2 to Bb3. CROWN (bar); C♯2 to F♯3. CLARA, Jake's wife (s); E3 to F♯4 (opt A4).

Lesser Roles. SERENA, Robbins' wife (s). MARIA (c). JAKE (bar), MINGO (t), ROBBINS (t), PETER (t), FRAZIER (bar), fishermen. ANNIE (m-s). LILY (m-s). STRAWBERRY WOMAN (m-s). JIM (bar). UNDERTAKER (bar). NELSON (t). CRAB MAN (t).

Chorus. SSAATBB. Residents of Catfish Row, fishermen, children, and stevedores.

Orchestra. 2 fl, 2 ob, 4 cl, bsn, 3 hrn, 3 trp, 2 trb, tuba, timp, perc (2 players), piano, strings.

Material. FS-P: TW (rent). VS: Ger $9.

Photographs. U.S. touring group: 12.15.52 pp. 12, 13. Broadway: 1.30.56 p. 31.

Performing Companies. Broadway (1942). Dallas (6.9.52). Tours, 1952–54.

116

◢ Prince Igor

Music by Alexander Borodin (1834–1887), completed by Rimsky-Korsakov, Liadov and Glazounov. Libretto in Russian by the composer based on a play by Stassov, from a 14th-century Russian poem of unknown origin, entitled "Song of the Army of Prince Igor." Premiere: St. Petersburg, November 4, 1890. Romance using folk melodies, Oriental themes and rhythms. Conventional harmonic structure; accompanied recitatives, set arias and numbers. Prominent chorus. Overture, march, dances. Setting: semi-legendary Russia, in 1185. Prologue and four acts, five scenes (142 min).

PROLOGUE: Public square of Poutivl (19 min). ACT I i: Court of Galitzky's house (15 min); ii: Jaroslavna's room (22 min). ACT II: The Polovtsian camp (34 min). ACT III: The Polovtsian camp (27 min). ACT IV: Public square of Poutivl (25 min).

Synopsis. Prince Igor of Seversk and his son Vladimir lead the Russian army against the Tartar tribe of Polovtsi, leaving Igor's wife, Jaroslavna, in the care of her brother, Galitzky, who will govern Poutivl in Igor's absence. Two deserters from Igor's army, Sulka and Eroshka, try to arouse the mob against Igor, and urge Galitzky to usurp his power. Igor's army is defeated, and the invasion of the city by the enemy under Khan Gzak is imminent. Igor and Vladimir are prisoners of Khan Kontchak in the Polovtsian camp, but are treated as honored guests. Vladimir falls in love with Kontchakovna, the Khan's daughter, but the lovers fear Igor will not approve. Igor, despondent, is offered a chance to escape by the Polovtsian Ovlour, but honor requires that he refuse. The Khan offers Igor liberty if he will vow not to make war, but Igor again refuses. The Polovtsians under Khan Gzak win a great victory and bring back many Russian prisoners. Igor is persuaded to sacrifice his honor and flee, to lead his army again. He escapes with Ovlour, but Vladimir is left behind when Kontchakovna, to keep her lover, arouses the camp. The Khan admires Igor's valor and accepts Vladimir as his son-in-law. Jaroslavna mourns her lonely state, but soon sees Igor returning, finally victorious. The two traitors, Sulka and Eroshka, slightly drunk in the fashion of Russian comedy characters, happen upon the rejoicing couple, and speedily repent, hurrying to the city to alert the populace to their ruler's return. They share in the glory of Igor's resumption of power and Galitzky's fall.

Major Roles. JAROSLAVNA (s); C♯3 to C5. KONTCHAKOVNA (c); has a florid aria; G♯2 to G4. VLADIMIR (t); E♭2 to B♭3. PRINCE IGOR (bar); A1 to G♭3. KHAN KONTCHAK (bs); F1 to E3. GALITZKY (bs); C2 to F♯3 (opt G3).

Lesser Roles. KHAN GZAK, Polovstian Khan (bs). OVLOUR (t). SULKA (bs) and EROSHKA (t), gudok players and traitors. Jaroslavna's NURSE (s). YOUNG POLOVTSIAN MAIDEN (s).

Chorus. SSAATTTTBBBB. Russian princes and princesses, boyars and wives, old men, Russian warriors and prisoners, young women, Polovtsian chiefs, Kontchakovna's women, Kontchak's slaves, Polovtsian soldiers.

Ballet. Polovtsian maidens and slaves, in Act II.

Orchestra. 2 fl (picc), 2 ob (Eng hrn), 2 cl (bs cl), 2 bsn, 4 hrn, 2 trp, 3 trb, bs tuba, timp, perc, harp, piano, strings.

117

Material. FS-P: B & H, Map (rent). VS: B & H (r, f, g) $15. Le $16. Tr: Procter-Gregg (TMC).

Photographs. Metropolitan: 12.30.40 p. 10.

Performing Companies. 156 (56–57).

🎵 I Quattro rusteghi · The School for Fathers or The Four Ruffians

Music by Ermanno Wolf-Ferrari (1876–1948). Libretto in Italian by Giuseppe Pizzola, based on Carlo Goldoni's "I Rusteghi." Premiere: (in German) Munich, March 19, 1906. Ensemble comedy in 18th-century opera buffa style. Accompanied recitative, set arias and concerted numbers. Light, graceful style; some dissonance. Brief prelude. Intermezzo between Acts I and II. Setting: Venice, about 1800. Three acts, four scenes (108 min).

ACT I i: Lunardo's house (24 min); ii: Marina's house (27 min). ACT II: Lunardo's house (36 min). ACT III: The same (21 min).

Synopsis. Four boorish townsmen rule tyrannically over their families. One of them, Lunardo, has a young daughter, Lucieta, whom he wishes to marry off to Filipeto, the son of his widower friend Maurizio. The fathers agree to prevent the children from seeing each other before the wedding, and determine to squander no money on finery. Filipeto manages to sneak off to his Aunt Marina's house to tell her about the wedding, before he is sent away by her husband, Simon. Indignant at the secrecy, Marina and her friend Felice, Canciano's wife, scheme to have Filipeto appear at Lucieta's home disguised as a girl, as it is carnival time and people may go about freely in masks. The plot is carried out despite the misgivings of Margarita, Lucieta's stepmother. Filipeto reveals his identity to Lucieta and the young people fall in love at first sight. But the men appear too soon, to await the arrival of Maurizio and his son, and Filipeto with his "escort" Riccardo, a friend of Felice's, must hide. Maurizio enters, distraught at his son's mysterious disappearance. Soon the masqueraders are discovered and there is great confusion. Lunardo proposes to break off the marriage plans, and the men discuss various means to punish their wives. Felice interrupts and makes the ladies' position quite clear. The men are cowed; Lunardo relents; the lovers are united.

Major Roles. LUCIETA (lyr s); youthful quality; C3 to C5. MARINA (s); trill; B2 to C5. FELICE (s); trill; B2 to C5. MARGARITA (m-s); low tessitura; Bb2 to G4. FILIPETO (t); young, romantic; high tessitura; E2 to A3. RICCARDO (t); C♯2 to A3. LUNARDO (bs); should have high falsetto; E1 to A3. MAURIZIO (bs); E1 to F3. SIMON (bs); should have high falsetto; E1 to A3. CANCIANO (bs); E1 to E3.

Lesser Role. MAID to Marina (m-s).

Orchestra. 2 fl (picc), 2 ob (Eng hrn), 2 cl, 2 bsn, 4 hrn, 3 trp, 3 trb, tuba, timp, perc (3 players), harp, strings.

Material. FS-P: G Sc (rent). VS: G Sc (g, e — Dent) $12.

Photographs. Sadler's Wells: 2.26.51 p. 15. Holland: 12.15.58 p. 27.

Performing Companies. 334 (10.18.51).

◪ The Rake's Progress

Music by Igor Stravinsky (1882–   ). Libretto in English by W. H. Auden and Chester Kallman, suggested by Hogarth's drawings. Premiere: Venice, September 11, 1951. A fable resembling a morality play. Contemporary score, formalized according to 18th-century practice, of great transparency and rhythmic diversity. Arias, recitatives, and ensembles. All solo parts are written in florid style and present formidable difficulties. Brief prelude. Three acts, nine scenes, and epilogue (140 min).

ACT I i: The garden of Trulove's cottage, a spring afternoon; ii: Mother Goose's, a London brothel, summer; iii: Same as I i, autumn night (45 min). ACT II i: Morningroom of Rakewell's house in London, autumn afternoon; ii: Street before Rakewell's house, autumn dusk; iii: Same as II i, winter morning (35 min). ACT III i: Same as II i, spring afternoon; ii: A churchyard, the same evening; iii: Bedlam (60 min). Epilogue: before the curtain.

Synopsis. Anne Trulove's father does not approve of the improvident Tom Rakewell as a suitor. Tom determines to live by his wits and makes a wish for money, summoning Nick Shadow to his aid, thereby beginning a life of moral deterioration. This Mephisto-like character, Nick, serves his new master in the inevitable path through false glory to damnation. Tom's adventures lead him away from Anne to the brothel of Mother Goose and a life of luxury. His second wish: to be happy. Shadow interprets this as marriage to the bearded Baba the Turk, who, however, succeeds only in boring Tom by her incessant chatter. He claps an enormous wig over her head to silence her. Out of a dream he makes his third wish: a machine to turn stones into bread. Nick supplies it, but like all his gratifications, it is a fraud. Now Tom, bankrupt and loveless, must pay his soul in debt to Shadow. Shadow gives him another chance — to guess three cards; but even though Tom succeeds, his evil genius cheats him again, taking away his sanity. Anne visits him in the madhouse, but it is too late. In an epilogue, all the principals sing the moral: "The Devil finds work for idle hearts and hands to do."

Major Roles. ANNE (lyr s); a very difficult aria demands agility and strength in extremes of range; B2 to C5. TOM RAKEWELL (t); large share of florid passages, dramatic effects; C2 to A3. NICK SHADOW (bar); acting ability valuable to show forceful character, sly, suave and plausible; C2 to E3. BABA THE TURK (m-s); needs great flexibility and stamina; B2 to F♯4.

Lesser Roles. TRULOVE (bs); A1 to D3. MOTHER GOOSE (m-s); A2 to A4. SELLEM, the auctioneer (t); E2 to G3. KEEPER OF THE MADHOUSE (bs); D2 to D♭3.

Chorus. SATB. Whores, roaring boys, servants, citizens, madmen.

Ballet. A dance possible though not necessary in Act I ii.

Orchestra. 2 fl (picc), 2 ob (Eng hrn), 2 cl, 2 bsn, 2 hrn, 2 trp, timp, piano, strings.

Production Problems. Cuckoo clock, synchronized with 12 beats in orchestra. Disappearance of Nick into grave. Many elaborate props.

Material. FS-P, CP: B & H (rent). VS: B & H (e, g) $15.

Photographs. La Scala: 1.28.52 p. 29; 2.9.53 p. 13. Vienna: 10.13.52 p. 10;

2.9.53 p. 12. Strasbourg: 2.9.53 p. 12. Metropolitan: 2.9.53 pp. 17, 19 (sketches); 10.19.53 2nd cover. Paris and Edinburgh: 10.19.53 p. 20.

Performing Companies. 329 (2.14.53 — Amer prem; 53–54). 197 (5.53). 53 (5.26.55; 56–57). 475 (56–57). 275 (57–58). 104 (2.12.59).

🎭 The Rape of Lucretia

Music by Benjamin Britten (1913–   ). Libretto in English by Ronald Duncan after the play, "Le Viol de Lucrèce," by André Obey. Premiere: Glyndebourne, July 12, 1946. Tragedy. Set numbers; recitative; demanding vocal line with difficult skips; orchestra extremely exposed, instruments of solo quality; several complicated ensembles. Setting: Rome, 6th century B.C. Two acts, four scenes, two prologues — within a frame provided by the Male and Female Chorus sitting at either side of the stage; in prologues and interludes a front cloth conceals the scenes (120 min).

ACT I prologue: Before the front cloth; i: The Army camp outside Rome; ii: Lucretia's house. ACT II prologue: Before the front cloth; i: Lucretia's bedroom; ii: Same as I ii.

Synopsis. Lucretia, wife of the Roman general Collatinus, is the only lady to remain chaste as the rule of the Tarquins debauches the city. Another general, Junius, jealous of Collatinus, slyly incites the libertine Prince Tarquinius to test Lucretia's virtue. Arriving at night, when the lady is alone with her maid and nurse, Tarquinius ravishes his hostess by force. Collatinus, arriving with Junius the next morning and hearing Lucretia's confession, wishes to forgive her, but she cannot bear to live with her sin and stabs herself. According to the historian Livy, her fate is the final incentive for the Romans to throw off Etruscan rule.

Roles. MALE CHORUS (high t); C2 to B♭4. FEMALE CHORUS (s); B2 to A♭4. These two "ideal spectators" explain, comment upon, and sometimes anticipate the story, yet do not take part. They are not dispassionate, but prejudiced, and, being outside time and space, interpret pre-Christian happenings from a Christian point of view. LUCRETIA (c); dramatic, sustained, extremes of range; touches E2 and A4. COLLATINUS (bs); noble in bearing; B1 to E3. JUNIUS (bar); E1 to G♭3. PRINCE TARQUINIUS (bar); sustained, forceful, considerable high tessitura; B1 to G3. BIANCA, Lucretia's nurse (m-s); A2 to F♯4. LUCIA, Lucretia's maid (high s); florid passages; B2 to B4.

Chorus. SATB. Can be added in II i and between II ii and iii.

Orchestra. fl (picc and bs fl), ob (Eng hrn), cl (bs cl), bsn, hrn, perc, harp, string qt, cb. Recitatives accompanied by piano can be played by conductor.

Material. FS-P: B & H (rent). VS: B & H $15. Li: B & H $1. Analytical bklt: B & H $1.

Photographs. St. Louis Opera Guild: 5.9.49 p. 24; N.Y. City Opera: 12.15. 58 p. 5. *Mus. Amer.* Academy of Vocal Arts, Philadelphia: 7.59 p. 31.

Performing Companies. 137 (1947 — Amer prem). Ziegfeld Theatre, New York (1948). 447 (7.51). 338A (2.52). 398A (6.53). 233 (10.53). 496 (4. 15.54). 68 (56–57). 416 (56–57). 334 (10.23.58). 147 (3.1.59). 439 (1959).

🎵 Richard Coeur de Lion · Richard the Lionhearted

Music by André Grétry (1741-1813). Libretto in French by Michel Jean Sedaine, based on a supposedly historical incident found in an old French trouvère's ballad. Premiere: Paris, October 21, 1784. Romantic comedy. Melodious; simple, conventional harmonic structure; set numbers; dialogue. Orchestral introduction, entr'actes before Acts II and III, orchestral finale to Act I. Setting: Germany, end of 12th century. Three acts, four scenes (or three scenes) (approx 90 min).

ACT I: Outside the walls of a castle. ACT II: Garden of the castle. ACT III i: A room in the castle; ii: Outside the castle. (Note: If battle is held offstage, Act III can be in one scene inside. Tanglewood production showed battle in silhouette behind interior by using scrim and lighting, then returned to interior.)

Synopsis. Richard I, King of England, is a prisoner in Germany. His minstrel Blondel, disguised as a blind man, has spent a year searching for his master, accompanied by the youth Antonio. Hearing a song which Richard has composed, Blondel recognizes his voice and determines to rescue him. Marguerite, Countess of Flanders and Artois, is in love with Richard. Blondel tells her of Richard's captivity and enlists her aid. Florestan, governor in charge of Richard and the castle, loves Laurette, daughter of the English Sir William. Blondel assembles a band of English soldiers outside the castle and lures Florestan to the scene with the bait of a meeting with Laurette. The soldiers attack; Richard is freed and reunited with his courtiers and his love. (Note: This is the third version of the plot, preferred by Grétry, employed in the Heugel score and in the Tanglewood production.)

Major Roles. MARGUERITE (s); high tessitura; D3 to A4. LAURETTE (lyr s); agile voice; D3 to A4. RICHARD (t); high tessitura; long florid phrases; D2 to B3. BLONDEL (bar); requires trill; acting ability; B1 to G3.

Lesser Roles. ANTONIO (m-s). SIR WILLIAM (bs). FLORESTAN (bs).

Bit Parts. LE SENECHAL, majordomo to Marguerite (speaking). MATHURIN and MATHURINE, aged peasant couple celebrating their anniversary (t, s). CHARLES GUILLOT and URBAIN, companions of Sir William (bar, bs). COLETTE, peasant girl (s). BEATRIX, lady-in-waiting to Marguerite (speaking).

Chorus. SSTTBB. Peasants, soldiers, officers, knights, members of Marguerite's entourage.

Orchestra. 2 fl, 2 ob, 2 bsn, 4 hrn, 2 trp, 3 trb, timp, perc, strings. (Brief violin solo supposedly played by Blondel.)

Material. FS-P: Pr (Mer − Heu) (rent). VS: Pr (Mer − Heu − f) $9.25. Tr: Goldovsky and Caldwell (T13).

Photographs. Tanglewood: 11.2.53 p. 6; 2.15.54 p. 5.

Performing Companies. 205 (8.10.53).

🎵 Rigoletto

Music by Giuseppe Verdi (1813-1901). Libretto in Italian by Francesco Maria Piave, based on the play "Le roi s'amuse" by Victor Hugo. Premiere:

Venice, March 11, 1851. Melodrama. Music unusually apt in portraying character and dramatic situation. Set numbers, accompanied recitative; highly melodious, often dramatic vocal line. Prelude. The opera changes the locale of the play (the court of Francis I) to Mantua in the 16th century. Four acts (originally three acts, four scenes) (95 min).

ACT I: Ballroom of the ducal palace (16 min). ACT II: The house of Rigoletto (21 min). ACT III: The private rooms of the Duke in the palace (27 min). ACT IV: Sparafucile's desolate inn near the river, both interior and exterior visible (31 min).

Synopsis. Rigoletto, jester in the court of the Duke of Mantua, mocks Count Monterone as the latter denounces the Duke for dishonoring his daughter. The old count curses Rigoletto, who is himself a father. He is very careful to protect his daughter, Gilda, from all the evil of the world, but the Duke has already found her – though he does not know her parentage. With the connivance of the nurse, Giovanna, the Duke, disguised as a student, is smuggled into Rigoletto's house for a rendezvous. Later, the corrupt courtiers, believing Gilda to be Rigoletto's mistress, kidnap her. Finding her at the palace, Rigoletto swears vengeance on the Duke, although Gilda, enamored of her fickle lover, tries to dissuade him. Rigoletto at last resorts to a hired assassin, Sparafucile, but Gilda intervenes, substituting herself for the beloved victim. Discovering her body instead of the libertine's, the distraught father acknowledges the power of Monterone's curse.

Major Roles. DUKE OF MANTUA (lyr t); needs lightness and flexibility, also considerable sustained power; C2 to B3. GILDA (col s); girlish appearance; requires both lyric tenderness and brilliant coloratura; trill; touches C♯5 (E5 often sung is not in score). RIGOLETTO (bar); one of the great acting and singing roles; requires physical stamina to simulate hunchback, as well as vocal strength and subtlety throughout wide range; dramatic, declamatory, and sustained; trill; B♭1 to G3. SPARAFUCILE (bs); sinister appearance, low tessitura; F1 to F♯3. MADDELENA, his sister (m-s or c); seductive gypsy; B2 to F♯4.

Lesser Roles. COUNT MONTERONE (bs). GIOVANNA (m-s). COUNT CEPRANO (bar), BORSA (t), and MARULLO (bar), courtiers. COUNTESS CEPRANO (m-s or s). A PAGE (m-s).

Chorus. SATB, TTBB. Courtiers and their ladies.

Ballet. Short dance in Act I.

Orchestra. 2 fl (picc), 2 ob (Eng hrn), 2 cl, 2 bsn, 4 hrn, 2 trp, 3 trb, tuba, timp, perc, strings. *Stage:* band, usually orchestrated for available players.

Materials. FS-P: Ka, Map, Ri, TW (rent). MS: Br (i) $17.50. CP: Map (i, e) (rent). VS: B & H (i, e – Oxenford) $4.50; Map (rent); TW (e – Martin) (rent); Pet (i, g) $4; Ri (i) $5; Ri (i, e – Machlis) $5; G Sc (i, e) $4. O Tr: Caldwell and Goldovsky (T13); Carpenter and Norton (Univ. of Oklahoma); Matz (Ru); Rachleff (T17). Li: Ox (e – Dent) $1.50.

Photographs. ACT I: Metropolitan: 1.26.42 p. 16; (at Baltimore) 3.16.42 p. 8; 12.3.51 p. 19. Indiana Univ.: 4.16.51 p. 21. La Scala: 3.1.54 p. 8. ACT II: Metropolitan: 12.13.43 p. 19; 12.3.51 p. 17. Florence: 2.6.50 p. 15. ACT III: Metropolitan: 1.26.42 p. 17; 12.3.51 p. 19. ACT IV: Metropolitan: 12.13.43

p. 21; 12.3.51 p. 19. Bob Jones Univ.: 11.15.54 p. 12. *Mus. Amer.* Central City: 8.57 p. 12.

Performing Companies. Approx 78; 1956–57 only 14, 37, 64, 70, 82, 182, 216, 295, 324, 329, 334, 394, 449, 478, 487.

🎵 Der Ring des Nibelungen · The Ring of the Nibelungs

Music and text by Richard Wagner (1813–1883). Composed as a stage festival to be performed over a 4-day period. Story based on German mythology as used in the "Nibelungenlied," circa 1160, and on legends from Icelandic literature, especially the Volsunga Saga of the 12th and 13th centuries. Premiere as cycle: Bayreuth, August 13, 14, 16, 17, 1876. Heroic saga with philosophical implications. Continuous texture of full, chromatic harmonies; heavy orchestration employing complicated interlocking system of leading motives, highly symbolic, and representing characters, moods, objects, actions. Largely declamatory vocal line integrated into orchestral structure, often submerged. Setting throughout: remote legendary antiquity. Four complete and self-sufficient, although interconnected, music dramas.

🎵 Das Rheingold · The Rhinegold

Prologue to the main body of "Der Ring des Nibelungen." Premiere: Munich, September 22, 1869. Epic tale of intrigue, setting in motion events of succeeding dramas. Orchestral prelude and postlude to each of four continuous scenes. One act (132 min).

Scene i: At the bottom of the Rhine (22 min); ii: Open space on heights bordering the Rhine (40 min); iii: Caverns of Nibelheim (22 min); iv: Same as ii (48 min).

Synopsis. At the bottom of the Rhine, the mystic gold, symbol of purity, has been protected for years by the carefree Rhinemaidens. While teasing the boastful dwarf Alberich, they inadvertently reveal to him the gold's secret: anyone who renounces love forever can forge the gold into a ring which will give him universal power. Alberich utters the fearful renunciation and steals the gold. Wotan, king of the gods, has hired the giants Fasolt and Fafner to build him a mighty fortress, Valhalla, the payment for which is to be Freia, goddess of youth and beauty. Fricka, Wotan's wife, joins the protest against paying this fee; but Wotan can see no way out of his bargain until Loge, god of fire, tells him of Alberich and the wealth he has accumulated. The giants agree to accept the dwarf's hoard in lieu of Freia. Wotan and Loge descend to Alberich's realm, and by trickery kidnap him and make him yield his entire treasure, including the Ring. When released, Alberich places a fearful curse on the Ring. The giants demand the Ring as part of their payment; Erda, the earth goddess, advises Wotan to yield it; the curse operates and Fafner kills his brother. As Donner, god of thunder, clears the air with a thunderbolt,

123

Wotan, disturbed by these events, leads the gods over a rainbow bridge into Valhalla as Loge laughs and the Rhinemaidens lament their loss.

Major Roles. FRICKA (m-s); dramatic intensity; C♯3 to F♯4. LOGE (t); bright quality; C2 to G3. WOTAN (bar); strong, warm voice; A♭1 to F3. ALBERICH (bar, sometimes sung by bs-bar); sinister; A♯1 to G♭3.

Lesser Roles. FREIA (s); E3 to C♭5. ERDA (m-s); dark. WOGLINDE, WELLGUNDE, FLOSSHILDE, Rhinemaidens (s, s or m-s, m-s). FROH, god of the fields (t). DONNER (bar). MIME, a Nibelung, Alberich's brother (t). FASOLT (bar). FAFNER (bs). NIBELUNGS (shout, groan, etc., but do not sing).

Orchestra. 3 fl, picc, 3 ob, Eng hrn, 3 cl, bs cl, 3 bsn, 8 hrn, (2 t tuba, 2 bs tuba), 3 trp, bs trp, 3 trb, cont bs trb, cont bs tuba, timp, perc, 18 anvil, 7 harp (or fewer), augmented strings (16.16.12.12.8).

Production Problems. Swimming of Rhinemaidens; shifts of scene without break; Alberich's becoming invisible, a serpent, and a frog; rising of Erda from the earth; rainbow bridge and entrance into Valhalla.

Material. FS-P: Ri, TW (rent). VS: AMP (Sch – g) $8.50; G Sc (g, e) $5. MS: Pet (Eu – g, f, e) $25.

Photographs. Metropolitan (Simonson): 1.22.51 pp. 18 (sketch), 20; 1.21.57 pp. 18, 19; 2.25.57 p. 24. Bayreuth: 10.19.53 p. 8. Stuttgart: 1.23.56 p. 3. Vienna: 2.23.59 p. 28.

Performing Companies. 329 (50–51, 56–57). 32B (57–58).

🎵 Die Walküre · The Valkyrie

Premiere: Munich, June 26, 1870. Music drama of epic proportions. Orchestral preludes and postludes, Magic Fire Music. Setting: near the Rhine. Three acts (193 min).

ACT I: Interior of Hunding's hut (59 min). ACT II: A wild, rocky height (75 min). ACT III: Valkyries' rock atop a mountain (59 min).

Synopsis. The exhausted Siegmund, son of Wotan (whom he knows only as Wälse) staggers into the hut of the warrior Hunding. He is succored by Sieglinde, Hunding's wife, who is, unknown to him, his twin sister. At supper Hunding recognizes Siegmund as his hereditary enemy, but promises the weaponless hero the traditional hospitality of one night before battle to the death. Sieglinde gives Hunding a sleeping potion, then shows Siegmund the sword Nothung, buried by Wotan deep in a tree trunk, the sword which can protect him and avenge her forced marriage to Hunding. Siegmund wrests the sword from the tree; the lovers rush into the spring night. Wotan wishes to protect his hero-son, but the law-abiding Fricka demands that Hunding be allowed his vengeance in the name of marital fidelity. Sadly Wotan summons his favorite daughter, Brünnhilde, a Valkyrie, and bids her bring Siegmund to his death. When she confronts the hero, guarding his exhausted sister-bride, he refuses to join her in Valhalla without Sieglinde. Brünnhilde is so touched by his devotion that she tries to protect him. Wotan interferes, and Hunding kills Siegmund, shattering his sword, only to be himself killed by the scornful god. Brünnhilde meanwhile spirits Sieglinde to safety, telling her she bears in her

124

womb the hero Siegfried, and giving her the pieces of the sword. Wotan pursues Brünnhilde to punish her for her disobedience. Despite the frightened pleas of the other eight Valkyries, he divests Brünnhilde of godhood and puts her to sleep, a prey for anyone to awaken and claim. As a final gesture he surrounds her rocky couch with a ring of magic fire, to repel all but a fearless hero, then bids his beloved child farewell.

Major Roles. SIEGLINDE (dram s); lyrical passages; B2 to B♭4. BRUNNHILDE (dram s); strong, superhuman quality; trill; A2 to C5. SIEGMUND (dram t); heroic, strong throughout range; C2 to A3. WOTAN (bar or bs-bar); warm, expressive voice; F1 to G♭3.

Lesser Roles. FRICKA (s or m-s); dramatic voice; C♭3 to A♭4. HUNDING (bs); harsh, dark; G1 to E♭3. HELMWIGE (s), ORTLINDE (s), GERHILDE (s), WALTRAUTE (m-s), SIEGRUNE (m-s), ROSSWEISE (m-s), GRIMGERDE (m-s), SCHWERTLEITE (m-s), Valkyries.

Orchestra. 3 fl, picc, 3 ob, Eng hrn, 3 cl, bs cl, 3 bsn, 8 hrn (2 t tuba, 2 bs tuba), 3 trp, bs trp, 3 trb, cont bs trb, cont bs tuba, timp, perc, 6 harp (or fewer), augmented strings (16.16.12.12.8). *Stage:* 2 Stierhorn (or trb).

Production Problems. Sword in tree; magic fire; two rams to pull Fricka's cart (usually not used).

Material. FS-P: Map, Ri, TW (rent). VS: G Sc (g, e) $5. Tr: Chapin (T24).

Photographs. Metropolitan: ACT I: 3.25.46. p. 18; (Simonson) 1.19.48 p. 18 (sketch); 1.24.49 p. 18; 1.28.57 p. 18. ACT II: (Jorgulesco) 12.1.41 p. 14 (sketch); (Simonson) 1.19.48 p. 18 (sketch); 1.24.48 p. 19. ACT III: (Jorgulesco) 12.1.41 p. 17; 2.22.43 p. 17 (sketch); (Simonson) 1.19.48 p. 20 (sketch); 1.24.49 pp. 19, 20; 3.13.50 cover. Bayreuth: 11.7.38 p. 8; 1.19.48 p. 10; 12.6.48 pp. 6, 7; 10.15.51 p. 23; 10.19.53 p. 9. Vienna: 10.14.57 p. 4.

Performing Companies. 329 (50–51, 53–54, 56–58). 321A (3.12.55; 57–58). 72 (10.3.56). 86 (56–58). 130 (56–57). 32B (57–58). 481 (11.59).

▶ Siegfried

Premiere: Bayreuth, August 16, 1876. Orchestral preludes and postludes, Forest Murmurs. Setting: near the Rhine. Three acts, four scenes (215 min).

ACT I: Rocky cave in a forest (75 min). ACT II: Depths of the forest (66 min). ACT III i: Wild area at foot of rocky mountain (continuous with) ii: Valkyries' rock atop a mountain (74 min).

Synopsis. Sieglinde has died giving birth to Siegfried. The young hero has been raised in a cave by the dwarf Mime, brother of the same Alberich who forged and then cursed the Ring. Mime hopes to weld the fragments of Siegmund's sword, Nothung, into an invincible weapon for Siegfried, with which the fearless youth can retrieve Alberich's treasure. The hoard, including the Ring, is guarded by the giant Fafner, who has transformed himself into a monstrous dragon. A strange wanderer, Wotan in disguise, who hopes for deliverance from the curse by the free action of an independent hero, now confronts the dwarf and predicts the forging of Nothung and the death of

125

Mime at the hands of one who has never known fear. Siegfried hammers Nothung into a gleaming sword and then, at Mime's urging, finds and kills Fafner and takes the Ring. He accidentally tastes the dragon's blood, which lets him understand the language of animals and the innermost thoughts of man. He thus divines Mime's hidden malevolence and kills him. A forest bird tells of Brünnhilde behind her Magic Fire; Siegfried sets off to find her. His way is blocked by the world-weary Wotan, but when Nothung shatters the god's spear, Wotan lets Siegfried pass, returning to Valhalla to await his inevitable doom. Siegfried braves the flames, which subside as he awakens Brünnhilde, an awakening which leads to mutual adoration.

Major Roles. BRUNNHILDE (dram s); trill, heroic quality; B2 to C5. SIEGFRIED (dram t); long role, strong, heroic voice; C2 to C4. MIME (t); strength throughout range; A1 to A3 (opt B3). DER WANDERER (bs or bs-bar); noble, mature quality; G♯1 to F♯3.

Lesser Roles. ALBERICH (bs). FAFNER, disguised as a dragon (bs). VOICE OF THE FOREST BIRD (s). ERDA (c).

Orchestra. 2 fl, picc, 3 ob, 2 Eng hrn, 3 cl, bs cl, 3 bsn, 8 hrn, (2 t tuba, 2 bs tuba), 3 trp, bs trp, 3 trb, cont bs trb, cont bs tuba, timp, perc, 6 harp (or fewer), augmented strings (16.16.12.12.8). *Stage:* hrn, Eng hrn.

Production Problems. Forging of sword; Fafner as a dragon; Erda's appearance out of rocks; magic fire.

Material. FS-P: Map, Ri, TW (rent). VS: G Sc (g, e) $5. MS: Pet (Eu — g, f, e) $25.

Photographs. Metropolitan (Simonson): 2.3.51 pp. 18, 19; 2.11.57 pp. 18–20. Covent Garden: 10.31.49 p. 13. Bayreuth: 10.18.54 p. 6.

Performing Companies. 329 (50–51, 56–57).

🎭 Götterdämmerung · Twilight of the Gods

Premiere: Bayreuth, August 17, 1876. Orchestral preludes and postludes, Rhine Journey, Siegfried's Funeral Music. Setting: near the Rhine. Prologue and three acts, five scenes (227 min).

PROLOGUE: The Valkyries' rock (34 min). ACT I i: Hall of the Gibichungs on the Rhine (39 min); ii: Valkyries' rock (29 min). ACT II: The Rhine before the Gibichungs' hall (55 min). ACT III i: Rocky valley on the Rhine (43 min); ii: Hall of the Gibichungs (27 min).

Synopsis. Three Norns predict the death of the gods. Siegfried leaves his bride, Brünnhilde, in search of adventure, after placing the Ring on her finger. He journeys to the hall of the Gibichungs — Gunther, his sister Gutrune, and his half-brother Hagen, the evil son of Alberich. Hagen plots to regain the Ring. Gutrune gives Siegfried a potion of forgetfulness. Under its power, Siegfried agrees to marry her and to win Brünnhilde for Gunther. He succeeds, unconscious of his guilt, despite the recriminations of Brünnhilde, who has been forewarned by Waltraute, a Valkyrie. Siegfried swears his innocence, and Brünnhilde vows vengeance on him for his perfidy. She reveals to Hagen Siegfried's one weakness: a blow on the back will prove fatal.

126

On a hunting trip Siegfried meets the Rhinemaidens, who beg for the return of the Ring he wrested from Brünnhilde, before he succumbs to its curse. He refuses. Hagen gives Siegfried a memory-restoring potion. As Siegfried tells the story of his life, he realizes his guilt. Two ravens, Wotan's messengers, arise to fly to Valhalla. As Siegfried turns to watch them, Hagen plunges his spear into the hero's back. He dies, calling Brünnhilde's name. His body is borne back to the hall of the Gibichungs, where Brünnhilde bids a pyre be prepared. Hagen kills Gunther and tries to seize the Ring, but the dead Siegfried's hand rises in warning, and Hagen falls back. Brünnhilde takes the Ring and bids farewell to her husband and the universe, and rides her horse, Grane, into the fire. The flames rise until Valhalla is ignited and the hall destroyed. The Rhine overflows, extinguishing the fire, while the Rhinemaidens reclaim the gold and drown Hagen. The day of the gods is over.

Major Roles. BRUNNHILDE (dram s); sustained power, trill, G2 to C5. SIEGFRIED (dram t); strong voice throughout range; B♯1 to C4. HAGEN (bs); dark, evil; F1 to G3.

Lesser Roles. GUTRUNE (s); C3 to C♭5. GUNTHER (bs or bs-bar); A1 to F3. ALBERICH (bs); A1 to F3. WALTRAUTE (m-s); G2 to A4. THREE NORNS (c, m-s, s). WOGLINDE, WELLGUNDE, FLOSSHILDE, Rhinemaidens (s, m-s, c).

Chorus. STTBB. Gibichung vassals and women (several solo lines).

Orchestra. 3 fl, picc, 3 ob, Eng hrn, 3 cl, bs cl, 3 bsn, 8 hrn (2 t tuba, 2 bs tuba), 3 trp, bs trp, 3 trb, cont bs trb, cont bs tuba, timp, perc, 8 harp (or fewer), augmented strings (16.16.12.12.8). *Stage:* 2–3 Stierhorn (or trb).

Production Problems. Ravens; immolation scene (funeral fire, burning of Valhalla, Rhine overflowing, collapse of Gibichung hall).

Material. FS-P: Map, Ri, TW (rent). VS: G Sc (g, e) $7.50. MS: Pet (Eu − g, f, e) $25.

Photographs. Metropolitan: (Simonson) 2.12.51 pp. 18–19; 12.31.51 pp. 18–19; 2.25.57 pp. 18–20. Bayreuth: 2.15.54 pp. 6, 7; 10.18.54 p. 7; 10.17.55 p. 23. Covent Garden: 11.1.54 p. 22. Appia design: 2.15.54 p. 7.

Performing Companies. 329 (50–52, 56–57).

▨ Roméo et Juliette · Romeo and Juliet

Music by Charles Gounod (1816–1893). Libretto in French by Jules Barbier and Michel Carré, based on Shakespeare's drama. Premiere: Paris, April 27, 1867. Romantic tragedy. Set numbers, arias, and ensembles; melodious vocal line over conventional harmony. Prelude. Setting: Verona, 14th century. Five acts, seven scenes (125 min).

Prologue introduces the characters in tableau (6 min).

ACT I: Ballroom in the Capulets' house (30 min). ACT II: Beneath Juliette's balcony (23 min). ACT III i: Frère Laurent's cell (9 min); ii: A street (20 min). ACT IV: Juliette's bedroom (19 min). ACT V: The tomb of the Capulets (18 min).

Synopsis. Roméo, scion of the house of Montague, falls deeply in love with Juliette at a ball in the house of her father, a Capulet. Because of a long-

127

standing feud between their families, the two lovers meet only secretly. They are married in the cell of Frère Laurent, who hopes to end the feud. But bitterness is intensified when the Capulet Tybalt kills Mercutio, and Roméo, avenging his friend, slays Tybalt and is banished from Verona. Juliette's father tells her she must marry Paris. Frère Laurent gives her a potion which produces a deathlike trance. Roméo comes from Mantua to visit her tomb and, believing her dead, drinks poison. Awaking to find him dying, Juliette plunges his dagger into her own heart.

Major Roles. JULIETTE (lyr s); florid passages; high tessitura; top D5. ROMEO (lyr t); top B3. MERCUTIO, a Montague (bar); top F♯3.

Lesser Roles. FRERE LAURENT (bs). STEPHANO, Roméo's page (s or m-s); top C5. GERTRUDE, Juliette's nurse (m-s). TYBALT, Capulet's nephew (t). COUNT CAPULET (bs); top F3. GREGORY, a Capulet (bar). BENVOLIO, a Montague (t). THE DUKE OF VERONA (bs). COUNT PARIS, Juliette's fiancé (bar).

Chorus. SATB. Montagues, Capulets, citizens.

Ballet. Dances in ballroom scene; also in Act IV (often omitted).

Orchestra. 2 fl, 2 ob, 2 cl, 2 bsn, 4 hrn, 2 trp, 3 trb, tuba, perc, timp, harp, strings, organ.

Material. FS-P: Map, Ka, TW (rent). VS: Pet (f) $8.50; G Sc (f, e) $5. CP: Map (f, e) (rent). Tr: Mead (Ha).

Photographs. Metropolitan: 1.21.46 pp. 18–22. San Francisco: 10.21.46 p. 16.

Performing Companies. 478 (4.50). 82 (1951). 32B (1.53). 33 (11.15.55). 321A (1.8.56). 304 (5.1.56; 56–57).

♨ Der Rosenkavalier · The Knight of the Rose

Music by Richard Strauss (1864–1949). Libretto in German by Hugo von Hofmannsthal. Premiere: Dresden, January 26, 1911. Highly melodious vocal line wedded to complex continuous orchestration and occasionally patterned after speech. Brief prelude. Setting: Vienna, mid-18th century during the reign of Maria Theresa. Three acts (176 min).

ACT I: The Marschallin's boudoir (67 min). ACT II: The main hall in Faninal's house (52 min). ACT III: A private diningroom at an inn (57 min).

Synopsis. A tender love scene between the young cavalier Octavian and the older Marschallin is interrupted by Baron Ochs, the Marschallin's provincial cousin. He brings news of his betrothal to Sophie von Faninal, daughter of a nouveau riche nobleman. Octavian hides, then vainly tries to escape disguised as a maid, but is prevented by the lecherous Ochs, who attempts to arrange an assignation. Ochs asks the Marschallin for a suitable emissary to deliver a silver rose to Sophie as a sign of his troth. She mischievously appoints Octavian, who at last manages to depart. The Baron remains during her hectic morning household levée, then Octavian returns for a few stolen moments. The Marschallin begins to realize that she will soon lose her boyish lover and meditates with resignation on the sadness of fleeting youth. Octavian, presenting the rose to Sophie, falls in love at first sight. Sophie, revolted by the Baron's

128

uncouth behavior, becomes increasingly interested in the young stranger. Octavian challenges the Baron and inflicts a tiny wound on him, whereupon he demands attention from Faninal's entire household. Meanwhile, Octavian has arranged a meeting for the Baron with the "maid," Mariandel, at an out of the way inn. Impersonating Mariandel, the young cavalier devises a series of pranks to plague the old roué, whose servant finally summons the Marschallin, to Octavian's discomfiture. With great dignity and presence of mind, the Marschallin smooths over the situation, leaving the stage to the rapturous young lovers.

Major Roles. PRINCESS VON WERDENBERG, THE MARSCHALLIN (dram s); needs warmth and expressiveness in voice and personality; B♭2 to B4. OCTAVIAN (m-s, often s); high tessitura; lengthy role requiring youthful ardor and impetuosity; B♭2 to A4. SOPHIE (lyr s); very high tessitura; B2 to C♯5. BARON OCHS VON LERCHENAU (bs); long buffo role requires bluff, broad comic sense; D1 (opt C1) to F♯3 (opt G♯3).

Lesser Roles. HERR VON FANINAL (bar); G1 to G♯3. SINGER (t); short but difficult role; A3 to C♭4. MARIANNE, Sophie's duenna (s). VALZACCHI, an Italian intriguer (t). ANNINA, his partner (c).

Bit Parts. POLICE COMMISSIONER (bs). MARSCHALLIN'S MAJORDOMO (t). FANINAL'S MAJORDOMO (t). ATTORNEY (bs). INNKEEPER (t). THREE NOBLE ORPHANS (s, m-s, c). MILLINER (s). ANIMAL VENDOR (t). FOUR FOOTMEN (2 t, 2 bs). FOUR WAITERS (t, 3 bs). SCHOLAR, FLUTEPLAYER, HAIRDRESSER, HIS ASSISTANT, A WIDOW, MAHOMET, a black page (mute).

Chorus. SAATTBB. Footmen, couriers, waiters, guests, musicians, two watchmen, four little children, etc.

Orchestra. 3 fl (picc), 3 ob (Eng hrn), 3 cl, basset hrn (bs cl), 3 bsn (cont bsn), 4 hrn, 3 trp, 3 trb, tuba, timp, perc (3 players), 2 harp, celeste, strings. *Stage:* 2 fl, ob, 3 cl, 2 bsn, 2 hrn, trp, side drum, piano, harmonium.

Production Problems. Manifestation and disappearance of pranksters in Act III.

Material. All B & H. FS-P (rent). VS (g, e) $15. Li (g, e) $1. Analytical bklt $1. Tr: Gutman (B & H); Pryce-Jones (T1); Levin (T26).

Photographs. ACT I: San Francisco: 10.21.40 p. 21 (sketch). Metropolitan: 2.14.44 p. 18. Cincinnati: 10.25.48 p. 18. ACT II: Metropolitan: 2.14.44 p. 19. N.Y. City Opera: 11.28.49 p. 14. Munich: 10.16.50 p. 12. New Orleans: 12.22.52 p. 3. Zurich: 10.18.54 p. 22. ACT III: Metropolitan: 2.14.44 p. 20. La Scala: 12.9.46 p. 9. Metropolitan (Gérard): 2.13.56 pp. 18–20 (sketches); 3.17.58 pp. 18–20.

Performing Companies. 198A (1951). 127B (4.22.54 – conc). 334 (10. 20.54). 444 (11.11.54). 258 (12.54). 283 (7.26.55 – conc). 127A (8.6.55). 329 (55–56, 57–58, 59–60). 72 (10.28.55). 391 (56–57). 481 (2.2.58). 76 (8.26.58).

⚜ The Saint of Bleecker Street

Music and libretto in English by Gian-Carlo Menotti (1911–   ). Premiere: New York City, December 27, 1954. Tragedy with social and religious significance. Continuous texture with a few set numbers; heavily orchestrated in modern idiom. Setting: present-day New York City. Three acts, five scenes (approx 110 min).

ACT I i: A cold-water flat on Bleecker Street; ii: An empty lot on Mulberry Street. ACT II: An Italian restaurant on Bleecker Street. ACT III i: Passageway in a subway station; ii: the Bleecker Street flat.

Synopsis. Annina, known to her neighbors as the Saint of Bleecker Street because of the stigmata on her hands, is gravely ill. Her one great desire is to take the veil before she dies. Her agnostic brother, Michele, believes her "voices" to be part of her illness, and antagonizes the neighbors by forbidding Annina to take part in their religious rites. At a wedding feast to which she has not been invited, Desideria, Michele's sweetheart, demands that he recognize her publicly. He refuses because of Annina, whereupon Desideria accuses him of an unnatural love for his sister. In a drunken rage Michele stabs Desideria, who dies in Annina's arms. Knowing she can no longer help her brother, Annina determines to take the veil immediately. Michele pleads with her in vain and finally curses her. Annina summons up her last strength to go through the ceremony whereby she becomes Sister Angela. She dies as Michele returns for a last vain appeal.

Major Roles. ANNINA (s); frail appearance, voice strong throughout range; C3 to C5. DESIDERIA (m-s); earthy warmth and fire in voice, seductive appearance; A2 to A4. MICHELE (t); high tessitura; D♭2 to C4. DON MARCO, parish priest (bs); B♭1 to E3.

Lesser Roles. ASSUNTA, a neighbor (m-s). CARMELA, Annina's closest friend (s). MARIA CORONA, a neighbor (m-s). SALVATORE, Carmela's fiancé (bar).

Bit Parts. Maria Corona's DUMB SON (mute). CONCETTINA, 5-year-old child (speaking). YOUNG MAN (t). OLD WOMAN (s). BARTENDER (bs). NUN (mute). YOUNG PRIEST (mute).

Chorus. SSAATTBB. Neighbors, guests (many with solo lines).

Orchestra. 3 fl, 2 ob, Eng hrn, 2 cl, bs cl, 2 bsn, cont bsn, 4 hrn, 3 trp, 3 trb, tuba, timp, perc, harp, piano, strings.

Material. All G Sc. FS-P (rent). CP (rent). VS $7.50. Li 75¢.

Photographs. St. John's Univ., Collegeville, Minn.: 11.19.56 p. 5.

Performing Companies. 345 (12.27.54; 5.15.55). 333 (4.55). 48 (12. 2.55). 476 (12.2.55). 477 (1955). 254 (4.13.56). 229 (5.13.56). 420 (7.20.56).

🎭 Samson et Dalila · Samson and Delilah

Music by Camille Saint-Saëns (1835–1921). Libretto in French by Ferdinand Lemaire, based on the Book of Judges. Premiere: Weimar, December 2, 1877 (in German). Set pieces, recitative; passages of Oriental flavor. Brief prelude. Biblical drama set in Gaza, in Palestine; 1150 B.C. Three acts, four scenes (120 min).

ACT I: Square in Gaza, in front of the temple of Dagon (48 min). ACT II: Garden of Dalila's house (39 min). ACT III i: Prison yard (8 min); ii: Temple of Dagon (25 min).

Synopsis. Samson, leader of the captive Israelites in Gaza, arouses his people to active resistance against the Philistines. Dalila, young priestess of Dagon, promises the High Priest to find the secret of Samson's strength and render him helpless. Samson cannot resist her; he reveals to her his secret: his long hair. Dalila cuts his hair; he loses his power and is taken prisoner by the Philistines. Blinded, he is forced to entertain the triumphant enemy. At the height of their ceremony he gathers all his strength and wrecks the temple, burying himself together with the Philistines.

Major Roles. SAMSON (dram t); needs strength and sustained tone for consistently high tessitura; E2 to Bb3. DALILA (m-s or c); both lyric and dramatic passages; needs smooth legato, seductive appearance; wide range; Ab2 (F2 opt) to A4 (Bb4 and B4 opt). HIGH PRIEST TO DAGON (bar); dramatic and expressive; high tessitura; C2 to F♯3.

Lesser Roles. ABIMELECH, commissioner of Gaza (bs). AN OLD HEBREW (bs).

Chorus. SSAATTBB. Philistines, priestesses, priests, Hebrews.

Ballet. Dance of the priestesses in Act I; bacchanale in Act III ii.

Orchestra. 3 fl (picc), 2 ob, Eng hrn, 2 cl, bs cl, 2 bsn, cont bsn, 4 hrn, 2 trp, 2 cornet, 3 trb, tuba, 2 ophicleide (usually hrn or bsn), perc (4–5 players), timp, 2 harp, strings.

Material. FS-P: Map, Ka, TW (rent). CP: Map (f, i) (rent); G Sc (e) $1.50. CS: Map (e) (rent). VS: G Sc (f, e) $5. Tr: Procter-Gregg (T2).

Photographs. San Francisco: 10.4.43, cover. Flint Civic Opera: 12.8.47 p. 26. Metropolitan: 11.21.49 pp. 19, 20; 12.21.53 p. 9; 4.7.58 p. 19.

Performing Companies. 220A (4.4.51; 4.12.53). 476 (4.4.51 — conc). 443 (11.21.52). 129 (3.7.53). 177A (5.3.54). 435 (8.7.54). 443B (10.26. 54). 329 (55–56, 57–58). 149 (56–57).

ꙮ Die Schweigsame Frau · The Silent Woman

Music by Richard Strauss (1864–1949). Libretto in German by Stefan Zweig adapted from "Epicoene" by Ben Jonson. Premiere: Dresden, June 24, 1935. Comedy. Complex harmonic structure with occasional dissonance. Dialogue over musical accompaniment; accompanied recitative and set numbers. Setting: the London suburbs about 1780. Overture. Three acts (N.Y. City Opera production: 129 min).

ACT I: A room in Sir Morosus' house (44 min). ACT II: The same (51 min). ACT III: The same, in the process of redecoration (34 min).

Synopsis. Sir Morosus, a cantankerous retired seaman who was once in the midst of an ear-splitting explosion, wishes to spend his declining years in seclusion with a quiet wife to care for him. He is constantly tormented by his talkative housekeeper and his barber, who determines to find him a wife. Sir Morosus's nephew, Henry, appears with a troupe of opera singers, among them Aminta, his young bride. The couple wish to get the old man's blessing and his inheritance, but they and their noisy friends win only his fury. The barber disguises the three female members of the troupe as candidates to

131

wed Sir Morosus. He chooses the third (Aminta), as she appears gentle and devoted. The marriage ceremony is performed by two singers disguised as priest and notary. Although Aminta dislikes the part she is playing in the deception, she feigns a shrewish talkativeness, so that Sir Morosus quickly wishes to be rid of her. Various legal complications are advanced by the impostors as the old man's anxiety mounts. Finally the hoax is brought to its end, and Sir Morosus gladly welcomes his nephew and niece. He can now laugh at the joke and find contentment in celibacy.

Major Roles. AMINTA (col s); demands great agility; constant very high tessitura; B2 to E5. HENRY MOROSUS (t); long lyrical line, high tessitura; romantic appearance; C2 to C4. CUTBEARD, a barber (bar); great flexibility; F1 to G3. SIR BLUNT MOROSUS (buf bs); requires good comic acting ability; Db1 to F♯3.

Lesser Roles. HOUSEKEEPER (c). ISOTTA (col s), and CARLOTTA (m-s), MORBIO (bar), VANUZZI (bs), and FARFALLO (bs), members of the troupe.

Chorus. SATTBB. Members of the troupe, neighbors.

Orchestra. 3 fl, 3 ob, 3 cl, bs cl, 3 bsn, 4 hrn, 3 trp, 3 trb, tuba, timp (2 players), perc, celeste, organ, harp, strings.

Material. FS-P: B & H (rent). VS: B & H (g) $15 (typescript − e). Li: Bedford (e − PPC).

Photographs. N.Y. City Opera: 11.10.58 p. 9. *Mus. Amer.* N.Y. City Opera: 11.1.58 p. 3.

Performing Companies. 334 (10.7.58 − Amer prem).

✉ Simon Boccanegra

Music by Giuseppe Verdi (1813–1901). Libretto in Italian by Francesco Maria Piave, revised by Boito, based on a play by Antonio Gutiérrez. Premiere: (1st vers) Venice, March 12, 1857; (2nd vers, used now) Milan, March 24, 1881. Melodrama. Accompanied recitative, set arias and numbers. Conventional harmonic structure. No overture. Setting: in and near Genoa, mid-14th century. Prologue, three acts, four scenes (130 min).

PROLOGUE: A square in Genoa (23 min). ACT I i: Garden of Grimaldi Palace, 25 years later (32 min); ii: Doge's council chamber (21 min). ACT II: Doge's apartment (27 min). ACT III: Hall in the Doge's palace (27 min).

Synopsis. Simon Boccanegra, a Genoese corsair, has been the lover of Maria, daughter of the current Doge, Fiesco. She has borne him a daughter, but Fiesco still refuses the plebeian Simon as son-in-law. Boccanegra accepts nomination as Doge by the People's Party, led by the conspirators Paolo and Pietro, hoping thereby to win Maria. At the moment of his election he discovers Maria dead and his child gone. Twenty-five years pass, and in Amelia Grimaldi, the ward of a man known as Andrea, but actually Fiesco himself, Boccanegra recognizes his long-lost daughter, Maria. She is in love with the young nobleman Gabriele Adorno. Paolo wishes to marry Amelia but when she refuses him, he plots with Pietro to ruin the Doge and kidnap Amelia, an act Fiesco and Gabriele blame on Boccanegra. Gabriele tries to stab the Doge,

132

but Amelia escapes in time to prove her father's innocence. Gabriele and Fiesco are imprisoned; in jail they are urged by Paolo to murder Boccanegra. They refuse, but Paolo and Pietro have already poisoned the Doge's decanter. Gabriele overhears a tender scene between Boccanegra and Amelia, and again tries to use his dagger; but their true relationship is revealed to him, and he asks forgiveness. Fiesco also forgives Boccanegra, who dies of the conspirators' poison, whereupon Gabriele is named the new Doge.

Major Roles. AMELIA GRIMALDI (MARIA BOCCANEGRA) (s); long, soaring line; trill; Bb2 to C5. GABRIELE ADORNO (t); C2 to Bb3. SIMON BOCCANEGRA (bar); lengthy, dramatic role; C2 to Gb3. FIESCO (bs); rich quality, long line, dignified; F1 to F3. PAOLO ALBIANI (bar); B1 to F3 (opt G3).

Lesser Roles. PIETRO (bar). Amelia's MAID (s or m-s). A CAPTAIN (t).

Chorus. SSAATTTBB. Noblemen, seamen, monks, councilors, attendants, populace.

Orchestra. 2 fl (picc), 2 ob, 2 cl, bs cl, 2 bsn, 4 hrn, 2 trp, 3 trb, tuba, timp, perc, harp, strings. *Stage:* 2 or more trp, harp, 2 trb, bells.

Material. FS-P: Ri (rent). VS: Ri (i) $10. Tr: Tucker (T2); Ducloux (T10).

Photographs. Metropolitan: ACT I: 1.23.50 p. 19; 3.19.51 p. 19; ACT II: 1.23.50 pp. 20, 21. Sadler's Wells: 10.15.51 p. 6. Rome: 3.30.53 p. 10.

Performing Companies. 329 (49–50, 59–61). 72 (10.9.56). 130 (1959).

▶ Sir John in Love

Music by Ralph Vaughan Williams (1872–1958). Libretto in English, based on Shakespeare's "The Merry Wives of Windsor," with the addition of lyrics from Elizabethan poets. Premiere: London, 1929. Comedy. Occasional use of folk tunes in musical texture; arias, many ensembles. Setting: Windsor, England; 15th century. Four acts, seven scenes (120 min).

ACT I: A street in Windsor. ACT II i: A room in Page's house; ii: A room at the Garter Inn. ACT III i: A field near Windsor; ii: A room in Ford's house. ACT IV i: A room in Ford's house; ii: Windsor Forest. (II i, III i, and IV i can be played in front of curtains.)

Synopsis. The story is the familiar one of Falstaff's encounter with the "merry wives," their trickery, and his eventual discomfiture. (See "The Merry Wives of Windsor" by Nicolai and "Falstaff" by Verdi.)

Major Roles. SIR HUGH EVANS, a Welsh parson (high bar). SLENDER, a foolish young gentleman, in love with Anne (t). PAGE, a citizen of Windsor (bar). SIR JOHN FALSTAFF (bar). NYM, Falstaff's attendant (bar). PISTOL, Falstaff's attendant (bs). ANNE PAGE (s). MRS. PAGE (s). MRS. FORD (m-s). FENTON, Anne's successful suitor (t). DR. CAIUS, a French physician, also in love with Anne (high bar). MRS. QUICKLY, his housekeeper (m-s or c). HOST OF THE GARTER INN (bar). FORD, a citizen of Windsor (bs). (If necessary, SHALLOW and CAIUS may be doubled.)

Lesser Roles. (May be played by chorus members.) SHALLOW, a country justice (t or bar). PETER SIMPLE, Slender's servant (t or bar). BARDOLPH, Falstaff's attendant (t). RUGBY, Caius's servant (bs). JOHN, ROBERT, Ford's servants (both bar).

Speaking Roles. ROBIN, Falstaff's page. WILLIAM, Mrs. Page's son. WILLIAM'S FRIENDS. ALICE SHORTCAKE, Bardolph's sweetheart. JENNY PLUCKPEARS, Nym's sweetheart.

Chorus. SATB. Townspeople, fairies.

Ballet. In Act IV. As elaborate as desired.

Orchestra. 2 fl, 2 ob, 2 cl, 2 bsn, 2 hrn, 2 trp, trb, timp, perc, harp, strings.

Material. FS-P: Ox (rent). VS: Ox (e, g) $9.50 (also rent).

Performing Companies. 302 (1.20.49). 197 (1955).

♬ Six Characters in Search of an Author

Music by Hugo Weisgall (1912–   ). Libretto in English by Denis Johnston, based on the play by Luigi Pirandello. Premiere: New York, April 26, 1959. Symbolical drama contrasting illusion and reality, in modern idiom. Some dissonance and atonality, some conventional harmonic structure. Continuous texture embodying arias and set numbers. No overture. Time and place unspecified. Three acts (128 min).

ACT I: Bare stage of a provincial opera house (48 min). ACT II: The same (45 min). ACT III: The same (35 min).

Synopsis. A new opera is in rehearsal. Six Characters (Father, Mother, Son, Stepdaughter, Boy, Little Girl) interrupt, claiming to be characters in an unfinished opera seeking someone to complete their drama and give them life. The Director substitutes their opera for the one in rehearsal. The Characters turn out to be at odds with each other, and entangled in a complex web of elopement, illegitimacy, jealousy, and general discord. In the course of acting out their scenes, the Director substitutes two of his singers, and the Characters resent being parodied by professionals. After many arguments the Little Girl drowns in a fountain and the Boy shoots himself. The remaining characters disappear in a blackout, and the professional company suggests that the whole thing has been a figment of the Director's imagination. The Characters are seen in a funeral procession from which the Stepdaughter runs laughing. The Director sees nothing, but hears the laughter. No one answers his, "Is there anyone there?"

Major Roles. Real People: THE DIRECTOR, Burt Betts (t); C2 to B3. THE COLORATURA, Lili Klein (col s); wide intervals; D3 to F5. The Characters: FATHER (bar); mature, weighty; G1 to A♭3. STEPDAUGHTER (dram s); young; A2 to C5. MOTHER (m-s); mature; B♭2 to A4.

Lesser Roles. Real People: TENORE BUFFO, Terrence O'Flaherty (t); D2 to A3. ACCOMPANIST, Sam Stein (bar); must play piano onstage; B1 to E3. BASSO CANTANTE, Pasquale Subito; F1 to F3. STAGE MANAGER, Mike Pampanickli (buf bs); F1 to E3. PROMPTER, Gertrude Glubb (s); C♯3 to B♭4. MEZZO, Gwen Thomas (m-s); B2 to G4. WARDROBE MISTRESS (c); A2 to F4. The Characters: THE SON (lyr bar); B1 to A♭3. MADAME PACE, owner of dress shop where a scene of the Characters' play takes place (c); D3 to F4. THE BOY, age 12, and THE LITTLE GIRL, age 5 (mute).

Chorus. SSAATTBB (ad lib.). Actors, carpenters, electricians, ushers, front-office men, actresses, cleaning women, seamstresses, secretaries. Seven Deadly Sins: PRIDE (s); ENVY (s); SLOTH (c); LUST (c); ANGER (t); AVARICE (bar); GLUTTONY (bs). THE UNHEARD-OF SIN (t). *Note:* The opera can be performed with as few as eight choristers (Sins), as specified above, if principals join in when they are onstage.

Orchestra. 2 fl (alto fl, picc), 2 ob (Eng hrn), 2 cl (bs cl), 2 bsn (cont bsn), 2 hrn, 2 trp, 2 trb, tuba, timp, perc, celeste, strings. *Stage:* upright piano.

Material. FS-P: Pr (Mer) (rent). VS: Pr (Mer) $12.

Photographs. Mus. Amer. N.Y. City Opera: 5.59 p. 8.

Performing Companies. 334 (4.26.59 — prem).

✄ La Sonnambula · The Sleepwalker

Music by Vincenzo Bellini (1802–1835). Libretto in Italian by Felice Romani. Premiere: Milan, March 6, 1831. Romantic melodrama in florid bel canto style. Lyrical; simple harmonic structure; accompanied recitative, formal arias and numbers. Setting: a Swiss village; early 19th century. Short prelude. Two acts, four scenes (120 min).

ACT I i: The village green; ii: Rodolfo's room at the inn. ACT II i: Woods between the village and the castle; ii: The village outside Teresa's mill.

Synopsis. The betrothal of Amina to Elvino, a rich young landowner, is celebrated by all the villagers except Lisa, the innkeeper, who had hoped to marry Elvino herself. A stranger (actually Count Rodolfo, lord of the castle) arrives and wishes the couple well, but his attentions to Amina arouse Elvino's jealousy. Teresa, Amina's stepmother, reminds the crowd of the village's nocturnal apparition, and they quickly disperse for the night. Rodolfo retires to Lisa's inn, where he is recognized by Lisa. She visits him in his room, but flees when she hears a noise, leaving her handkerchief behind. Amina enters, walking in her sleep and talking of her forthcoming marriage. Rodolfo leaves the room, but Amina is discovered there by Elvino, whom Lisa has summoned, and by the villagers, who come to pay their respects to the Count. Elvino breaks the engagement, leaving Amina dazed and grief-stricken, and he refuses to believe the Count's protestations of her innocence. Elvino is about to marry Lisa, but is again disillusioned when Teresa produces the handkerchief Lisa left in Rodolfo's room. At that moment Amina appears from the mill, again sleepwalking. The Count explains somnambulism, and, to everyone's satisfaction, Elvino awakens Amina and begs forgiveness.

Major Roles. AMINA (col s); high tessitura with frequent C5's, demands trill and complete command of florid style; C3 to Eb5. LISA (s); high tessitura, needs coloratura technique; C3 to C5. ELVINO (lyr t); high tessitura, trill, florid style; C2 to C4. RODOLFO (bs); florid passages; G1 to Eb3.

Lesser Roles. TERESA (m-s). ALESSIO, peasant in love with Lisa (bs). NO-TARY (t).

135

Chorus. SSATTBB. Villagers. Of great importance throughout the opera.
Orchestra. 2 fl, 2 ob, 2 cl, 2 bsn, 4 hrn, 2 trp, 3 trb, tuba, timp, perc, strings.
Stage: military band.
Material. FS-P: Ka, Map, Ri, TW (rent). CP: Map (i) (rent). VS: Ri (i) $4; G Sc $4; Map (rent).
Photographs. Sketch of old production: 1.5.59 p. 8.
Performing Companies. 350A (12.20.54). 297 (1.25.55). 33 (4.19.55).

🎼 Susannah

Music and libretto in English by Carlisle Floyd (1926–   ). Premiere: Florida State University, Tallahassee, Fla., February 24, 1955. Realistic folk tragedy. Music has strong folk flavor, although no folk tunes as such are employed; vocal line often patterned after speech; several set numbers. No overture. The story of Susannah and the Elders is transferred from the Apocrypha to a primitive Tennessee mountain valley of today or yesterday. Two acts, ten scenes (95 min).

ACT I i: New Hope Valley churchyard; ii: Polk farmhouse exterior; iii: Woods close to Polk farm; iv: Same; v: Polk farmhouse exterior. ACT II i: Polk farmhouse exterior; ii: New Hope Valley church interior; iii: Polk farmhouse exterior; iv: New Hope Valley church interior; v: Polk farmhouse exterior. Four sets can be very simple.

Synopsis. Susannah Polk has incurred the jealousy of the pious womenfolk by her appeal to all men, even the itinerant preacher, Olin Blitch. When the Elders discover Susannah bathing in the creek they wanted to use for baptism, they denounce and ostracize her. Her gentle and ineffectual brother Sam offers little comfort. Unwillingly, she takes his advice and attends a prayer meeting, where the impassioned eloquence of Blitch over the relentless chanting of the congregation nearly sweeps her into a "confession." Blitch follows her home. In her lassitude and despair she does not resist him. When Susannah tells Sam of the seduction, he kills the preacher in the midst of a baptismal ceremony. The outraged crowd converges on Susannah's house; she repulses them with a gun. Then, making advances to Little Bat, weak-witted son of Elder McLean, she slaps him viciously when he responds. She is left alone, an embittered woman.

Major Roles. SUSANNAH POLK (spin s); two major arias; several passages in very high tessitura, one with three B4's shows optional B3's; touches Gb2. SAM (lyr t); sustained, not extremely exacting. OLIN BLITCH, evangelist (bs-bar); calls for impassioned acting, dramatic singing; G1 to G3. LITTLE BAT MC LEAN (t or speaking).

Lesser Roles. ELDER MC LEAN (bs). ELDER GLEATON (t); top Ab4. ELDER HAYES (t); top Bb4. ELDER OTT (bs). MRS. MC LEAN (m-s). MRS. GLEATON (s). MRS. HAYES (s). MRS. OTT (c).

Chorus. SATB. Churchgoers.

Ballet. Several sets of squaredancers.

Orchestra. 2 fl (picc), 2 ob (Eng hrn), 2 cl (bs cl), 2 bsn (cont bsn), 4 hrn, 2 trp, 3 trb, tuba, timp, perc, celeste, harp, xyl, strings. *Reduced vers*: 2 fl (picc), ob (Eng hrn), 2 cl (bs cl), bsn, 2 hrn, 2 trp, 2 trb, timp, perc, harp, strings.

Material. All B & H. FS-P (rent). VS $10.

Performing Companies. 110A (2.24.55 — prem). 334 (56–59). 1956–57: 48, 50, 75, 216. 449 (12.4.58). 198A (5.5.59).

The Sweet Bye-and-Bye

Music by Jack Beeson (1921–   ). Libretto in English by Kenward Elmslie; fictitious but suggested by Aimee Semple McPherson's story. Premiere: New York, November 22, 1957. Tragicomedy. Simple harmonic structure in modern idiom. Accompanied recitative, set numbers. No overture; short interludes between scenes. Setting: Atlantic City and New York City, late 1920's. Two acts, five scenes (105 min).

ACT I i: Beach, Atlantic City; ii: Penthouse in Hotel Paradise Arms, New York. ACT II i: Boardwalk, Atlantic City; ii: Inside the Lifeshine Ark; iii: The Miracle Room.

Synopsis. Sister Rose Ora Easter, founder and leader of the Lifeshine Gospel, is believed to have drowned while swimming in the sea, and is mourned by her followers, who chide bathers on the beach for failing to show proper respect. Mother Rainey, who reared Sister Rose Ora, suspects that she was spirited away by a certain man, and questions Sister Gladys, her close friend. Rose Ora has indeed run off with Billy Wilcox, with whom she plans to go to the Holy Land on Lifeshine Gospel money. Mother Rainey and Sister Gladys follow Rose Ora to a New York hotel, and, while Billy is out, persuade her to return to her flock. Back in Atlantic City Rose Ora is telling her followers how she was kidnapped when she again decides to break away and reveal the truth. She explains that her vows were made as a child; she has now grown up and awakened to love, and bids her followers to wake up also. She and Billy are about to flee when Mother Rainey confronts them with a gun. She shoots Billy, feeling justified in "saving" Rose Ora and reclaiming the Gospel's money. Billy dies in Rose Ora's arms as the flock pledges its faith to the Sister-Elect.

Major Roles. SISTER ROSE ORA EASTER (spin s); magnetic personality; C3 to Bb4. SISTER GLADYS (col s); strong middle range, occasional high tones; C♯3 to D5. MOTHER RAINEY (m-s); low tessitura, mature quality; Ab2 to G4. BILLY WILCOX (t); D2 to Bb3.

Lesser Roles. SISTER REES, the Sister-Elect (s). MARY JANE RIPLEY, First Bather and Beauty Contest Winner ("pop" s); dancer. BROTHER SMILEY of the Lifeshine Ark (bs).

Bit Parts. SECOND AND THIRD BATHERS (t, bs-bar). FIRST BEAUTY CONTEST JUDGE (bar). THREE BATHING BEAUTIES (s, s, a). WOMEN'S TRIO (s, a, a). MEN'S TRIO (t, b, b).

Chorus. SSAATTBB. Members of the Lifeshine Ark, beauty contest judges, waiter, children, etc. *Note:* Bit parts can be sung by chorus soloists.

Ballet. Sinners, pantomime roles of photographers, gangsters, gunmoll, etc.
Orchestra. 2 fl (2 picc), ob, 2 cl (bs cl), bsn, 3 hrn, trp, trb, timp, harp,
celeste, perc, piano, strings.
Material. FS-P: Mi (rent). VS: Mi (rent).
Performing Companies. 321 (57–58 – prem).

🎭 The Taming of the Shrew

Music by Vittorio Giannini (1903–   ). Libretto in English by Vittorio
Giannini and D. Fee, based on Shakespeare's "The Taming of the Shrew,"
with additions from "Romeo and Juliet" and the sonnets. Premiere: Cincinnati, January 31, 1953. Comedy. Melodic vocal line with accompanied recitative in continuous texture. Short overture. Setting: Padua, 16th century. Three
acts, four scenes (153 min).

ACT I: The street outside Baptista's house (36 min). ACT II i: The garden
of Baptista's house; ii: The garden of Baptista's house (40 min). ACT III:
A room in Petruchio's house (37 min).

Synopsis. Baptista, a wealthy gentleman of Padua, has determined not to
let his younger daughter Bianca marry until her older and sharp-tongued sister
Katharina has a husband. Three suitors, Hortensio, Lucentio and Gremio,
pursue Bianca. Through the ruse of disguising himself as her tutor, Lucentio
woos her and finally wins her hand. Meanwhile, Petruchio has come from
Verona to seek a wealthy wife. He decides to marry Katharina in spite of her
violent disposition. By treating her in a high-handed fashion he tames her
and wins her love.

Major Roles. BAPTISTA (bs); C♯2 to D3. KATHARINA (dram s); E2 to B4.
BIANCA (lyr s); G2 to G4. PETRUCHIO (bar); B♯1 to G3. HORTENSIO (bar);
D♭2 to F3. LUCENTIO (t); E♭2 to B3. GREMIO (t); E2 to G♯3.

Lesser Roles. VINCENTIO, Lucentio's father (bs). TRANIO, Lucentio's servant
(bar). BIONDELLO, Lucentio's servant (bs). GRUMIO, Petruchio's servant (t).
CURTIS, Petruchio's servant (bs). A PEDANT (t). A TAILOR (t).

Chorus. SATB. Servants of Baptista, maids of Katharina, citizens.

Orchestra. 4 fl (picc), 4 ob (Eng hrn), 4 cl, 3 bsn, 4 hrn, 3 trp, 3 trb, 2
tuba, perc, timp, harp, celeste, xyl, strings. *Reduced vers:* 3 fl (picc), 2 ob
(Eng hrn), 2 cl, 2 bsn, 4 hrn, 3 trp, 2 trb, bs trb, tuba, timp, perc, harp,
piano, strings.

Material. FS-P: Ri (rent). VS: Ri (e) $10.

Photographs. Cincinnati: 3.2.53 p. 10. Chicago: 12.6.54 p. 11.

Performing Companies. 390 with 392 (1.31.53 – prem). 373 (12.53).
333 (3.13.54). 130 (11.3.54). 334 (1958). 283 (1959). 245 (58–59).

🎭 Tannhäuser

Music by Richard Wagner (1813–1883). Libretto in German by the composer, based on a medieval legend. Premiere: Dresden, October 19, 1845.

For Paris premiere (1861), Wagner revised the Venusberg scene and added a ballet. Romantic drama with theological implications. Heavy orchestration; some use of leitmotifs. Set pieces, extended accompanied recitative; important chorus. Overture. Setting: the Venusberg, and in and around the Wartburg; early 13th century. Three acts, four scenes (177 min).

ACT I i: Venusberg (47 min); ii: A valley near Wartburg Castle (21 min). ACT II: A hall in Wartburg Castle (58 min). ACT III: The valley near the castle (51 min).

Synopsis. The troubadour Tannhäuser, who had renounced the world for the pleasures of Venus, decides to return to earth. Informed by his friend Wolfram that the Landgrave's niece, Elisabeth, still loves him, he enters a singing contest with her hand as prize, horrifying the assembled guests by hymning praises to carnal love. Elisabeth protects him from the anger of the throng. Remorseful, he sets out to seek absolution from the Pope. Despite Elisabeth's prayers, he returns despairing and unforgiven; not until the pontiff's staff sprouts leaves can he expect pardon from the Almighty for his sins. Once more he invokes Venus, but repents when Wolfram tells him of Elisabeth's death. Her funeral cortege appears. Grief-stricken, Tannhäuser begs her spirit to pray for him, and then dies. A band of pilgrims arrives, bearing the Pope's staff which has miraculously grown leaves, thus assuring Tannhäuser's salvation.

Major Roles. ELISABETH (dram s); needs great strength at top of range (B2 to B4). VENUS (dram s, frequently sung by m-s); sensual quality; C3 to B4. TANNHAUSER (dram t); long, taxing role; high tessitura consistently; D2 to A3. WOLFRAM VON ESCHENBACH, a minstrel knight (bar); A♯1 to F♯3. HERMANN, Landgrave of Thuringia (bs); needs dark voice conveying authority; E1 to F3.

Lesser Roles. WALTHER VON DER VOGELWEIDE (t), BITEROLF (bs), HEINRICH DER SCHREIBER (t), REINMAR VON ZWETER (bs), minstrel knights. YOUNG SHEPHERD (s).

Bit Parts. FOUR NOBLE PAGES (SSAA).

Chorus. SSAATTBB. Thuringian nobles, knights, ladies, elder and younger pilgrims, sirens, naiads, nymphs, and bacchantes.

Ballet. Elaborate bacchanale in I i.

Orchestra. 2 fl, picc, 2 ob, 2 cl, 2 bsn, 4 hrn, 3 trp, 3 trb, tuba, timp, perc, harp, strings. *Stage:* Act I i: 2 fl, 2 ob, 2 cl, 2 bsn, 4 hrn, harp; ii: Eng hrn, 12 hrn (can be arranged for fewer). Act II: 12 trp (can be fewer). Act III: 2 orch, each of picc, 2 fl, 2 ob, 3 cl, 2 bsn, 2 hrn, perc (either condensed or played in pit).

Material. FS-P: Map, Ri, TW (rent). MS: AMP $10; Pet (Eu − g, e, and i) $25 (g − 2 vols incl Paris vers) $25. VS: Map, TW (rent); Pet (g − Mottl) $6.50; G Sc (g, e) $5. CP: G Sc (g, e) 60¢. Tr: Peltz (Ru).

Photographs. ACT I i: Metropolitan: 12.30.40 p. 17; 1.4.54 p. 20 (sketch, Gérard); 1.24.55 p. 18. ACT I ii: Metropolitan: 2.9.42 p. 18; 12.14.42 p. 19; 1.4.54 p. 20 (sketch); 1.24.55 p. 19. Covent Garden: 2.13.56 p. 29. ACT II: Metropolitan: 12.11.39 p. 18; 1.4.54 p. 20 (sketch); 4.26.54 p. 7. Florence:

3.15.54 p. 15; 2.11.57 p. 12. ACT III: Metropolitan: 12.11.39 p. 21; 1.4.54 p. 20 (sketch); 1.24.55 p. 20.

Performing Companies. 129 (11.17.51). 329 (53–55; 60–61). 72 (1958). 487 (2.59). 180 (10.59).

♭ The Tender Land

Music by Aaron Copland (1900–   ). Libretto in English by Horace Everett. Commissioned by Rodgers and Hammerstein for the League of Composers' 30th anniversary. Premiere: New York City, April 1, 1954. Revised. Folklike drama. Set numbers including important quintet; recitative and dialogue; in modern idiom. Setting: a lower middle-class farm in the American Midwest, in June of the early '30's. Three acts, three scenes (100 min).

ACT I: Outside the Moss home. ACT II: A party at the Moss home. ACT III: Outside the Moss home.

Synopsis. Laurie Moss, overprotected all her life by her Ma and Grandpa, is about to graduate from her rural high school. When Martin and Top, two roving farmhands of doubtful character, appear seeking work on Grandpa Moss's farm, Laurie immediately falls in love with Martin. The lovers plan to elope graduation morning, following a party in Laurie's honor. Top persuades Martin that their nomadic existence is not right for Laurie or for marriage, and the pair slip off before dawn. Disillusioned and disappointed, Laurie leaves home, feeling she must make her own way in the world. Ma turns her protectiveness toward Laurie's younger sister, beginning the cycle all over again.

Major Roles. LAURIE (lyr s); fresh young voice; C3 to C5. MA MOSS (c); warm, matter-of-fact quality; G2 to G4. MARTIN (lyr t); romantic, youthful voice and appearance; C2 to B3. TOP (bar); harsh cynicism needed in voice; A1 to F♯3. GRANDPA MOSS (bs); old quality; F1 to E3.

Lesser Roles. BETH MOSS (child); mostly speaking. MR. SPLINTERS, postman (t). MRS. SPLINTERS (m-s). MR. JENKS (bar), MRS. JENKS (s), neighbors. THREE GUESTS (s, t, bs).

Chorus. SATB. Party guests.

Ballet. Several sets of squaredancers. Can be choristers.

Orchestra. 2 fl (picc), ob, Eng hrn, 2 cl (bs cl), 2 bsn, 2 hrn, 2 trp, 2 trb, perc (2 players), harp, piano (ad lib.), strings.

Material. FS-P: B & H (rent). VS: B & H $7.50.

Photographs. Tanglewood: 11.1.54 p. 17.

Performing Companies. 334 (4.1.54 – prem). 205 (8.2.54). 411 (5.20.55). 212 (56–57). 233 (56–57).

♭ Thaïs

Music by Jules Massenet (1842–1912). Libretto in French by Louis Gallet, from a novel by Anatole France. Premiere: Paris, March 16, 1894. Lyric drama. Simple harmonic structure; accompanied recitatives, set arias and scenes. Brief prelude. Meditation between II i and ii, solo violin and orchestra. Setting: Egypt, end of the 4th century. Three acts, seven scenes (approx 120 min).

ACT I i: Cenobite retreat on the banks of the Nile; ii: Terrace of Nicias' house at Alexandria. ACT II i: Interior of Thaïs' home; ii: Outside Thaïs' house. ACT III i: An oasis; ii: Cenobite retreat; iii: Convent garden.

Synopsis. Athanaël, a Cenobite monk, is distressed by the sensation in Alexandria caused by the courtesan Thaïs, whom he had known in his earlier, prereligious days. He resolves to convert her from a life of dishonor to piety. At Alexandria he is received by Nicias, an old friend and Thaïs' current lover, and is invited to a banquet which Thaïs will attend. Two slaves, Crobyle and Myrtale, array the monk in appropriate dress. At first Thaïs mocks Athanaël; later she invites him to her home to hear him further. On the verge of acquiescing to his wish, she temporizes and sends him away. The "Meditation" suggests her thoughts. Undiscouraged, Athanaël waits at her threshold. In a few hours Thaïs appears, her conversion finally complete. In spite of the efforts of a crowd of revelers to prevent her going she follows Athanaël to a convent. After the nuns have led her away, Athanaël realizes that he loves her desperately. In a dream he sees her dying. He hurries to the convent where Thaïs is, indeed, in her final extremity. The frustrated monk confesses his earthly love as his convert dies a holy death.

Major Roles. THAIS (s); high, sustained tessitura; B2 to E♭5. ATHANAEL (bar); lengthy, lyrical role; C2 to F♯3. NICIAS (t); E♭2 to B♭3.

Lesser Roles. CROBYLE (s) and MYRTALE (m-s), slaves. ALBINE, an abbess (m-s). SERVANT of Nicias (bar). PALEMON, old Cenobite (bs). LA CHARMEUSE, dancer (s).

Chorus. SSSATTTTBB. Cenobites, actors, comedians, philosophers, friends of Nicias, populace, nuns.

Orchestra. 2 fl, picc, 2 ob, Eng hrn, cl, bs cl, 2 bsn, cont bsn, 4 hrn, 2 trp, 3 trb, tuba, timp, perc, harp, strings. *Stage:* fl, Eng hrn, cl, 2 harp, harmonium; stage band: ob, Eng hrn, piano, timp, perc.

Material. FS-P: Ka, Map (rent). VS: Pr (Mer) $12. Tr: Klein (Pr).

Photographs. Riverside Opera: 11.6.44 p. 26 (costumes).

Performing Companies. 390 (5.52). 189 (4.20.56). 130 (1959).

🎭 Tosca

Music by Giacomo Puccini (1858–1924). Libretto in Italian by Luigi Illica and Giuseppe Giacosa, based on "La Tosca," a play by Victorien Sardou. Premiere: Rome, January 14, 1900. Melodrama. Continuous texture with a few set numbers; highly descriptive orchestra with recurring motival material. Setting: Rome; June, 1800. No overture. Three acts (112 min).

ACT I: Church of Sant' Andrea della Valle (43 min). ACT II: Scarpia's apartment in the Farnese Palace (42 min). ACT III: Terrace of Sant' Angelo Castle (27 min).

Synopsis. Floria Tosca, a famous singer, is beloved by the painter Mario Cavaradossi, and desired by Baron Scarpia, evil chief of Roman police. At work on a painting of the Madonna in the church of Sant' Andrea della Valle, Mario helps to conceal an escaped political prisoner, Angelotti, whose sister, the Marchese Attavanti (Mario's model), has left their family chapel open. Tosca enters and expresses her jealousy of the Attavanti, but Mario reassures her. After her departure, Cavaradossi sends Angelotti to hide at his villa, just before Scarpia and his henchmen arrive. When Tosca returns, her jealousy is revived by the lecherous Scarpia, who shows her a fan left in the chapel by the Attavanti. Cavaradossi is arrested and tortured in Tosca's hearing, until she reveals Angelotti's whereabouts. Attempting to make amends, she offers herself to Scarpia in return for a pardon for Cavaradossi and a safe-conduct. Scarpia agrees, but insists that a mock execution take place. As he advances amorously towards Tosca, she stabs him, extricates the passport from his hand and rushes to the Castel Sant' Angelo where her lover awaits execution. They share a moment of joy before the "mock" execution. Too late Tosca realizes the bullets were real. Her grief is interrupted by the arrival of Scarpia's henchman Spoletta, who has discovered the baron's body. In final despair Tosca leaps over the parapet to her death.

Major Roles. FLORIA TOSCA (lyr spin s); high tessitura, many notes above the staff; compelling personality, must radiate the aura of a prima donna; C3 to C5. MARIO CAVARADOSSI (t); should have high pianissimo, long flowing line; D2 to B3. BARON SCARPIA (bar); one of the most controversial acting roles; dark, menacing vocal quality; must convey subtle cruelty; B1 to G♭3.

Lesser Roles. CESARE ANGELOTTI (bs). SACRISTAN (bar, usually sung by buf bs). SPOLETTA, a police agent (t). SCIARRONE, Scarpia's orderly (bs). A JAILER (bs). A SHEPHERD BOY, offstage (s, m-s, or boy s).

Chorus. SSATTBB. Ladies, nobles, police agents, soldiers, citizens, a cardinal, a judge, an executioner, a scribe, an officer, a sergeant. Boys' choir.

Orchestra. 3 fl (picc), 2 ob, Eng hrn, 2 cl, bs cl, 2 bsn, cont bsn, 4 hrn, 3 trp, 3 trb, tuba, timp, perc, bells, small bells, celeste, harp, strings. *Stage:* organ, bells, side drums, fl, vla, harp.

Material. FS-P: Map, Ka, Ri, G Sc (rent). VS: Ri (i, e – Machlis) $6 (i) $10 (f) $10; G Sc (i, e – Gutman) $6. CP: G Sc (i, e) 60¢. Li: Ri (i, e) 60¢. O Tr: Ashbrook (254); Reese (T31); Levin (T26).

Photographs. ACT I: San Francisco: 2.2.42 p. 16. Metropolitan: 4.3.44 p. 10; 1.2.56 p. 18. ACT II: Metropolitan: 2.2.42 p. 18; 1.2.56 p. 19. Houston: 4.1.57 p. 26. ACT III: Metropolitan: 4.3.44 p. 12; 1.2.56 p. 20. Covent Garden: 2.26.51 p. 14. Florence: 3.15.54 p. 15 (sketch).

Performing Companies. Approx 58. 1956–57 only: 6, 64, 72, 130, 148, 173, 295, 324, 329, 391, 398, 443B, 460, 481.

🎭 La Traviata

Music by Giuseppe Verdi (1813–1901). Libretto in Italian by Francesco Maria Piave, based on "La Dame aux Camélias," play by Alexandre Dumas, *fils*, after his novel by the same name. The play is known in English as "Camille." Premiere: Venice, March 6, 1853. Romantic tragedy. Set numbers; recitative. Setting: Paris; time, about 1850. Originally in three acts; present-day productions usually in four acts, dividing the original Act II (116 min).

ACT I: Violetta's Paris salon, luxuriously furnished (31 min). ACT II: A villa near Paris (33 min). ACT III: Ballroom in Flora's mansion (22 min). ACT IV: Violetta's bedroom (30 min).

Synopsis. At one of her brilliant supper parties, the beautiful but frail demi-mondaine, Violetta Valéry, meets the well-born Alfredo Germont, and for love of him abandons her feverish life of pleasure. Alfredo's father intrudes on their idyllic existence in the country and, although realizing her sincerity, persists in his demand that Violetta renounce Alfredo. Violetta determines to make the sacrifice and departs, leaving only a note for Alfredo. She appears at a ball in Flora's house on the arm of an old admirer, Baron Douphol, to the fury of Alfredo. The two men play at cards; Alfredo wins consistently. Unable to persuade Violetta to go with him, Alfredo insults her and is challenged by the Baron. Violetta becomes ill, and all her friends desert her, leaving her virtually penniless. Alfredo at last returns. His father has told him of Violetta's noble renunciation, and urged him to seek her forgiveness. Overjoyed at the sight of him, Violetta attempts to rise. But it is too late. As Germont and the doctor enter, Violetta dies in Alfredo's arms.

Major Roles. VIOLETTA VALERY (lyr s; has been sung by dram, lyr, and col s); coloratura passages of great brilliance in Act I; demands dramatic expression; D3 to C5 ("Sempre Libera" to Db5). ALFREDO GERMONT (lyr t); chief aria, "Demiei bollenti spiriti," sustained; several Bb3's. GIORGIO GERMONT (bar); top Gb3.

Lesser Roles. FLORA BERVOIX (s or m-s). BARON DOUPHOL (bar). GASTONE, Viscount de Letorières (t). MARQUIS D'OBIGNY (bs). DOCTOR GRENVILLE (bs). ANNINA, Violetta's maid (m-s).

Bit Parts. JOSEPH, a servant (t). COMMISSIONAIRE (bs). FLORA'S SERVANT (bs).

Chorus. SSATTBB. Guests of Violetta and Flora, some as matadors and gypsies. Servants and gypsies (mute).

Ballet. Spanish ballet in Act III, as elaborate as desired.

Orchestra. 2 fl, 2 ob, 2 cl, 2 bsn, 4 hrn, 2 trp, 3 trb, tuba, timp, bs drum, triangle, nakers (drums) and tambourine, strings. *Stage:* band, orchestrated to fit existing conditions; often played from pit.

Material. FS-P: Map, Ka, Ri, TW (rent). CP: Ka, Map, Ri, TW (rent). VS: Map, TW (e — Martin) (rent); Ri (i) $5, (i, e — Machlis) (in prep); G Sc (i, e) $4. Stage guide: Map, TW (rent). O Tr: Dent (Ox) $1.50; Mead (Ha); Norville (138A); Reese (Car); Treash (358); Stoessel (T22); Bowe (T22).

Photographs. ACT I: Metropolitan: (Jorgulesco) 12.18.39 p. 20; 11.30.42 p. 11; (Smith) 4.1.57 pp. 16, 18. Portland: 10.6.41 p. 10. Flint: 3.12.51 p. 30. Scranton: 10.20.47 p. 9. Hartford: 4.5.48 p. 12 (modern dress). Stockholm: 4.1.57 p. 10. Puerto Rico: 4.1.57 p. 12. Brooklyn: 4.1.57 p. 12. ACT II: Metro-

143

politan: (Jorgulesco) 12.27.43 p. 19; (Smith) 4.1.57 pp. 14, 19. Flint: 11.4. 46 p. 19. Houston: 4.1.57 p. 26. Palermo: 4.1.57 p. 10. ACT III: Metropolitan: (Jorgulesco) 12.18.39 p. 21; 4.2.51 p. 9 (ballet); (Smith) 4.1.57 p. 19. San Carlo: 11.8.48 p. 7 (ballet). Moscow: 4.1.57 p. 12. Buenos Aires: 4.1.57 p. 12. ACT IV: Metropolitan: (Jorgulesco) 11.24.41 p. 28; (Smith) 4.1.57 pp. 8, 20. Paris: 10.15.51 p. 16; 4.1.57 p. 10. Florence: 4.1.57 p. 11.

Performing Companies. Approx 142. 1956–57 only: 35, 39, 58, 70, 92, 96, 122, 130, 157, 185, 216, 283, 290, 295, 313, 324, 329, 334, 378, 391, 415, 443B, 449, 462, 479, 481.

📖 A Tree on the Plains

Music by Ernst Bacon (1898–   ). Libretto in English by Paul Horgan, commissioned by the League of Composers. Premiere: Spartanburg, S.C., 1942. Revised 1958. Folk drama. Folklike music, no set arias but many songs; vocal line patterned after speech; dialogue. Needs knowledge of American styles on the part of all performers, although no special vocal problems appear. One set: a house on the plains; one act or two. Passing of time can be indicated by lighting. Very brief prelude and interlude (approx 120 min).

Synopsis. It is a blazing hot morning on the prairie. Mom's father has died, and the neighbors gather for the funeral. Lou, the cowboy, hopes that Corrie, the daughter of the house, will see him and the earth for the reality and love they can bring, but her heart is set on city ways, and she dreams of luxuries. Her college-boy brother, Buddy, too has ambitions – to be a tough cookie. Taut emotions eventually erupt – the men squabbling because the drought is so fierce, Lou and Buddy fighting over Corrie's future. At the height of the tension a storm breaks, bringing blessed relief. The little elm tree in the yard, which had seemed about to die, perks up, and everyone's spirits are lightened. Pop and Mom go off for a ride, while Lou comes seriously courting Corrie. She yields to his love and the sweetness of the night, and they run off to be married by the jolly Reverend. Buddy, hearing the call of civilization in the drone of an airplane, departs. The next morning Lou and Corrie return, to be welcomed warmly by the parents. Everyone sings praise.

Roles. LOU (bar). POP, owner of the homestead (bs). CORRIE MAE (s). MOM (c). BUDDY (low t or high bar). A NEIGHBOR (t). ANOTHER NEIGHBOR (t or s). LITTLE SHIRLEY, a neighbor's child; tapdancer. THE REVEREND (speaking).

Chorus. SATB. As large as desired. Men and women from neighboring ranches.

Orchestra. 2 fl (picc), 2 ob (Eng hrn), 2 cl, 2 bsn, 2 hrn, 2 trp, 2 trb, tuba, harp, piano (or 2), timp, perc, xyl, bells, celeste, strings. Guitar, accordion desirable.

Production Note. Lighting could be very elaborate. Rain, mill. Sound effects (plane, crickets, etc.).

Material. Composer.

Performing Companies. 457 and 457A (1942 – prem). 376 (7.20.42). 214A (8.52).

144

▶ Il Trionfo del onore · The Triumph of Honor

Music by Alessandro Scarlatti (1659–1725). Libretto in Italian by Francesco Antonio Tullio. Premiere: Naples, November 26, 1718. Adapted by Virgilio Mortari. Comedy. Highly melodic; set numbers; patter recitative; two quartets. Overture (sinfonia). The single setting is a small piazza on the outskirts of Pisa, late 17th century. Three acts (approx 90 min).

Synopsis. A typical plot of entangled affections. Riccardo is engaged to Leonora but has won the love of Dora, fiancée of Leonora's brother Erminio, and deserted her as well. Flaminio has promised to wed the wealthy Cornelia but slyly woos her maid Rosina. Captain Bombarda, Riccardo's companion-at-arms-and-amour, also seeks Rosina's favors. She likes neither man. The two adventurers seek money from Flaminio, Riccardo's uncle; the two forsaken damsels seek advice from Cornelia, Dora's aunt. Everyone's perfidy is revealed; everyone's honor is at stake. To solve the problem in true comic opera style, with a happy ending, Riccardo is restored to Leonora, Dora to Erminio, Flaminio to Cornelia, while Rosina is perforce paired off with the Captain.

Roles. RICCARDO ALBENORI, a young rake (t). LEONORA DORINI, his abandoned fiancée (m-s). ERMINIO, her brother (bar). DORA ROSSETTI, his fiancée (lyr s). FLAMINIO, Riccardo's uncle, engaged to Cornelia (lyr t). CORNELIA, Dora's aunt (light s). ROSINA, Cornelia's maid (m-s). CAPTAIN BOMBARDA, a friend of Riccardo (bar). No problems of range, but all singers need command of sustained vocalism as well as flexibility for florid passages and recitative.

Orchestra. Strings, harpsichord.

Material. FS-P: B & H (Ca) (rent). VS: B & H (Ca – i) $3. Tr: William Murray and Hibbard James (T32); Dunn (T3); Zytowski (30).

Photographs. London Opera Club: 4.16.51 p. 7.

Performing Companies. 97E (8.8.54). 445 (4.5.58). 321 (58–59).

▶ Tristan und Isolde · Tristan and Isolde

Music by Richard Wagner (1813–1883). Libretto in German by the composer, based on a medieval legend. Premiere: Munich, June 10, 1865. Romantic tragedy. Heavy emphasis on orchestra; fully developed idiom of leitmotifs and symphonic construction, predominantly chromatic; continuous texture. Vocal line is extremely exacting with difficult intervals and great demands on strength and stamina. Prelude. Setting: on board ship, in Cornwall, and in Brittany; time, legendary. Three acts (199 min).

ACT I: A ship en route to Cornwall (74 min). ACT II: A garden in King Marke's castle in Cornwall (65 min). ACT III: Tristan's castle Kareol, in Brittany (60 min).

Synopsis. The Irish princess Isolde is being escorted by the knight Tristan to marry his uncle, King Marke. Out of loyalty to his uncle, Tristan maintains his reserve, although Isolde passionately recounts the circumstances that first brought them together: she nursed him to health although he had slain her betrothed, and feels that he returns her love. In despair, she bids her maid

145

Brangäne prepare a poisonous potion which she intends to share with him. Brangäne substitutes a love philter, and Tristan and Isolde succumb immediately to its magic. In the very shadow of Marke's towers they meet to fulfill their passionate devotion; there, despite Brangäne's warning, they are surprised by Marke. Treacherously wounded by his one-time friend, Melot, Tristan returns to Brittany with his trusted retainer, Kurvenal. His feverish longing for Isolde inflames his illness. At last she arrives, in time for only a brief, ecstatic reunion before he dies. Isolde murmurs a final expression of transfigured love and joins Tristan in rapturous death.

Major Roles. ISOLDE (dram s); needs tremendous power throughout wide range; A2 to C5. BRANGANE (m-s — Wagner suggests s); high tessitura; C3 to A4. TRISTAN (dram t); prototype of heroic tenor; C♯2 to A3. KURVENAL (bar); consistently high range; A1 to G3. KING MARKE (bs); needs dark, rich timbre; G1 to E3.

Lesser Roles. MELOT (t). A SHEPHERD (t). A STEERSMAN (bar). A SAILOR'S VOICE (t).

Chorus. TTBB. Sailors, knights, attendants.

Orchestra. 3 fl, 2 ob, Eng hrn, 2 cl, bs cl, 3 bsn, 4 hrn, 3 trp, 3 trb, bs tuba, timp, perc, harp, strings. *Stage:* Act II: 3 trp, 3 trb, 6 hrn; Act III: Eng hrn (at Metropolitan, latter part of solo played on tarogato).

Material. FS-P: Ri, TW (rent). FS: Br (g) $25. MS: Pet (e, f, g) $15, $17.50. VS: Pet (g — Mottl) $6.50; G Sc (g, e) $5. Tr: Spaeth and Cowdry (T22); Mead (Ha); Chapin (T24).

Photographs. Metropolitan: ACT I: 12.6.43 p. 18; 4.9.45 p. 30; 12.12.49 p. 18; ACT II: 12.6.43 p. 19; 12.12.49 p. 19; ACT III: 12.6.43 p. 21; 12.12.49 p. 20. Stuttgart: 3.10.52 p. 8 (Act I). Bayreuth: 10.14.57 p. 8 (Act II). Hamburg: 3.2.53 p. 14 (Act II). Vienna: 10.13.52 p. 11 (Act I).

Performing Companies. 329 (47–51, 52–53, 54–55, 57–58, 59–61). 130 (1958). 392 (57–58).

🎭 Troilus and Cressida

Music by William Walton (1902–   ). Libretto in English by Christopher Hassall, based on Greek legend as interpreted by Boccaccio and Chaucer. Premiere: London, December 3, 1954. Romantic tragedy. Modern idiom; abundantly melodic, set numbers, accompanied recitative. No overture. Setting: Troy, 12th century B.C. Three acts (134 min).

ACT I: Before the temple of Pallas (42 min). ACT II: Room in Pandarus's house, and orchestral interlude (46 min). ACT III: The Greek camp overlooking Troy (46 min).

Synopsis. Calkas, Trojan High Priest, is discouraged after ten years' siege by the Greeks, and deserts his people, leaving his daughter, Cressida, in Troy. Troilus, son of Priam, loves Cressida, but she fears to return his love. Pandarus, Cressida's uncle, persuades Cressida to send Troilus her red scarf as a token and arranges for the pair to meet at his home. Cressida's resolution gone, the two vow a new life and love. Their idyll is interrupted by the arrival of the

146

Greek prince Diomede, bearing a royal decree for the exchange of Cressida for Antenor, a captive Trojan warrior. The lovers must part. Troilus returns Cressida's scarf as sign of their eternal faith, and promises to communicate secretly with her. Ten weeks later Cressida has had no word from Troilus: her treacherous maid Evadne has burned all his messages. Calkas pleads with Cressida to accept Diomede's offer of marriage, to save their lives. Having finally lost faith in Troilus, she yields, even giving Diomede the scarlet scarf. Just before the wedding Troilus and Pandarus arrive to bring Cressida back to Troy. Confronted by the Greek prince wearing the scarf, Troilus draws his sword and attacks Diomede, but is mortally wounded by Calkas. Diomede sends Calkas back to Troy in chains and orders Cressida to remain in the camp as a whore. The disgraced Cressida kills herself on Troilus' sword.

Major Roles. CRESSIDA (s); requires strong voice throughout wide range; A2 to C5. TROILUS, Prince of Troy (t); virile, romantic; D2 (opt C♯2) to C4. PANDARUS, brother of Calkas (buf t); needs high falsetto, flowery style; D2 to B3. DIOMEDE, Prince of Argos (bar); high tessitura, some staccato passage-work; A1 to G3. CALKAS (bs); G1 to E3.

Lesser Roles. EVADNE, Cressida's servant (m-s). ANTENOR, captain of Trojan spears (bar). HORASTE, friend of Pandarus (bar).

Bit Parts. WOMAN'S VOICE within the temple (speaking). TWO PRIESTS (t, bar). TWO SOLDIERS (t, bar). THREE WATCHMEN, offstage (t, bar, bar).

Chorus. SSSSAAAATTTTBBBB. Priests, priestesses, soldiers, Trojan citizens, slaves, camp followers.

Orchestra. 3 fl, 3 ob (Eng hrn), 3 cl (bs cl), 2 bsn (cont bsn), 4 hrn, 3 trp, 3 trb, tuba, timp, perc (4–5 players), 2 harp, celeste, strings. *Stage:* hrn, 4 trp, bells, 2 drum.

Material. FS-P: Ox (rent). VS: Ox $16.50 (also rent). CP: Ox (rent). Li: Ox $1.

Photographs. San Francisco: 10.31.55 p. 6. N.Y. City Opera: 11.14.55 p. 17.

Performing Companies. 72 (10.7.55 — Amer prem). 334 (10.55).

⚑ Il Trovatore · The Troubadour

Music by Giuseppe Verdi (1813–1901). Libretto in Italian by Salvatore Cammarano, based on a play by the same name by Antonio Garcia Gutiérrez. Premiere: Rome, January 19, 1853. Tragic melodrama. Almost unbroken sequence of melody with both dramatic and lyrical vocal line; arias, ensembles, and important choruses. No overture. Setting: Spain, 15th century. Four acts (each with a title), eight scenes (130 min).

ACT I (The Duel) i: Hall of the Guards in Aliaferia Castle (10 min); ii: Castle gardens (17 min). ACT II (The Gypsy) i: Gypsy camp in the Biscay Mountains (24 min); ii: Convent cloisters (18 min). ACT III (The Gypsy's Son) i: Military camp of Count di Luna near Castellor (12 min); ii: Room in Castellor fortress (10 min). ACT IV (The Penalty) i: Outside the prison tower of Aliaferia Castle (21 min); ii: Inside the prison (18 min).

Synopsis. Ferrando, Captain of the Guards, relates to his companions on night watch the tragedy that has happened before the opera begins. The present Count di Luna's brother has presumably been thrown into the flames by the gypsy Azucena in revenge for her mother's similar death. In reality it was Azucena's own son who perished, but she conceals this even from the young nobleman, who thereafter is known as Manrico, the troubadour. As the opera opens, Manrico and the Count are rivals for Leonora, who prefers the troubadour. The two enemies duel; Manrico obeys an inexplicable impulse to spare his adversary. He is bitterly reprimanded for this weakness by Azucena, who reminds him of her mother's fate. Half-crazed, she partially reveals the truth about his birth, but puts off his horrified questioning. He learns that Leonora, believing him dead, has retreated to a convent, from which he rescues her after a skirmish with the Count. Then, lodged in the Fortress Castellor, he makes an unsuccessful foray to rescue Azucena from the Count, who has captured her in his camp. The Count seems the victor, with all three in his power. Leonora begs for Manrico's release with her own person as the reward. Manrico refuses her sacrifice furiously, but his suspicions are refuted as she dies in his arms, having taken poison to insure that the Count shall possess only her lifeless body. The Count's ultimate revenge is thwarted as the dying Azucena informs him that the man he has just executed is in reality his own brother.

Major Roles. MANRICO (dram t); robust quality, with lyric interludes; sustained; E2 to A3 (top B3 of "Di quella pira" most often taken as C4). COUNT DI LUNA (bar); both sustained line and agility; C2 to G3. LEONORA (dram s); flexibility for fioriture required, as well as long, dramatic vocal arch; A♭2 to D♭5. AZUCENA (c or m-s); needs strength throughout wide range; animation and vigor; D2 to C5.

Lesser Roles. FERRANDO, Di Luna's captain of the guard (bs). INEZ, confidante of Leonora (m-s). RUIZ, soldier in Manrico's service (t).

Chorus. SATB. Soldiers, gypsies, nuns, guards, monks.

Orchestra. 2 fl (picc), 2 ob, 2 cl, 2 bsn, 4 hrn, 2 trp, 3 trb, tuba, timp, perc, organ, bells, harp, strings. *Stage:* harp, hrn, side drum. Anvils.

Material. FS-P: Map, Ri, TW, Ka (rent). FS: Br (i) $17.50. CP: Map (i, e) (rent). VS: Pet (i, g) $6.50; Ri (i) $5; G Sc (i, e) $4. Li: Ox (Dent) $1.50. O Tr: Rachleff (T17).

Photographs. Metropolitan: 1.6.41 cover (Act II ii), p. 9 (sketch, Act IV i), p. 16 (Act III i), p. 17 (Acts I ii and II i); 3.13.44 p. 18 (Act I i), p. 20 (Act IV ii), p. 24 (Act III ii); 1.8.51 p. 21 (Act IV ii). Covent Garden: 12.1. 47 p. 14. Jackson, Miss., Opera Guild: 1.17.49 p. 28.

Performing Companies. Approx 56. 1956–57 only: 39, 72, 92, 113, 130, 216, 244, 295, 301, 324, 329, 334, 391, 526.

📧 Turandot

Music by Giacomo Puccini (1858–1924). Libretto by Giuseppe Adami and Renato Simoni, based on the drama of the same name by Carlo Gozzi. Left

148

unfinished by Puccini, the last act was completed, from the point where Turandot and Calaf are left alone, by Franco Alfano. Premiere: Milan, April 25, 1926. A tale of legendary China. Vocal line often patterned after speech with occasional set numbers enclosed in continuous orchestral texture; Oriental atmosphere pervades. The music of the three ministers is in light, conversational style in contrast to the highly emotional dramatic music of the principals. No overture. Three acts, five scenes (99 min).

ACT I: At the gates of Pekin (30 min). ACT II i: Pavilion in the Imperial Palace; ii: A square outside the palace (37 min). ACT III i: Gardens of the palace; ii: Same as II ii (32 min).

Synopsis. Turandot, Princess of Pekin, will marry only the prince who can solve three riddles. Should he fail, his life is forfeit. Many have attempted the contest and failed before Calaf, exiled Prince of Tartary, determines to win. His ancient father Timur, who has found his way to Pekin accompanied by the female slave Liu, attempts to dissuade him, but Calaf is madly in love with Turandot. He answers the riddles correctly. But the Princess still refuses to marry him in spite of her father's protests at the breaking of her oath. Calaf resolves the situation by propounding his own riddle: if Turandot can correctly name him by dawn, he will give up his life. Through the restless night the Princess seeks his name, discovering at last that only Liu and the old man Timur know it. Torture will not wring the name from the girl's lips. She plunges a knife in her breast rather than reveal it. Turandot, still adamant, is nevertheless shaken by this frail girl's powers of resistance. After the body is carried away, Turandot and Calaf are left alone. He boldly takes her in his arms and kisses her. This completes the Princess's softening; she no longer wishes revenge. But Calaf tells her his name of his own accord. She summons the court, revealing that the stranger's name is — Love.

Major Roles. TURANDOT (dram s); extremely exacting, constant high tessitura; C#3 to C5. CALAF (t); robust, but many sustained and lyrical passages; top B3 (opt C4). LIU (lyr s); top B♭4.

Lesser Roles. TIMUR (bs). PING (bar), PANG (t), and PONG (t), three ministers of the court; descendants of the commedia dell' arte masked figures; demand great style and precision in ensemble. THE EMPEROR ALTOUM (t). A HERALD (bar).

Chorus. SATTB. People of Pekin, courtiers, children.

Orchestra. 3 fl (picc), 2 ob, Eng hrn, 2 cl, bs cl, 2 bsn, cont bsn, 4 hrn, 3 trp, 3 trb, tuba, timp, perc, Chinese gong, tubular bells, celeste, 2 xyl, 2 harp, strings. *Stage:* brass, cont sax.

Material. FS-P: Ri (rent). VS: Ri (i, e) $10. Tr: Elkin (T1).

Photographs. Covent Garden: 12.1.47 p. 14. N.Y. City Opera: 5.1.50 p. 3. San Francisco: 11.16.53 p. 13. San Carlo, Naples: 1.4.54 p. 13. Verona: 10.18.54 p. 17. San Antonio: 3.12.56 p. 14. Trieste: 12.22.58 pp. 30, 32. Metropolitan: 3.4.61 pp. 16, 24, 25.

Performing Companies. 334 (1950, 1957, 1958, 1959). 72 (1952, 1954). 391 (7.27.55; 7.12.56). 180 (12.1.56; 10.23.58). 487 (2.4.56). 1956–57: 31, 64, 92. 130 (1958, 1959). 329 (60–61).

149

🎭 Il Turco in Italia · The Turk in Italy

Music by Gioacchino Rossini (1792–1868). Libretto in Italian by Felice Romani. Premiere: Milan, August 14, 1814. Comedy. Simple harmonic structure, melody alternating between extremely florid and typical quick patter; set numbers, recitative. Overture. Setting: Naples; 18th century. Two acts, six scenes (Goldovsky vers, seven scenes) (150 min).

ACT I i: By the sea; ii: At the house of Don Geronimo; iii: By the sea. ACT II i: The Sultan's lodgings at an inn; ii: A ballroom; iii: By the sea.

Synopsis. Fiorilla, married to a considerably older man, is looking for amorous diversion. Sultan Selim of Turkey debarks on the shores of Naples, and Fiorilla finds him the exactly right — and most willing — object for her purpose. However, her husband, Geronimo, and Narciso, also in love with her, frown on the flirtation. The trouble is compounded by the gypsy Zaida, who is revealed to be an old flame of Selim's. The height of confusion is reached at a masked ball during which Fiorilla and Zaida are dressed alike, while Narciso and Geronimo appear as Turks (as, of course, does Selim). A poet in search of a plot, who has been following the proceedings throughout with the greatest delight, now lends a hand to achieve the happy ending: Fiorilla returns to her husband, and the Sultan embarks homeward with Zaida.

Major Roles. THE SULTAN SELIM OF TURKEY (bs); extremely florid; A1 to F3. DON GERONIO (originally GERONIMO) (buf bs); A1 to E3. FIORILLA (col s); D3 to B4. NARCISO (lyr t); high tessitura, needs great flexibility; D2 to B3. THE POET (bs-bar); very high tessitura; A1 to G3. ZAIDA (s or m-s); B2 to G4. *Note:* Fiorilla, Zaida, and Narciso are actually written down to A1, but octave transpositions are commonly used in Rossini.

Bit Parts. ISAURA, companion of Zaida (s); G3 to G4. ALBAZAR, a gypsy (t).

Chorus. SATTB. Sailors, gypsies.

Orchestra. 2 fl, 2 ob, 2 cl, 2 bsn, 2 hrn, 2 trp, trb, timp, strings.

Material. FS-P: Pr (Mer — Goldovsky) (rent). VS: Pr (Mer — e — Goldovsky and Wolfes) (rent). Tr: Goldovsky and Caldwell (T13); Jacobs (T8).

Photographs. Tanglewood: 10.11.48 p. 28. San Carlo, Naples: 4.18.55 p. 30.

Performing Companies. 205 (8.9.48). 279A (4.55). 397 (5.20.58).

🎭 The Turn of the Screw

Music by Benjamin Britten (1913–   ). Libretto in English by Myfanwy Piper, based on a novel of the same title by Henry James. Premiere: Venice, September 14, 1954. Supernatural drama. The work is constructed as a theme and 15 variations. Continuous texture with a few set scenas and numbers. Scenes are connected by orchestral theme and variations. Orchestra is extremely exposed and requires 13 expert players. Vocal line also demanding, with difficult intervals. Setting: in and around Bly, an English country house, mid-19th century. Prologue and two acts, sixteen scenes (105 min). Timings below are for intervals only based on the blackout of each scene to the fade-in of the next in the N.Y. College of Music production.

PROLOGUE: In front of a curtain (45 sec). ACT I i: Interior of a coach —
The Journey (30 sec); ii: The porch at Bly — The Welcome (28 sec); iii: The
porch near a window of the house — The Letter (1 min, 40 sec); iv: The house
— The Tower (27 sec); v: Hall at Bly — The Window (1 min, 8 sec); vi:
Schoolroom at Bly — The Lesson (1 min); vii: In the park — The Lake (1 min,
10 sec); viii: The house and tower — At Night (entire act, approx 53 min).
ACT II i: Nowhere — Colloquy and Soliloquy (40 sec); ii: Churchyard — The
Bells (28 sec); iii: Schoolroom — Miss Jessel (1 min, 5 sec); iv: Miles —
The Bedroom (15 sec); v: Miles's bedroom — Quint (1 min, 10 sec); vi: Par-
lor — The Piano (45 sec); vii: The lake — Flora (50 sec); viii: Outside the
house — Miles (entire act, approx 52 min).

Synopsis. A Governess is given complete charge of Miles and Flora, orphaned brother and sister, on an English country estate, and is forewarned by
their guardian not to bother him with any problems. She immediately senses
an air of mystery about the household which Mrs. Grose, the housekeeper, is
unable to explain. The children seem angelic, but the Governess soon discovers
that they are haunted by the ghosts of Peter Quint, former caretaker, and
Miss Jessel, their previous governess, who exercise an evil control over the boy
and girl, striving to possess their souls. As the situation comes to a dangerous
climax, the Governess dispatches Flora to the guardian in care of Mrs. Grose.
Miles remains behind. When, at the Governess's insistence, he attempts to
exorcise the ghost, he dies.

Major Roles. GOVERNESS (s); occasional high tessitura; B2 to C5. MRS.
GROSE (s); elderly type; Bb2 to A4. MISS JESSEL (s); Bb2 to Cb5. PETER
QUINT (t); long, florid passagework, Db2 to Ab3. MILES (boy s); Bb2 to A4.
FLORA (s); Eb3 to A4.

Lesser Role. PROLOGUE (t); sung by man who plays Quint.

Orchestra. fl (bs fl, picc), ob (Eng hrn), cl (bs cl), bsn, hrn, harp, perc,
piano (celeste), 2 vln, vla, vcl, cb.

Production Problems. Many scenes and complicated lighting. A Poe-like
eeriness should be suggested.

Material. All B & H. FS-P (rent). VS $12. Li $1.

Photographs. Mus. Amer. Stratford, Ont.: 9.57 p. 22.

Performing Companies. 533 (1957). 336 (3.19.58). 47 (4.59). 24 (12.59).

✠ Vanessa

Music by Samuel Barber (1910–   ). Libretto in English by Gian-Carlo
Menotti. Premiere: New York, January 15, 1958. Melodrama in neo-roman-
tic style. Accompanied recitative, set arias and numbers. Setting: Vanessa's
country estate in a "northern country," about 1905. No overture; prelude
to Act IV. Four acts, five scenes (121 min).

ACT I: Drawingroom (26 min). ACT II: The same (31 min). ACT III: Entrance hall and staircase with ballroom beyond (21 min). ACT IV i: Erika's
bedroom (18 min); ii: Drawingroom (25 min).

Synopsis. On a snowy evening Vanessa awaits the arrival of Anatol, her lover of 20 years before. Erika, her niece, helps prepare for his coming. The Baroness, Vanessa's mother, watches in the stony silence she has maintained for many years toward her daughter, having disapproved of her dismissal of Anatol and her closely kept seclusion. When the guest arrives Vanessa is horrified to discover he is a stranger, and rushes from the room. Anatol explains to Erika that he is the son of Vanessa's Anatol, who has died, and he has come to meet the woman he has heard so much about. He and Erika dine together. A month later Vanessa and Anatol have become close friends. Erika tells the Baroness that Anatol seduced her that first night and she is carrying his child, but she refuses his superficial offer of marriage. At a ball the old family doctor announces Vanessa's betrothal to Anatol. Erika and the Baroness refuse to attend. Erika finally appears, faints, recovers, and disappears into the snowy night. Hours later she is found by a search party led by Anatol. Erika tells the Baroness the child will not be born; the Baroness now refuses to talk to Erika as well. Vanessa and Anatol are married and prepare to depart for Paris. Erika refuses to tell Vanessa the real reason for her attempted suicide, but swears it was not because of Anatol, as she does not want to mar Vanessa's long-awaited happiness. The couple leave and Erika remains to take care of her silent grandmother and to wait in seclusion for her true love, as Vanessa had done so many years before.

Major Roles. VANESSA (s); demands florid singing, trill; Bb2 to C5 (opt D5). ERIKA (m-s); youthful appearance, intensity, no special vocal requirements; B2 to Bb4. ANATOL (t); Db2 to Cb4 (opt C4). DOCTOR (bar or bs-bar); warm personality; A1 (opt G1) to Gb3.

Lesser Roles. OLD BARONESS (c). NICHOLAS, Majordomo (bs). FOOTMAN (bs). YOUNG PASTOR (mute).

Chorus. SATB. Servants, guests, peasants.

Ballet. Ballroom dancing in Act III.

Orchestra. 2 fl, picc, 2 ob, Eng hrn, 2 cl, bs cl, 2 bsn, 4 hrn, 3 trp, 3 trb, tuba, timp, perc, celeste, harp, strings. *Stage:* bells (Act I), organ (Act II), dance orchestra (Act III), fl, ob, 2 cl (Eb cl), 2 bsn, 2 hrn, trp, sn drum, accordion, strings; horn (Act IV) imitates dog.

Material. All G Sc. FS-P (rent). VS (e, g) $10. Vocal selections 60¢, 75¢. Li 75¢.

Photographs. Metropolitan: 1.27.58 pp. 19, 20.

Performing Companies. 329 (57–59).

🖢 Werther

Music by Jules Massenet (1842–1912). Libretto in French by Édouard Blau, Paul Milliet and Georges Hartmann, based on Goethe's novel, "The Sorrows of Young Werther." Premiere: (in German) Vienna, February 16, 1892. Lyric tragedy with strong romantic atmosphere. Delicate, simple melodic line; conventional harmonic structure; accompanied recitatives, set arias and scenes. Setting: in and around Wetzlar, near Frankfurt, from July to December in the 1870's. Four acts (120 min).

ACT I: Garden outside Le Bailli's house, July (39 min). ACT II: Village Square in Wetzlar, October (30 min). ACT III: Albert's home, Christmas Eve (33 min). ACT IV: Werther's apartment, Christmas Eve (18 min). (Acts III and IV are usually played without intermission.)

Synopsis. The death of Le Bailli's wife has left Charlotte, their eldest daughter, in charge of the younger children and bound by a promise to her mother to marry Albert, a conventional young man who has been away for several months as the opera begins. Le Bailli is rehearsing a Christmas carol with the children as Charlotte prepares to attend a dance with the young poet Werther. While they are at the ball Albert returns and discusses plans for his marriage with Charlotte's younger sister, Sophie. Charlotte and Werther return, obviously deeply absorbed in one another. Their mood is shattered when Le Bailli announces Albert's presence. Werther declares he will die if Charlotte marries Albert.

Three months after Charlotte's marriage, Werther reaffirms his loyalty to both, though Albert knows the true situation. Werther is drawn irresistibly to Charlotte, who begs him to go away. On Christmas Eve Charlotte, rereading Werther's letters, realizes that her suppressed feelings for him have at last emerged. Werther suddenly appears and evokes an expression of love from Charlotte, but she retreats, leaving him in despair. He writes that he is going on a long journey, asking to borrow Albert's pistols. Albert gives them to Charlotte to send. She realizes the meaning too late, rushing to Werther's apartment only to find him dying. At last she admits her love for him as he dies in her arms. The children are heard singing their Christmas carol in the distance.

Major Roles. CHARLOTTE (m-s); high tessitura, long flowing line; C3 to A4 (opt A♯4). SOPHIE (lyr s); light agile voice, youthful appearance; C♯3 to A4. WERTHER (lyr t); long line, young, romantic appearance; F2 to A♯3 (opt B3). ALBERT (bar); staid quality; C2 to F3.

Lesser Roles. LE BAILLI (bar or bs). SCHMIDT, friend of Le Bailli (t). JOHANN, friend of Le Bailli (bar or bs).

Bit Parts. A PEASANT, A SERVANT (mute).

Chorus. SSA. Townsfolk, children (Fritz, Max, Hans, Karl, Gretel, Clara). In final chorus women sing with children.

Orchestra. 2 fl, ob, Eng hrn, 2 cl, E♭ alto sax, 2 bsn, 4 hrn, 2 trp, 3 trb, tuba, timp, perc, harp, strings.

Material. All Pr (Heu). FS-P (rent). VS $11. Tr: Tucker (T2).

Photographs. Trieste: 3.17.52 p. 9. San Francisco: 11.2.53 p. 6. Sadler's Wells: 3.24.52 p. 12.

Performing Companies. 72 (52–53). 350 (5.25.54). 180 (56–57). 338 (56–57). 443B (11.22.57).

❦ The Wife of Martin Guerre

Music by William Bergsma (1921–   ). Libretto in English by Janet Lewis, based on her novel about an actual incident found in the records of the court

153

of Toulouse for the year 1560. Premiere: New York, February 15, 1956. Melodrama in modern idiom. Mostly conventional harmonic structure; continuous texture without break between scenes, embodying set numbers, and accompanied recitative. No overture. Setting: France in mid-16th century. Three acts, twelve scenes (approx 120 min).

ACT I i, ii, iii: Martin Guerre's cottage in Artigues. ACT II i, ii, iii, iv, v: The same. ACT III i: The same; ii: Courtroom at Rieux; iii: Outside courtroom at Toulouse; iv: Courtroom at Toulouse.

Synopsis. Afraid of his father's wrath because he has stolen grain, Martin Guerre deserts his wife, Bertrande, and his infant son, Sanxi, and disappears. Eight years later, his vengeful father now dead, Martin returns, strangely different in manner and bearing. The farm prospers, everyone is happy again, and Bertrande becomes pregnant. She alone feels a strange unrest about her husband, but he humors her, attributing her doubts to her condition. After her baby is born, Bertrande is increasingly uneasy and finally accuses her husband of being an impostor. She has him arrested and brought to trial, although her entire family considers her mad. She loves Martin, but claims he has led her into adultery. Martin is judged an impostor and sentenced to hang. He appeals and is granted a second trial, during which the real Martin Guerre appears. He arrogantly declares Bertrande responsible for her sin, although the imposter claims he alone is to blame. Bereft of her husband's love and that of the man she has come to love, who must die for his deceit, Bertrande goes off alone and embittered.

Major Roles. BERTRANDE (s); strong voice throughout range, sustained role; C2 to B4. MARTIN GUERRE, THE IMPOSTOR (bar); winning personality; A1 to F♯3.

Lesser Roles. CATHERINE, servant in Martin's household (c); G2 to E♯4. UNCLE PIERRE (bs); G1 to E3. DIANE (col s) and ANNETTE GUERRE (m-s), Martin's sisters. FATHER ANTOINE, priest at Artigues (t). OLD GUERRE, Martin's father (bs-bar); also plays role listed on program as Third Soldier, really the true Martin Guerre. SANXI, Martin's son (boy s).

Bit Parts. (May be doubled as indicated by the composer as follows): STEWARD and JUDGE II (t). YOUNG SOLDIER and CRIER I (t). CARTER and CRIER II (bs). SOLDIER FROM ROCHEFORT and JUDGE I (bs).

Bit Parts from Chorus. WOMAN (m-s). ESPAGNOL (t). BAGPIPER (t). SHEPHERD (t). JEAN DU TILH (bar). WORKER (bar). MAN (bar). WORKER (bs). MUSICIAN (bs). MEN-AT-ARMS (bs).

Chorus. SATB. Neighbors, workers, maidservants, spectators.

Orchestra. 2 fl (picc), ob, cl (bs cl), bsn, trp, hrn, harp, perc, strings. (String parts written for solo players: 2 vln, vla, 2 vcl, cb; but should be reinforced in a large hall.) *Stage:* fife, shawm, bagpipe.

Production Problem. Action must be kept flowing by use of separately lighted areas on stage.

Material. FS-P, VS: Comp through Ga.

Photographs. Juilliard: 3.12.56 pp. 32, 33 (sketch).

Performing Companies. 321 (1.11.56 – prem).

🎭 Wozzeck

Music by Alban Berg (1885–1935). Libretto in German by the composer, adapted from Georg Büchner's play. Premiere: Berlin, December 14, 1925. Psychological and sociological tragedy. Atonal (departs from atonality only in last entr'acte, and is truly dodecaphonic in only one instance). Orchestra in set musical forms: sonata, rondo, variations, etc. Employs *Sprechstimme* (speech set forth in terms of intonation and rhythm, but which retains quality of spoken word). Continuous texture; no set numbers. No overture. Scenes separated by orchestral interludes. Setting: Germany in the 1830's. Three acts, fifteen scenes (89 min).

ACT I i: The captain's room; ii: An open field; iii: Marie's room; iv: The doctor's study; v: Street outside Marie's house (34 min). ACT II i: Marie's room; ii: The town square; iii: Street outside Marie's house; iv: A beergarden; v: The barracks (33 min). ACT III i: Marie's room; ii: A pond; iii: A tavern; iv: A pond; v: Street outside Marie's house (22 min).

Synopsis. Wozzeck, a downtrodden German soldier in a small provincial town, is the constant butt of both fate and man. His sadistic Captain victimizes him, and he is made a guinea pig for unorthodox experiments by the incompetent regimental doctor. His only joy is his mistress, Marie, by whom he has a son. Even she betrays him: she yields to a pompous Drum Major, who aggravates the situation by taunting poor Wozzeck and then beating him. Driven almost mad, Wozzeck stabs Marie; then, searching for the lost knife, he wanders distractedly into a pond and drowns. His orphaned son, understanding nothing, rides his hobbyhorse after the children that go to gape at his mother's body.

Major Roles. MARIE (s); earthy type; high tessitura, difficult skips; G2 (opt E2) to C5. CAPTAIN (t); trill; Bb1 (opt Ab1) to C♯4 (opt G♯4). DRUM MAJOR (dram t); C2 to Bb3. WOZZECK (bar); extremely dramatic role; Gb1 (opt E1) to A3. DOCTOR (buf bs); D1 to F3; (opt F♯3 and falsetto A3). (Ranges given are those of actual singing parts. Pitch of *Sprechstimme* in some cases is higher or lower than singing ranges. All major roles are difficult.)

Lesser Roles. MARGRET, Marie's neighbor (m-s or c). ANDRES, Wozzeck's friend (t). Marie's CHILD (child s). Two APPRENTICES (bs and bar). FOOL (t). SOLDIER (t). TOWNSMAN (t).

Chorus. SATTBBBB. Soldiers, maids, servants, children.

Orchestra. 4 fl (picc), 4 ob (Eng hrn), 4 cl, bs cl, 3 bsn, cont bsn, 4 hrn, 4 trp, 4 trb, tuba, harp, celeste, timp (2 players), perc, xyl, strings. *Stage:* Act I: military band (picc, 2 fl, 2 ob, 2 cl (Eb), 2 bsn, 2 hrn, 2 trp, 3 trb, tuba, bs drum, side drum, triangle). Act II iv: 2 vln, cl, accordion, guitar, small tuba (bombardon), upright piano. Act III iii: chamber orch (usually played by pit): fl (picc), ob, Eng hrn, Eb cl, A cl, bs cl, bsn, cont bsn, 2 hrn, string quintet.

Production Problems. Drowning of Wozzeck in pond; quick changes of scenery necessary to fit orchestral interludes.

Material. FS-P: AMP (UE) (rent). FS: AMP (UE) deluxe $20. VS: AMP (UE) (g) $20. Tr: Harford and Blackall (A Ka).

Photographs. Covent Garden: 3.3.52 p. 8. La Scala: 10.13.52 p. 13. Munich: 10.14.57 p. 3. 3.9.59 (entire issue).
Performing Companies. 334 (1952). 329 (58–59, 60–61).

▨ Wuthering Heights

Music by Carlisle Floyd (1926–   ). Libretto in English by the composer after the novel by Emily Brontë. Commissioned by the Santa Fe Opera Company. Premiere: Santa Fe, July 16, 1958. Drama. Vocal line mostly declamatory in first two acts, with orchestra heightening the drama; third act contains more melodious passages and several dramatic ensembles; small amount of dialogue. Brief prelude; interludes between Prologue and I i; II i and ii. Setting: the moor country of northern England; time, 1835 and 1817–21. Prologue and three acts, seven scenes (140 min).

PROLOGUE: Livingroom (with moors outside) and kitchen of Wuthering Heights, 1835. ACT I i: The same, 1817; ii: The same, three months later; also the moor and outside of Thrushcross Grange with a suggestion of the interior (40 min). ACT II i: Wuthering Heights, four weeks later; ii: The same, one month later (45 min). ACT III i: Thrushcross Grange livingroom and drawingroom, three years later; ii: The same, one month later; iii: The same, six months later (55 min).

Synopsis. In the Prologue, Lockwood, the tenant at Thrushcross Grange, is forced by a storm to take refuge in Wuthering Heights, where he is received ungraciously by Heathcliff, now master of the Earnshaws' former estate. In the night, the guest is visited by the apparition of Cathy, who still haunts her former home and her lover. The opera takes place as a flashback. In the motherless Earnshaw household, managed only by the patient servant Nelly, Cathy runs wild; her favorite playmate is the strange gypsy boy, Heathcliff, whom Mr. Earnshaw insists on treating as one of the family despite his son Hindley's opposition. In a quarrel with Hindley, his father suddenly collapses and dies, leaving the household to Hindley's revengeful management. Heathcliff is at once demeaned, but still sees Cathy in stolen moments. On one of their meetings, they approach Thrushcross Grange, the Lintons' home. Cathy sprains her ankle and is offered hospitality by Edgar and Isabella Linton and their parents. When she comes home, she is changed, disposed to listen to Edgar's suit; finally, in a fit of anger at Heathcliff, she accepts Edgar. Her life with him is not happy, not unhappy; she seems always to be waiting. At last Heathcliff reappears; it is evident where her thoughts have been. The former ragamuffin is now a man of the world, wealthy and arrogant. He has come for one purpose only: to take Cathy away with him. Still divided, she refuses to go, but it is evident that her love for him has only been a banked fire. Yet she resists Heathcliff, and in a cold temper, he proposes to Isabella, who has always admired him. Cathy, about to bear Edgar's child, becomes dangerously ill. Heathcliff comes to see her once more, to take her into the air and light she has missed so sorely, but it is her last moment of joy. Life ends for her,

156

but her anguished cry haunts the surly Heathcliff and his pitifully deranged wife till their last days.

Major Roles. CATHERINE EARNSHAW (s); 17 at the opening of the opera; intensely volatile, dramatic and lyric by turns; needs sustained power throughout range; A2 to C5. HEATHCLIFF (bar); must indicate change from wild youth to imperious man; some high tessitura; G1 to A3. NELLY (m-s); middle-aged, kindly; G♯2 to G4. EDGAR LINTON (t); light, fair, well-dressed; E♭1 to B3. ISABELLA LINTON (s); E♭3 to A♯4. HINDLEY (t); occasional high tessitura; E♭2 to B♭3.

Lesser Roles. MR. EARNSHAW (bs); B♭1 to F3. JOSEPH, the Earnshaws' crabbed servant (t). LOCKWOOD (t); top A♭3. MR. LINTON (mute). MRS. LINTON (mute). SERVANT (mute).

Chorus. SATB. Party guests, Act III.

Ballet. Minuet and waltz in Act III.

Orchestra. 2 fl (picc), 2 ob (Eng hrn), 2 cl (bs cl), 2 bsn, 2 hrn, 2 trp, 2 trb, timp, perc, harp, strings.

Material. FS-P: B & H (rent). VS: B & H $12.

Photographs. Santa Fe: 10.27.58, cover, pp. 18, 19. *Mus. Amer.* Santa Fe: 9.58 p. 12. N.Y. City Opera: 5.59 p. 8.

Performing Companies. 275 (7.16.58 — prem). 334 (4.9.59). 283 (7.31. 59). 133 (59–60).

🎭 Die Zauberflöte · The Magic Flute

Music by Wolfgang Amadeus Mozart (1756–1791). Libretto in German by Emanuel Schikaneder. Premiere: Vienna, September 30, 1791. Lyric drama with mystic overtones. Set numbers; melodic elements embrace folk, romantic, consecrational, and dramatic; dialogue. Overture. Setting: in and near the temple of Isis at Memphis at the time of Rameses I. Two acts, seventeen scenes (159 min).

ACT I i: Rocky pass; ii: The sky; iii: Rocky pass; iv: Room in Sarastro's palace; v: Gateway of the temples; vi: Court outside the three temples (71 min. Scenes are continuous). ACT II i: The sanctuary of the priests; ii: Subterranean passage; iii: Temple garden; iv: Subterranean passage; v: Crypt; vi: Subterranean passage; vii: Garden beyond the temple; viii: Caverns of fire and water; ix: A garden; x: Below the temple walls; xi: The Temple of the Sun (88 min).

Synopsis. The principles of good versus evil are embodied in a complicated story: good is represented by Sarastro, evil by the Queen of the Night. Prince Tamino falls in love with Pamina's portrait and is sent by her mother, the Queen of the Night, to rescue her from Sarastro, the Priest of Isis, long the Queen's enemy. Papageno, the bird-catcher, is sent with Tamino. They receive respectively a magic flute and magic bells to guard them against danger. In Sarastro's temple Pamina resists the advances of the evil slave Monostatos, who is frightened off by Papageno's arrival. Papageno and Pamina flee. Tamino meanwhile has encountered Sarastro's followers and decides to join them. Tamino and Pamina finally meet. Sarastro orders them to pass the tests that will prove them worthy. In spite of all temptations, the Prince remains faithful to Sarastro. The Queen of the Night, furious at the turn of events, tries to induce Pamina to stab Sarastro, but Sarastro calmly reassures and comforts the girl. The Queen's last attempt at revenge is foiled by the coming of dawn, which dispels the forces of night. Pamina and Tamino are united within the Sacred Order; and even Papageno finds a Papagena for his very own.

Major Roles. QUEEN OF THE NIGHT (dram-col s); demands power and facility in high range; B2 to F5 (often E♭5). PAMINA (lyr s); high tessitura; flowing, lyric line; C♯3 to B♭4. TAMINO (lyr t); long, lyrical phrases; F2 to A3. PAPAGENO (bar); light comic role; B♭1 to E3. SARASTRO (bs); true basso profundo, extremely low tessitura; weighty, dignified line; F1 to E♭3.

Lesser Roles. PAPAGENA (s); must imitate old woman. MONOSTATOS (t); character role. THREE LADIES (s, s, m-s); complicated ensembles. THREE GENII (s, m-s, c). SPEAKER OF THE TEMPLE (bs). TWO PRIESTS (t, bs). TWO MEN IN ARMOR (t, bs).

Chorus. SATTBB. Priests of the temple, slaves, attendants.

Orchestra. 2 fl, 2 ob, 2 cl (2 basset hrn), 2 bsn, 2 hrn, 2 trp, 3 trb, timp, keyboard glockenspiel (sometimes also celeste), strings.

Production Problems. Appearances and disappearances of Queen of the Night. Transformation of old woman into Papagena. Trial by fire and water. Appearance of serpent.

Material. FS-P: Map, Ri, G Sc, TW (rent). FS: Br (g) $17.50. MS: Pet (Eu − g) $6, $10. CP: Map (g, e) (rent); G Sc 60¢. VS: B & H (g, e − Dent) $4, $5; G Sc (g, e − Martin) $5. Li: Ox (e − Dent) $1.50; G Sc (g, e − Martin) 75¢. O Tr: Auden and Kallman (Random House); Blatt (215).

Photographs. Metropolitan: 1.17.41 cover, pp. 18, 22, 23, 26 (designs); 1.5.42 pp. 14, 15, etc.; 12.21.42 p. 12 (design); 3.27.44 pp. 18, 19, etc.; 11.20.50 pp. 18, 20; 2.27.56 pp. 18, 19, etc. (sketches); 3.4.57 cover, pp. 18–21. Juilliard: 12.1.41 p. 7. Stockholm: 2.15.54 p. 5. Wiesbaden: 1.24.55 p. 11. Budapest: 4.23.56 p. 28. Glyndebourne: 11.5.56 p. 26. Florence: 3.4.57 pp. 10, 11.

Performing Companies. Approx 41; 1956–57 only: 295, 313, 329, 346, 371, 380, 395, 440, 447, 448. 5 (58–59).

📧 Der Zigeunerbaron · The Gypsy Baron

Music by Johann Strauss (1825–1899). Libretto in German by I. Schnitzer from a story by Maurus Jókai. Premiere: Vienna, October 24, 1885. English version by Maurice Valency for the Metropolitan Opera, 1959–60. Comedy. Set numbers and dialogue. Overture. Setting: the Austro-Hungarian monarchy, mid-18th century. Three acts (Metropolitan vers, approx 120 min).

ACT I: Road in front of Zsupán's house and Czipra's hut. ACT II: Gypsy camp by the ruins of an old tower. ACT III: Vienna (or often same as Act I).

158

Synopsis. Barinkay returns from exile to take possession of his father's lands. The gypsy Czipra prophesies for him a wife and a treasure. He asks for the hand of Arsena, the daughter of his neighbor Zsupán, a man who cannot read or write but who prides himself on breeding the finest swine in the country. Arsena, who is secretly in love with Ottokar, says she will not marry Barinkay until he becomes a baron. Led by Czipra, the gypsies swear loyalty to Barinkay as their liege lord. Barinkay now presents himself to Zsupán as a Gypsy Baron, but spurns Arsena's hand and declares he will marry Czipra's daughter Saffi. With her help he finds buried treasure, but Czipra's revelation that Saffi is of noble descent so upsets him that he joins the Hussars and gives his treasure to the fatherland. As he returns from the war, he is officially decorated and created a nobleman. His marriage to Saffi, originally entered into beneath the starlit sky with two nightingales as witnesses, is officially sanctioned by the court; all ends in happiness.

Major Roles. SANDOR BARINKAY, THE GYPSY BARON (strong lyr t); E♭2 to A3. CZIPRA, an old gypsy woman (m-s); B2 to A4 (or at least G4). SAFFI, reared as Czipra's daughter (dram s); C♯3 to C5 (opt D5), or at least B4. ARSENA (light or col s); D3 to C5 (or at least A4). KALMAN ZSUPAN (buf bar); highest notes can be transposed or omitted; D2 to A♭3.

Lesser Roles. OTTOKAR, in love with Arsena (light t); C2 to G3. COUNT PETER HOMONAY, recruiting officer for the Hussars (t; often sung by bs or bar); F♯2 to G3. CARNERO, Chairman of the Commission for Moral Decency (t, bar, or bs); C2 to E3. MIRABELLA, his wife (c); when aria is cut, only a bit part remains; G2 to E4.

Bit Parts. Several GYPSIES, depending on version (speaking).

Chorus. SSAATTBB. Peasants and gypsies.

Ballet. Opt in Act III.

Orchestra. 2 fl (picc), 2 ob, 2 cl, 2 bsn, 4 hrn, 2 trp, 3 trb, timp, bs drum, sn drum, harp, glockenspiel, strings.

Material. FS-P: Ka, Map (rent). CP: Map (g) (rent). VS: G Sc (e — Valency) (in prep). B & H (e — Martin) (in prep). Mead (Ha).

Photographs. Vienna: 2.28.49 p. 14. Metropolitan (sketches): 12.5.59 pp. 18, 20–22.

Performing Companies. 347 (7.7.55). 82 (56–57). 99 (56–57). 1957–58: 106A, 138A, 254A, 454A, 456A. 329 (59–60).

Short Operas

SHORT OPERAS

✒ Abu Hassan

Music by Carl Maria von Weber (1786–1826). Libretto in German, after a story from the Arabian Nights. Comedy. Set numbers, dialogue; strong Oriental flavor. Setting: Bagdad. One act (approx 55 min).

Synopsis. Abu Hassan, the favorite of the Caliph, has lived beyond his means and resorts to trickery to replenish his coffers. His wife, Fatima, aids him in a plot to make the Caliph and his wife, Zobëide, believe that one or the other has died, each receiving bounty. What they do not foresee is that the Caliph and his wife will both come at the same time to console the bereaved, thus discovering the deception. An old creditor of Abu Hassan's, Omar, becomes involved and is eventually the victim, being driven away while the Caliph forgives his favorite everything.

Roles. ABU HASSAN (t). OMAR (bs). FATIMA (s).

Speaking Roles. THE CALIPH, ZOBEIDE, MASRUR, Caliph's treasurer; ZEMRUD, Zobëide's confidential nurse.

Chorus. SATB.

Orchestra. 2 fl, 2 ob, 2 cl, 2 bsn, 2 hrn, 2 trp, trb, timp, perc, strings.

Material. FS-P: Ka, Ox (rent). VS: Ka (g) $8; Ox (rent). Tr: Balaban (T22); James Sutcliffe (Ka — in prep). David Harris (Ox), Li (Ox) $1.25.

Performing Company. 316 (3.17.61).

✒ Amahl and the Night Visitors

Music and libretto in English by Gian-Carlo Menotti (1911–   ) inspired by Hieronymous Bosch's painting "The Adoration of the Magi." Commissioned by the NBC-TV Opera Theatre. Premiere: NBC-TV Opera Theatre, December 24, 1951. Premiere stage version: Indiana University, February 21, 1952. A Christmas miracle. Arias, recitatives, ensembles. The set should show the interior of Amahl's cottage near Bethlehem and the fields outside with a suggestion of the star. One act (50 min).

Synopsis. The three kings, following the star to the newborn Christ, stop overnight with a poor woman and her crippled son, Amahl. Neighboring shepherds gather to bring food and to dance for the royal visitors. After the Kings are asleep the mother tries to steal some of their treasure to help her

163

boy. When the Kings magnanimously forgive her, Amahl offers his crutch as a gift to the Child, and goes off with the Kings on their pilgrimage, miraculously cured.

Roles. AMAHL (boy s); top A4. HIS MOTHER (m-s); top A4. KING KASPAR (t). KING MELCHIOR (bar). KING BALTHAZAR (bs).

Lesser Role. PAGE (bar).

Chorus. SATB. Shepherds.

Ballet. Three or more dancers, primitive folkdancing and folk ritual.

Orchestra. 2 fl, ob, cl, bsn, hrn, trp, harp, piano, perc, strings.

Production Note. ". . . anachronistic characters are seen in the paintings of Flemish and Italian primitives. Three kings magnificently clad; Balthazar and the Page are Nubian." (From the vocal score.)

Material. All G Sc. FS-P (rent). Two-piano score, stage guide (rent). VS $3.50. CP 60¢. Li 50¢.

Photographs. Santa Barbara: 12.31.56 p. 2. NBC-TV: 1.7.57 p. 32. *Mus. Amer.* 1.1.52 pp. 3, 10.

Performing Companies. Approx 258. 1956–57 only: 194, 274, 357, 370, 392, 397, 401, 405, 422, 431, 432, 438, 450, 453, 454, 459, 470, 482, 484, 489, 490, 492, 501, 504, 509, 518, 527, 530.

◪ Amelia al ballo · Amelia Goes to the Ball

Music and libretto in Italian by Gian-Carlo Menotti (1911–   ). Premiere: Curtis Institute, Philadelphia, April 1, 1937. Farce, satire on women's foibles. Continuous texture parodying grand opera; set numbers embedded; patter recitative. Prelude. Setting: a European city at the beginning of the century. One act: the boudoir of a young society matron (62 min).

Synopsis. Amelia is dressing for a ball when her husband storms into her boudoir, having found a letter from her lover. Amelia warns the lover (who lives upstairs) but cannot concentrate on his problems because of her anxiety to go to the ball. At last, frantic with frustration, she hits her husband over the head with a vase, summons the police chief, hands over her lover as the assailant, and sweeps off to the ball on the arm of the policeman.

Major Roles. AMELIA (lyr s); exacting role; flexibility; high tessitura; B2 to B4. THE HUSBAND (bar); high tessitura; G1 to E3. THE LOVER (t); top A3.

Lesser Roles. AMELIA'S FRIEND (m-s or c). CHIEF OF POLICE (bs). FIRST AND SECOND MAIDS (both s).

Chorus. SATB. Neighbors.

Orchestra. 3 fl, 2 ob, 2 cl, 2 bsn, 4 hrn, 3 trp, 3 trb, tuba, timp, perc, celeste, xyl, harp, strings. *Reduced vers*: 2 fl, ob, 2 cl, bsn, 2 hrn, 2 trp, trb, timp, perc, celeste, xyl, harp, strings.

Material. FS-P: Ri (rent). VS: Ri (i, e) $6. Tr: Mead (Ha).

Photographs. Curtis Institute: 2.21.38 cover; (sketch) 2.21.38 p. 2. San Remo: 1.9.39 p. 12. Central City: 10.29.51 p. 11. New Orleans: 11.14.55 p. 13.

Performing Companies. 441A (4.1.37 prem; 1.49). 329 (37–39). 166

(3.15.51). 82 (7.51). 140 (1.52). 375A (5.52). 447 (7.52). 179A (4.53). 373 (4.53). 475 (5.53). 6 (11.53). 411 (5.6.55). 179B (9.22.55). 404A (2. 23.56). 145 (5.18.56). 420 (7.6.56). 501 (10.10.56). 194 (11.57). 148 (11. 57). 60 (56–57).

🎭 L'Amore Medico · Doctor Cupid

Music by Ermanno Wolf-Ferrari (1876–1948). Libretto in Italian by Enrico Golisciani after Molière's "L'amour médecin." Premiere: Dresden, December 4, 1913. Comedy; a satire on the medical profession of the author's time. Simple harmonic structure; highly melodic; set numbers; accompanied recitative. Overture; Intermezzo before Act II. Setting: just outside Paris in the reign of Louis XIV. Two acts (90 min).

ACT I: A garden of Signor Arnolfo's villa near Paris. ACT II: A sumptuous room in the villa.

Synopsis. Arnolfo's entire household is sunk in gloom because of the mysterious illness of his daughter Lucinda, whom he has jealously tried to keep forever a child. She has been suffering from an unknown malady for two months, and no one seems able to cure her. Lucinda's companion Lisetta says that all she needs is a man, but Arnolfo refuses to allow his daughter to marry. He calls in four doctors, but none of them benefits Lucinda. Her secret lover Clitandro, however, presents himself disguised as a doctor and prescribes a mock marriage as the remedy. Naturally he hires a real notary; the marriage turns out to be real, and Arnolfo, perforce, agrees to give the couple his blessing.

Major Roles. ARNOLFO (bar); A1 to E3. LUCINDA (s); E2 to C5. CLITANDRO (t); Eb1 to A3. LISETTA (s); E2 to C5.

Lesser Roles. TOMES (bar), DESFONANDRES (bar), MACROTON (bar), and BAHIS (t), doctors. A NOTARY (bar).

Chorus. SSTB. Friends, servants.

Orchestra. 2 fl, picc, 2 ob, Eng hrn, 2 cl, bs cl, 2 bsn, 4 hrn, 3 trp, 3 trb, tuba, timp, perc, harp, celeste, strings.

Material. FS-P: G Sc (Wein) (rent). VS: G Sc (Wein – i, g) $12. Tr: Aveling (Wein). Li: G Sc (i, e) 50¢.

Performing Company. 343 (8.19.52).

🎭 Angélique

Music by Jacques Ibert (1890–   ). Libretto in French by Nino (Michel Weber). Premiere: Paris, January 28, 1927. Farce. Set numbers, dialogue, many ensembles. Brief prelude. One act: Exterior, houses on a waterfront (55 min).

Synopsis. Angélique quarrels with her old husband, Boniface, making his life miserable, breaking his china. He advertises her for sale. Three customers appear in turn — an Italian, an Englishman, and a Moor. But all demand their

165

money back. In despair, Boniface wishes her to the Devil, who promptly obliges. The bereaved husband and suitors forget their grievances and rejoice together, but all too soon the Devil also repents of his bargain — his establishment and his disposition are not proof against such a temper. Reluctantly Boniface takes back Angélique, who promises to behave. After the final celebration, the curtain rises again, and Boniface informs the public: "She is still for sale."

Major Roles. ANGELIQUE (s); florid with many skips; high tessitura; touches D♭5. BONIFACE, a china merchant (high bar); top F3.

Lesser Roles. FIRST COMMERE (s). SECOND COMMERE (m-s). CHARLOT, a servant (bar). AN ITALIAN (lyr t). AN ENGLISHMAN (t). A MOOR (bs). THE DEVIL (t).

Chorus. Neighbors who do not sing but speak in rhythm.

Orchestra. 2 fl, ob, cl, bsn, hrn, trp, trb, timp, perc, piano, strings.

Material. FS-P: Pr (Mer — Heu) (rent). VS: Pr (Mer — Heu — f) $7. Tr: Ezra Rachlin — typescript (Pr); Harris (T3).

Photographs. Juilliard: 10.25.48 p. 14. London: 10.16.50 p. 16. Hamburg: 1.17.55 p. 29.

Performing Companies. 32 (1.50). 137A (6.52). 358 (6.12.52). 254 (5.54). 389 (7.22.54). 524 (9.1.55; 8.56). 80 (56–57).

◪ Der Apotheker · The Apothecary

Music by Franz Josef Haydn (1732–1809). Libretto in German, adapted by Robert Hirschfeld from the play, "Lo Speziale," by Carlo Goldoni. Premiere: Esterhazy, 1768. Comedy. Highly melodious; set numbers over consonant accompaniment; recitative; several passages in "Turkish" style. No overture. One act: Sempronio's apothecary shop (50 min). Full-length vers, three acts (90 min) from Henle Publ. (Germany) given by Actors' Opera in New York, May 8,1961. Uses all material in Henle edition plus alternate aria for Grilletta given to Sempronio, love duet from Haydn's "Orlando Paladino," and extra recitatives, all added in Act III.

Synopsis. Mengone has entered the service of the apothecary Sempronio in order to be near the old man's ward Grilletta. His progress in wooing is slow, for Sempronio seldom leaves Grilletta alone. Another suitor, the rich young fop Volpino, tries to bribe Sempronio by promising him a post as the Turkish Sultan's apothecary. Sempronio accepts but, not wishing to meet the condition of Grilletta's marriage to Volpino, sends Mengone for a notary, thinking to marry her himself. Volpino enters, disguised as a notary; immediately afterwards Mengone perpetrates the same masquerade. Sempronio dictates the marriage contract, which each notary adapts to his own purpose. When the ruse is discovered, Volpino disappears, to return later disguised as the Sultan. When he attempts to carry off Grilletta, Sempronio protests, whereupon the false Turks begin to break up the shop. Mengone saves the situation and wins the frightened Sempronio's promise of Grilletta's hand. Volpino retires, baffled, and the "Turks" and neighbors join in the jubilation.

Roles. MENGONE (t); A♯1 to C4. GRILLETTA (s); needs trill; C3 to B4 (one C5). VOLPINO (m-s); A♯2 to A♭4 (one B♭4). SEMPRONIO (bs); G1 to G3. All have florid passages. In full-length vers, Sempronio is sung by a tenor, A1 to C4.

Chorus. B (unison). Turks. Touches D1 (D2 opt); needs trill; florid. SATB in finale.

Orchestra. fl, 2 ob, bsn, 2 trp, strings. *Full-length vers:* fl, 2 ob, 2 hrn, bsn, harpsichord, strings.

Material. FS-P: AMP, Map (rent). VS: AMP (UE − g) $4; Map (rent). *Full-length vers:* 293 (rent).　　　All Henle.

Performing Companies. 285A (5.28.48). 214A (52–53). 182 (3.25.56). 211 (56–57). 368 (7.10.56). 323 (10.19.59).

🎭 Arlecchino · Harlequin

Music and libretto in German by Ferruccio Busoni (1866–1924). Premiere: Zurich, May 11, 1917. Fantasy in commedia dell' arte style. Vocal line largely declamatory, occasionally melodious; set numbers; recitative; dialogue. Short prelude. Setting: Bergamo, Italy; 18th century. One act (70 min).

Synopsis. Arlecchino, or Harlequin, plays four parts: as a rogue, he makes love to the wife of Matteo, the tailor, while the latter is reading nearby. As a soldier, he recruits Matteo into the army. As a husband, he quarrels with his wife and attacks her lover. As a conqueror, he elopes with Matteo's wife just as the old tailor returns from the army.

Major Roles. (No special vocal problems.) COLOMBINA, Arlecchino's wife (m-s). SER MATTEO DEL SARTO, master tailor (bar). ABBE COSPICUO (bar). DOTTOR BOMBASTO (bs). LEANDRO, Colombina's lover (t). ARLECCHINO, needs acting experience (speaking).

Mute Roles. ANNUNZIATA, Matteo's wife. TWO SOLDIERS.

Orchestra. 3 fl, 2 ob, Eng hrn, 2 cl, bs cl, 2 bsn, cont bsn, 4 hrn, 4 trp, 3 trb, tuba, perc (2 players), timp, celeste, strings.

Material. FS-P: AMP (BH) (rent). VS: AMP (BH − g) $4. Tr: Dent (T1).

Photographs. Glyndebourne: 10.18.54 p. 20.

Performing Company. 389 (5.13.57).

🎭 Bastien and Bastienne

Music by Wolfgang Amadeus Mozart (1756–1791). Libretto in German by F. W. Weiskern, based on Marie Justine Benoite Favart's parody of Jean Jacques Rousseau's "Le Devin du Village." Premiere: Vienna, probably September 1768. Pastoral tale of 18th-century Europe. Arias, duets, one trio; recitative; dialogue. One act (35 min).

Synopsis. Bastienne, a shepherd girl, is in love with Bastien, but, as she complains to the magician Colas, he loves a wealthy girl. Colas advises her to arouse Bastien's jealousy. A lover's quarrel ends with reconciliation.

Roles. BASTIEN, a shepherd (t). BASTIENNE, a shepherdess (s). COLAS, a magician (bs).

Orchestra. 2 fl, 2 ob, 2 hrn, strings.

Material. Ka, Map, Ri (rent). VS: AMP (Sch − e) $3, (UE − e) $2.50; Map (rent); Ri (i, g) $2.50. Tr: Dunn (T4); Paul (Mar); Bartusek and Bair (T25); Weiler (T22).

Photographs. Greensboro, N.C.: 1.18.43 p. 28. Rock Hill, S.C.: 1.16.50 p. 15.

Performing Companies. Approx 25, including 376 (7.21.42). 394 (6.27.53; 5.15.54). 154 (2.54). 389 (11.20.55). 164 (12.7.55). 299A (3.11.56). 236A (5.8.56). 66 (6.8.56). 16 (7.56). 211 (8.24.56). 98 (56–57).

▨ Beauty and the Beast

Music by Vittorio Giannini (1903–). Libretto in English by R. A. Simon. Premiere: Columbia Broadcasting System, 1939. Fantasy based on the well-known fairy tale. Continuous texture, embodying several set numbers; melodious. One act, two scenes (60 min).

ACT I i: Father's home; ii: Garden outside the Beast's castle. Transitions can be made by lights.

Synopsis. Beauty's two selfish sisters plague their father for finery, but Beauty asks only for one red rose. The father finds the flower in the Beast's garden, but the Beast exacts Beauty's hand in exchange. After only a short time as his bride, she goes home, but dreams that the Beast is lonely, returns to comfort him, and finds him changed into a prince by her love.

Major Roles. THE FATHER (bar). BEAUTY (s). THE BEAST (t).

Lesser Roles. THE STORYTELLER (m-s or speaking). FIRST DAUGHTER (m-s). SECOND DAUGHTER (c). THE GARDENER (t). VOICES OFFSTAGE (2 t; 1 bs). Concluding ensemble enlists entire cast, others ad lib.

Orchestra. 2 fl, ob, 2 cl, bsn, 2 hrn, 2 trp, 2 trb, timp, perc, strings.

Material. FS-P: Ri (rent). VS: Ri $4.

Photographs. Hartt College: 4.22.46 p. 28.

Performing Companies. 326 (4.5.48). 499A (8.6.55). 304 (3.4.56). 225 (1959).

▨ The Bell Tower

Music by Ernst Krenek (1900–). Libretto in English by the composer, after a story by Herman Melville. Premiere: University of Illinois, March 17, 1957. Horror story. Continuous texture based on twelve-tone harmony; vocal line largely declamatory. Orchestral interludes between scenes. One act, three scenes (56 min).

ACT I i: Bannadonna's workshop; ii: The same, with the bell visible; iii: Interior of the bell tower.

Synopsis. Bannadonna, a mixture of genius and madness, casts a great bell for a city that already fears him, suspecting sorcery. Enraged when the work-

168

men wish to flee, Bannadonna kills his faithful assistant, Giovanni. The superstitious workmen believe Giovanni's blood has entered the alloy of the bell. Giovanni's daughter, Una, mourns him, but is drawn to Bannadonna and finally accepts his love. He smuggles her into the tower to witness his triumph as the bell first strikes, but when he boasts to townspeople that he has killed her father, she awakes from the spell he has cast upon her and makes an attempt on his life. Her own is the price; the wizard turns her to stone, to be the instrument first to strike the bell. Instead, she fells him with a mortal blow. And when the bell is struck at last, it breaks, to reveal human flesh in its composition, Una's face on its surface.

Major Roles. BANNADONNA (bar); some high tessitura; top F♯3. UNA (s); C♯3 to B4.

Lesser Roles. GIOVANNI (bar). SENATOR I (t). SENATOR II (bar). WORKMAN I (t). WORKMAN II (t).

Chorus. Scene i: TB. Scene iii: SATB.

Orchestra. fl, ob, cl, trp, trb, perc, piano, strings. *Stage:* 2 trp, trb.

Material. All B & H. FS-P, VS, CP (rent).

Photographs. Univ. of Illinois: 4.15.57 p. 15. *Mus. Amer.* Univ. of Illinois: 4.57 p. 8.

Performing Companies. 147 (3.17.57 – prem). 138 (56–57).

🏛 Blennerhasset

Music by Vittorio Giannini (1903–   ). Libretto in English by Philip Roll and Norman Corwin. Commissioned for the Columbia Radio Workshop. Premiere: CBS, 1940. Historical drama. A radio opera, but stage production possible. Continuous texture, embodying a few set numbers; melodious; small amount of dialogue. One act: a house on the mainland near the island of Blennerhasset, 1806 (approx 30 min).

Synopsis. Stephen, one of the followers of Aaron Burr in his conspiracy to create a new republic in the Southwest, gathers his forces on the island of Blennerhasset in the Ohio River near Parkersburg, West Virginia. He bids farewell to his fiancée, Madeleine, with a foreboding of doom. Madeleine discloses his rendezvous, believing that General Wilkinson means to bring Stephen and his men safely back; instead, it is Wilkinson who has betrayed Burr and set the militia on the Blennerhasset gathering. Stephen returns, wounded, and dies in Madeleine's arms. The conspiracy is foiled; Aaron Burr's cause is lost.

Major Roles. STEPHEN (t); top A3; one B♭3. MADELEINE (s); top A4, one B♭4 (one opt C5).

Lesser Roles. WILKINSON (bar). ANNE (m-s) and MRS. FIELD (c), wives of Stephen's colleagues. MESSENGER (t).

Orchestra. 2 fl (picc), 2 ob (Eng hrn), 2 cl, 2 bsn, 4 hrn, 2 trp, 2 trb, piano, harp, timp, perc, strings.

Material. All Ri. FS-P (rent). VS (rent).

Performing Companies. 390 (2.10.48). 373 (11.50). 380 (5.53).

⛝ Bluebeard's Castle

Music by Béla Bartók (1881–1945). Libretto in Hungarian by Béla Balász. Premiere: Budapest, 1918. Fantasy based on the fairy tale.
One act: Bluebeard's grim castle hall, with seven doors (66 min).

Synopsis. Judith, Bluebeard's fourth wife, reiterates her love for him even after entering his gloomy castle and discovering what lies behind six of the seven doors: a torture chamber, an arsenal, fabulous riches, a garden, a sunny and endless countryside, and grey waters swelled by mournful tears. But when she insists on opening the seventh door, her doom is sealed. Back into darkness she must follow the three former wives who emerge.

Roles. JUDITH (s or m-s); demands dramatic ability; generally low tessitura but with top A4's. BLUEBEARD (bs-bar). Both roles have difficult intervals against dissonant accompaniment. THE BARD (speaking). BLUEBEARD'S THREE FORMER WIVES (mute).

Ballet. In N.Y. City Opera vers, dancers appear as Bluebeard's wives and as symbols of what is behind doors.

Orchestra. 4 fl, 3 ob, 3 cl, 4 bsn, 4 hrn, 4 trp, 4 trb, tuba, timp, perc, 2 harp, celeste, organ, strings. *Stage:* 4 trp, 4 trb.

Material. All B & H. FS-P (rent). VS (g, h) $7.50. Li (Kallman) 40¢. Tr: Chester Kallman (B & H); Hassall (T5).

Photographs. N.Y. City Opera: 11.24.52 p. 2.

Performing Companies. 477 (1.8.49 – conc). 334 (10.2.52; 3.19.53). 127B (1.31.52 – conc). 232A (11.28.52 – conc). 398A (12.13.54). 154 (10.2.55). 73 (4.5.57). 444 (11.18.60 – conc). 477A (3.2.61).

⛝ The Boor

Music by Dominick Argento (1927–   ). Libretto in English by John Olon Scrymgeour, after the Chekhov play of the same name. Premiere: Eastman School of Music, Rochester, May 6, 1957. Musical and stage spoof. Style shifts with each change of the mood of the play. Setting: drawingroom of the widow's house in the country, about 1890. One act (55 min).

Synopsis. The old servant has almost succeeded in cheering his mistress, who has spent a year mourning her late husband, when a neighbor, the Boor, forces his way into her drawingroom, demanding payment for a debt – ironically, for oats her husband bought for the horse Toby, who conveyed the unfaithful man to many a rendezvous. Inimical at first, the wife refuses to pay; the Boor threatens to stay until she does. At last she goes to fetch her husband's pistols – she will challenge him to a duel. Impressed by her spirit, the Boor confesses that he has at this late date fallen in love again. He kneels at her feet, begging for her hand. With a few final threats to shoot, she relents, drops the pistol, and falls into his arms.

Roles. THE WIDOW, young and pretty (s). THE BOOR, middle-aged (bs-bar); a few florid passages; G1 to F♯3. THE SERVANT, an old man (t).

Orchestra. fl (picc), ob (Eng hrn), 2 cl (bs cl), bsn, 2 hrn, trp, piano, perc, strings.

Material. FS-P: B & H (rent). VS: $6.

Photographs. Rochester: 11.11.57 p. 18.

Performing Companies. 358 (5.6.57). 302 (3.18.58).

La Cambiale di matrimonio · Marriage by Promissory Note

Music by Gioacchino Rossini (1792–1868). Libretto in Italian by Gaetano Rossi. Premiere: Venice, March 11, 1810. Farcial comedy. Melodic; simple harmonic structure; set numbers; accompanied recitative. Overture. Setting: England, 18th century. One act: a room in Tobias Mill's house (approx 50 min).

Synopsis. Tobias Mill, an English merchant, anticipates the arrival in England of his American business associate, Slook, to whom he is in debt. Slook has also announced his willingness to marry anyone recommended by Tobias. Tobias plans to cancel his debt to Slook by giving him his daughter Fanny in marriage. Fanny, however, is in love with Edward Milfort, and they are upset when Norton, Mill's assistant, informs them of Slook's letter. Slook arrives and is captivated by Fanny. She and Edward try to dampen his joy by pointing out the horrors of matrimony. When Norton tells Slook that Fanny may be the "capital" he has been led to expect, he withdraws his offer. Learning that Fanny and Edward are in love, he decides to give Edward his note of credit against Tobias, who is enraged at this turn of events and demands satisfaction for his honor. The sight of his adversary cools him, however; Edward presents his claim for payment, and Tobias gives his daughter to him, while Slook basks in the happiness he has created.

Major Roles. TOBIAS MILL (buf bs); B1 to F3. FANNY (s); requires extreme agility and coloratura technique; D#3 to B4. EDWARD MILFORT (t); several difficult florid passages; D2 to G3. SLOOK (bs); high tessitura; requires facile articulation and flexibility; C2 to G3. NORTON (bs); C2 to Eb3. CLARINA (m-s); one aria with coloratura; E3 to G4.

Orchestra. fl, 2 ob, 2 cl, bsn, 2 hrn, strings.

Material. FS-P: Ri (rent). VS: Ri (i, e — Mead in prep).

Performing Companies. 324A (10.27.49). 317 (5.22.58).

Il Campanello · The Night Bell

Music by Gaetano Donizetti (1797–1848). Libretto in Italian by the composer. Premiere: Naples, June 7, 1836. Comedy. Recitatives, arias, duets, one trio. Brief prelude with chorus. Setting: Foria, a suburb of Naples, about 1835. One act (50 min).

Synopsis. An elderly Neapolitan apothecary, Don Annibale, marries young and pretty Serafina. Enrico, a gay young blade, plans revenge. Three times, as the old man is ready for bed, Enrico rings the bell that an apothecary may not ignore. First he simulates a Frenchman who demands wine; next, a singer who has lost his voice and needs lozenges; last, a doddering old man who lists his wife's illnesses ad infinitum. The opera ends as the dawn breaks and the bell is rung for the last time to announce the coach and horses which will drive Don Annibale to Rome, where his presence is needed to settle a will. He loses Serafina's dowry because the marriage has not been consummated in the time required by law.

Major Roles. DON ANNIBALE PISTACCHIO (buf bs); B♭1 to G3. SERAFINA (s); lyric, florid; C♯3 to G♯4 (one A4). ENRICO (bar); needs agility in wide range; trill on B♭3; G1 to B♭3 (falsetto E4 and A4). MADAMA ROSA, Serafina's mother (m-s); D♯3 to G♯4.

Lesser Role. SPIRIDONE (t).

Chorus. SATTB.

Orchestra. 2 fl, 2 ob, 2 cl, 2 bsn, 2 hrn, 2 trp, 3 trb, timp, strings.

Material. All Ri. FS-P (rent). VS (i) $10. Tr: Zytowski (30); McBride and Schaeche (66).

Performing Companies. 350 (5.22.57). 61 (56–57). 282 (1.16.58).

☙ La Canterina · The Songstress

Music by Franz Josef Haydn (1732–1809). Libretto in Italian. Premiere: for Count Esterhazy, 1767. Comedy. Highly melodious; set pieces; recitative has been replaced by dialogue. No overture. Two acts, one set: a room in the house of an 18th-century musician (35 min).

Synopsis. Gasparina and her duenna, Apollonia, make sport of their benefactor, the singing teacher Don Pellagio. Don Ettore, the merchant's son, steals his mother's jewels to give to Gasparina and wins her favor temporarily. Pellagio is infuriated when he hears the women mocking him immediately after he has proposed marriage to Gasparina. He summons the bailiff to put her out. But she faints so pitifully that he must forgive her. Ettore too contributes to her happiness — his mother's jewels.

Roles. GASPARINA (s); needs trill; several florid passages; D3 to B4. APOLLONIA (s); C3 to G4. DON PELLAGIO (buf t); B♭1 to B3. DON ETTORE (s or t). Haydn wrote this part in the soprano clef, but at the first performance a tenor sang it, probably in falsetto. Can be sung by a soprano or young boy or girl. Needs trill; C3 to A4.

Bit Parts. BAILIFF (mute). PORTERS (mute).

Orchestra. 2 ob, strings.

Material. All Pr (Mer – Heu). FS-P (rent). VS (e – Karl Geiringer) (rent).

Performing Companies. 127D (6.3.55). 154 (57–58).

☙ Cavalleria rusticana · Rustic Chivalry

Music by Pietro Mascagni (1863–1945). Libretto in Italian by C. Targioni-Tozzetti and G. Menasci after the story and play by Giovanni Verga. Pre-

172

miere: Rome, May 17, 1890. Tragic drama of common village folk. Set numbers woven into tightly knit texture; highly dramatic accompanied recitative; vocally taxing. Prelude; orchestral intermezzo. Setting: the square in a Sicilian mountain village; time, late 19th century. One act (68 min).

Synopsis. It is Easter morning. Turiddu, son of the innkeeper, Lucia, has abandoned Santuzza, with whom he had consoled himself for the loss of his former sweetheart, Lola. Lola had married Alfio during Turiddu's military service, but now is flirting again with Turiddu. Santuzza, rejected and jealous, informs Alfio of his wife's faithlessness. The famous Intermezzo proclaims the peace of Easter, shattered by Alfio's challenging Turiddu. The two men duel offstage, and a villager brings to Lucia the tragic news of her son's death.

Roles. SANTUZZA (dram s); needs dramatic force and vocal strength; top C5. TURIDDU (t), requires sustained power, high tessitura; top Bb3. LOLA (m-s). ALFIO (bar); demands flexibility; top F3 (one F#3, one Gb3). LUCIA (m-s or c).

Chorus. SSATTB, as large as possible.

Orchestra. 2 picc, 2 fl, 2 ob, 2 cl, 2 bsn, 4 hrn, 2 trp, 3 trb, bs tuba, timp, perc, 2 harp, strings. *Stage:* organ, harp.

Material. FS-P: Ha, Ka, Map, G Sc, TW (rent). CP: Ha, Ka, Map, TW (rent); G Sc (i, e) 75¢. VS: AMP (Son — i) $7; Ha (e — Mead), Map, TW (rent); G Sc (i, e) $4.

Photographs. Metropolitan: 1.27.41 p. 12; 2.23.48 p. 18; 2.16.51 p. 18; (Armistead) 4.2.51 p. 13; 4.8.57 p. 18; (Gérard) 1.29.58 pp. 18, 19. San Antonio: 3.31.52 p. 15.

Performing Companies. Approx 92; 1956–57 only 37, 39, 188, 215, 218, 221, 252, 253, 303, 313, 324, 329, 331, 341, 354, 449, 460, 471, 487, 517, 521.

🐓 Chanticleer

Music by Seymour Barab (1921–   ). Libretto in English by Mary Caroline Richards after a story by Geoffrey Chaucer. Premiere: Aspen, Colo., August 4, 1956. Comedy. Classical method and forms in romantic idiom with modern overtones. Set numbers. One act: A farmyard, on one side a cottage, on the other a henhouse; just before dawn (40 min).

Synopsis. The Widow wakens, and is dismayed not to hear the voice of her treasured rooster, Chanticleer, who is still under the influence of a terrible dream — a creature resembling a hound yet with a bushy tail has been stalking him. His wife Pertelote berates him for his foolishness and with the Widow begs him to sing the day in. The Fox, disguised as a hunter, comes to beg an egg from Pertelote, and tries to capture her in his butterfly net, but she is saved by the Widow's appearance. Chanticleer is not so lucky; the Fox's flattery traps him. In turn, he tricks his captor and brings him near enough to the Widow's broom for punishment. Chanticleer is a hero.

Roles. CHANTICLEER (t). PERTELOTE (s). WIDOW (m-s). FOX (bar).

Orchestra. fl, ob, cl, bsn, hrn, trp, trb, perc, harp, strings.

Material. All B & H. FS-P (rent). VS (in prep).
Performing Companies. 155 (7.11.57). 10 (1.22.58). 337 (4.21.58). 325 (4.28.58). 85A (4.1.59). 502A (11.12.60).

🎵 A Childhood Miracle

Music by Ned Rorem (1923–   ). Libretto in English by Elliott Stein after an idea suggested by Hawthorne's "The Snow Image." Premiere: New York, May 10, 1955. Fairy tale. Vocal line melodious; a few set numbers linked by melodic exposition; brief recitatives, dialogue. Brief prelude. One act: Garden in the wintertime, also the front parlor of house; any country during the past hundred years (40 min).

Synopsis. On a snowy winter day, Emma comes to visit her sister, who sits comfortably by the fire, complacent with her little family (the husband rather stern, the two teen-age daughters very imaginative). The father goes to town on an errand, and the two women sit gossiping by the fire. Peony and Violet, the daughters, revel in the snowstorm and build a snowman. They endow him with life: he is their brother. Impatient with Peony, the younger, Violet sends her away to build another snowman, and tells her "brother" her deepest secret — the terror she experienced at the funeral of her Aunt Elizabeth. Deeply absorbed, she does not notice her father's return. He hurries the girls into the house, despite their protests. Seated in front of the fire, the snowman expires. The two girls rush out into the storm. When their distraught parents find them, they are frozen into statues like their beloved "brother."

Roles. PEONY (s); several coloratura passages; top C♯5. VIOLET (m-s); needs flexibility. SNOWMAN (t); E1 to B♭3. AUNT EMMA (m-s). MOTHER (c). FATHER (bs-bar).

Orchestra. fl, ob, cl, bsn, 2 hrn, trp, perc, piano, string qt.

Material. FS-P: So (rent). VS: So (rent).

Performing Companies. 343 (5.10.55 – prem). 441A (2.56 – TV).

🎵 I Combattimento di Tancredi e Clorinda · The Duel between Tancred and Clorinda

Music by Claudio Monteverdi (1567–1643). Libretto in Italian, based on Torquato Tasso's verses 52–68, Canto XII of "Gerusalemme liberata." Premiere: Venice, 1624. Drama (called by Monteverdi a "madrigal"). Simple harmonic structure, dramatic recitative, no arias. No overture. Setting: the battlefield of the combat between Tancred and Clorinda in 1099. One act (25 min).

Synopsis. Testo, the narrator, describes how Tancred, a Christian knight, has fallen in love with the Saracen maiden Clorinda. Dressed as a man, Clorinda has led a successful attack on a Christian fortress. In revenge, Tancred has challenged her to mortal combat, believing she is a man. Clorinda accepts his challenge, and the two meet in combat as the music vividly describes the battle. Clorinda is finally run through by Tancred's sword, and she falls dying at his feet. She forgives him and asks Tancred to baptize her. When he lifts her visor, he sees his beloved, and he baptizes her as she sings of heavenly peace.

Major Roles. TESTO (t); the principal role; a few florid passages; C2 to G3. TANCRED (t); D2 to F♯3. CLORINDA (s); E3 to F♯4.

Orchestra. (Malipiero vers) string qt, cb, clavicembalo (or piano, harp, celeste in large hall). (Ghedini vers) harp, harpsichord, 3 vla, vcl, cb.

Material. FS-P: AMP (SZ — Ghedini vers) (rent); G Sc (Ch — Malipiero vers) (rent). VS: AMP (SZ — Ghedini vers — i) $3.50; G Sc (Ch — Malipiero vers; e — Peter Pears) (rent). O Tr: Harris (411).

Photographs. English Opera Group: 10.15.51 p. 12.

Performing Companies. 193 (11.16.54). 270B (4.29.55). 297 (3.15.55). 290A (6.17.55). 316 (3.4.56). 254 (6.15.56). 443 (56–57).

🎭 Comedy on the Bridge

Music by Bohuslav Martinu (1890–1958). Libretto in Czech after the play by V. K. Klicpera. English version by Walter Schmolka. Commissioned by Prague Radio. Premiere: Prague Radio, 1937. Zurich (stage premiere) 1952. Satire. Music is wryly satirical; continuous texture; a few set pieces. Short prelude. Setting: a bridge separating two warring armies; early 19th century. One act (35 min).

Synopsis. Five persons are trapped one by one as the sentries on either side let them onto the bridge but not off. Josephine, charming village coquette who has been searching for her brother, presumed killed in action, is first. Next, a brewer, who steals a kiss from Josephine and is surprised by Johnny, her fiancé, as well as his own wife. The ensuing quarrel is interrupted by the arrival of the schoolmaster, deeply perplexed by an unsolved riddle told him by his colonel. All of them forget their immediate troubles as the battle resumes. Suddenly comes victory; Josephine's brother is alive; the riddle has an obvious answer; everyone is happy.

Major Roles. JOSEPHINE (s). BEDRON, brewer (bs). NANCY, his wife (c). JOHNNY, Josephine's fiancé, fisherman (bar). SCHOOLMASTER (t).

Speaking Roles. Captain, soldier, sentry.

Orchestra. fl, ob, cl, bsn, 2 hrn, trp, trb, perc, timp, piano, strings.

Material. All B & H. FS-P: (rent). VS (g, e) $5.

Photographs. Mannes School: 10.29.51 p. 20. Venice: 11.12.51 p. 15.

Performing Companies. 290 (56–57). 389 (56–57).

🎭 Les Deux Avares · The Two Misers

Music by André Grétry (1741–1813). Libretto in French by Fenouillet de Falbaire. Premiere: Paris, 1770. Comedy. Very melodious; set numbers, recitative; dialogue; consonant harmonies. Overture. Two acts, one set: a square in Smyrna, with houses on three sides, a pyramid near one, a well in the center.

Synopsis. Gripon, a moneylender who has fled France for Turkey, bringing along his niece Henriette, lives opposite another miser, Martin, whose nephew Jérome loves Henriette. Martin devises a plan to secure the treasure he is sure was buried with the Mufti in a nearby pyramid, and admits the willing Gripon to his scheme. Both curse their young relatives: they may want to marry and demand an accounting of their inheritances. Jérome overhears a plot to kill him and decides to take action. But Madelon, Henriette's nurse and confidante, counsels caution. She obtains Gripon's keys and brings out his hidden fortune. While she is in the house searching for more, the lovers embrace so enthusiastically that the jewels and money fall into the well. Jérome goes after them, but just as the women are about to draw him up, the uncles appear. They force their way into the pyramid, but the only treasure is the hat and mantle of the Mufti, which Gripon throws into the well. He lowers the grill to the tomb, shutting Martin in, then is forced to hide in a window embrasure as some janissaries, drunk on forbidden wine, meet for their nightly patrol. Drawing up water to quench their inner fires, they are confronted with Jérome, dressed as the Mufti, and promptly scatter, knocking down the ladder on which Gripon ascended. Madelon takes advantage of the misers' plight to wring from them consent to the young couple's marriage and an admission that there are better things to cherish than gold and diamonds.

Major Roles. (All need agility for florid passages.) GRIPON (t); trill; top B3. MARTIN (bar); trill, high tessitura; top G3. HENRIETTE (s); trill; top B4, touches C5 and D5. JEROME (t); top A♭3.

Lesser Roles. MADELON (m-s). ALI, first janissary (bs).

Chorus. TTB. Mustapha, Osman, and other janissaries.

Orchestra. 2 fl, 2 ob, 2 cl, 2 bsn, 2 hrn, mandolin, strings.

Material. FS-P: Pet (Chou) (rent). VS: Pet (f) $5. Tr: Weiler (Ha).

Performing Company. 203A (4.10.53).

✠ The Devil and Daniel Webster

Music by Douglas Moore (1893–   ). Libretto in English by Stephen Vincent Benét, based on his story of the same title. Premiere: New York, May 18, 1939. Folk opera. Spoken dialogue, solos, and choruses. Setting: the home of Jabez Stone, Cross Corners, New Hampshire; the 1840's. One act (60 min).

Synopsis. Neighbors have assembled to celebrate the marriage of Jabez and Mary Stone. The guests sing of the happy couple and of the unaccountable new prosperity of the bridegroom, whose family had always been poor. The party becomes merry, there is squaredancing, with the fiddler calling the figures. The distinguished Daniel Webster, another neighbor, arrives and is hailed as New England's pride. An unexpected guest slips in, calling himself Scratch, a Boston lawyer. His coming puts the fiddle out of tune, and the merriment of the guests changes to anxiety. A lost soul, in the form of a moth, flutters out of a small box that Scratch carries, and thus the guests know

176

that Scratch is the Devil, come to claim Jabez, who has sold his soul for earthly success. A trial ensues. Webster volunteers to defend his old friend, Jabez; and Scratch conjures up a ghostly jury of long-dead rascals. Before this biased tribunal, Scratch almost triumphs, but Webster wins by appealing for the noble things that human beings cherish. The neighbors rush in for a merry charivari, drive Scratch out, and sing with pride of the great New England dish, pie for breakfast.

Major Roles. JABEZ STONE (bs); F1 to E♭3. MARY STONE (m-s or s); C3 to A4. DANIEL WEBSTER, Secretary of State (bar); B♭1 to G♭3. MR. SCRATCH (THE DEVIL) (t); E♭2 to A♭3.

Lesser Roles. CLERK (bar). VOICE OF MISER STEVENS (THE MOTH) (t). BLACKBEARD TEACH (bar), KING PHILIP (bar), SIMON GIRTY (bs), jurors.

Speaking Parts. A FIDDLER, JUSTICE HATHORNE, WALTER BUTLER.

Chorus. Neighbors — SATB(B). Jurymen — TB(B). Several solo parts.

Ballet. Several sets of squaredances.

Orchestra. 2 fl (picc), 2 ob (Eng hrn), 2 cl (bs cl), 2 bsn (cont bsn), 2 hrn, 2 trp, trb, harp, timp, perc, strings. A score for small orchestra is also available.

Material. FS-P: B & H (rent). VS: B & H $5. CP: B & H $1.

Photographs. Eugene, Ore.: 10.27.52 p. 19. Sturbridge, Mass.: 11.2.53 p. 8.

Performing Companies. 390 (5.2.49). 53 (3.51). 57 (6.51). 212A (11.1. 51). 289A (12.51). 432 (4.52). 112 (7.52; 5.53). 343 (7.52). 179D (3.53). 153 (5.13.53). 375 (5.53). 502A (5.53). 211A (7.53). 404A (5.6.54). 164 (5.13.54). 433 (5.19.54). 259 (7.16.54). 97C (8.24.54). 407 (3.10.55). 96A (5.14.55). 524 (9.1.55). 400 (5.19.56). 41 (56–57). 206 (56–57). 334 (4.5. 59).

⚰ The Devil Take Her

Music by Arthur Benjamin (1893–1960). Libretto in English by Alan Collard and John B. Gordon. Lyrics for Blind Beggar's Song and Drinking Song by Cedric Cliffe. Premiere: London, December 11, 1931. Fantasy. Melodic; vocal line patterned after speech; set numbers. Setting: London, 15th century. One act, with spoken prologue (60 min).

Synopsis. The scene is the livingroom of the Poet, opening onto the street. The Poet's beautiful wife has been speechless since birth. A famous surgeon comes to town and, at the Poet's urging, performs an operation that enables the wife to speak. At once she becomes a virago; she slaps the Doctor, drives out the neighbors, belabors the kitchen maid with a broom and reviles the Poet. Appeals are in vain, and at length the Poet, tried beyond endurance, cries out "The Devil take her!" Instantly the Devil appears, but he too is soon crying for help. The Poet gladly escapes with the Devil through a trap door, and the wife is left alone to explain the moral: "Be rather dumb than scold like me."

Major Roles. THE WIFE (m-s). THE POET (t); some florid passages. THE NEIGHBOR (bar). THE DOCTOR (bs). THE DEVIL (bs). The Doctor and the Devil can double. THE MAID (s).

Lesser Roles. FIRST WOMAN (s). SECOND WOMAN (m-s). THIRD WOMAN (c).
A SWEEP (bar). A BLIND BEGGAR (bar). DOCTOR'S FIRST ATTENDANT (bs).
DOCTOR'S SECOND ATTENDANT (s).

Bit Parts. WATCHMAN (bar). AN ORANGE SELLER (c). BIRD SELLER (mute).

Orchestra. 2 fl, 2 ob, 2 cl, 2 bsn, 4 hrn, 2 trp, 3 trb, tuba, timp, perc, piano,
strings.

Material. All B & H. FS-P (rent). VS: $3.75.

Performing Companies. 321 (2.13.41 — Amer prem). 309A (58–59).

◪ Dido and Aeneas

Music by Henry Purcell (1658–1695). Libretto in English by Nahum Tate,
based on Book IV of Virgil's "Aeneid." Commissioned by Josias Priest's School
for Young Ladies. Premiere: London, probably September, 1689. Classic
tragedy, containing every element of grand opera in its brief span: recitative,
arias, ensembles, choruses, ballet, and instrumental interludes. The music,
though of great dramatic intensity, is fairly simple in range and style, having
been designed for young girls. Prelude. Setting: Carthage, after the fall of
Troy. Three acts (approx 85 min; Dent vers 75 min).

ACT I i: The palace at Carthage; ii: The witches' cave. ACT II: The grove.
ACT III: The ships.

Synopsis. Dido, Queen of Carthage, falls in love with Aeneas, the Trojan
hero who has been cast on her shore after the fall of Troy. A sorcerer in the
guise of Mercury, messenger of the gods, informs Aeneas he must leave Dido
and go with his men to found Rome. Dido laments the loss of her love and
dies, brokenhearted.

Major Roles. DIDO, Queen of Carthage (dram s or m-s); powerfully descriptive dramatic role, sustained passages; C#3 to G4. AENEAS, Trojan hero, legendary founder of Rome (bar). BELINDA, lady-in-waiting (light s).

Lesser Roles. FIRST WOMAN (s). SECOND WOMAN (m-s). SORCERESS (m-s).
FIRST WITCH (s). SECOND WITCH (s). SORCERER, disguised as Mercury (s).
SAILOR (t).

Chorus. Two groups, each SATB, preferable, one for courtiers, the other
for witches and crowd in alternate scenes, joining in last scene.

Ballet. In all scenes; Dido's women, furies, witches, sailors. Division into
two groups preferable.

Orchestra. Strings, continuo part written out for piano or cembalo.

Material. FS-P: Ka, Ox (rent). FS: Br (e) $7.50. CP: Ox (SATB) $1.25;
(treble only) $1; (school chorus) 75¢. VS: Ox (Dent — e, g, with historical
notes and production suggestions) $2.50.

Photographs. Cheltenham: 10.15.51 p. 10. Sketch, Mermaid Theatre, London: 3.24.52 p. 31; 3.9.53 p. 4. Yale: 3.30.53 p. 14. Sarah Lawrence College:
4.26.54 p. 27. *Mus. Amer.* Boston Conservatory: 5.59 p. 35.

Performing Companies. 203A (3.50). 129 (11.5.50). 343A (1.52). 389
(2.52). 242 (5.52). 409A (5.52). 97A (2.53). 336 (3.53). 181A (4.53).
297 (4.54; 12.13.56). 53 (5.54). 32 (6.6.54). 474B (12.1.54). 186 (2.21.

55). 270C (3.22.55). 122A (4.28.55). 518 (5.20.55). 278 (6.12.55). 288A (4.21.56). 97D (4.30.56). 449B (5.10.56). 1956–57: 26, 52, 177, 205, 209, 219, 240, 248, 315, 337, 371, 468, 510.

✠ Don Perlimplin

Music by Vittorio Rieti (1898–   ). Libretto in Spanish after the play by Federico Garcia Lorca. Premiere: Chicago (conc), 1952; Paris (stage), 1952. Tragedy. Modernization of the traditional Italian opera; occasional set numbers embedded in continuous texture. No overture. Setting: Don Perlimplin's home in Spain; end of 18th century. Prologue: A square in front of Belisa's house; scene i: Bedroom in Don Perlimplin's house; ii: Don Perlimplin's diningroom; iii: Don Perlimplin's garden (65 min).

Synopsis. Rich Don Perlimplin marries young Belisa, but feels that she is not happy. He builds up an imaginary character, a lover who sends her flowers and poetry. Instead of revealing that he is the dream man, he kills himself because he cannot live up to the ideal.

Major Roles. (No special difficulties.) DON PERLIMPLIN (bs). WIFE, BELISA (s). MARCOLFA, housekeeper (m-s).

Lesser Roles. BELISA'S MOTHER (m-s). TWO SPRITES (may be dancers).

Orchestra. 2 fl, 2 ob, 2 cl, 2 bsn, 4 hrn, 2 trp, 2 trb, timp, perc, harp, celeste, strings. *Reduced vers*: fl, ob, 2 cl, bsn, 2 hrn, 2 trp, trb, timp, perc, harp, strings.

Material. FS-P: AMP (rent). VS: AMP (e – James Graham Luján) (rent).

Performing Companies. 24 (57–58). 316 (57–58). 317 (3.18.59).

✠ Don't We All?

Music by Burrill Phillips (1907–   ). Libretto in English by Alberta Phillips. Premiere: Rochester, April 1949. Comedy. Light, melodic, great emphasis on vocal line; informal pattern of solos and ensembles. Brief prelude. An unspecified setting just before Christmas in an unspecified year. One act: interior of a farm kitchen, in any style (28 min).

Synopsis. On a cold December night, Nell and Tom, snug in their farm kitchen, fall into an argument about who shall bar the door — Tom, who has settled down in comfort, or Nell, who is mixing her Christmas pudding. Thoroughly exasperated, they vow that whoever speaks first shall perform the small chore. In the midst of their silence their neighbors Amy and Ralph pay a visit. Noticing the tense atmosphere, they tease their hosts, bringing them to a pitch of fury. At last they depart. Tom and Nell are on the point of making up when Nell remembers that Tom spoke first and lost the wager. When you argue with a woman, he reasons, you lose — don't we all?

Roles. (No vocal problems.) NELL (c). TOM (bar). AMY (s). RALPH (t).

Orchestra. fl, ob, 2 cl, bsn, 2 hrn, trp, trb, piano, strings. P-Yes.

Material. C44.

Photographs. 10.31.49 p. 22. 1.16.50 p. 15.

Performing Companies. Approx 100, including 138 (1950). 172 (5.1.51). 502A (3.3.54). 17 (2.13.56).

The Door

Music by Irving Mopper (1914–). Libretto in English by Margaret Matthews Hordyk, based on the story, "The Sire de Maletroit's Door" by Robert Louis Stevenson. Premiere: Newark, December 2, 1956. Drama. Vocal line largely declamatory, with occasional melodic passages. Very brief prelude. One act: the Great Hall of the de Maletroit mansion in Paris, 1429 (50 min).

Synopsis. Alain, the Sire de Maletroit, learning that his niece, Blanche, is infatuated with a captain she has seen only in church, determines to disgrace her by marrying her to the first man that enters his door. The "victim" is a young soldier, Denis. Alain offers him the choice of marriage or hanging. Gallantly Denis intends to die, although he is smitten with Blanche. The girl, swallowing her pride, asks him to marry her. His pride, too, is quickly appeased. The two are locked in an embrace as Alain reappears, overjoyed at the success of his plot. The family priest blesses the union of the two young people.

Major Roles. ALAIN, SIRE DE MALETROIT (t); B♭1 to G3. DENIS DE BEAULIEU (bar); high tessitura; B♭1 to G♭3 (one G3). BLANCHE DE MALETROIT, Alain's niece (s); C3 to B♭4 (one C5).

Bit Parts. A PRIEST (bs). Several MEN-AT-ARMS (mute).

Chorus. Optional TTBB. Brief offstage passages (in French).

Orchestra. 3 fl, ob, 2 cl, 2–3 bsn, 4 hrn, 2 trp, 2 trb, tuba, timp, perc, harp, strings.

Material. C40.

Performing Company. 308 (3.19.57).

Double Trouble

Music by Richard Mohaupt (1904–1957). Libretto in English by Roger Maren, after Plautus's "Menaechmi." German text by Louis A. Bornemisza. Commissioned by the Louisville Philharmonic Society, Inc. Premiere: Louisville, December 4, 1954. Farce. Vocal line patterned largely after speech; a few ensembles. The time is undefined; the style of playing, commedia dell' arte, with masks. One set, a Mediterranean island street. One act with prologue, epilogue, and two choral interludes (65 min).

Synopsis. Hocus and Pocus, twin sons of Docus and Crocus, have been separated in youth, when Docus took Hocus on a "business" trip and lost him. Hocus has grown up, married Naggia, has a daughter, Cynthia, and is involved with the courtesan Erotia at the time Pocus arrives, seeking his long-lost brother. Pocus is, of course, mistaken for Hocus: first by Erotia, who asks him to repair a fur coat and diamond brooch Hocus has stolen from Naggia to give her; next by Cynthia and her lover, Lucio (son of Dr. Antibioticus), who secure his permission to marry, although Hocus has always refused; and finally by Naggia, who demands her coat and jewelry and drags him into the house. When the brothers finally come face to face, all is explained. Hocus bids Dr. Antibioticus auction off all his goods and keep Naggia for himself; whereupon he sets off with Pocus to return to their parents.

Roles. HOCUS (bs-bar); needs trill; A1 to F♯3; POCUS, his twin brother (bs-bar); G1 to E3 (one opt G3). NAGGIA, a shrewish type (m-s); A♭2 to A♭4. EROTIA (col s); flashy, seductive; florid, needs trill; D3 to B♭4 (one B4). CYNTHIA (s); D3 to A4. DR. ANTIBIOTICUS (buf t); D♭2 to B♭3. LUCIO (t); D2 to A3.

Chorus. SATB. Introduces action and comments ironically on it.

Orchestra. 2 fl (picc), ob (Eng hrn), cl (bs cl), bsn (cont bsn), 2 hrn, 2 trp, 2 trb, timp and perc (3 players), 2 piano, strings. Piano reduction by the composer.

Material. FS-P: AMP (rent). VS: AMP (e, g) $7.50.

Photographs. Kentucky Opera: 11.14.55 p. 19.

Performing Company. 176 (12.4.54 – prem).

♨ Down in the Valley

Music by Kurt Weill (1900–1950). Libretto in English by Arnold Sundgaard. Premiere: Indiana University, July 12, 1948. Folk drama. Simple vocal line can be performed by nonprofessionals; arias and ensembles; dialogue. One act (45 min).

Synopsis. The leader of the chorus, like his counterpart in Greek drama, introduces and explains the action of the plot. Brack Weaver is in jail for the murder of Thomas Bouché, but escapes to see his love Jennie. Flashbacks show the crime at the Shadow Creek Cafe, the church, and Jennie's home. Finally, assured that Jennie really loves him, Brack gives himself up to the posse.

Roles. BRACK WEAVER (t or high bar); top G3. JENNIE PARSONS (s). THOMAS BOUCHE (bs). THE LEADER (bar). THE PREACHER (bar). GUARD, PETERS, JENNIE'S FATHER, TWO MEN, TWO WOMEN (speaking).

Chorus. SSAATTBB.

Ballet. American folkdancing and squaredancing.

Orchestra. 2 fl, ob, 2 cl, 2 sax (alto and tenor), bsn, 2 hrn, 2 trp, 2 trb, guitar, piano, perc, strings (no violas). (Second flute, oboe, bassoon, and horns may be omitted.)

Production Note. "The physical production can be as simple as a 'dramatic' concert performance where the principals act their scenes in front of the chorus, without any help of scenery. If scenery is used, it should consist of simple painted frames, indicating the place of action (jail, porch, church, etc.), which are placed in front of the chorus." (Sundgaard.)

Material. All G Sc. FS-P (rent). VS $3. CP 60¢.

Photographs. Los Angeles City College: 10.31.49 p. 16. Pepperdine College: 12.28.53 p. 9.
Performing Companies. Approx 300.

🎵 The Dress

Music and libretto in English by Mark Bucci (1924–   ). Premiere: New York, December 8, 1953. Comedy. Melodious, with vocal line occasionally patterned after speech; a few set numbers, recitative, dialogue. Brief overture. Setting: a one-room apartment in the city, as simple or elaborate as desired; time, the present. One act (28 min).

Synopsis. While David is out of town, Vicki spends the rent money for a glamorous new dress whose most distinctive feature is a collar that fastens with a padlock. While modeling the dress for her neighbor Sylvia, she drops the key out the window. David returns unexpectedly, having misplaced his own keys. Vicki quickly conceals the dress under a robe. Discovering that David has found her key, she resorts to several ruses to recover it, but does not succeed until he has fallen asleep. The ordeal of telling him about her rash purchase is postponed till next day.

Roles. VICKI (s); needs flexibility, trill; D3 to C5. SYLVIA (s); B♭2 to F♯4. DAVID (bar); B♭1 to E3.
Orchestra. fl, ob (Eng hrn), 2 cl (bs cl), bsn, trp, perc, piano, strings.
Material. FS-P: MTI (Fra) (rent). VS: MTI (Fra) $3.50.
Photographs. Theatre Marquee, N.Y.: 12.29.58 p. 28.
Performing Companies. 313A (12.8.53 — prem). 444A (5.23.56). 154 (56–57). 400 (56–57). 254 (57–58). 183 (4.23.58).

🎵 Une Éducation manquée · An Incomplete Education

Music by Emmanuel Chabrier (1841–1894). Libretto in French by Eugene Leterrier and Albert Vanloo. Premiere: Paris, May 1, 1879. Comedy in the manner of "Candide." Set numbers, mainly in the form of couplets connected by dialogue. Setting: a small salon in the chateau of Count de Boismassif in the reign of Louis XVI. One act (45 min).

Synopsis. The young Count Gontran de Boismassif brings his bride home, unaccompanied by the two older members of the family whose advice it was customary to seek about marital matters. Gontran's grandfather sends a letter, saying that he did very well without specific advice. Hélène's aunt finally arrives, but as she is an old maid, her advice is of little help. Nature, in the shape of a friendly storm, brings the young couple to each other. The Count makes Hélène believe that they can chase away the thunder if they stay close together. Master Pausanias, who has gone out to seek help, finds that he is no longer needed.

Roles. GONTRAN DE BOISMASSIF (light t); easy tessitura; top B♭3. HELENE DE LA CERISAIE (light s); top A4. MAITRE PAUSANIAS (buf bs); needs flexibility; top F3.

Orchestra. fl (picc), ob, cl, bsn, hrn, trp, timp, perc, strings.
Material. FS-P: En (rent). VS: So (rent). Tr: Reese (T31). Dvorkin (BMI).
Performing Companies. 37B (12.2.52). 524 (8.53). 205 (8.53). 202 (9.53). 147 (4.54). 254 (5.30.54). 176 (10.28.54). 180A (12.10.54). 294 (1954). 322 (3.57). 350 (5.22.57). 57–58: 198A, 364, 501. 461A (4.13.59).

☙ L'Enfant prodigue · The Prodigal Son

Music by Claude Debussy (1862–1918). Libretto in French by E. Guinaud based on the parable in Luke 15. Premiere: Rome, 1884. Opera-cantata. Complex harmonic structure, impressionistic style; continuous texture; accompanied recitative and arias. Brief introduction. Setting: a village near the Lake of Gennesaret in biblical times. One act (30 min).

Synopsis. Lia mourns the absence of her son Azaël, who has left home and is wasting his life in riotous living. Simeon, her husband, chides her for giving way to grief and encourages her to join a group of village merrymakers to forget her sorrow. Azaël has returned home secretly. From his hiding place he watches his former friends dancing, and laments his wasted life. Exhausted and sick, he falls to the ground. Lia returns and at first does not recognize Azaël, but soon recognizes him as her long-lost son, and rejoices. Simeon enters with some happy villagers, welcomes his son, and bids wine brought and the fatted calf killed to celebrate Azaël's return. All give thanks to God and sing His praises.
Major Roles. LIA (s); C3 to B4. SIMEON (bar); C2 to F3. AZAEL (t); D2 to A3.
Chorus. STB. Village neighbors.
Orchestra. 3 fl, 2 ob (Eng hrn), 2 cl, 2 bsn, 4 hrn, 2 trp, 2 trb, tuba, timp, perc, 2 harp, strings.
Material. FS-P: El-V (Du) (rent). VS: El-V (Du – f, e – Nita Cox) $4. O Tr: Fattey (358).
Performing Companies. 43 (3.50). 439 (6.50). 429A (2.52). 435A (1.53). 140 (3.53). 296A (52–53). 205 (8.53). 138 (11.53). 358 (3.54). 254 (5.54). 180A (4.29.55). 16 (7.17.55 – conc; 7.56; 56–57). 287 (2.3.56). 503B (55–56). 17 (56–57). 337 (56–57).

☙ L'Enfant et les sortilèges · The Bewitched Child

Music by Maurice Ravel (1875–1937). Libretto in French by Colette. Premiere: Monte Carlo, March 21, 1925. Comic fantasy. Continuous texture, melodic; passages of witty and satirical brilliance. No overture. Difficult to stage because of the large number of inanimate objects which come alive and must be acted and sung. The setting is an old-fashioned Norman country house in the present. One act, two scenes without break (45 min).
ACT I i: The child's room; ii: The garden of the house.

Synopsis. A naughty child is scolded and punished by his mother for bad behavior. In a fit of temper, he kicks over the chairs and table and tears up his books. Suddenly, the objects he has treated so badly come to life. The fire refuses to warm him; a princess from his fairytale book emerges and tells him she is through with him. His chair refuses to let him sit down. A white and a black cat wander into the room and sing a charming duet in cat language. The child follows them out into the garden which is bathed in moonlight. Frogs are heard and several animals gather to tell the child how naughty he is. Terrified, the child calls for his mama; all the animals rush to attack him. In the fray, a squirrel is wounded, and the child bandages it. Impressed with his kindness, the animals join in a chorus and help him call to his mama.

Major Role. THE CHILD (m-s); D3 to G4.

Lesser Roles. MAMA (c). THE SHEPHERDESS (s). THE CHINESE CUP (c). THE FIRE (lyr s). THE PRINCESS (lyr s). THE WHITE CAT (m-s). THE DRAGONFLY (m-s). THE NIGHTINGALE (lyr s). THE BAT (s). THE SCREECH-OWL (s). THE SQUIRREL (m-s). A COUNTRY LASS (s). A HERDSMAN (c). THE ARMCHAIR (bs). THE CLOCK (bar). THE TEAPOT (t). THE BLACK CAT (bar). A TREE (bs). THE TREE FROG (t). THE LITTLE OLD MAN (t). (All may be doubled; the last two should be sung by the same singer.)

Chorus. SSAATTBB. Shepherds, herdsmen, tree frogs, animals, trees. Children: the Bench, the Sofa, the Stool, the Wicker Chair, the Numbers.

Orchestra. 3 fl, 2 ob, Eng hrn, 4 cl, 3 bsn, 4 hrn, 3 trp, 3 trb, tuba, timp, large perc, celeste, harp, strings.

Material. FS-P, CP: El-V (Du) (rent). VS: El-V (Du – f, e – Katherine Wolff) $9.

Photographs. Indiana Univ.: 1.16.56 p. 32. *Mus. Amer.* Juilliard: 4.57 p. 29.

Performing Companies. 148 (1955). 321 (3.22.57). 304 (56–57).

🎵 Escorial

Music by Marvin Levy (1932–   ). Libretto from Lionel Abel's English version of the play by Michel de Ghelderode. Commissioned by the "Music in Our Time" series, New York. Premiere: New York, May 4, 1958. Melodrama. Cyclic in form; vocal line mostly lyric recitative; a few melodic passages; dialogue. Orchestra evocative of the drama, unconventional harmony and sonorities. Brief prelude. One act: a sepulchral room in the palace of the Escorial in Spain (45 min).

Synopsis. The last of his unhealthy race, the half-mad King delights in dismal solitude. He has decreed that bells shall no longer toll, in spite of the monk's protest. His Queen has sought solace elsewhere, in the love of the court jester. Now she is dying, poisoned by her husband. The King baits the jester, who cannot rise to his usual sportiveness and who finally confesses his weariness and begs for pity. The King demands a farce. The jester frantically relates the story of the beggar made king, and snatches the crown from the King's head. Now they are both men. The jester almost strangles the King, who pretends to think the farce amusing and carries it further. Now deeper in each other's roles, they face the truth — the Queen has loved where no love is allowed. The farce plays itself out as the monk comes to announce the death of the Queen. Summoning the executioner and gloating as his powerful hands strangle the fool, the King laughs wildly — "A queen is not hard to find," he tells the monk in mock remorse, "but a clown . . ."

Major Roles. THE KING (bar); a portrait by El Greco, wan, sickly, and unkempt; a powerful role demanding a wide range of characterization; high tessitura; C2 to G♯3. FOLIAL, the jester (t); should be athletic, with twisted legs; top C4.

Lesser Role. THE MONK (bs); top D3.

Bit Part. EXECUTIONER (mute), dressed in scarlet, should appear to have huge, hairy fingers. Also several voices speaking offstage.

Orchestra. fl (picc), ob (Eng hrn), cl (alto sax), bsn (cont bsn), hrn, trp, piano, harp (celeste, organ), perc, string qt, cb. *Stage:* sound effects on tape, including bell, dogs, cannon.

Material. FS-P: B & H (rent). VS: B & H (in prep).

Performing Companies. 330A (5.4.58 — prem). 353 (57–58).

✎ The Fair at Sorochinsk

Music by Modest Mussorgsky (1839–1881). Libretto in Russian by the composer, based on an episode from Gogol's "Evenings on a Farm near Dekanka." Incomplete at composer's death; completed in several different versions by Cui and Tcherepnin. Premiere (in concert form): St. Petersburg, December 30, 1911. Revised, translated, and orchestrated version by Josef Blatt, uses only music intended by Mussorgsky, plus several passages from "Night on Bald Mountain" and two motives from "Red Jacket" (a demon, who is the subject of the gypsy's tale), compressed into two acts from the previous three. Folk comedy. Conventional harmonic structure incorporating folk idiom of Ukraine. Accompanied recitative, set arias and numbers. Introduction. Setting: the Ukraine; mid-19th century. Three acts (Blatt vers, two acts — 53 min).

ACT I: Marketplace of Sorochinsk (Blatt vers — 23 min). ACT II: Interior of Tcherevik's farmhouse (Blatt vers — 30 min). ACT III: (not in Blatt vers) Village square before Tcherevik's house (or a forest).

Synopsis. Tcherevik, a pots-and-pans salesman, brings his daughter Parassia to the fair for the first time. There she meets Gritzko, a wealthy young Cossack, who falls in love with her. Their betrothal is heartily approved by Tcherevik, but his wife Khivria, Parassia's stepmother, forbids the marriage. Alone, Gritzko is approached about buying a horse by Tzigane, the gypsy, who promises to help the Cossack wed Parassia. The lovers manage to hold a secret tryst. Khivria contrives to get her husband and stepdaughter out of their house in order to welcome her lover, Afanasi, the priest's son. The clandestine meeting is interrupted by a group of peasants, among them Tcherevik and Tzigane. Afanasi hides on top of the porcelain stove. The men drink wine, and Tzigane tells a fantastic tale of a devil (Red Jacket) who made love to a farmer's wife in Sorochinsk. The trembling Afanasi comes crashing down, illustrating the fable and giving himself away. Khivria's despotism is broken. (In the Tcherepnin version Gritzko goes to search for Parassia, who has wandered away. She is alone and despondent in the woods, and is about to end her life when the search party finds her.) Parassia and Gritzko are united, and all ends gaily in a hopak.

Major Roles. PARASSIA (s); romantic, lyrical line; C♯3 to A4. KHIVRIA (m-s); heavy, shrewish quality; B2 to G♯4. GRITZKO (t); C♯2 to B♭3. TCHEREVIK (bs); B♭1 to F♯3.

Lesser Roles. AFANASI (t). TZIGANE (bs). TCHEREVIK'S CRONY (bs); called compère in score. Latter two combined into one major role in Blatt vers. Additional in Blatt vers: TWO GUESTS (both t). TWO JEWS (both t). TWO GYPSIES (both bs).

Chorus. (Blatt vers) SSAATTBB. Young men and women, gypsies, merchants, Cossacks, etc.

Ballet. In finale of Blatt vers: folk-type dances.

Orchestra. (Blatt vers). 2 fl, 2 ob, 2 cl, 2 bsn, 2 hrn, 2 trp, trb, timp and perc (3 players), small string group.

Material. VS: G Sc (e — Blatt) (rent).

Photographs. Zurich: 3.30.53 p. 12.

Performing Company. 215 (56–57).

🎭 La Favola di Orfeo · The Fable of Orpheus

Music by Alfredo Casella (1883–1947). Libretto in Italian by "Poliziano" (Angelo Ambrogini). Premiere: Venice, September 6, 1932. Drama. Melodious; set numbers, recitative. Short overture. One act: antiquity (approx 40–45 min).

Synopsis. The story is the Orpheus legend with a different ending from that in other operatic versions. Orfeo, after losing Euridice the second time, curses women and is killed by the Bacchantes, who employ his severed head as the centerpiece of an orgiastic sacrifice to Bacchus.

Major Role. ORFEO (t); sustained, high tessitura; D2 to A♭3 (B3 opt).

Lesser Roles. EURIDICE (s). VOICE OF ARISTAEUS, young shepherd (bar); high tessitura; top F3. PLUTO (bs). DRYAD (m-s) and BACCHANTE (m-s), can be doubled. MERCURY (speaking).

Chorus. SA. Dryads and bacchantes (in pit).

Ballet. Bacchantes (female).

Orchestra. fl, ob, cl, bs cl, bsn, trp, trb, timp, perc, harp, strings.

Material. FS-P: B & H (Ca) (rent). VS: B & H (Ca — i, g) $6. Tr: Reese (T31); P. P. Fuchs (178).

Performing Company. 178 (11.12.57).

🎭 Gallantry

Music by Douglas Moore (1893–   ). Libretto in English by Arnold Sundgaard. Premiere: New York, March 19, 1958. A "soap opera," satire on

186

present-day television, also a spoof on grand opera. Set pieces, recitative, dialogue. No overture. Should be performed with complete seriousness. One setting, a television studio with a doctor's operating room set on one side, the commercial on the other. One act (35 min).

Synopsis. This is a dramatic moment in the daily soap opera's eternal suspense. Dr. Gregg, the eminent surgeon, declares his long-suppressed love for anesthetist Lola at an inopportune moment — just before an operation. The patient is none other than Donald, whom Lola truly loves. As he goes under the anesthetic, Donald inquires after the health of Gregg's wife. Lola, righteously indignant because the doctor has not seen fit to divulge the fact of his marriage, spurns his advances, while Donald lies breathing heavily. It is obvious that Dr. Gregg cannot be allowed to operate on Lola's beloved. Frantically, she revives Donald and sends for another surgeon. The story is naturally interrupted several times for commercials.

Roles. ANNOUNCER (m-s); seductive type; B♭2 to E♯4. DR. GREGG (bar), no longer young; B1 to F3. LOLA (s), young and lovely; D3 to G♯4 (two A4, one B4). DONALD (t); D2 to G♯3.

Ballet. Billy Boy Girls, three dancers.

Orchestra. 2 fl, ob, 2 cl, bsn, 2 hrn, 2 trp, trb, perc, harp, strings.

Material. FS-P: G Sc (rent). VS: G Sc $3.50.

Performing Companies. 302 (3.19.58 — prem). 187 (57–58; 8.7.58). 395 (57–58). 225 (8.20.58). 47 (11.19.58). 481 (1.28.59). 259 (2.4.59). 16 (58–59). 185 (11.8.59).

🎵 A Game of Chance

Music by Seymour Barab (1921–   ). Libretto in English by Evelyn Manacher, suggested by the play, "All on a Summer's Day," by Florence Ryerson and Colin Clements. Premiere: Rock Island, Ill., January 11, 1957. Comedy. Set numbers, recitative, over orchestra using satirical dance rhythms and other expressive devices; dialogue. Short overture. One act: A garden; the present (35 min).

Synopsis. A Representative, the eternal messenger of fate, brings to each of three young women her dearest wish — to one a fortune; to the second, fame; to the third, love. Each discovers she has not asked for enough: the rich woman misses real friends; the famous author yearns for love; the matron finds marriage an unending chore. Even the Representative is dissatisfied: he needs an assistant in his tough job. The moral: we all want too much or too little.

Roles. FIRST NEIGHBOR (lyr s); needs trill, agility; C3 to C5. SECOND NEIGHBOR (s); C3 to G♯4. THIRD NEIGHBOR (m-s); G2 to F4 (A♭4 opt). THE REPRESENTATIVE (bs-bar); G1 to E3.

Orchestra. 2 fl, 2 ob, 2 cl, 2 bsn, 2 hrn, timp, perc, strings.

Material. FS-P: B & H (rent). VS: B & H $4.50.

Performing Companies. 145 (1.11.57 — prem). 237 (5.3.57). 374 (6.28.57). 241 (4.17.58). 325 (4.28.58). 289B (4.10.59). 88A (8.13.59).

📀 Gianni Schicchi

Music by Giacomo Puccini (1858–1924). Libretto in Italian by Gioacchino Forzano, suggested by a passage in Dante. Part of a "triptych" which includes "Suor Angelica" and "Il Tabarro." Premiere: New York, December 14, 1918. Comedy. Highly melodious; set numbers with fully developed recitatives giving impression of continuous texture; many ensembles. Short introduction. Setting: the bedchamber of Buoso Donati's house, Florence, 1299. One act (48 min).

Synopsis. Buoso Donati has died and left his considerable estate to charity. His grasping relatives, deeply shocked, decide to accept Rinuccio's advice and ask help of Gianni Schicchi, a well-known local rogue and the father of Rinuccio's sweetheart Lauretta. Schicchi's approach is direct: the deceased is removed and Schicchi takes his place in bed. When even the doctor is fooled, the delighted relatives call in a notary to hear "Donati" make a new testament. The delight turns to helpless rage, however, as the resourceful Schicchi wills the bulk of the old man's property to himself. He chases them all out of his newly acquired house, all except, of course, his son-in-law to be, Rinuccio, who remains with Lauretta in their future home.

Major Roles. LAURETTA (lyr s); young, innocent; D♭3 to B♭4 (opt D♭5). RINUCCIO (t); high tessitura; D2 to B3. GIANNI SCHICCHI (buf bar); A1 to G3. ZITA, Buoso's cousin (m-s); A♭2 to A♭4.

Lesser Roles. GHERARDO, Buoso's nephew (t). NELLA, Gherardo's wife (s). BETTO, Buoso's cousin (bar). SIMONE, Buoso's cousin (bs). MARCO, Simone's son (bar). LA CIESCA, Marco's wife (s). MASTER SPINELLOCCIO, physician (bs). AMANTIO DI NICOLSO, notary (bs).

Bit Parts. GHERARDINO, son of Gherardo and Nella (m-s or boy). PINELLINO, shoemaker (bs). GUCCIO, dyer (bs).

Orchestra. 2 fl, picc, 2 ob, Eng hrn, 2 cl, bs cl, 2 bsn, 4 hrn, 3 trp, 3 trb, bs trb, timp, perc, harp, celeste, bells, strings. *Reduced vers:* 2 fl, ob, 2 cl, bsn, 2 hrn, 2 trp, trb, timp, perc, celeste, bells, harp, strings.

Material. FS-P: Ri (rent). VS: Ri (i, e — Grossman) $6.50. O Tr: Blatt (215); NBC-TV (333); Ann and Herbert Grossman (Ri); Rachleff (T17).

Photographs. Metropolitan: 2.7.44 p. 12; 3.7.49 p. 18; 1.14.52 p. 18. Chautauqua: 1.8.45 p. 13. Univ. of Texas: 3.14.49 p. 11. Univ. of Louisville: 10. 29.51 p. 22. Florence: 2.20.56 p. 12.

Performing Companies. Approx 43, including 1956–57 only 8, 80, 115, 321, 373, 387, 471, 482, 495.

📀 Hello Out There

Music by Jack Beeson (1921–   ). Libretto in English by William Saroyan, from his play of the same title. Premiere: Columbia University, New York, May 27, 1954. Contemporary tragedy in modern idiom. Continuous texture; dialogue (also over music); accompanied recitative; a few set numbers. No overture. One act: cell in the jailhouse, Matador, Texas; the present (40 min).

Synopsis. A vagrant Young Man, imprisoned in a small-town jail for raping another man's wife, strikes up a conversation with the jail's cook, a local girl in her teens, and attracts her strongly. Afraid that he will be attacked in the deserted jail by the offended Husband, the Young Man sends the Girl home to get her father's gun. While she is away the Husband and a group of his friends appear. The Young Man reveals that the wife is a slut, but the incredulous Husband shoots him. The Girl returns as the angry mob carries off the Young Man's body.

Major Roles. GIRL (s); young, naive; C3 to B♭4 (opt C5). YOUNG MAN (bar); appealing quality; B♭1 to F♯3.

Lesser Roles. HUSBAND (t). ANOTHER MAN (speaking). WIFE (speaking). THIRD MAN (mute).

Orchestra. fl (picc), ob, cl, bsn, hrn, trp, perc, piano (harmonium), string quintet (can be enlarged).

Material. FS-P: Mi (rent). VS: Mi $6.

Photographs. Peabody Institute, Baltimore: 3.18.57 p. 32.

Performing Companies. 302 (5.27.54 — Amer prem). 254 (5.20.55; 4.17. 56). 447 (7.55). 193 (1956).

▉ L'Heure espagnole · The Spanish Hour

Music by Maurice Ravel (1875–1937). Libretto in French by Franc-Nohain. Premiere: Paris, May 19, 1911. Comedy. Complex harmonic structure; highly melodic; continuous texture. Brief introduction. Setting: Toledo, Spain; 18th century. One act: the clock shop of Torquemada (50 min).

Synopsis. Torquemada, an absent-minded clockmaker, is reminded by his wife, Concepcion, that it is Thursday and time for him to wind all of the government clocks. She usually takes advantage of this weekly absence to entertain her lovers. Ramiro, a muleteer who has entered the shop to have his watch repaired, is left behind with Concepcion, who is annoyed because she expects an admirer. When Gonzalve arrives, she quickly hides him in a grandfather clock and asks Ramiro to carry it to her room. Don Inigo, a banker and admirer of Concepcion, also comes for a tryst, and he too is hidden in a clock. A switch of clocks effects a change in lovers, and a farcical situation results. Meanwhile, Concepcion has begun to admire the virile Ramiro, and she takes him to her room. When Torquemada returns, she explains that Gonzalve and Inigo are merely customers, and he sells them each a clock. He chooses to overlook his wife's indiscretions, and they all sing a sparkling quintet.

Major Roles. CONCEPCION (s); B♯2 to B4. GONZALVE (t); D♯2 to C4. TOR-QUEMADA (t); D♯2 to A3. RAMIRO (bar); C2 to G♯3. DON INIGO (bs); G1 to F3.

Orchestra. 3 fl, 2 ob (Eng hrn), 3 cl, 2 bsn, 4 hrn, 2 trp, 3 trb, tuba, timp, perc, 2 harp, celeste, strings.

Material. FS-P: El-V (Du) (rent). VS: El-V (Du — f, e — Katharine Wolff) $9. O Tr: Simon (321), Levin (T26).

Photographs. N.Y. City Opera: 1.30.56 p. 30 (sketch). *Mus. Amer.* N.Y. City Opera: 10.52 p. 3.

Performing Companies. 334 (1952). 156 (7.22.53). 176 (1953). 441 (3.6.54). 368 (56–57).

🎭 Hin und Zurück · There and Back

Music by Paul Hindemith (1895–   ). Libretto in German by Marcellus Schiffer. Premiere: Baden-Baden, July 17, 1927. "Sketch with music," a tour de force which depends for effect on its construction. Halfway through, the action reverses itself, and the music correspondingly reverses the order of its themes, while avoiding the complications of a crab canon. The music is in various styles, but brilliantly unified. Prelude. Setting: a contemporary living-room. One act (12 min).

Synopsis. Helen comes in to have breakfast near her deaf aunt, who is knitting. She pours tea and sings of her joy in the lovely morning. Her husband, Robert, enters with a birthday present for her. The maid brings her a note which she hides. Robert demands to know who wrote it. She finally confesses it is from her lover, whereupon he shoots her. The aunt uses her ear trumpet too late to hear, and goes back to her knitting. Robert jumps out the window. A doctor and an orderly remove Helen's body. Then a bearded sage rises through a trapdoor, saying that it matters little if a man lives from cradle to grave, or if he dies first and follows from death to birth. The action reverses itself: Robert jumps in the window; Helen's body is carried back, and so on to the Aunt's first sneeze.

Major Roles. ROBERT (t); D2 to Ab3. HELEN (s); a few florid passages; needs trill; D3 to Ab4.

Lesser Roles. A BEARDED SAGE (t); B1 to Gb3. DOCTOR (bar). ORDERLY (bs). AUNT EMMA (mute). MAID (speaking).

Orchestra. fl, cl, Eb alto sax, bsn, trp, trb, piano – 2 hands, piano – 4 hands. *Stage:* harmonium.

Material. FS-P: AMP (Sch) (rent). VS: AMP (Sch – g, e – Marion Farquhar) $3.25. O Tr: Hammond (T22).

Photographs. Hartt College: 11.9.42 p. 22. Los Angeles City College: 11.10.58 p. 17.

Performing Companies. 432 (1949). 389 (2.52). 321 (2.53). 164 (5.53). 270D (5.53). 127C (6.53). 140 (11.53). 10 (3.54). 179A (4.1.54). 225 (7.54). 202 (7.27.54). 138 (2.14.55). 468 (3.14.55). 178 (11.18.55). 233 (11.19.55). 327 (12.7.55). 193 (1956). 529A (2.26.56). 186 (4.20.56). 496 (57–58).

🎭 L'Histoire du soldat · The Soldier's Tale

Music by Igor Stravinsky (1882–   ). Libretto in French by C. F. Ramuz. Premiere: Lausanne, September 28, 1918. Tragicomedy to be read, played, and danced. Chamber orchestra of paramount importance; complex harmonic structure; dissonant. No overture. Two acts, usually played in five scenes (30 min).

ACT I i: The edge of a stream; ii: The soldier's village; iii: Scene with narrator. ACT II i: The palace; ii: At the edge of the village.

Synopsis. The narrator begins his tale. A soldier lurches in with his knapsack. The Devil offers him a book on the secret of success in exchange for his violin and invites him to be his guest for three days. The soldier accepts, putting himself in the Devil's power. The soldier returns to his village, but no one recognizes him. Disguised as a beggar, the Devil appears again with a knapsack resembling the soldier's. The narrator tells the soldier to get the Devil drunk and lose at gambling with him in order to go free. The soldier, seeing a proclamation that whoever can cure the king's daughter can marry her, rushes to the palace. By playing his violin, he cures the princess, and they embrace. But the Devil knows that the soldier is safe only as long as he does not cross the border. As he steps across the frontier, the Devil seizes his violin and fastens on his prey.

Major Roles. No singing roles. THE READER (speaking). THE DEVIL, THE SOLDIER, THE PRINCESS (mimes or dancers).

Orchestra. vln, cb, cl, bsn, cornet-à-pistons, trb, timp.

Material. FS-P: G Sc (Che) (rent). VS: G Sc (Che – f, e, g) (rent). Tr: Michael Flanders and Kitty Black (G Sc); Newmarch (G Sc).

Photographs. Aspen: 11.1.54 p. 30. N.Y. City Opera: 11.19.56 p. 9.

Performing Companies. 193 (4.22.52; 11.16.54). 358 (7.15.54; 56–57). 80 (8.15.54; 56–57). 446A (11.8.54). 353 (12.18.54; 56–57). Also 1956–57: 94, 199, 326, 327, 334, 348, 416, 482, 497.

▶ In a Garden

Music by Meyer Kupferman (1926–   ). Libretto in English by Gertrude Stein. Premiere: New York, December 29, 1949. A fable. Parodies elements of grand opera; melodious; vocal line largely mock declamation and recitative over unconventional harmony with the effect of satirical pomp. Very brief prelude. One act: a garden suitable to a Gertrude Stein fable. The only indispensable property is a rack in the rear, from which hang kitchen and garden implements (15 min).

Synopsis. Lucy Willow, a young girl with a dream, pretends she is a queen. Each of two boys, Philip, sentimental, and Kit Raccoon the First, self-assertive, begs her to be his queen. She doubts if they are kings. They prove it by donning crowns. This leads her to doubt if she is a queen, but she soon reassures herself. Still, she is in a quandary. The two kings decide to fight for her hand, and equip themselves with garden and kitchen tools. They kill each other. Now Lucy has two crowns and knows how lovely it really is to be a queen.

Roles. LUCY WILLOW (s); top Bb4. PHILIP HALL (t); needs some agility; top G3. KIT RACCOON THE FIRST (bar); low F♯1 (F♯2 opt).

Orchestra. fl, ob, cl, bsn, hrn, trp, trb, timp, perc, harp, strings.

191

Material. FS-P: Pr (Mer) (rent). VS: Pr (Mer) $2.75.

Photographs. Emporia: 2.16.53 p. 7.

Performing Companies. 294 (12.29.49 – prem; 6.14.50; 1956; 56–57). 15 (11.52). 150 (4.51). 164 (5.52). 338A (2.53). 441 (6.54). 225 (7.54). 124A (10.27.54). 472A (4.30.56). 368 (7.7.56). 337 (57–58).

◪ Le Jeu de l'amour et du hasard · The Game of Love and Chance

Music by Pierre Petit (1922–   ). Libretto in French by Charles Clerc, after a play by the same name by Marivaux. Premiere: Paris, July 3, 1946. Lyric comedy. Several ensembles, but not a "set number" opera; neo-classic dissonance, yet conventional. Suited for young singers, though music is sophisticated. Setting: a Parisian salon, about 1730. One act (25 min).

Synopsis. Sylvia, a bored young noblewoman, decides to change places with her maid, Lisette. A stranger is announced as Bourginon, valet to Dorante. He and Sylvia become interested in each other, whereupon he reveals that he is really Dorante. The maid enters and declares that she and the true valet have also discovered a reciprocal interest.

Roles. SYLVIA (s); not difficult, touches top of range only once (D3 to Bb4). LISETTE (s); range is the same as Sylvia's, but part is not so exacting, nor tessitura so high. DORANTE (t); light and lyric; some sustained passages could be sung by bar; Bb2 to G3.

Orchestra. fl, picc, 2 ob, 2 cl, bs cl, 2 bsn, 2 hrn, 2 trp, trb, timp, celeste, harp, sn and bs drum, strings.

Material. All Pr (Mer – Heu). FS-P (rent). VS (f) $5.50; (f, e – Feist) $5.50.

Performing Companies. 16 (1954, 1955, 1959). 302 (56–57).

◪ The Jumping Frog of Calaveras County

Music by Lukas Foss (1922–   ). Libretto in English by Jean Karsavina, after the story by Mark Twain. Premiere: University of Indiana, Bloomington, May 18, 1950. American idiom unselfconsciously employed; set numbers. One act, two scenes (45 min).

Scene i: Uncle Henry's saloon; ii: Village square.

Synopsis. A mustachioed stranger challenges Smiley's jumping frog, Daniel Webster. Left alone, the stranger feeds Dan'l with buckshot while the boys are outside laying bets. In the square, the stranger makes up to Lulu, and the local boys are jealous. Needless to say, Dan'l is defeated in the great jumping match. After the stranger has left with all the money, Dan'l's extra weight is discovered; he is upended and disgorges the buckshot. The crapshooters rush off to bring back the stranger, their money is restored, and Lulu smiles once more on Smiley.

192

Major Roles. SMILEY (t). UNCLE HENRY (bar). LULU, Uncle Henry's niece (m-s). THE STRANGER, a roving gambler (bs).

Minor Roles. CRAPSHOOTERS (t and bs). GUITAR PLAYER (bar).

Chorus (opt). SATB, TTBB, unison. Townspeople.

Orchestra. fl, ob, 2 cl, bsn, hrn, 2 trp, trb, tuba, perc, piano, strings.

Material. All Fi. FS-P (rent). VS $4.

Photographs. Univ. of Alabama: 2.20.56 p. 31.

Performing Companies. 294 (6.50). 389 (2.4.51). 53 (3.51). 156 (7.51). 32 (3.52). 140 (3.53). 164 (5.53). 179C (5.53). 87 (7.53). 397 (11.5.54). 41 (1.25.55). 475 (2.3.55). 8 (4.22.55). 468 (12.8.55). 378 (55–56). 159 (2.9.56). 449 (10.56). 59 (56–57).

⚑ Let's Build a Town

Music by Paul Hindemith (1895–   ). Libretto in German by R. Seitz (English by George List). Premiere: 1931. A play for children intended for experience rather than entertainment. Number of participants and duration optional.

Synopsis. All the children decide to build a brand new town. Two groups perform different functions: building the houses, laying streetcar tracks, etc. A stranger asks what sort of people come to the town. The children tell him: all kinds, and they come in all conveyances and from everywhere. They name their own occupations; they gossip; they play cops and robbers — they are all children; the grownups take second place. Even the traffic cop is a child.

Orchestra. Number of instruments opt, with a minimum of 3 — 1 high part, 2 lower. Additions may double outer parts in octaves; percussion may also be added.

Material. FS-P: AMP (Sch) (rent). VS: AMP (Sch – e) $1.25.

Performing Company. 288 (4.19.56).

⚑ A Letter to Emily

Music by Lockrem Johnson (1924–   ). Libretto in English adapted by the composer from the play "Consider the Lilies," by Robert Hupton. Premiere: Seattle, April 24, 1951. Revised vers, prem: Interlochen, July 26, 1951. Drama; an incident in the life of the poetess Emily Dickinson. Set numbers, recitative, arias, ensembles, small amount of accompanied and unaccompanied dialogue. Vocal line patterned after speech inflections; interpretative style indicated by composer as "similar to that of the art song." Brief overture; intermezzo before ii. Setting: the Dickinson home in Amherst, Mass., the morning and afternoon of August 16, 1870. One act, two scenes (35–40 min).

Synopsis. Emily Dickinson, living quietly in Amherst, has had some correspondence with Colonel Higginson in Boston, to whom she has sent several of her poems unbeknown to her tyrannical, overbearing father. Colonel Higginson comes to call and invites Emily to Boston. Her own introverted nature prompts her to refuse, although her sister urges her to mingle with the famous men and women there. Her sensitivity is irreparably wounded when the colonel reveals a fundamental lack of appreciation for her true quality as a poet. With her father's taunts ringing in her ears, Emily retires further into her introspective imagination.

Roles. EMILY DICKINSON (lyr s); C3 (one Bb2) to A4 (one Bb4). LAVINIA, her sister (m-s); Ab2 to F♯4. MR. EDWARD DICKINSON, her father (bs-bar); Gb1 (opt F1) to E2 (falsetto to G4). COLONEL HIGGINSON, her adviser and critic (bar); A1 to E3. (Note: All voices with possible exception of Mr. Dickinson's should be relatively light and lyric.)

Orchestra. fl, cl, string qt, piano (opt cb). P-Yes.

Material. FS-P: Pr (Mer) (rent). VS: Pr (Mer) (rent).

Performing Companies. 511A (4.24.51 — prem). 225 (7.26.51 — revised vers). 400 (5.16.53). 333A (10.26.54). 338 (1.25.55). 404 (4.56).

☙ The Little Harlequinade

Music by Antonio Salieri (1750–1825). A comedy intermezzo from ACT III of the opera, "Azur, King of Ormus" (libretto in Italian by Giambattista Casti; premiere: Vienna, January 8, 1788), which was rewritten from the original opera, "Tarare" (libretto in French by Pierre Augustin de Beaumarchais; premiere: Paris, August 6, 1787). In the present adaptation by Fritz Schröder the Introduction is taken from the second theme of the overture to "Azur"; the accompaniment to the concluding Vaudeville Canon is from C. G. Neefe's piano reduction. Simple and melodious. Setting: an interior, or a formal garden in the rococo period. The style is commedia dell' arte. One act (12 min).

Synopsis. Harlequin and Brighella, both suitors for Columbine's hand, agree to draw straws to determine the winner. When, however, the straws are presented by Columbine in the guise of an old witch, both men refuse. Columbine is happily rid of them, warning them to look beneath the surface for true worth.

Roles. COLUMBINE (s). HARLEQUIN (t). BRIGHELLA (bar). All wear domino costumes and half-masks. Columbine carries a fan; the men, wooden swords. No vocal problems.

Orchestra. Orig: 2 fl, 2 ob, 2 bsn, 2 hrn, timp, strings. Also arranged for strings only.

Material. P: AMP (Sch) $7.50. VS: AMP (Sch — e — Greta Hartwig) $2.

Performing Companies. 321 (52–53). 321B (6.3.55). 368 (6.25.55). 178 (11.18.55). 282 (56–57). 404 (56–57).

☙ The Little Sweep · Let's Make an Opera

Music by Benjamin Britten (1913–   ). Libretto by Eric Crozier. Premiere: Aldeburgh, England, June 1949. "The Little Sweep" is the final section, the "opera" of the entertainment for young people called "Let's Make an Opera," a play which illustrates the preparation and rehearsal of an opera. Professionals or gifted amateurs are essential for adult roles, real children for children's parts. Set numbers and ensembles; dialogue. Four songs are to be sung by audience and must be rehearsed. Music retains atmosphere of simplicity although sophisticated rhythmically and harmonically. Setting: the children's nursery of Iken Hall, Suffolk; time, 1810. Three scenes (40 min).

Synopsis. Eight-year-old Sam has been sold to a brutal pair of chimney sweeps, who take him to a job in Iken Hall. The children of the house and their visiting cousins from Woodbridge befriend the boy, without the knowledge of the housekeeper, but with the help of the visitors' nurserymaid. They bathe and feed him and finally bundle him off in a trunk to Woodbridge, which is also his home.

Major Roles. SAM (boy s). MISS BAGGOTT, housekeeper (c). JULIET BROOK, age 14 (s). GAY BROOK, 13 (boy s). SOPHIE BROOK, 10 (s). ROWAN, Woodbridge nurserymaid (s).

Lesser Roles. BLACK BOB, sweep-master (bs). CLEM, his son and assistant (t). Double with TOM, coachman (bs). ALFRED, gardener (t). JONNY CROME, 15 (boy s). HUGH CROME, 8 (boy s). TINA CROME, 8 (s).

Orchestra. Solo string qt, piano (4 hands), perc (1 player). Arr for piano duet in VS. String parts are difficult.

Material. All B & H. FS-P (rent). VS $5. Audience participation songs 15¢.

Photographs. Aldeburgh: 11.14.49 p. 16. Ithaca College: 10.29.51 p. 20.

Performing Companies. 415A (1.15.51). 289A (3.51). 439 (4.51). 164 (11.51). 249A (3.53). 110A (4.53). 247 (5.53). 259 (3.19.54). 518 (4.10. 54). 198A (5.20.54). 30 (56–57). 90 (56–57). 480 (56–57).

⚄ The Loafer and the Loaf

Music by Henry Leland Clarke (1907–   ). Libretto in English by Evelyn Sharp. Premiere: Los Angeles, May 1, 1956. Fantasy. Continuous texture; melodious; many ariosos; occasionally suggestive of English folkdance; consonant harmony with occasional asperities and modal passages. Short overture. One act: a street in a "city that never was" (45 min).

Synopsis. The Loafer steals a loaf from the Baker's Boy's cart and is caught by the Prosperous Citizen. The Poet's Wife comes to his defense — he may be a poet. She herself supports her Poet, which the Prosperous Citizen thinks a disgrace. She also steals a loaf, which the Prosperous Citizen eventually reclaims. The Baker's Boy denounces him as a thief to the Watchman, whose insistence on "evidence" over logic and truth leads everyone to accusation and counter-accusation and results in utter confusion. The Loafer settles it: "If [the Prosperous Citizen] had not stolen my loaf before I ever set eyes on it, I should not be hungry now." The Poet's Wife embraces him — this Poet is her husband after all. The innocent Baker's Boy is about to be made the scapegoat but pacifies everyone with creamcakes.

Roles. (No problems of range.) BAKER'S BOY (s). LOAFER (t). PROSPEROUS

195

CITIZEN (bar). POET'S WIFE (m-s). WATCHMAN (bs). MINSTREL (mime), should seem to play the flute.

Ballet. Entire performance can be choreographed.

Orchestra. fl (picc), ob, cl (bs cl), trp, trb, 2 vln, vcl, cb. P-Yes (can also be performed with fl and piano).

Material. All ACA: FS-P, VS (rent).

Performing Company. 47 (5.1.56 — prem).

🖤 Lord Byron's Love Letter

Music by Raffaelo de Banfield (1922–   ). Libretto in English by Tennessee Williams. Premiere: New Orleans, January 19, 1955. Lyric drama. Vocal line patterned after speech; one aria. Short overture. The scene is New Orleans in the late 19th century. One set, a parlor in a faded house in the French Quarter, with a scene of the Acropolis behind a scrim. One act (70 min).

Synopsis. An old lady, living with her spinster granddaughter, possesses a letter from Lord Byron and a diary which she shows to tourists for money. A couple enter, the woman eager to see the letter but dominated by her husband, who cares only for the more obvious charms of the Mardi Gras. The spinster shows the letter and reads from the diary about the day her grandmother met the poet on the steps of the Acropolis. This scene is acted out partly in pantomime behind a scrim. The old woman sings the familiar phrases to the point of rhapsody, but her passion finds no echoes in the visitors. They depart unceremoniously to see a parade, leaving no money. The gaiety of the Mardi Gras passes the two recluses by. The spinster believes for a moment that she has found romance as a stray young man bursts in at the door, but he moves on quickly. "You have dropped your grandfather's letter!" the old woman exclaims.

Major Roles. OLD WOMAN (dram s or m-s); B♭2 to B♭4 (one B4). SPINSTER (s), a woman of 40; demands character acting; some high tessitura; B2 to B4.

Lesser Roles. THE MATRON (c). THE HUSBAND, middle-aged, slightly drunk (t).

Bit Parts. YOUNG MAN (mute). Pantomime: MIDDLE-AGED WOMAN (c); YOUNG GIRL (s); HANDSOME YOUNG MAN (LORD BYRON) (mute), can be dancer; can double with YOUNG MAN.

Orchestra. 3 fl, 3 ob, 2 cl, 2 bsn, 4 hrn, 3 trp, 3 trb, tuba, timp, perc, celeste, harp, strings.

Material. All Ri. FS-P (rent). VS $5.

Photographs. Chicago: 1.2.56 p. 33 (sketch).

Performing Companies. 180 (1.19.55 — prem). 130 (11.21.55).

🖤 The Lowland Sea

Music by Alec Wilder (1907–   ). Libretto in English by Arnold Sundgaard. Premiere: Montclair State College, N.J., May 1952. Folk drama suggested

196

by sea stories and songs. Melodious, simple structures, songs, ensembles, and dialogue. Designed for college and community groups. The scene shifts from land to shipboard by means of lighting and groupings and very simple properties. Only production requirements are a table, a bench, and two chairs. The main scene is Scarlet Town, about 1845. One act (55 min).

Synopsis. Dorie Davis loves the sailor, Johnny Dee, who must always sail away. Faithfully she waits until news comes that his ship has gone down with all hands. After a year, she yields to the pleas of Nathaniel, a widower with several children, and marries him. But Johnny is still alive: he had been put off the ship ill with malaria. He returns to find his love married but still in love with him. He sails away again.

Major Roles. DORIE DAVIS (s or m-s); Bb2 to Ab4 (A4 opt). JOHNNY DEE (bar); A1 to F#3. NATHANIEL HAZARD (t); Eb2 to F3. CAPTAIN JESSE, captain of the *Scarlet Sail* (bs-bar); A1 to C3.

Lesser Roles. HANNAH (m-s or s). BELINDA (s). Speaking Roles: AMOS, SHIP'S DOCTOR, NATHANIEL'S CHILDREN (if three boys, ABRAHAM, ISAAC, and MORDECAI; if three girls, DELIGHT, PATIENCE, and SUBMIT).

Chorus. SSATTBB. Townsfolk, sailors. Men should dance simple hornpipe.

Orchestra. fl, ob, 2 cl, bsn, 2 hrn, 2 trp, 2 trb, timp, perc, piano (and/or harp), strings.

Material. FS-P: G Sc (rent). VS: G Sc $3.

Photographs. Ithaca College: 11.2.53 p. 21.

Performing Companies. Approx 84; 1956–57 only 28, 40, 54, 63, 79, 143, 183, 247, 249, 250, 261, 272.

▶ Malady of Love

Music by Lehman Engel (1910–   ). Libretto in English by Lewis Allen. Premiere: New York, May 27, 1954. Light comedy. Melodic; set pieces, recitative; small amount of dialogue; parodies of various dance forms. No overture. One act: a psychoanalyst's office (26 min).

Synopsis. Emily Brown comes to consult young Dr. Barlow. She is disturbed: her dreams reveal a preoccupation with the opposite sex – at a cocktail party the glasses turn into men; she is a scantily dressed electric sign and the doctor, another sign, drinks an old-fashioned in a toast to her; she is Eve in the Garden of Eden and the doctor is the Serpent; next she is back at the party and an ice cube changes into a man. Now it is the doctor's turn to be disturbed. Emily confesses what is plain to everyone but him: she loves him. It is mutual, and they agree to combine their libidos.

Roles. DR. STANLEY BARLOW (bar). EMILY BROWN (s). Two dancers resembling the singers mime the dream sequences.

Orchestra. fl, cl, trp, hrn, trb, drums, piano, string qt. 2 P-Yes (rent).

Material. FS-P: Fl (rent). VS: Fl $3.

Performing Companies. 302 (5.27.54 – prem). 447 (5.11.56). 180A (57–58). 225 (6.30.59). 237A (11.24.58).

🎵 Les Malheurs d'Orphée · The Sorrows of Orpheus

Music by Darius Milhaud (1892–   ). Libretto in French by Armand Lunel, adapted from Greek mythology. Premiere: Brussels, May 7, 1926. Romantic tragedy of pastoral nature. Recitatives, set arias, and ensembles in neo-classic style; some dissonance. No overture. Setting: unspecified country village; unspecified time. Three acts (45 min).

ACT I: Outskirts of a country village. ACT II: Sheltered spot in a forest. ACT III: Orpheus' house and pharmacy in the village.

Synopsis. Orpheus has deserted his neighbors to live in the woods with his animal friends, whom he comforts and nurses to good health. Now he returns to his village to await the arrival of his bride, Eurydice. A gypsy, Eurydice has been warned by her people against marrying Orpheus, but defies them and goes to live with him in the woods. Eurydice falls ill, and Orpheus laments that all his scientific knowledge cannot cure her. She asks to be buried in the woods and begs the faithful animals to continue their devotion to Orpheus. Eurydice dies vowing that she and Orpheus will meet again. The animals carry her off to a shady spot, as she requested. Orpheus returns to the village and busies himself in his apothecary shop, but continues to mourn for Eurydice. Her three gypsy sisters appear to berate Orpheus. Finding no peace on earth, he sees a vision of Eurydice and welcomes the end of his torment. As he dies the sisters finally recognize that he truly loved their sister.

Major Roles. EURYDICE (lyr s); sweet, flowing quality; D3 to B4. ORPHEUS (bar); high tessitura; light, lyrical line; Bb1 to F#3.

Lesser Roles. FARRIER, blacksmith (t); WHEELWRIGHT (bar); BASKET WEAVER (bs), villagers. FOX (s), WOLF (c), BOAR (t), BEAR (bs), animal friends of Orpheus and Eurydice. TWIN SISTER (s), SECOND SISTER (m-s), OLDER SISTER (c) of Eurydice, gypsies.

Orchestra. fl, ob (Eng hrn), cl, bs cl, bsn, trp, timp, perc, harp, solo strings.

Production Note. Four animal costumes.

Material. FS-P: Pr (Mer) (rent). VS: Pr (Mer) $6. Tr: Aron (Pr – Mer); Charles C. Cushing (24).

Photographs. Mus. Amer. Hunter College: 6.58 p. 17.

Performing Companies. 340 (5.10.54). 317 (5.22.58). 364 (57–58). 47 (3. 16.59). 24 (5.14.59).

🎵 Les Mamelles de Tirésias · The Bosom of Thérèse

Music by Francis Poulenc (1899–   ). Libretto in French by Guillaume Apollinaire, from his early 20th-century play. Premiere: Paris, June 3, 1947. Farce. Continuous texture primarily in declamatory style; a few set ensembles; dialogue. Setting: an imaginary town on the French Riviera between Nice and Monte Carlo, about 1910. Prologue, entr'acte and two acts (50 min).

PROLOGUE: Before an inner curtain. ACT I: Main square of Zanzibar. ENTR'-ACTE: Before the inner curtain. ACT II: Same as Act I with numerous cradles added.

198

Synopsis. This opera has no consistent plot: it is a series of sketches with the battle of the sexes as general theme. In the Prologue the Manager attempts to explain the play's significance. In Act I Thérèse deserts her Husband to become a male. She dresses herself as a man and her Husband as a woman. A pair of drunkards, Lacouf and Presto, argue and kill each other in a duel. A gendarme comes to investigate, and courts the Husband, thinking him a woman. He is soon enlightened. The Husband declares he will make children if his wife will not. In Act II the Husband, with the aid of an incubator, has produced thousands of children in a single day. He tells a reporter of the successful careers of several of the offspring. He "makes" a son who turns out to be a blackmailer. The gendarme complains of a food shortage owing to the sudden increase in population. The Husband suggests feeding the people with cards (ration cards). The gendarme thinks he means playing cards. Thérèse appears as a card-reader, having become a woman again. She and the Husband are reunited, and all the participants urge the audience to go and have children.

Major Roles. THERESE and CARD-READER (s); high tessitura; Cb3 to D5. HUSBAND (bar); needs high falsetto, high tessitura; A1 to A3. GENDARME (bar); needs high falsetto; G1 to G3. MANAGER (bar); A1 to G3.

Lesser Roles. NEWSPAPER SELLER (m-s). ELEGANT WOMAN (m-s). LARGE WOMAN (m-s). PRESTO (bar). LACOUF (t). NEWSPAPERMAN (t). SON (bar). BEARDED MAN (bs).

Chorus. SSAATTBB. Citizens of Zanzibar, newborns. Citizens dance in entr'acte.

Orchestra. 3 fl, 2 ob (Eng hrn), 2 cl, bs cl, 3 bsn, 4 hrn, 3 trp, 3 trb, tuba, timp, perc, 2 harp, piano, strings.

Material. All Pr (Mer). FS-P (rent). VS $13.50. Tr: (Goss).

Photographs. American Opera Society: 4.8.57 p. 15.

Performing Companies. 212 (6.13.53 – Amer prem). 297 (56–57; 59–60).

✄ The Marriage

Music by Bohuslav Martinu (1890–1959). Libretto in German by the composer, after Gogol. Premiere: NBC-TV, February 7, 1953. Comedy. Music is often highly satirical; vocal line mostly patterned after speech; small amount of melody; dialogue; no special vocal problems. Setting: St. Petersburg in the early 19th century. Two acts (75 min).

ACT I i: Podkolyosin's bachelor apartment; ii: Agafya's livingroom. ACT II i: Agafya's room; ii: Podkolyosin's apartment.

Synopsis. Podkolyosin, a government official, is of two minds about getting married. The matchmaker Fyokla introduces him to Agafya, a merchant's daughter, who soon dismisses her other suitors in his favor. At the last moment he yields to fright and jumps out the window, escaping matrimony – at least for the time being.

Major Roles. PODKOLYOSIN (bar). FYOKLA IVANOVNA (m-s). AGAFYA (s); needs flexibility.

199

Lesser Roles. STEPHAN, Podkolyosin's servant (speaking). KOCHKARYOV, Podkolyosin's friend (t). ARINA, Agafya's aunt (s). DUNYOSHKA, her maid (speaking). Three suitors of Agafya: IVAN, a government official (bs); ANUCH-KIN, a retired army officer (t); ZHEVAKIN, a retired naval officer (t).

Orchestra. 2 fl, 2 ob, 2 cl, 2 bsn, 2 hrn, 2 trp, tuba, timp, perc, piano, strings.

Material. All B & H. FS-P (rent). VS (e, g) (rent).

Performing Companies. 333 (2.7.53 — prem). 83 (5.26.56).

ᴟ Mavra

Music by Igor Stravinsky (1882–   ). Libretto in Russian by Boris Kochno, after Pushkin's "The Little House in Kolomna." Premiere: Paris, June 3, 1922. Comedy of rustic Russia. Set numbers, arias, and ensembles based on native themes. One act: livingroom of a relatively comfortable village family in early Russia (25 min).

Synopsis. Vasili, a young hussar, makes love to his neighbor, Parasha, unbeknown to her mother, who is preoccupied with the loss of a cook. Parasha disguises her lover; the new "cook" is welcomed rapturously and introduced as Mavra to the mother and a gossipy neighbor. Mavra begins to shave in order to maintain the deception, but is surprised by the mother, and flees. Parasha is left without her Vasili.

Roles. PARASHA (lyr s); D3 to B4. THE NEIGHBOR (m-s); B2 to G4. THE MOTHER (c); A2 to D4. THE HUSSAR (t); C2 to B3.

Orchestra. 2 fl, picc, 2 ob, Eng hrn, 3 cl, 2 bsn, 4 hrn, 4 trp, 3 trb, tuba, timp, strings (10).

Material. FS-P: B & H (rent). VS: B & H (f, g, e — Craft) $7.50. O Tr: Mead (Ha).

Photographs. Univ. of Illinois: 2.16.53 p. 4.

Performing Companies. 202 (11.51). 338A (2.53). 225 (7.54). 129B (5. 12.55). 468 (7.12.55). 156 (7.20.55). 68 (56–57).

ᴟ Médée · Medea

Music by Darius Milhaud (1892–   ). Libretto in French by Madeleine Milhaud, based on Greek legend and the play of Euripides. Premiere: Antwerp, October 7, 1939. Classic tragedy. Polytonal; continuous texture; vocal line patterned after speech. Brief prelude. Setting: Corinth in the classical past. Three tableaux, nine scenes (approx 60 min).

TABLEAU I: A square in Corinth before the palace of Creon and the house of Medea. TABLEAU II: The den where Medea prepares her sorceries. TABLEAU III: Same as I.

Synopsis. Medea, wife of Jason, is endowed with supernatural powers, which she has used to help her husband secure the Golden Fleece. They have fled to Corinth, where Jason has deserted Medea for Creusa, daughter of King Creon. As the opera opens, Creusa is preparing for her marriage to Jason. Creon tells Medea she must leave Corinth, for he fears her terrible vengeance.

200

Medea begs him to let her have her two children for a brief time before she leaves. At last he relents. When Jason appears, Medea upbraids him for his ingratitude. She invokes Hecate, spirit of evil, to assist her vengeance and prepares a poisoned robe which she sends to Creusa as a wedding gift. The robe burns Creusa to death; Creon dies also while attempting to save his daughter. As a last act of revenge, Medea slaughters her children and reveals them to the devastated Jason.

Major Roles. MEDEA (s); several difficult sustained dramatic passages; C3 to B♭4. CREUSA (s); F♯3 to B4. CREON (bar); B1 to F3. JASON (t); E2 to B♭3.

Lesser Role. NURSE (c); A2 to F3.

Chorus. SSAATTBB. Men and women of Corinth, used as in Greek tragedy to comment upon the action.

Orchestra. 2 fl (picc), 2 ob (Eng hrn), 2 cl, bs cl, E♭ alto sax, 2 bsn, cont bsn, 2 hrn, 3 trp, 3 trb, tuba, timp, perc, harp, strings.

Material. FS-P: Pr (Mer − Heu) (rent). VS: Pr (Mer − Heu) $7.50.

Photographs. Brandeis Univ.: 12.5.55 p. 14.

Performing Company. 212 (6.11.55).

✄ The Medium

Music and libretto in English by Gian-Carlo Menotti (1911–   ). Commissioned by the Alice M. Ditson Fund of Columbia University. Premiere: New York, May 8, 1946. Melodrama. Melodic, simple harmonic structure; continuous texture embodying several set pieces; dialogue. Short prelude. Setting: outside a large city; the present. Two acts (75 min).

ACT I: A squalid room in a flat. ACT II: The same.

Synopsis. Madame Flora (Baba) is a charlatan medium who uses her daughter Monica and a mute gypsy boy, Toby, to assist in her frauds. One night during a séance which she holds for Mr. and Mrs. Gobineau and Mrs. Nolan, who want to communicate with their dead children, Flora suddenly feels a hand around her throat. Terrified, she dismisses her clients and accuses Toby of trying to frighten her. When the Gobineaus and Mrs. Nolan return, she repels them, screaming that she is a fraud. Again she questions Toby and whips him when he does not confess. Half-drunk and in terror, she chases Toby out of the house and locks Monica in her room when she tries to protect the boy. Toby slips back in to see Monica and hides behind the curtain in the medium's booth as Flora awakes. She senses an alien presence, draws a gun, and shoots toward the booth, wounding Toby. As Monica rushes for help, the crazed woman demands of the dying mute, "Was it you, was it you?"

Major Roles. MADAME FLORA (BABA) (c); requires intense dramatic ability; A2 to A♭4. MONICA (s); D3 to C5.

Lesser Roles. MRS. GOBINEAU (s). MR. GOBINEAU (bar). MRS. NOLAN (m-s). TOBY (mute) (may be a dancer).

Orchestra. fl, ob, cl, bsn, hrn, trp, perc, piano, strings. 2 P-Yes.

Material. FS-P: G Sc (rent). VS: G Sc (e, f) $3.50.

Photographs. Univ. of Georgia: 3.17.52 p. 15.

Performing Companies. Approx 120. 1956–57 only 7, 12, 42, 98, 107, 150, 152, 153, 156, 164, 170, 175, 182, 203, 288, 406, 409, 412, 420, 500, 501, 503.

The Mighty Casey

Music by William Schuman (1910–   ). Libretto in English by Jeremy Gury. The poem "Casey at the Bat," by Ernest L. Thayer, is incorporated in the text. Premiere: Hartford, Conn., May 4, 1953. Satiric comedy. Simple harmonic structure, set pieces, dialogue. Brief overture. Setting: Mudville, U.S.A., in the recent past. One act, three scenes (80 min).

ACT I i: Main Street (backdrop); ii: Outside the stadium; iii: Inside the stadium.

Synopsis. It is the day of the Big Game — the state championship is at stake, and Centerville is playing against Mudville for the title. The band marches off to the stadium where the crowd begins to gather. The great Casey enters to wild cheering, and we follow him into the stadium. In the last half of the ninth inning things look bad for the Mudville team. If only Casey could get to the plate! Finally Casey comes to bat and — strikes out. The fallen hero is comforted by a fan and by his girl, Merry.

Major Roles. There are no major singing roles. The role of Casey is pantomimed by either actor or dancer.

Lesser Roles. MERRY, Casey's girl (s). THE WATCHMAN (bar). THATCHER, Centerville's catcher (bar). FIREBALL SNEDEKER (bar). CHARLIE, a fan (t). THE CONCESSIONAIRE (bar). UMPIRE (bar). THE CATCHER (bar). MALE FAN (t). FEMALE FAN (s). MEMBERS OF THE TOWN BAND (mute). MEMBERS OF THE MUDVILLE TEAM (speaking).

Chorus. SATB. Players, girls, hawkers, fans. Very important in suggesting crowd atmosphere.

Ballet. Optional, dance of the hawkers, rhubarb dance. The game is played in pantomime and may be choreographed, the crowd movements as well.

Orchestra. fl, ob, 2 cl, bsn, 2 trp, 3 trb, perc, piano, strings.

Material. FS-P: G Sc (rent). VS: G Sc $4.50. CP: G Sc 85¢.

Performing Companies. 94 (5.4.53 — prem). 47 (11.19.58). 225 (1959).

Miranda and the Dark Young Man

Music by Elie Siegmeister (1909–   ). Libretto in English by Edward Eager. Premiere: Hartford, May 9, 1956. Comedy. Highly melodious; set pieces, recitative. One act: a comfortable home (showing livingroom and Miranda's bedroom) at the turn of the century (60 min).

Synopsis. Miranda, 17, seeks to demolish the wall of protection with which her stern father has surrounded her. Her frisky Aunt Nan has a plan: at various times she falsely informs the father of indiscretions committed by a dark young man who passes the house each day. The young man, repeatedly the innocent victim of the father's indignation, at last investigates, climbing

202

the tree he has been accused of climbing, and meeting the far-from-unwilling lady he had hitherto never dreamed of.

Roles. (No vocal problems.) MIRANDA (lyr s). HER FATHER (bs-bar). AUNT NAN (m-s). THE DARK YOUNG MAN (lyr bar or t). THE FAIR YOUNG MAN and THE MIDDLE-AGED MAN (mute).

Orchestra. fl, ob, 2 cl, bsn, 2 hrn, 2 trp, 2 trb, perc, piano, strings.

Material. FS-P: Te (rent). VS: Te (rent).

Performing Companies. 94 (5.9.56 — prem; Columbus, O. 4.30.57).

🎵 The Nightingale

Music and libretto in English by Bernard Rogers (1893–), after the fairy tale by Hans Christian Andersen. Premiere: New York City, May 10, 1955. Fantasy. Impressionistic; tonal merging into bitonal, emphasis on pentatonic. Set numbers; vocal line patterned largely after speech except for Nightingale's songs. Short prelude and interludes in Chinese manner. Setting: ancient China. Prologue, one act, three scenes (65 min).

PROLOGUE: The palace kitchen; i: Clearing in the forest, shore of a lake; ii: The Emperor's reception hall; iii: The Emperor's bedchamber.

Synopsis. The little gray Nightingale in the woods is persuaded to sing for the Emperor and his court, who are deeply impressed. But a mechanical bird, the gift of the Emperor of Japan, soon supplants the living songster in the fickle affections of the court. Only when the Emperor is mortally ill, with Death kneeling on his chest and the mechanical bird broken and helpless, does the Nightingale return. His song banishes Death and restores the Emperor to full health.

Major Roles. THE NIGHTINGALE (col s); sustained and florid passages; top B4 (C♯5 and C5 opt). EMPEROR OF CHINA (bar or bs-bar).

Lesser Roles. KITCHEN MAID (s). GENTLEMAN-IN-WAITING (t). FISHERMAN (t). DEATH (bs).

Bit Parts. CHINESE CHAPLAIN (bar). MUSICMASTER (speaking). COURTIER (t). MESSENGER FROM JAPAN (t).

Chorus. SATB. Phantoms, ladies and gentlemen of the court.

Orchestra. picc, ob, Eng hrn, cl, bsn, hrn, trp, trb, perc (2 players), timp, piano (opt), harp, strings.

Material. FS-P: So (rent). VS: So (rent).

Performing Companies. 343 (5.10.55 — prem). 358 (56–57). 178 (58–59).

🎵 Noye's Fludde · Noah's Flood

Music by Benjamin Britten (1913–). Libretto, a Chester miracle play in 16th-century English. Premiere: Aldeburgh, England, June 18, 1958. Medieval miracle play designed to be performed by both professionals and children. Simple vocal line over unconventional accompaniment, often dissonant. Many forms employed: march, passacaglia, hymn, waltz, etc. No overture. One act: a bare stage or platform on which the ark is built (50 min).

Synopsis. The voice of God proclaims his displeasure with the people of the earth and warns Noye to build an ark against the oncoming flood. Noye and his sons comply with alacrity and all is rapidly shipshape. The animals enter, two by two. Soon everyone is aboard but Mrs. Noye, who, slightly tipsy, refuses to leave her dear Gossips. The three sons have to carry her forcibly to the craft. Apparently she recovers her good spirits during the 40-day voyage. At the appointed time Noye sends off a raven and a dove, and when the latter appears with an olive branch, the company moves back onto the shore, praising God.

Major Roles. THE VOICE OF GOD (speaking); not necessarily professional, but should have rich, sincere delivery; should be high, away from stage. NOYE (bs-bar). MRS. NOYE (c). Both should be experienced singing actors. No vocal problems. SEM, HAM, JAFFETT (all boy s). MRS. SEM, MRS. HAM, MRS. JAFFETT (all girl s). Should have well-trained voices, lively personalities. Jaffett, the elder, may be a tenor; Mrs. Jaffett is a little older. MRS. NOYE'S GOSSIPS (all girl s); older with strong voices especially in lower register. RAVEN, DOVE (child dancers).

Chorus. Children, SATB. Animals and birds — as many as possible to approach the 49 species referred to in libretto. Can range widely in age. Seven well-balanced groups are necessary. The congregation (audience) joins in the hymns.

Orchestra. Professional: solo string quintet; solo treble recorder, piano (4 hands), organ, timp. Children (or amateurs): 2 descant recorders, treble recorders, 4-pt bugles, 12 handbells (6 players), strings, perc (6 players), wind machine, whip (clappers).

Material. FS-P: B & H (rent). FS: $12.50. VS: B & H $5 (with production notes). CP: 30¢.

Production Notes. Should be played in church or large building other than a theater. Four property men are necessary to help build the Ark, move waves (painted flats), and hoist rainbow (painted linen fan). A large breakaway tree to be used as the mast. Costumes for animals can be heads, masks, or merely symbols.

Photographs. Aldeburgh: 9.29.58 p. 13.

Performing Company. Union Theological Seminary (3.16.59 — Amer prem).

✠ L'Oca del Cairo · The Goose of Cairo

Music by Wolfgang Amadeus Mozart (1756–1791). Libretto in Italian by Diego Valeri after the original text of Abbate Varesco. Unfinished; completed and adapted by Virgilio Mortari. Comedy. Set numbers: arias, ensembles, recitative. Overture. Setting: Ripasecca, capital of Marchesato, at an unspecified time. One act, two scenes (75 min).

ACT I i: A room in Don Pippo's castle; ii: Garden of the castle.

Synopsis. Don Pippo has confined his daughter Celidora and her companion Lavina in a tower. He promises Biondello that he may marry Celidora if he can gain entrance to the tower. Biondello and his friend Calandrino conceal themselves in a large artificial goose which Don Pippo purchases for the girls — a variation on the wooden horse of the Greeks — and win their brides.

Roles. DON PIPPO (buf bs); A1 to F♯3. CELIDORA (s); trill, flexible; B2 to B♭4. BIONDELLO, a rich gentleman (t); B1 to G3. CALANDRINO (t); B♭1 to G3. LAVINA (s); B2 to B♭4. CHICHIBIO, Don Pippo's majordomo (bs); F1 to G♯3 (many G3's). AURETTA, his wife (s); B2 to A4.

Chorus. SATB. Guards and servants, finale only.

Orchestra. 2 fl, 2 ob, 2 cl, 2 bsn, 2 hrn, 2 trp, timp, strings.

Material. FS-P: AMP (Sch) (rent); B & H (Ca) (rent); Pr (rent). VS: B & H (Ca — i) $7. Pr (f) $8.

Photographs. Buenos Aires: 12.31.56 p. 14.

Performing Companies. 347A (5.27.56).

🎭 Oedipus Rex

Music by Igor Stravinsky (1882–   ). Libretto in French by Jean Cocteau translated into Latin by J. Danielou, based on Sophocles' play of the same name. Premiere: Paris, May 30, 1927. Opera-oratorio. Complex harmonic structure, intensely dramatic. No overture. Setting: Thebes in the classical past. Two acts (50 min).

ACT I: A tableau-like grouping of principals and chorus before a backdrop of the Acropolis (25 min). ACT II: The same (25 min).

Synopsis. Oedipus, the son of Jocasta and Laius, King of Thebes, had been left on a mountain to die because of the oracle's prediction that he would kill his father. Adopted by Polybus, King of Corinth, Oedipus is unaware that Polybus is not his real father. On a journey from Corinth, Oedipus has met, quarreled with, and killed a stranger who turns out to be his real father, Laius. Oedipus has solved the riddle of the Sphinx and is now King of Thebes. He has also unwittingly married his own mother, Jocasta. Thebes is being ravaged by a terrible plague, and the people implore Oedipus to save them. Creon, Oedipus's brother-in-law, returns from Delphi, where the oracle has demanded that the murderer of Laius be punished. Oedipus questions the seer Tiresias, who tells him that the assassin of the king is a king. Jocasta tries to settle the dispute by telling them that her husband was killed by thieves at the crossing of the roads from Daulis and Delphi. Oedipus realizes that he has killed his father and committed incest with his mother. Jocasta hangs herself, and Oedipus puts out his eyes. The Thebans drive Oedipus away to roam the world in expiation for his heinous crime.

Major Roles. OEDIPUS (t); several difficult coloratura passages; E2 to A3. JOCASTA (m-s); A2 to A4. CREON (bs-bar); A♭1 to E♭3. TIRESIAS (bs); F♯1 to D3.

Lesser Roles. SHEPHERD (t). MESSENGER (bs-bar), can double with Creon

Chorus. TTBB. Thebans.

Orchestra. 3 fl (picc), 2 ob, Eng hrn, 3 cl, (E♭ cl), 2 bsn, cont bsn, 4 hrn, 4 trp, 3 trb, tuba, timp, perc, harp, piano, strings.

Material. FS-P: B & H (rent). VS: B & H (speaker, f, g, e − E. E. Cummings, commissioned by Juilliard Opera Theatre; chor, Latin) $7.50.

Photographs. N.Y. City Opera: 10.31.59 p. 12. *Mus. Amer.* Zurich: 2.59 p. 259.

Performing Companies. 308A (7.25.59). 334 (9.24.59).

🎭 The Old Maid and the Thief

Music and libretto in English by Gian-Carlo Menotti (1911–   ), originally commissioned by NBC as a radio opera and broadcast April 22, 1939. Stage premiere: Philadelpha, February 11, 1941. Grotesque comedy. Continuous texture, simple melodic line. Overture. Setting: a small American town in the present. One basic set is generally used to represent the house, the parlor, bedroom, and kitchen, and the street, the liquor store, and front porch. One act, fourteen scenes (60 min).

Synopsis. Miss Todd, a middle-aged spinster, lives alone with her young servant Laetitia. While she is entertaining her friend Miss Pinkerton, a handsome beggar comes to the door; Laetitia persuades Miss Todd to ask him to stay overnight. The following day Miss Todd meets Miss Pinkerton on the street and learns that a criminal has escaped from the local prison; his description fits that of Bob, her beggar guest. But she is already infatuated with him and determines to protect him from the police. Laetitia also loves Bob; together the two women rob a liquor store to give him spending money. Furious because Bob will not return her love, Miss Todd goes for the police, though she has discovered he is not the escaped convict. While she is gone Laetitia persuades him that his only safety lies in marrying her and running away. Together they ransack Miss Todd's house and elope in her car.

Roles. MISS TODD (c); G2 to G♯4. LAETITIA (s); C3 to D5. MISS PINKERTON (s); D3 to A4. BOB (bar); A1 to G♯3.

Orchestra. 2 fl, ob, cl, bsn, 2 hrn, 2 trp, trb, perc, strings.

Material. FS-P: Ri (rent). VS: Ri $5.

Photographs. Univ. of Denver: 10.31.49 p. 17. Cosmos Theatre, Vienna: 12.15.52 p. 13. Univ. of Oregon: 2.16.53 p. 4. Univ. of Texas: 11.2.53 p. 21.

Performing Companies. Approx 54; 1956–57 only 14, 17, 104, 133, 145, 163, 368, 457, 498, 531.

🎭 L'Osteria portoghese · The Portuguese Inn

Music by Luigi Cherubini (1760–1842). Anonymous libretto in Italian, based on a play by St. Aignan. Premiere: Paris, 1798. Revised by Giulio Confalonieri. Comedy. Set numbers; patter recitative. No overture. Setting: an inn near the Portuguese-Spanish frontier; 17th century. One act.

Synopsis. Gabriela has fled her home, accompanied by her servant Ines, to meet her lover, Carlos, and also to escape her guardian, Roselbo. They stop at the inn of Rodrigo, who suspects that Gabriela is the wife of a Spanish governor. When Carlos arrives, Rodrigo, believing him to be a secret agent, sidetracks him. Roselbo comes in pursuit of Gabriela, and Rodrigo confides that two Spanish ladies are under his protection. Roselbo suggests that he escort them to Lisbon. The dismay of the ladies when confronted with Roselbo is assuaged by the timely arrival of Carlos with a royal decree annulling Gabriela's guardianship. Roselbo is foiled and Rodrigo punished for his interference.

Major Roles. GABRIELA (lyr s); needs flexibility; C3 to Bb4. RODRIGO (buf bs); Bb1 to D♯3. DON CARLOS (t); E2 to A3. ROSELBO (buf bar); C2 to F3 (falsetto to Bb3). INES (s); soubrette; D3 to A4.

Lesser Roles. INIGO, Rodrigo's servant (buf t); C2 to E3. PEDRILLO, Carlos' servant (bar); top F3.

Chorus. SATB.

Orchestra. 2 fl, 2 ob, 2 cl, 2 bsn, 2 hrn, 2 trp, 2 trb, perc, strings, piano for recitatives.

Material. All Al. Li (52 − i, e − Gutman) 40¢.

Photographs. San Francisco: 11.15.54 p. 7.

Performing Company. 72 (9.24.54 − Amer prem).

▶ Pagliacci

Music by Ruggiero Leoncavallo (1858–1919). Libretto in Italian by the composer. Premiere: Milan, May 21, 1892. Melodrama (verismo). Highly melodious; continuous texture embodying set numbers; vocal line occasionally patterned after speech. Short instrumental prelude; short interlude between acts. Vocal prologue before curtain. Setting: a southern Italian village, Montalto, between 1865 and 1870. Two acts (73 min).

Synopsis. A troupe of strolling players arrives in the village. Canio, actor-manager, becomes suspicious of his young wife Nedda when Tonio, another actor, tells him that he saw her with a lover. Nedda, in fact, plans to elope with Silvio, a young villager. They are surprised in their rendezvous by Canio, but Silvio escapes unidentified. In the show that evening, a situation similar to real life is enacted, with Columbine hiding her lover from her jealous husband. Canio, beyond control, demands the name of his wife's lover. When she refuses to tell, he stabs her. Silvio rises in horrified protest, whereupon Canio stabs him also, then turns to the audience and sobs that the comedy is finished.

Major Roles. CANIO (lyr t); needs dramatic force, sustained power; D2 to A3 (one Bb3). NEDDA (lyr s); occasional dramatic passages; C3 to Bb4 (two B4's). TONIO (bar); needs ability as actor as well as strong voice throughout range; several florid passages; trill; Bb1 to F♯3.

Lesser Roles. SILVIO (lyr bar); C2 to G3. BEPPE, one of the players (light t); Bb1 to A3.

Chorus. SSTTBB. Boys, villagers.

Orchestra. 2 fl, picc, 2 ob (Eng hrn), 2 cl, bs cl, 3 bsn, 4 hrn, 3 trp, 3 trb, tuba, timp, perc, 2 harp. *Stage:* bells, ob, vln, bs drum, trp.

Material. FS-P: AMP (Son), Ka, Map, G Sc, TW (rent). MS: Br (i) $17.50. VS: AMP (Son – i) $7.50; Ri (i) $4; G Sc (i, e – H. G. Chapman) $5. CP: Map (i, e – rent). Tr: Mead (Ha); Rosing (T22).

Photographs. Metropolitan: 1.27.41 p. 13; (Armistead) 2.26.51 p. 20; 4.8.57 p. 22; (Gérard) 12.29.58 pp. 20–21. William C. de Mille film: 2.23.42 p. 28. Jackson, Miss., Opera Guild: 1.20.47 p. 11.

Performing Companies. Approx 73; 1956–57 only 129, 218, 252, 303, 313, 324, 329, 341, 354, 378, 449, 487.

🎵 Le Pauvre Matelot · The Poor Sailor

Music by Darius Milhaud (1892–   ). Libretto in French by Jean Cocteau. Premiere: Paris, December 16, 1927. Melodrama. Continuous texture. Difficult vocal line. Short prelude. Setting: a seaport; time: the present. Three acts, one set: a street with a tavern stage right, a wineshop stage left, the sea in the background (45 min).

Synopsis. A woman waits for her sailor husband, who has been away fifteen years. She is so sure that he will return with a fortune that she refuses to marry his friend, who keeps a shop across the street from her rundown bar. Her father's urging cannot move her. The sailor returns, but decides to see his friend first. He has changed so greatly that he is not recognized. He asks to spend the night in his wife's bar, telling her that her husband will soon return. He tells a story: both he and her husband were courted by a savage queen; her husband refused and will return as a poor man, but he acceded and received a priceless pearl necklace as a souvenir. He goes to sleep. The woman steals in and kills him with hammer blows. She will have the necklace to pay her husband's debts and start them on a happy life again.

Roles. SAILOR (t); some high tessitura, needs flexibility; top A♯3. HIS WIFE (s); top B♭4. HIS FATHER-IN-LAW (bs). HIS FRIEND (bar).

Orchestra. fl, ob, cl, bsn, hrn, trp, trb, timp, perc, 2 vln, vla, vcl, cb.

Material. FS-P: Pr (Mer – Heu) (rent). VS: Pr (Mer – Heu – f) $5.50. Tr: Finley (Pr – Mer).

Photographs. Juilliard: 10.31.49 p. 20. Univ. of Illinois: 10.27.52 p. 18.

Performing Companies. 177A (10.53). 338A (2.53). 279 (5.54). 225 (7.54). 180A (11.4.55). 30 (55–56). 411 (5.18.56). 193A (57–58). 518 (57–59).

🎵 Pepito

Music by Jacques Offenbach (1819–1880). Libretto in French by L. Battu and J. Moinaux. Premiere: Paris, 1853. English version by Robert A. Simon, recitatives prepared from original dialogue by William Tarrasch. Premiere: New York, March 20, 1959. Comedy. Melodious, set pieces, arias, ensembles, recitative. Overture. One act: an Italian inn (55–60 min).

Synopsis. Manuelita, owner of an inn, carries on a rivalry with Vertigo, proprietor of a nearby bistro, who vainly seeks her love. She is faithful to Pepito, who went away to war some years ago. At last a buddy of Pepito's,

208

Miguel, comes with news. He has had a letter from Pepito, who has married. Manuelita is at first furious, then heartbroken, then somewhat reconciled. After all, Miguel is right there, very attractive, and very much in love.

Roles. MANUELITA (light s); C5 opt. MIGUEL (lyr t); top B3. VERTIGO (buf bs-bar); needs acting ability, also should dance; vocally agile, particularly in an aria that satirizes "Largo al Factotum"; top F3 opt.

Orchestra. 2 fl, ob, 2 cl, 1–2 bsn, 2 hrn, 2 trp, trb, timp, perc, strings, piano for recitatives.

Material. VS: Map (g, f). Tr: Simon (T29); Hammond (T22).

Performing Company. 317 (3.20.59 — Amer prem).

✠ The Pet Shop

Music by Vittorio Rieti. Libretto in English by Claire Nicolas after a story by Vittorio Rieti. Premiere: New York, April 14, 1958. Farce. Lively and melodious; set pieces, accompanied recitative. Very brief prelude. Setting: a pet shop on Lexington Avenue, New York; the present. One act (approx 40 min).

Synopsis. The stylish Mrs. Camouflage seeks a new dog to replace her dead Mimi. It must match her costume in the Dog and Dowager Parade. Her daughter Trixie accompanies her to the pet shop, owned by the personable Mr. Canicular. While Mrs. Camouflage takes several dogs (mimed by dancers) out for trial runs, the two young people confess that they have fallen in love at sight. Mrs. Camouflage is persuaded to give her blessing when Mr. Canicular reveals himself as a judge of the style show.

Roles. MRS. CAMOUFLAGE, youngish society matron (c); A2 to F♯4. TRIXIE (high s); C3 to C5. MR. CANICULAR (t); C♯2 to B♭3. DOGS (three mimes).

Orchestra. fl, ob, cl, hrn, trp, trb, perc, piano, strings.

Material. FS-P: G Sc (rent). VS: G Sc (rent).

Photographs. Mus. Amer. Mannes College: 5.58 p. 39.

Performing Company. 327 (4.14.58 — prem).

✠ Pimpinone

Music by Georg Philipp Telemann (1681–1767). Libretto by (Albinoni?) Pietro Pariati partially translated into German by Praetorius for Telemann. Premiere: Hamburg, 1725. Comedy. Melodious; set numbers, arias, duets; patter recitative. No overture. One act: three parts (intermezzi) (40 min).

Synopsis. Pert Vespetta seeks a place as maid to a rich bachelor; Pimpinone seems ideal. With her clever prompting, he soon believes that marriage would be a still happier state. But after the ceremony, his demure bride turns into an extravagant, pleasure-loving shrew. Beleaguered by her tantrums, he gives in to her every wish, at last recognizing his helplessness.

Roles. VESPETTA (col s); florid passages, needs trill; D3 to B♭4. PIMPINONE (buf bs); needs trill, agility; C2 to F3 (one F♯3), falsetto to C4.

Orchestra. Strings, harpsichord.

Material. FS-P: AMP (Sch) (rent). VS: AMP (Sch — g, i, e — Norman Platt) $3.75.

Photographs. Univ. of Maryland: 2.10.58 3rd cover.

Performing Companies. 327 (4.14.58). 193A (57–58).

🎭 Le Portrait de Manon · The Portrait of Manon

Music by Jules Massenet (1842–1912). Libretto in French by Georges Boyer. Premiere: Paris, November 24, 1894. Drama; a sequel to "Manon." Highly melodious; set numbers over lyrical consonant accompaniment; recitative and dialogue. Many echoes of the music of "Manon." Short prelude. One act: a rather severely furnished apartment in a chateau near Paris (appropriate to show both exterior and interior so that chorus of revelers may be seen); time, circa 1750 (40 min).

Synopsis. The Chevalier des Grieux, now grown old, but still in love with the memory of Manon, has a ward, Jean, who is in love with a young girl, Aurore. Des Grieux, who has never seen her, bitterly opposes the marriage, resisting even the pleas of his lifelong friend Tiberge. The young lovers find a portrait of Manon. Aurore appears before Des Grieux in the costume of the portrait (that worn by Manon in the first act of the opera) and breaks down the old man's opposition. He is further mollified when Tiberge reveals that Aurore is Lescaut's daughter, therefore Manon's niece.

Major Roles. CHEVALIER DES GRIEUX (high bar or t); lyric, high tessitura for bar; sustained; C#2 to F3. JEAN, VICOMTE DE MORCERF (m-s); not taxing; C3 to F4.

Lesser Roles. TIBERGE (t); D2 to E3. AURORE (lyr s); light, needs flexibility at top; D3 to B4.

Chorus. SATB. Offstage at opening; humming ensemble at close.

Orchestra. 2 fl, 2 ob (Eng hrn), 2 cl, 2 bsn, 4 hrn, timp, perc, harp, harmonium, strings.

Material. FS-P: Pr (Mer — Heu) (rent). VS: Pr (Mer — Heu — f, e) $5.50. Tr: Feist (T30).

Photographs. Havana: 12.8.58 p. 2.

Performing Companies. 501A (4.49). 190A (51–52). 364 (57–58). 368 (57–58). 386 (1.17.59).

🎭 The Pot of Fat

Music by Theodor Chanler (1902–   ). Libretto in English by Hester Pickman. Premiere: Boston, May 9, 1955. Satire. Continuous texture; vocal line patterned after speech. No overture. Six scenes (50 min).

PROLOGUE: In front of curtain. i: Cat's room; ii: In front of curtain; iii: Cat's room; iv: Same; v: Same; vi: Interior of church. EPILOGUE: In front of curtain.

Synopsis. A Cat and a Mouse marry for love. The Narrator, skeptical at first, begins to believe that a golden age has arrived. But his skepticism is

210

fully justified. The Cat pretends to attend three christenings, secretly dipping into a pot of fat he and his bride have stored in a church against winter. Discovery by the trusting mouse of her hungry husband's perfidy brings the inevitable denouement, and wife becomes dinner.

Roles. NARRATOR (bs-bar — t in revised vers), G2 to F3 (one A3, two B3s). MOUSE (s), B2 to A4. CAT (bs-bar), G2 to F3 (one F♯3).
Orchestra. fl, ob, cl, bsn, hrn, trp, piano, perc, strings.
Material. FS-P: AMP (rent). VS: AMP (rent).
Photographs. After-Dinner Opera: 4.2.56 p. 33.
Performing Companies. 197A (5.9.55 — prem). 294 (2.22.56).

✍ Il Prigioniero · The Prisoner

Music by Luigi Dallapiccola (1904–   ). Libretto in Italian by the composer, from "La Torture par l'espérance" by Count Villiers de l'Isle-Adam and "La Légende d'Ulenspiegel et de Lamme Goedzak" by Charles de Coster. Premiere: Turin, December 1, 1949. Psychological melodrama in dodecaphonic style. Continuous texture with a ballad and an aria. No overture. Setting: Saragozza, Spain; second half of the 16th century. Prologue and one act (seven sections) (50 min).

(1): Prologue: Before a black curtain. (2): First choral intermezzo. (3): Cell in Inquisitor's jail. (4): The same. (5): Passageway leading from the cell. (6): Second choral intermezzo. (7): Large garden with cedar tree.

Synopsis. A Flemish patriot has been imprisoned and tortured by the Spanish Inquisition. His mother visits him and sees a vision of King Philip. The Prisoner tells her of his torture and of the words "my brother," spoken by his kindly Jailer, which renewed his hope. The Mother leaves as the Jailer appears, bringing encouraging news of a turning tide for the Flemish. He again urges the Prisoner to hope. When the Jailer leaves, the Prisoner finds his cell door open and starts down a long, dark passageway. He hides from two priests who do not stop him. Finally he reaches a vast, springlike garden and believes himself free, but the Grand Inquisitor (who was the Jailer) appears from behind the tree and holds him fast, saying "my brother." The Prisoner recognizes his final torture has been hope, as he is led off to the stake.

Major Roles. THE MOTHER (dram s); A2 to B4. JAILER and GRAND INQUISITOR (must be played by same person) (t); B1 to B3. THE PRISONER (bar); G1 to G3.
Lesser Roles. TWO PRIESTS (t, bar). FRA REDEMPTOR (mute).
Chorus. SSAATTBB. Offstage. Should be large.
Orchestra. 3 fl, 2 ob, 3 cl, 2 bsn, 4 hrn, 3 trp, trb, tuba, 2 sax, timp, perc, 2 harp, piano, strings. *Stage:* organ, 2 trp, trb. *Reduced vers:* 2 fl, 2 ob, 2 cl, 2 bsn, 4 hrn, 2 trp, trb, tuba, timp, harp, piano, strings. *Stage:* organ, 2 trp, trb.
Material. FS-P: AMP (SZ) (rent). VS: AMP (SZ — i) $6. Tr: Harold Heiberg (AMP).
Photographs. Essen: 1.3.55 p. 32.
Performing Companies. 321 (3.16.51). 334 (9.29.60).

211

✄ Prima Donna

Music by Arthur Benjamin (1893–1960). Libretto in English by Cedric Cliffe. Premiere: London, February 23, 1949. Comedy. Set pieces, arias, ensembles, recitative, dialogue; considerable satire on conventional forms. The place, Florindo's house in Venice; mid-18th century. One act and prologue (60 min).

Synopsis. The profligate Florindo, expecting a visit from his rich uncle, Count Rinaldo, takes the advice of his friend, Alcino, and borrows from moneylenders to lay out a rich feast. The Count, a spry old countryman of sixty, requests the presence of Filomela, the opera star, but Florindo sends for his current favorite, Olimpia, instead. Unbeknown to him, Alcino sends for his own lady-love, Fiammetta. In consequence, the old man sees and hears "double" but is persuaded that his drunkenness is responsible. When he demands the company of "Filomela," the two haughty singers, already exasperated by their rivalry in song, would refuse, but Bellina dons one of their costumes and further deceives the inebriated Count. The young men pacify their own ladies as the curtain falls.

Major Roles. FLORINDO (bar); top F♯3. ALCINO, his friend (t); top A3. THE COUNT, Florindo's uncle (bs-bar); needs agility in all parts of range; G1 to F♯3 (G3 opt). OLIMPIA and FIAMMETTA, of the opera chorus (both col s); top D♯5.

Lesser Roles. BELLINA, Florindo's maid (light m-s); needs flexibility for birdlike song. A PASTRYCOOK, ASSISTANTS, FURNITURE REMOVERS, TWO NEGRO PAGES (mute).

Orchestra. 2 fl, 2 ob, 2 cl, 2 bsn, 4 hrn, 2 trp, 3 trb (1 opt), timp, perc, piano (celeste opt), guitar (harp opt), strings. *Reduced vers* (material in Italy): fl, ob, cl, bsn, 2 hrn, trp, trb, timp, perc, piano (celeste opt), guitar (harp opt), solo strings. *Stage:* fl, vln, vla, vcl, guitar (or harp or harpsichord).

Material. All B & H. FS-P (rent). VS $10.

Performing Companies. 518 (12.52). 165 (5.53). 517 (10.53). 441 (12. 53; 4.27.55; 56–57). 140 (2.54). 279 (4.54). 156 (7.21.54). 322 (3.57). 85A (12.3.58).

✄ The Princess and the Pea

Music by Ernst Toch (1887–   ). Libretto in German by Benno Elkan after a fairy tale by Andersen. Premiere: Baden-Baden, July 17, 1927. Arias, ensembles, small amount of dialogue; brief prelude and interludes. Setting: a mythical kingdom. Two sets: throneroom of the palace; a royal bedroom. One act (48 min).

Synopsis. According to the familiar fairy story, a true princess is being sought as the bride for a blasé young prince. The King is old, and wants to see an heir to his kingdom; the Queen is willing to marry off her son but insists that any candidate be tested to determine her genuineness. A strange Princess duly presents herself, truly haughty and imperious. The Nurse at last devises a sure

212

method to try her: she places a tiny pea between the bottom mattresses of a huge bed. The Princess tosses and turns — her bruises reveal her to possess the extreme sensibility known only to royalty. The entire court, including the now-captivated Prince, welcomes her as a fitting consort.

Roles. KING (bs); F1 to D3 (one E3). QUEEN (s); Db3 to Bb4. PRINCE (t); C2 to Bb3. PRINCESS (s); some high tessitura; D3 to Bb4. NURSE (m-s or s); C3 to A4. CHANCELLOR (bar); A1 to E3. MINISTER (t); D2 to A3.

Chorus. SATBB. Court ladies, servants, pages.

Orchestra. 2 fl (picc), ob, cl, bsn (cont bsn), hrn, trp, tuba, timp, perc, strings.

Material. FS-P: AMP (Sch) (rent). VS: AMP (Sch — e — Marion Farquhar) $3.

Performing Companies. 48 (5.51). 476 (2.21.52). 197 (3.5.54). 179A (4.1.54). 205 (7.54). 479A (11.19.54). 398A (3.55). 412 (4.20.55). 389 (5.55). 321 (3.7.56). 478 (4.20.56).

🎵 El Retablo de maese Pedro · Master Peter's Puppet Show

Music by Manuel de Falla (1876–1946). Libretto in Spanish adapted by the composer from an episode in "Don Quixote" by Miguel de Cervantes. Premiere: Paris, June 25, 1923. Satirical comedy. Declamatory vocal line, simple harmonic structure. Prelude: "Master Peter's Symphony." Setting: Spain, 17th century. One act: an inn stable near Aragon in which Master Peter has his puppet show (50 min).

Synopsis. Don Quixote comes with Sancho Panza, his servant, to see Master Peter's puppet show. The puppets represent scenes from the life of Charlemagne in the days of knight errantry, and a boy announces the action as it takes place on the stage. Don Quixote, in his usual fashion, gets so carried away with his resolve to avenge all wrongs that he leaps out of his seat and attacks the puppets, leaving Master Peter's business in ruins.

Major Roles. DON QUIXOTE (bs or bar); C2 to F3. MASTER PETER (t); Bb2 to E3. THE BOY (NARRATOR) (boy s); sings in the manner of street cries; C♯3 to F4.

Lesser Roles. SANCHO PANZA, INNKEEPER, PAGE, SCHOLAR (all mute). Figures in the puppet show (large puppets, with voices offstage, or living actors wearing masks): CHARLEMAGNE, DON GAYFEROS, DON ROLAND, MELISENDRA, KING MARSILIUS, THE MOOR, HERALDS, KNIGHTS, SOLDIERS, ETC.

Orchestra. fl, 2 ob, Eng hrn, cl, bsn, 2 hrn, trp, timp, perc, piano, harp, strings.

Material. FS-P: G Sc (Ch) (rent). VS: G Sc (Ch — s, f, e — J. B. Trend) (rent).

Photographs. Mus. Amer. San Francisco Symphony: 4.57 p. 10.

Performing Companies. 323 (11.8.53). 398A (3.55). 1956–57: 74, 193, 297.

🎵 Riders to the Sea

Music by Ralph Vaughan Williams (1872–1958). Libretto in English, the play by J. M. Synge. Premiere: London, 1937. Drama. Vocal line patterned largely after speech, occasionally unaccompanied; modal and melodic passages. One act: a cottage kitchen on an island off the west coast of Ireland (30 min).

Synopsis. Maurya, who lives in the village on the wild seacoast, has seen her husband and four of her six sons drowned. The fifth, Michael, is missing and the sixth, Bartley, rides away to a horse fair. The daughters, Cathleen and Nora, try to keep from their mother a shirt and sock taken from the body of a drowned man — they are Michael's. Bartley leaves without his mother's blessing. The old women begin to enter the cottage, keening. Bartley has been thrown into the sea by his horse. Now all the sons are gone; Maurya has no more fear of the sea, no more hope in the world. She sits desolate and alone, while her daughters are powerless to comfort her.

Major Roles. (No problems of range.) MAURYA (c). BARTLEY (bar). CATHLEEN (s). NORA (s).

Lesser Role. A WOMAN (m-s).

Chorus. SSAA (wordless). Group of men and women (mute).

Orchestra. 2 fl, ob, Eng hrn, bs cl, bsn, 2 hrn, trp, timp, bs drum, sea machine, strings (not more than 6.6.4.4.2).

Material. FS-P: Ox (rent). VS: Ox $4.25. CP: Ox 50¢.

Photographs. Northwestern Univ.: 2.16.53 p. 12. Alabama Univ.: 11.14.55 p. 21.

Performing Companies. Approx 32; 1956–57 only 17, 145, 164, 254, 317, 364, 375, 395, 511, 518.

🎵 Rita

Music by Gaetano Donizetti (1797–1848). Libretto in Italian by Gustavo Vaez. (Originally "Rita, ou Le Mari Battu — Deux Hommes et une Femme.") Premiere: Paris, 1860. Revised by Umberto Cattino. Comedy. Set pieces, arias, ensembles; dialogue. Setting: an inn; time, immaterial. One act (45 min).

Synopsis. Rita, the owner of an inn, quarrels incessantly with her husband, Beppo. A rough stranger, Gasparo, discloses himself as her former husband. He and Beppo play a game of drawing straws for the wife. Beppo loses and is delighted. But when he attempts to leave, Rita promises to behave and persuades Gasparo to move on. Beppo, now with the upper hand, resigns himself to his fate.

Roles. RITA (s); considerable florid singing; B♭2 to B4. BEPPO (t); D2 to B3 (one important C♯4). GASPARO (bar); A1 to F3. BARTOLO, a servant (speaking).

Orchestra. 2 fl (picc), 2 ob, 2 cl, 2 bsn, 2 hrn, 2 trp, 3 trb, timp, strings.

Material. FS-P: Ri (rent). VS: Ri (i, e — Mead) $7.50.

Performing Company. 326 (5.14.57 — Amer prem).

☙ The Robbers

Music by Ned Rorem (1923–   ). Libretto in English after a verse from Chaucer's Pardoner's Tale: "Thus ended these two homicides in woe; Died thus the treacherous poisoner also." Premiere: New York, April 14, 1958. Melodrama. Vocal line declamatory over unconventional harmonies. One aria. Short prelude. One act: a sordid second-story room in a 14th-century inn (28 min).

Synopsis. Three thieves have just murdered a stranger for his gold. The Young Novice already repents, but the Leader and his servile Companion threaten him. He rests apart from them while they divide the gold — into two piles. When he brings them a drink of wine, they stab him. But the wine was poisoned, and the murderers themselves are murdered.

Roles. THE LEADER (bs-bar); G1 to E3. HIS COMPANION (t); C2 to B♭3. A YOUNG NOVICE (lyr bar); difficult role, wide range, some florid passages; F1 to F♯3. A corpse lies stage center throughout.

Orchestra. fl (picc), ob (Eng hrn), 2 cl (bs cl), bsn, hrn, timp, perc, piano (celeste), string qt, cb.

Material. FS-P: B & H (rent). VS: B & H (rent).

Performing Company. 327 (4.14.58 – prem; 12.30.58).

☙ The Rope

Music by Louis Mennini (1920–   ). Libretto in English by the composer after the play by Eugene O'Neill. Commissioned by the Koussevitzky Foundation. Premiere: Tanglewood, August 8, 1955. Rural drama. Vocal line mostly declamatory, often highly dramatic, with occasional melodic passages. Orchestra is evocative of the dramatic elements. Brief prelude. One act: interior of an old barn on a high headland at the seacoast; time, before the First World War (45 min).

Synopsis. Abraham Bentley spends his days cursing the absent Luke, his son by a second marriage, and making his daughter Annie, her husband Pat, and their daughter Mary miserable. Abe prophesies that Luke will return and hang himself, and keeps a noosed rope in the old barn against that day. Pat persuades a lawyer to divulge that Abe has left the farm to Luke, but the whereabouts of a thousand dollars in gold pieces remains a mystery. Luke returns unexpectedly. He gives Mary a silver dollar and encourages her to skip it off the cliff into the sea, to the consternation of her parents. Abe appears glad to see Luke at first, then returns to his demand that Luke hang himself. In horror, Pat takes the old man to the house, then returns to the barn to plot the old man's downfall with Luke over a bottle of whiskey. If Abe won't disclose his hiding place, Luke will resort to torture. They go off to put their plan into action. Mary sneaks into the barn, puts a chair beneath the noose, and takes a big swing on the rope. The rope parts, bringing down on the girl a dusty bag, from which spill dozens of shiny gold pieces. In glee Mary skips them one by one into the sea.

Roles. ABRAHAM BENTLEY (bs); shabby, rheumatic, about 65; A1 to E3. ANNIE (m–s); worn out, about 40; C3 to A4. PAT SWEENEY (t); stocky, Irish, mean; C2 to A3. LUKE BENTLEY (bar); coarse, good-natured, weak; A1 to F3 (one F♯3). MARY (speaking — short passages can be hummed); scrawny, aimless, expressionless.

Orchestra. fl, ob, 2 cl, bsn, 2 hrn, trp, trb, timp, perc, strings.

Material. C34a.

Performing Companies. 205 (8.8.55 – prem). 358 (5.14.56).

📓 R.S.V.P. or A Musicale at Mr. Cauliflower's

Music by Jacques Offenbach (1819–1880). English version adapted and translated from the original libretto, "Monsieur Choufleuri," by Dino Yannopoulos. Composed in 1861. Premiere Yannopoulos version: Chicago Musical College, May 6, 1951. Farce. Very melodious; set numbers, dialogue. One act: the contemporary livingroom can suggest the past in decorative detail; the time of the "opera within the opera" is 1833. A piano is necessary (50 min).

Synopsis. The contemporary Stuart Offenbach, although probably no descendant of Jacques, possesses a trunkful of Offenbachiana. One night while his opera-loving wife is out, Stuart decides to write his own opera based on a party invitation from a Monsieur Choufleuri found in the trunk. The opera unfolds while Stuart looks on, directs, interprets, and comments — not always favorably. The pompous Mr. Cauliflower receives only regrets from the singers he has invited for a soirée. Ernestine, his lively daughter, suggests her lover, the bassoon-playing Chrysodule Babylas, as one substitute, while she and her father also disguise themselves as opera singers. This makes the opportunity for a showy trio à l'Italienne, which is so successful that Mr. Cauliflower, under the threat of being ridiculed if Babylas' true identity is revealed, consents to the marriage of the bassoonist-cum-tenor to Ernestine. Even Stuart tries to join in the ensuing celebration, although his wife's voice offstage reminds him he cannot sing.

Major Roles. ERNESTINE (col s); wide range; top D5. CHRYSODULE BABYLAS (t); top C4. MR. CAULIFLOWER (bar); considerable agility needed.

Lesser Roles. PETERMAN, an English butler (t); one solo couplet, joins ensemble. BALANDARD, a guest (t). MRS. BALANDARD, a guest (s). MEINHERR REGEULSMAN, accompanist (mute). STUART OFFENBACH (speaking). MRS. STUART OFFENBACH (offstage, speaking).

Chorus. SSTTBB. May be eliminated by adding 1 B and 1 S to ensemble as guests.

Orchestra. 2 fl (picc), 2 ob, 2 cl, 2 bsn, E♭ sax, B♭ sax (bs cl), 2 hrn, 2 trp, 2 trb, timp, perc, strings.

Material. FS-P: G Sc (rent). VS: G Sc (f, e) $2.50. "M. Choufleuri": Map (rent). Pr (f) $5.

Photographs. Emporia College, Kans.: 3.18.57 p. 32.

Performing Companies. 240 (4.51). 321 (5.22.53). 517 (51–54). 164 (5.52; 56–57). 279 (52–53; 57–58). 6 (52–53). 164 (52–53). 380 (3.53).

400 (5.53). 10 (5.54). 497A (5.54). 150B (7.55). 161 (11.55). 81A (4.22. 56). 286 (56–57). 294 (57–58). 29 (7.21.59). 9A (10.59).

⚑ The Ruby

Music by Norman Dello Joio (1913–   ). Libretto in English by William Mass, after the play, "A Night at an Inn," by Lord Dunsany. Premiere: Indiana University, May 13, 1955. Lyric melodrama. Vocal line patterned largely after speech; one lyrical duet. Intensely dramatic orchestration. Short prelude with curtain up. Setting: A lonely house, a hunting lodge, uninhabited for years, on the English moors at the turn of the century. One act: (55 min).

Synopsis. Scott, an English gentleman gone to seed, is now the leader of a group of thugs, who have robbed an Eastern temple of a great ruby, which was set in the eye of an idol. They are hiding out in Scott's old hunting lodge, to which he has summoned his wife, Laura. Laura, still hopelessly in love with her renegade husband, believes his promises that he has reformed, but distrusts the others — Albert, a cold ruthless blusterer; Sniggers, a ratlike sneak; and Bull, a massive brute. The men fear three Indian priests who have inexorably followed them and who at last find even this retreat. Under Scott's leadership they kill the three priests, and while Laura looks on in horror Scott disposes of his cronies. But Nemesis is at hand; the idol itself comes to seek its missing eye, and Scott is doomed.

Roles. LAURA (s); D3 to A4. SCOTT (bar); B1 to F♯3. ALBERT (t); E2 to A3. SNIGGERS (t); F2 to A3. BULL (bs); B1 to E3. THREE INDIAN PRIESTS (mute — ideally dancers). IDOL, monstrous, like a juggernaut (mute).

Orchestra. 2 fl, picc, 2 ob, Eng hrn, 2 cl, bs cl, 2 bsn, 4 hrn, 3 trp, 2 trb, bs trb, tuba, timp, celeste, harp, perc, strings.

Material. FS-P: Ri (rent). VS: Ri $5.

Photographs. Mus. Amer. Manhattan School: 6.57 p. 22.

Performing Companies. 148 (5.13.55 — prem). 326 (5.14.57). 154 (57–58). 9A (5.13.61).

⚑ Salome

Music by Richard Strauss (1864–1949). Libretto in German by the composer, based on Hedwig Lachmann's translation of Oscar Wilde's play. Premiere: Dresden, September 9, 1905. Pathological drama. Continuous texture of complex, sometimes dissonant harmonic structure, with widely varied orchestral colors; recurring motives. Vocal line is difficult, following speech inflection in idealized form, often like instruments. No overture. Setting: a terrace of Herod's palace in Galilee; circa A.D. 30. One act (90 min).

Synopsis. Salome, daughter of the evil Herodias and stepdaughter of Herod, neurotic king of Palestine, is fascinated by a prisoner Herod has confined in a cistern. This is Jokanaan, John the Baptist, who proclaims the coming of the Messiah. Salome persuades the soldier Narraboth, who loves her, to let

217

her speak to the prophet. She passionately begs Jokanaan to satisfy her lust, ignoring Narraboth, who kills himself in despair at her wantonness. The prophet spurns and curses her, then returns to his dungeon. The lecherous Herod asks Salome to dance for him. She agrees on condition he grant her one wish. After her dance, she demands the head of Jokanaan, to the unholy glee of Herodias. Though disgusted and frightened, Herod is forced to keep his oath. The executioner is summoned and descends into the cistern. The prophet is slain; his severed head is presented to the princess on a silver charger. When Salome clutches the severed head and wildly kisses the dead lips, the horrified Herod orders her crushed beneath his soldiers' shields.

Major Roles. SALOME (dram s); requires great stamina and intensity of acting as well as singing; ability to convey the illusion of being a dancer unless the Dance of the Seven Veils is assigned to a ballerina; Gb2 to B4. HEROD (t); acting must sustain high dramatic level; vocal part difficult but beautiful voice not essential; A1 to Bb3. HERODIAS (m-s); voice should be harsh and darkly colored; C3 to Bb4. JOKANAAN (bar); needs dark, sepulchral quality, tonal vitality; Ab1 to F#3.

Lesser Roles. NARRABOTH, a young Syrian (t); Eb2 to A3. PAGE OF HERODIAS (c); A2 to G4.

Bit Parts. FIVE JEWS (4 t, bs). TWO NAZARENES (t, bs). TWO SOLDIERS (2 bs). CAPPADOCIAN (bs). SLAVE (s).

Orchestra. picc, 3 fl, 2 ob, Eng hrn, hecklephone, 4 cl, Eb cl, bs cl, 3 bsn, cont bsn, 6 hrn, 4 trp, 4 trb, tuba, timp (2 players), perc (6–7 players), 2 harp, celeste, strings. *Stage:* organ. *Reduced vers:* 3 fl, 2 ob, Eng hrn, 2 cl, bs cl, 3 bsn, 4 hrn, 3 trp, 3 trb, tuba, timp, perc (3 players), harp, celeste, strings.

Production Problems. Dance of the Seven Veils; appearance of Jokanaan from well.

Material. All B & H. FS-P (rent). VS: (g, e — Kalisch) $4.50. Li: (g, e) 75¢. O Tr: Polacheck (333).

Photographs. Metropolitan: 12.28.42 cover; 12.3.58 pp. 20–21. N.Y. City Opera: 4.7.47 p. 21 (sketch); 1.24.49 p. 11. Covent Garden: 1.2.50 pp. 27, 28. Munich: 10.16.50 p. 13. Stockholm: 10.18.54 p. 15. Dresden: 3.5.56 p. 33. Houston: 3.26.56 p. 32. *Mus. Amer.* NBC-TV: 2.57 p. 17.

Performing Companies. 182 (11.10.49). 391 (6.53). 72 (1954). 333 (5.8. 54). 185 (11.54). 329 (51–52, 54–55, 57–58). 334 (1954). 478A (11.23.54). 477 (11.23.54). 481 (1.19.56). 85 (3.26.56). 130 (56–57). 496 (56–57).

⚜ Savitri

Music and libretto in English by Gustav Holst (1874–1934). Premiere: London, November 5, 1916. Indian legend based on an episode in the Mahabharata. Intended for performance in the open air or in a small building where chorus, orchestra, and conductor are not visible to the audience. Continuous texture with rhythm patterned on speech; simple harmonic structure. No overture. Setting: a wood at evening (time and place otherwise unspecified). One act (30 min).

Synopsis. The voice of Death is heard calling to Savitri. He has come to take her husband, Satyavan, a woodcutter. When Satyavan returns home from his work in the woods, he finds Savitri trembling and lamenting the vanity of all things. Death claims Satyavan, and Savitri discovers that her fears are gone. Because she was not afraid of him, Death offers her a boon, on the condition that it not be Satyavan's life. Savitri asks for life — a request which includes the possibility of giving life to others through her life with Satyavan. Death grants her wish and restores her husband to life.

Major Roles. SATYAVAN (t); E2 to A3. SAVITRI (s); B2 to B4. DEATH (bs); B1 to F3.

Chorus. SSAA.

Orchestra. 2 string qt, 2 fl, cb, Eng hrn.

Material. FS-P: G Sc (Ch — Goodwin) (rent). VS: G Sc (Ch — Goodwin) (rent).

Photographs. Univ. of Illinois: 1.17.49 p. 12.

Performing Companies. 343A (5.28.48). 294 (12.29.49). 441 (3.6.54). 389 (9.54; 5.55). 122A (11.54). 297 (2.55). 61 (56–57). 428 (56–57).

▶ The Scarf

Music by Lee Hoiby (1926–   ). Libretto in English by Harry Duncan, based on a story by Chekhov. Commissioned by the Curtis Institute of Music. Premiere: Spoleto, Italy, June 20, 1958. Melodrama. Complex harmonic structure, continuous texture, dramatic but simple vocal line. Brief introduction. Setting: an isolated farmhouse; the present. One act: the kitchen-bedroom of the farmhouse (45 min).

Synopsis. During a fierce February blizzard, Miriam sits at her spinning wheel weaving a long scarlet scarf. Her elderly husband, Reuel, accuses her of casting a spell in order to attract a young man to the house. Every time she has sat at her wheel, a man has turned up to spend the night, and Reuel is sure she has bewitched them. Suddenly, out of the blizzard, a postman appears and begs refuge from the storm. Miriam's charm has worked again. The Postman falls asleep, and Miriam sings a wild incantation. Reuel can stand it no longer, wakes the Postman, and insists that he leave. While Reuel is out harnessing the horse, Miriam and the Postman embrace. She gives him the scarf and casts a spell which will bring him back to her. But her charms always fail — it is only Reuel who returns, wearing the scarf which the Postman gave to him. In a fury, Miriam strangles her husband with the scarf and rushes into the night.

Major Roles. MIRIAM (s); should give the impression of wild, dark beauty; taxing dramatically, needs strength and intensity; Bb2 to Bb4. REUEL (t); B1 to B3. POSTMAN (bar); A1 to F3.

Orchestra. ob, cl, bsn, 2 hrn, trp, trb, timp, perc, piano, celeste, strings.

Material. FS-P: G Sc (rent). VS: G Sc $3.50.

Performing Companies. 334 (4.5.59 — Amer prem). 196 (6.5.59). 225 (1959). 9A (1960).

⚑ Der Schauspieldirektor · The Impresario

Music by Wolfgang Amadeus Mozart (1756–1791). Libretto in German by Gottlob Stephanie the Younger. Composed for Emperor Joseph II. Premiere: Vienna, February 7, 1786. A pastiche, collected from other Mozart works (Mozart originally wrote only one overture and one terzett). A later version by Taubert and Schneider added several songs. The first version shows the manager, Frank, seeking members for his company; Mozart himself and Schikaneder, his librettist for "The Magic Flute," are introduced, as well as Mme. Hofer, his sister-in-law, who sang the Queen of the Night. Later versions are by Giovanni Cardelli and Rudolph Fellner. Several difficult vocal numbers; dialogue. One act, a theater manager's office, 18th century; can be freely interpreted (60 min).

Synopsis. A theater manager tries to recruit an operatic company for his playhouse. He encounters difficulties with two jealous prima donnas, as each is determined that she shall be the only singer he engages and scorns the accomplishments of the other. At last, M. Vogelgesang manages to placate the two and persuades them to sign contracts.

Roles. MADAME HERZ (s); C3 to F5. MADAME SILVERKLANG (s); C3 to D5. Both women need tremendous agility for the many florid passages. MONSIEUR VOGELGESANG (t); C2 to A3. BUFF (bs).

Orchestra. 2 fl, 2 ob, 2 cl, 2 bsn, 2 hrn, 2 trp, timp, strings.

Material. FS-P: G Sc, Map, TW, Ka (rent). MS: AMP (Ph) $3. VS: G Sc (g, e — Cardelli) $3; Ri (g) $3.75; Map (rent). O Tr: Blom (T2); Mead (Ha); Reese (T31); Weiler (T22).

Photographs. Los Angeles City College: 1.18.43 p. 30. Washington Univ., St. Louis: 2.1.54 p. 32. Ogelbay: 11.19.56 p. 21.

Performing Companies. Approx 46; 1956–57 only 19, 22, 258, 356, 368, 478, 482.

⚑ Die Schöne Galathea · The Beautiful Galatea · The Lovely Galatea

Music by Franz von Suppé (1819–1895). Libretto by "Poly Henrion" (L. Kohl von Kohlenegg). Premiere: Berlin, June 30, 1865. Farce. Highly melodious; set numbers; dialogue. Overture. One act: Pygmalion's studio in Athens, the Golden Age (60 min).

Synopsis. The sculptor Pygmalion and a chorus of worshipers are going to the temple of Venus at dawn, but Ganymede, Pygmalion's helper, prefers to sleep. In Pygmalion's absence, the moneylender Midas calls, and for a bribe is shown Pygmalion's new statue of Galatea. The sculptor returns and drives the rich old man away, then prays to Venus to bring the statue to life. His prayer is answered. Galatea, the maiden, falls in love with Pygmalion, the first man she sees, but soon after spies the younger and handsomer Ganymede and shifts her affections. Later she bewitches Midas and accepts his gifts without promising any return. Pygmalion discovers her intrigues and in despair prays that she be turned back to stone. The sculptor then sells his statue to Midas.

Roles. GANYMEDE (bar); A1 to B3. MIDAS (buf t); C2 to G♯3. PYGMALION (t); D2 (C♭2 opt) to A3 (B3, C4 opt). GALATEA (lyr col s); florid, needs trill; D3 to G5.

Chorus. SATTB.

Orchestra. 2 fl, 2 ob, 2 cl, 2 bsn, 4 hrn, 2 trp, 3 trb, timp, perc, strings.

Material. FS-P: Map (rent). VS: Dit (Pr — e — Willard Day); Ha (e — Mead) (rent).

Performing Companies. 82 (50–51). 94 (51–52). 366 (51–52). 481 (56–57). 85A (12.3.58).

🎭 School for Wives

Music by Rolf Liebermann (1910–   ). Libretto in German by Heinrich Strobel after Molière's "L'École des femmes." English adaptation by Elizabeth Montague. Commissioned by Louisville Philharmonic Society, Inc. Premiere: Louisville, December 3, 1955. Rondo buffo. Continuous texture, melodic. Overture. Setting: France, 17th century. One set: a street outside the house of Arnolphe. The façade of one of the two houses should lift or be transparent to show a girl's room. One act (orig 72 min; German vers in three acts, 90 min).

Synopsis. Poquelin (Molière), who sits in the center of the stage and makes comments on the action, is the author of the play and assumes several characters as needed. Arnolphe is an aging cynic who has boasted of his conquests with married women. For his own wife he has chosen a young country girl, Agnes, without parents and has educated her in a convent far from temptation. She now lives in seclusion next door to him. Horace, the son of Arnolphe's friend Oronte, has fallen in love with Agnes. Unwittingly he confides to Arnolphe his distress that she is being kept in tyrannical bondage by a lecherous old fool. Arnolphe is determined to outwit Horace. However, when Henry (played by Poquelin) unexpectedly arrives and announces that he is Agnes's father and intends to marry her to Horace, Arnolphe is forced to admit the failure of his plan to educate a women to be the model wife.

Major Roles. POQUELIN (Arnolphe's servant ALAIN, also OLD WOMAN and HENRY) (bar); B1 to F3. ARNOLPHE (bar); G♯1 to G♭3. AGNES (lyr s); E♭3 to D5. HORACE (lyr t); D2 to C4. GEORGETTA, Arnolphe's servant (c); A2 to E♭4.

Lesser Role. ORONTE (bs).

Orchestra. fl (picc), ob, cl, bsn, 2 hrn, trp, trb, timp, perc, harpsichord, strings. (German vers adds offstage wind orchestra.)

Material. FS-P: AMP (UE) (rent). VS: AMP (UE — e — Montague) $12.50.

Photographs. Salzburg: 10.14.57 p. 18.

Performing Companies. 176 (12.3.55 — prem). 334 (5.56). 47 (6.14.56). 178 (58–59). Many in Germany.

🎵 Il Segreto di Susanna · The Secret of Suzanne

Music by Ermanno Wolf-Ferrari (1876–1948). Libretto in Italian by Enrico Golisciani. Premiere: Munich, December 4, 1909. Comedy ("Interlude"). Continuous texture; melodic; simple harmonic structure. Overture. Setting: Piedmont circa 1910 — a handsome apartment in the Count's palace. One act (40 min).

Synopsis. Susanna, a pretty bride of a month, comes home after buying a package of cigarettes. Her husband, Count Gil, hates the smell of tobacco so she has concealed her fondness of smoking from him. Gil has seen her out alone against his wishes and rushes in to question her. When he smells the odor of tobacco, his suspicions are aroused — she must have an admirer! Susanna calms him, but just as he is about to embrace her, he smells tobacco again. After a furious quarrel, Susanna sends Gil to his club. Sante, the mute servant, brings her a cigarette. Suspecting that a man is hiding somewhere in the house, Gil hurries back, and Susanna hides her cigarette just in time. Gil leaves again, and Susanna lights up, just as Gil peeks through the window. Her secret is out. Gil asks her to forgive him. They each light a cigarette and retire happily.

Major Roles. SUSANNA, about 20 (s); several florid passages; D3 to A4. COUNT GIL, about 30 (bar); G1 to F3.

Lesser Role. SANTE, a servant, about 50 (mute).

Orchestra. 3 fl, 2 ob, 2 cl, 2 bsn, 4 hrn, 2 trp, 3 trb, timp, harp, strings.

Material. FS-P: G Sc (Wein) (rent). VS: G Sc (Wein — i, e — Claude Aveling) (rent). O Tr: Farquhar (T22).

Photographs. Newport, R.I.: 3.10.41 p. 26. Hartt College: 11.19.45 p. 18. Glyndebourne: 9.29.58 p. 25.

Performing Companies. Approx 29; 1956–57 only 51, 187, 192, 241, 457, 460.

🎵 La Serva padrona · The Maid Mistress and other titles

Music by Giovanni Battista Pergolesi (1710–1736). Libretto in Italian by Gennaro Antonio Federico. Premiere: Naples, August 28, 1733. Comedy. Melodious, vocal line light and pliant over conventional harmonies. Set numbers; patter and occasional accompanied recitative. No overture. Originally a two-part intermezzo to be played between the acts of an opera seria. One act: the home of Uberto (42 min).

Synopsis. Set in his ways, the bachelor Uberto resists the open attempts of his maid, Serpina, to marry him. But the idea of marriage is implanted. When the sly girl brings on Vespone in the disguise of a hot-tempered soldier, and claims he is her fiancé, Uberto is troubled. Can the engagement be broken? he asks. Only if he refuses to pay four thousand crowns as a dowry, she says. With this excellent way out, Uberto vows to marry her himself. He even forgives her stratagem when Vespone is unmasked.

Roles. SERPINA (s); needs flexibility and lightness; C3 (one B2) to A4.

UBERTO (buf bs); needs agility over wide range; high tessitura in recitatives; F1 (one E♭1) to F3. VESPONE (mute).

Orchestra. Harpsichord (or piano), strings. Or 2 hrn, 2 trb, harpsichord (or piano), strings.

Material. FS-P: AMP (UE), Ka, Map, Ri (rent). MS: AMP (Ph) $3.50. VS: AMP (UE – g) $1.50; Ri (i, e – Josef Furgiuele) $4. O Tr: Dunn (T3); Stoessel (A Ka); Farquhar (T22); Weiler (T22).

Photographs. Community Opera, Scranton, Pa.: 2.23.48 p. 30 (in modern dress). Univ. of Illinois: 1.17.49 p. 11.

Performing Companies. Approx 54; 1956–57 only 16, 51, 165, 275, 313, 319, 386.

⛤ The Shepherds of the Delectable Mountains

Music by Ralph Vaughan Williams (1872–1958). Libretto in English by the composer, based on Bunyan's "Pilgrim's Progress." Premiere: London, 1922. Pastoral episode. Melodic; simple accompaniment, largely modal. No overture. One act: an unspecified time and place (35 min).

Synopsis. A pilgrim seeking immortality comes upon three shepherds who invite him to stay with them in the Delectable Mountains and enjoy the birds' song. But a celestial messenger comes for him to take him to the master. He pierces the Pilgrim's heart with an arrow whose point is sharpened by love and bids him surmount the waters of the nearby river. The Shepherds anoint him with spices and pray for him as he makes the difficult crossing. The heavenly choir welcomes the new pilgrim, and the Shepherds rejoice.

Roles. (No special vocal problems.) PILGRIM (t). THREE SHEPHERDS (t, t, bs). A CELESTIAL MESSENGER (s or t). VOICE OF A BIRD (s), offstage.

Chorus. Boy ss. Offstage.

Orchestra. 2 fl, ob, Eng hrn, strings. *Stage:* 2 trp, harp, bells.

Material. FS-P: Ox (rent). FS: Ox $6. VS: Ox $3. CP: Ox 60¢.

Photographs. Sadler's Wells: 4.7.47 p. 19.

Performing Companies. 390 (12.16.49). 518 (11.29.55). 3 (57–58).

⛤ Slow Dusk

Music and libretto in English by Carlisle Floyd (1926–   ). Premiere: Syracuse University, Spring 1949. Rural tragedy. Folklike atmosphere; melodic vocal line; recitative and a few set numbers; simple harmonic structure. Prologue; interlude between scenes indicating passage of time. One act: front porch and yard of a farmhouse in the sandhills of the Carolinas; time, the present (40 min).

Synopsis. Sadie, a young farm girl, is determined to marry Micah, although she is a Disciple and he a Truelight, warring religious sects of the countryside, and she is better educated than he. Her Aunt Sue and brother Jess oppose the marriage. After a tender meeting in which the diffident Micah at last proposes and is accepted, he goes off fishing. Sadie storms out of the house when her news is angrily received by Aunt Sue. After an interval she returns to be met with the tragic news that Micah has drowned. Her happiness is turned to bitterest grief.

Roles. AUNT SUE (m-s); rough-hewn, middle-aged; B♭2 to F4. JESS (bar); rawboned, early 20's; A1 to E3. SADIE (s); B♭2 to B♭4. MICAH (t); D2 to G♭3 (one A3).

Orchestra. 2 fl (picc), 2 ob (Eng hrn), 2 cl (bs cl), 2 bsn, 2 hrn, 2 trp, 2 trb, timp, perc, harp, strings.

Material. FS-P: B & H (rent). VS: B & H $4.50.

Performing Companies. 145 (1.11.57). 520A (11.57). 325 (4.21.58). 395 (8.7.58). 63 (1.13.59). 259 (2.4.59). 7 (3.12.59). 91 (4.18.59). 225 (8.5.59). 9A (10.59).

✄ The Soldier

Music by Lehman Engel (1910–   ). Libretto in English by Lewis Allan, based on a story by Roald Dahl. Premiere: New York, November 25, 1956 (conc). Contemporary tragedy. Vocal line mostly patterned after speech; occasional set numbers; dialogue; dissonant. Brief prelude. The action is continuous; three scenes show a lonely country road, exterior of house, bedroom; time, the present (55 min).

Synopsis. Robert, a soldier returned from war, is beset by fears — of tomorrow, of the doctor and nurse who submit him to humiliating tests, even of his wife Edna, who has become impatient with his vagueness, his sudden withdrawn moods, and his clumsiness. He sees himself as a child, happily playing by the sea, then going home holding his mother's hand. He envisions scenes with the doctor, with his wife, and with two friends, who seem to him to behave strangely, recalling the days when he and Edna were happily in love. The soldier's sense of loss and persecution grows to madness and he threatens his wife with a kitchen knife. She disarms him, whereupon he begins to weep and once more sees the little boy that was. His wife phones the doctor to send "them" for him. He is alone in the dark, shadowless, black night.

Major Roles. THE MAN (ROBERT, the soldier) (bar); top G3. HE (t); top A3; SHE (m-s), friends of Robert and Edna. EDNA (speaking). DOCTOR (offstage bar, speaking). NURSE (offstage, speaking). CHILD, Robert as a boy (mime).

Orchestra. fl (picc), cl (bs cl), bsn, trp, hrn, trb, piano, perc, string quintet.

Material. FS-P: Ch (rent). VS: Ch $3.50.

Photograph. Jackson, Miss.: 1.5.59 p. 25.

Performing Companies. 237A (11.24.58 — stage prem).

✄ Solomon and Balkis · The Butterfly That Stamped

Music by Randall Thompson (1899–   ). Libretto in English by the composer, adapted from Kipling's "Just So Stories." Commissioned by League of

Composers, 1941. Premiere: CBS, March 29, 1942. Stage premiere: Cambridge, April 14, 1952. Fantasy. Melodic, often satirical mockery of classic composers; set numbers. Brief prelude. One act: King Solomon's gardens (43 min).

Synopsis. Solomon's 999 wives quarrel bitterly among themselves and make his life miserable. Balkis, his favorite, sees a chance to teach them a lesson. A Butterfly and his wife find their way to the garden where Solomon and Balkis sit; they also are quarreling. The Butterfly boasts that he can destroy the palace by merely stamping his foot. His wife laughs at him, and Balkis encourages her to test him. Solomon tells him to go ahead, and summons four djinns, whom he orders to spirit away the palace when the Butterfly stamps. The miracle works: the Butterfly's wife is full of respect, and Solomon's wives, seeing what can happen when a mere insect is angered by his spouse's nagging, fall down in awe and vow to mend their ways. The Butterfly stamps again, and the palace is restored, with it the happiness and peace of Solomon and Balkis.

Major Roles. KING SOLOMON (bar); G1 to F♯3. BALKIS, QUEEN OF SHEBA (m-s); B2 to F♯4 (A♭4 opt). THE BUTTERFLY (t); C♯2 to B♭3. BUTTERFLY'S WIFE (lyr s); D3 to A4. EGYPTIAN QUEEN (dram s); C♯3 to A♭4.

Lesser Roles. OTHER QUEENS, of Abyssinia, Ethiopia, Mesopotamia, Persia, India, China, representing the 999 wives of Solomon; (s) B♭2 to G4; (c) G2 to D4. FOUR DJINNS (mute).

Orchestra. fl, ob, 2 cl, bsn, 2 hrn, 2 trp, 2 perc, timp, strings.

Material. FS-P: E Sc (rent). VS: E Sc $2.50. 2 P-Yes (E Sc).

Performing Companies. 400 (4.54). 16 (7.55). 164 (2.28.57). 61 (1957).

🦋 Sotoba Komachi

Music by Marvin Levy (1932–). Libretto after the Noh play by Kan'ami Kigotsugu, translated by Sam Houston Brock. Premiere: New York, 1957. Oriental influence, from the esthetic of the Noh play. Can be performed with any of three elements most prominent: opera, ballet, or cantata. Prelude. One scene: typical Noh play, symbolistic, and as simple as desired; time, 16th-century feudal Japan (30 min).

Synopsis. The withered Komachi, once a beautiful and heartless poetess, muses on her past and on her present shame and misery, evoking her younger self as a vision. Seeing her as a beggar, two priests attempt to instruct and admonish her, but she remains untouched, and at last reveals her identity. The chorus tells of the Captain who loved Komachi desperately; the cruel beauty demanded that he visit her in his chariot a hundred nights before he should see her. He died just before his task was completed. His love and anger now possess Komachi's soul. The priests pray for her.

Roles. No special vocal demands. FIRST PRIEST (bs-bar). SECOND PRIEST (t). KOMACHI (s). CHORUS (m-s). THE YOUNG KOMACHI (female dancer). SHII NO SHOSHO, the Captain (male dancer).

225

Orchestra. fl, ob, vla, vcl, harp, timp (2), perc (gong, triangle, sn drum, woodblock, cymbal, temple blocks).
Material. FS-P: B & H (rent). VS: B & H (rent).

🎵 Sunday Excursion

Music by Alec Wilder (1907–   ). Libretto in English by Arnold Sundgaard. Premiere: N.Y. City, April 17, 1953. Curtain raiser; simple, nostalgic story. Melodic, set numbers; conventional harmonies; no vocal difficulties. Overture. The set (may be as simple as desired): a section of the excursion coach on the New York, New Haven, and Hartford Railroad, about 1910. One act (25 min).

Synopsis. Two boys and two girls are returning from an excursion to New York City. They are strangers at first, but manage to become acquainted before the candy butcher warns them that the train has stopped at their destination.
Roles. ALICE (s). VERONICA (c). HILLARY (t). MARVIN (bar). TIM, CANDY BUTCHER (bs-bar).
Orchestra. fl, ob, 2 cl, bsn, hrn, trp, perc, piano, strings.
Material. FS-P: G Sc (rent). VS: G Sc $2.50.
Photographs. Brigham Young Univ.: 11.15.54 p. 16.
Performing Companies. Approx 83; 1956–57 only 3, 15, 19, 126, 146, 239, 240, 242, 274, 292, 320, 425, 434, 451, 463, 482, 516 (prem − 378 − 4.17. 53 for Federation of Music Clubs).

🎵 Suor Angelica · Sister Angelica

Music by Giacomo Puccini (1858–1924). Libretto in Italian by Giovacchino Forzano. Premiere: New York, December 14, 1918. Lyric tragedy. Part of a "triptych" which includes "Il Tabarro" and "Gianni Schicchi." Set numbers; accompanied recitative; simple harmonic structure. No overture. Setting: the cloister of a convent near Siena, 17th century. One act (53 min).

Synopsis. Because of the scandal which she caused her noble family by having an illegitimate child, Sister Angelica has done penance in a convent for seven years. The Princess, her aunt, arrives to demand that Angelica sign a document which turns over her inheritance to her young sister, who is about to be married. When Sister Angelica inquires about her son, the Princess coldly tells her that he has been dead for two years. The Princess departs, refusing forgiveness. In despair, Angelica takes poison. Recognizing too late that she has committed a monstrous sin, she begs the Virgin to give her a sign of forgiveness before she dies. In a vision, the Virgin appears leading a little child, which she sends towards Angelica, while a heavenly chorus sings of her salvation.
Major Roles. SISTER ANGELICA (s); requires stamina for dramatic acting and high tessitura; A2 to C5. THE PRINCESS, stern and commanding (c); G♯2 to F♯4.

Lesser Roles. THE ABBESS (m-s). THE MONITOR (m-s). MISTRESS OF NOVICES (c). SISTER GENEVIEVE (s). SISTER OSMINA (m-s). SISTER DOLCINA (m-s). NURSING SISTER (m-s). TWO ATTENDING NUNS (m-s). TWO NOVICES (m-s). TWO LAY-SISTERS (s and m-s).

Chorus. SSSTB. Angels, children. Brief, backstage.

Orchestra. 2 fl, picc, 2 ob, Eng hrn, 2 cl, bs cl, 2 bsn, 4 hrn, 3 trp, 3 trb, bs trb, perc, harp, strings. *Stage:* piano, organ, 3 trp, picc, bells.

Material. FS-P: Ri (rent). VS: Ri (i, e — Herbert Withers) $6. O Tr: Reese (T31).

Photographs. Florence: 2.20.56 p. 12.

Performing Companies. 387 (3.10.50). 389 (3.13.50). 72 (1951). 338A (2.17.52). 496A (3.52). 249A (11.20.52). 57 (12.52). 333 (3.17.53; 12.5. 54). 475 (5.53). 129A (5.2.53). 140 (2.26.54). 343A (4.23.54). 499B (5.14. 54). 441 (12.10.54). 218A (3.55). 127A (5.22.55). 457 (1.14.56). 447 (3.56). 29A (5.27.56). 1956–57: 59, 223, 241, 314, 373.

▶ Il Tabarro · The Cloak

Music by Giacomo Puccini (1858–1924). Libretto in Italian by Giuseppe Adami after the play, "La Houppelande," by Didier Gold. Premiere: New York, December 14, 1918. Melodrama. Verismo style. Part of a "triptych" which includes "Suor Angelica" and "Gianni Schicchi." Set numbers; accompanied recitative. No overture. Setting: a barge on the Seine; 19th century. One act (54 min).

Synopsis. Michèle, owner of a barge, is in his fifties and married to Giorgetta, who is half his age. She has taken Luigi, one of the workmen on the barge, as her lover. At the end of the day, Giorgetta offers the workmen, Tinca, Talpa, and Luigi, a drink. They dance with her until Michèle arrives, whereupon Tinca and Talpa leave. Luigi remains to arrange a meeting that night with Giorgetta. The signal that all is safe will be a lighted match. Michèle sadly asks Giorgetta why they have grown apart; she tells him that it is merely that they are growing old. She pretends to go to bed, but Michèle realizes that she intends to meet a lover. As he ponders, he lights his pipe, unwittingly giving a signal to Luigi, who rushes out to meet Giorgetta. Michèle strangles him and hides him beneath his cloak. Giorgetta uneasily creeps on deck, discovers Michèle, and asks him to cover her with his cloak because she is cold. Michèle flings the cloak aside to reveal the body of her dead lover.

Major Roles. GIORGETTA (s); C3 to C5. MICHELE (bar); Bb1 to G3. LUIGI (t); D3 to Bb4. FRUGOLA, Talpa's wife (m-s); B2 to A4.

Lesser Roles. TINCA (t). TALPA (bs). TWO LOVERS (s and t). SONG VENDOR (t).

Chorus. STBB. Midinettes, stevedores. An organ grinder (mute). A harp player (mute).

Orchestra. 3 fl, 3 ob, 3 cl, 2 bsn, 4 hrn, 3 trp, 3 trb, tuba, timp, perc, small bells, celeste, hand organ, harp, strings. *Stage:* cornet, harp. *Reduced vers:* 2 fl, ob, 2 cl, bsn, 2 hrn, 2 trp, trb, timp, perc, small bells, celeste, harp, strings.

Material. FS-P: Ri (rent). VS: Ri (e – Machlis) $7.50. O Tr: Gaines (Ri); Goldovsky and Neway (T13); Levin (T26); Reese (T31); Vacano (148).

Photographs. Metropolitan: 12.31.45 p. 18 (sketch). Florence: 2.20.56 p. 11. *Mus. Amer.* La Scala: 5.59 p. 21.

Performing Companies. 390 (2.23.51). 333 (2.14.52). 338A (2.17.52). 447 (7.52; 5.54). 47 (4.53). 443 (5.21.53). 531 (10.53). 502A (3.3.54). 72 (1954). 397 (11.5.54). 148 (5.24.55; 12.16.55). 145 (5.19.55). 138 (11. 16.55). 403 (3.2.56; 56–57). 337 (6.1.56). 92B (5.56). 1956–57: 48A, 59, 115, 187, 281, 317, 358, 441.

🎵 Tale for a Deaf Ear

Music by Mark Bucci (1924–   ). Libretto in English (with one aria in Italian, one in German) by the composer, based on a story by Elizabeth Enright. Commissioned by Samuel Wechsler. Premiere: Berkshire Music Center, August 5, 1957. Contemporary tragedy with supernatural episodes. Vocal line partly recitative, partly melodic (arias), over dramatic orchestra, occasionally dissonant. Small amount of dialogue. Very brief prelude. Setting: the livingroom of Tracy and Laura Gates, the present. One act with three miracle sequences dramatized behind a scrim, on which lighting projections may be flashed (46 min).

Synopsis. After an acrimonious dispute between the suburban couple, Laura and Tracy Gates, in which many old wounds are reopened, Tracy dies of a heart attack. Laura penitently wishes him back. Her fervent plea is made at exactly 3:59 and three quarters on a winter Sunday afternoon; at that same moment Hypraemius, a mariner, had died centuries ago. So good was he that four miracles were allowed him, one each season. When a penitent pled for the return of a dear one at this exact moment, the wish was granted. This had already happened three times: in springtime, a son was restored to a noble-woman in Tuscany; in summer the plea of a Scottish girl in the Isle of Skye brought a much-needed cow back to life; and in an autumn during the Thirty Years' War, a soldier gave life to his young brother before dying himself. True to the pattern, Tracy is restored. But he is as cantankerous as ever, and in spite of Laura's efforts, they are soon quarreling bitterly again. Once more, Tracy dies. This time it is too late. The chorus comments: "The only death in life is the death of love."

Major Roles. LAURA GATES (s or m-s); C3 to G♯4 (B♭4 opt). TRACY GATES (bar); B1 to E3 (one F3).

Lesser Roles. FLORENTINE NOBLEWOMAN (dram s or m-s); C3 (B♯2 opt) to B♭4. SCOTTISH FARM GIRL (lyr s); C3 to A♭4. GERMAN SOLDIER (t); C2 to B♭3.

Bit Part. DOCTOR (speaking).

Chorus. SB. Generally unison. Behind scene; may be small as desired.

Orchestra. fl, ob (Eng hrn), 2 cl (bs cl), bsn, hrn, trp, perc, piano (celeste), harp, strings. 2-piano (celeste; harpsichord opt). 2-piano, as above, plus perc (2 players).

Production Problems. First miracle scene: crib must be visible; second: cow (papier maché with flexible neck); third: soldier's brother must be seen.

Material. FS-P: MTI (Fra) (rent). VS: MTI (Fra) $5, (inc Tr of i and g arias).

Photographs. Mus. Amer. N.Y. City Opera: 5.58 p. 30.

Performing Companies. 205 (8.5.57 – prem). 334 (1958).

◪ The Telephone

Music and libretto in English by Gian-Carlo Menotti (1911–   ). Written for Ballet Society. Premiere: New York, February 18, 1947. Comedy. Melodious; vocal line often patterned on speech. Prelude. Setting: Lucy's apartment, a phone booth outside; time, the present. One act (25 min).

Synopsis. Ben, in a hurry to catch a train and in despair because his Lucy won't put down the phone, goes out and phones her himself to propose marriage. She accepts immediately and makes him promise not to forget her phone number so he can call her every day while he is away.

Roles. LUCY (col s); high tessitura, needs trill; C3 to D5. BEN (bar); A1 to F3 (one G♭3, one G3 opt).

Orchestra. fl, ob, cl, bsn, hrn, trp, perc, piano, strings. 2 P-Yes.

Material. FS-P: G Sc (rent). VS: G Sc (e, f) $2.

Photographs. Univ. of Minnesota: 10.29.51 p. 19. Kentucky Opera Association: 3.16.53 p. 3. Wichita, Kans.: 11.14.55 p. 19.

Performing Companies. Approx 217; 1956–57 only 3, 20, 42, 44, 63, 97, 100, 108, 121, 133, 140, 143, 162, 163, 174, 175, 191, 195, 203, 220, 227, 233, 242, 254, 268, 274, 288, 289, 294, 304, 309, 314, 319, 356, 378, 381, 384, 392, 399, 412, 413, 417A, 436, 437, 454, 458, 467, 472, 483, 485, 498, 500, 505, 508, 528, 529.

◪ The Tenor

Music by Hugo Weisgall (1912–   ). Libretto in English by Karl Shapiro and Ernst Lert, based on the play, "Der Kammersänger," by Frank Wedekind. Premiere: Baltimore, February 11, 1952. Tragedy, embodying satire. Continuous texture, chromatic, occasionally mildly atonal; difficult vocal line; several ensembles. Brief prelude. One act: hotel room, the present (70 min).

Synopsis. Gerardo, the spoiled and cynical tenor, whose Tristan inspires women to follow him in droves and shower him with roses and champagne, finds his valet selling all the booty to the bellhop. A young girl has concealed herself in the room and steps out when Gerardo is alone. By her importunities she materially reduces the hour Gerardo has set apart for a rest before his departure to another city. Eventually Maurice, the manager, gets rid of her by sending her to an agent for a singing job. Maurice brings the rebellious Gerardo to heel by the effective threat to replace him by younger tenors. He

229

promises to break off a current affair with Helen, a married woman. But she appears, saying that she has left her husband for Gerardo. Her ardent plea rouses in the tenor the wish to abandon the false life of the stage, for his contract forbids him to marry. At the end of their impassioned duet, the phone rings. It is Maurice waiting. The spell is broken, and Gerardo prepares to depart. But it is the end for Helen — she shoots herself and falls across the threshold, blocking Gerardo's exit. In a daze, he gathers up his belongings, steps over her body, and rushes out of the room.

Roles. VALET (bar); Ab1 to E3 (F♯3 opt). BELLBOY (buf t); D♯2 to A3. GERARDO (dram t); several florid passages; considerable high tessitura, needs strength throughout range; C2 to Bb3 (B3 opt). YOUNG GIRL (lyr spin s); sustained passages, high tessitura; C3 to C5. MAURICE (bs-bar); G♯1 (one F♯1 opt) to Ab3. HELEN (dram s); Bb2 (one A2) to Bb4 (one C5).

Orchestra. fl (picc), ob (Eng hrn), 2 cl (Eb cl, bs cl), bsn, 2 hrn, trp, trb, perc (inc timp), piano, strings.

Material. FS-P: Pr (Me) (rent). VS: Pr (Me) $5.

Performing Companies. 193 (2.11.52 — prem). 333A (10.27.54).

⚓ The Tide

Music by Boris Blacher (1903–   ). Libretto in German by Heinz von Cramer. Premiere: Dresden, March 4, 1947. Fantasy. Vocal line patterned after speech, a few short set arias. No overture. One act: a sandbank near the wreck of a ship, today or yesterday (40 min).

Synopsis. A young fisherman, a girl, a rather irresponsible young man, and a wealthy old banker become stranded on a wreck as the tide rises. Believing themselves lost, the fisherman and the girl (formerly the banker's mistress) declare their love. The banker offers gold to anyone who will save them. The young man, wild with greed, murders the banker for his wealth. But now, unexpectedly the tide recedes. The girl, seeing the money in the young man's possession, goes off with him, leaving the idealistic fisherman dreaming vainly of her return.

Roles. FISHERMAN (bar); some high tessitura; C♯2 to E3. GIRL (s); C3 to Ab4. YOUNG MAN (t); F2 to Ab3. BANKER (bs); a few florid passages; A1 to D3.

Chorus. SATB. Comments on and describes action.

Orchestra. fl, cl, bsn, trp, trb, strings.

Material. FS-P: AMP (BB) (rent). VS: AMP (BB — g, e — Dorothy de Reeder) $6.

Performing Company. 197 (4.19.56) — Amer prem).

⚓ The Tower

Music by Marvin Levy (1932–   ). Libretto in English by Townsend Brewster. Premiere: Santa Fe, August 2, 1957. Comedy. Melodious, often parodies classical and dance forms, unconventional harmonies; set numbers: arias, ensembles, recitative. Short prelude. One act, five scenes (40 min).

Scene i: Solomon's throneroom; ii: Near the shore where the tower is being built; iii: A wasteland in winter; iv: A room in the tower; v: Outside the tower wall. Before each scene Reuel appears before the curtain.

Synopsis. Reuel prophesies that King Solomon will give his daughter Achlamah to the poorest in the land. To avoid the prophecy's being fulfilled, the wily Solomon builds a tower and imprisons the princess in it, guarded by seventy scholars. But Fate will not be denied: the poor youth Joash, finding shelter on a cold night in the skeleton of an ox, is transported to the tower roof and received warmly by the princess's nurse Tabitha, who believes in the prophecy. The two young people immediately fall in love. When they wish to sign a marriage contract, there is no ink — the old curmudgeon Nabarias has hoarded it all for himself. Joash cuts his finger, and the couple plight their troth in his blood. Solomon is forced to agree that the prophecy was right.

Roles. REUEL, a young prophet (bs-bar); needs agility; A1 to E♭3. KING SOLOMON (buf t); needs trill, considerable florid singing; C2 to B♭3. PRINCESS ACHLAMAH (lyr spin s); C♯3 to C5. TABITHA (m-s); G2 to G♯4. NABARIAS, an old scholar (bs); G1 to D3. ABIGAIL, Achlamah's maid (col s); one important aria; C♯3 E♭5. JOASH (lyr bar); high tessitura; B♭1 to G♭3.

Orchestra. fl (picc), ob (Eng hrn), cl, bsn, 2 hrn, trp, trb, timp, perc, harp, strings.

Production Problems. Frequent scene changes, which can be accomplished by drops. Ox skeleton prop. Eagle descending from sky.

Material. FS-P: B & H (rent). VS: B & H (rent).

Photographs. Santa Fe: 1.27.58 p. 28.

Performing Company. 275 (8.2.57 — prem).

✠ Trouble in Tahiti

Music and libretto in English by Leonard Bernstein (1918–   ). Premiere: Brandeis University, June 12, 1952. Domestic tragicomedy with satirical overtones. Melodic, with occasional jazz tunes and rhythms; set numbers, accompanied recitative. Orchestra acts mainly as accompaniment; diction is more important than vocal accomplishment. Interludes between i and ii. Sets can be as simple as desired; many effects can be achieved through lighting and simple, suggestive props. Setting: any American city and its suburbs; time, now. Seven scenes (40 min).

PRELUDE: Trio in front of curtain. i: Exterior and interior of little white dream house; ii: Sam's office; iii: Psychiatrist's office; ii a: Sam's office; iii a: Psychiatrist's office; i iv: Street in the rain; Interlude with trio; v: Gymnasium; vi: hat shop; v vi a: Exterior of little white house; vii: Interior of little white house.

Synopsis. A suburban couple, Dinah and Sam, have drifted apart without knowing why. Both are dissatisfied, vaguely longing to repair their relation but not knowing quite how. Both neglect their son, who is to appear in a play that afternoon. Dinah goes to the psychiatrist and then to a movie, "Trouble in Tahiti," which she describes at some length in a hat shop afterward. Sam leaves his office after various encounters which show up his faults, and plays in a handball tournament which he wins. The victory turns to dust when he has to go home. The couple makes one more abortive try at understanding then gives up and goes off to the movie. At various junctures the smiling, sophisticated trio comments sardonically on the blessings of suburban life in their pert, jazzy rhythms.

Roles. DINAH (m-s); in her early 30's; florid passages; G2 to G4. SAM (bs-bar); same age; G1 (touches F1) to F♯3, one passage whistled. THE TRIO, a Greek chorus born of the radio commercial (s or m-s, high t, high bar).

Orchestra. 2 fl, 2 ob, 2 cl, 2 bsn, 2 hrn, 2 trp, 2 trb, tuba, perc, harp, strings.

Material. FS-P: G Sc (rent). VS: G Sc $3.50.

Photographs. Mus. Amer. NBC-TV: 12.1.52 p. 21.

Performing Companies. Approx 31; 1956–57 only 140, 165, 416, 463, 478. 218B (10.57). 127D (11.3.58). 81A (8.18.59).

🎵 The Veil

Music by Bernard Rogers (1893–   ). Libretto in English by Robert Lawrence. Premiere: Indiana University, May 18, 1950. Melodrama. Continuous texture; several set numbers embedded; mainly atonal, expressionist style; vocal line patterned largely after speech. No overture. Setting: a madhouse outside London, 1825. One act: the combined office and cellblock (70 min).

Synopsis. Lucinda has been confined to a gloomy madhouse because she believes her brother wants her fortune. The attending doctor, Betts, already half mad himself, has become infatuated with Lucinda and determines to keep her with him in spite of her belief in her sanity, which is shared by a young consultant, Dr. Keane. Betts places a bridal veil on Lucinda's head and forces her to go through a gruesome ceremony with the maniacal inmates as witnesses. As Keane attempts to rescue her, Betts barricades the door and in a mad ecstasy strangles his "bride." Keane finds him standing over her body, shrouded with the bridal veil.

Major Roles. LUCINDA, about 22 (s); C3 to B4. MRS. FROHN, an attendant, about 40 (c); B♭2 to E♭4. DR. BETTS, 45–50 (bar); A1 to G3. DR. KEANE, about 30 (t); C♯2 to B♭3.

Lesser Roles. WILLIAM, an elderly keeper (bs). Maniacs: BOUND, stoop-shouldered, emaciated (t). BRAMBLE, huge, unshaven delinquent (bs). FLUFF, small, birdlike, with chirping voice (col s); top E♭5; trill on D5. ASPEN, fat, dirty, ragged, middle-aged (m-s); B2 to A4.

Chorus. SSATB. Small group of maniacs.

Orchestra. 2 fl (picc), 2 ob (Eng hrn), 2 cl (bs cl), 2 bsn, 2 hrn, trp, trb, timp, perc, harp, strings.

Material. All So. FS-P (rent). VS (rent).

Performing Company. 333A (10.27.54).

🎵 What Men Live By

Music by Bohuslav Martinu (1890–1959). Libretto after Leo Tolstoi's "Pastoral." Premiere: Hanover, 1953. Highly melodic. No vocal problems; vocal line patterned after speech; dialogue. The scene represents, not realistically, a basement room and a street separated by a wall. Should be staged in the manner of a miracle play, with action suggested rather than played. One act (40 min).

Synopsis. Martin, the cobbler, is told by voices to expect a visit from Christ. He watches eagerly for unfamiliar shoes to pass on the walk outside his basement window, but only an old peasant, a poor woman with a starving child, and an old woman and young boy appear. He befriends them all, then learns that "as he had done it unto the least of these brethren," so had he befriended Him.

Major Roles. MARTIN AUDEITCH, a cobbler (bar); high tessitura, top F3. AN OLD PEASANT PILGRIM (bs). STEPANITCH, an old soldier (bs). WOMAN WITH A CHILD (s); top Bb4. AN OLD WOMAN (c).

Lesser Roles. A BOY (speaking). SPEAKER (t); participates in action.

Chorus. SSAATB. Small. Takes part in action.

Orchestra. fl (2 opt), 2 ob, 2 cl (3 opt), 2 bsn, 2 hrn, trp, trb, perc, piano, strings.

Material. All B & H. FS-P (rent). VS (e, g) $4.50. CP (rent).

Performing Companies. 225 (7.31.54). 124A (1.10.55). 407 (3.10.55). 397 (4.15.55). 317 (5.20.55). 390 (1.29.56; 2.24.57). 249 (12.9.56). 156 (1.15.57). 140 (56–57). 16 (7.22.58).

Appendix

SUPPLEMENTARY LIST OF OPERAS

NOTE: The number of acts appears before the slash, the number of scenes after. The number in parentheses is the number of sets needed. "Lesser" refers to lesser roles. The last entry indicates the source of the opera: letter abbreviations are on pages 243–244, 247–250, numbers on pages 251–262.

LONG OPERAS

Acis and Galatea, J. Lully: heroic pastoral; 3/(3); 15 char, ch; Ba

Acres of Sky, A. Kreutz: folk dr; 2/(5); 135 min; 4 char, 9 sp; C30

Aegyptische Helena, Die, R. Strauss: dr; 2/; 150 min; 2 s, c, 2 t, bar, 6 lesser, ch; LO; B & H

Amadis de Gaulle, J. Lully: trag; Prol, 5/(5); 8 char, ch; Ba

Amfiparnasso, O. Vecchi: madrigal farce; 3/(1); 90 min; 13 char

L'Ange de Feu, S. Prokofiev: dr; 5/7; 2 s, m-s, 3 t, 2 bar, bs, 8 lesser, ch; LO; B & H

Armida, A. Dvořák: mystic dr; 4/; s, t, 2 bar, bs, lesser, ch; MO; B & H

Armide, J. Lully: trag; Prol, 5/(1); 12 char

Beatrice, L. Hoiby: dr; 3/; 90 min; B & H

Blonde Donna, The, E. Carter: com; 3/(4); 120 min; 2 s, 2 c, t, 6 bar, 2 bs; CPr

Blood Wedding, H. Smith: dr; 3/(5); 150 min; 2 s, 2 m-s, t, bs; C50

Boccaccio, F. von Suppé: com; 3/; s, 8 char, ch; Map

By Gemini, M. Baylor: (2); 150 min; 7 char; C4

Christopher Sly, T. Eastwood: com; 2/; 100 min; 2 s, 2 t, 2 bar, bs; Ox

Cinderella, J. Jarrett: fairy tale; 2/(2); 120 min; 9 char, ch; C23

Cowherd and the Sky Maiden, The, J. Verrall: Chin dr; 2/(1); 90 min; s, c, t, bar, bs, ch; SO; ACA

Daphne, R. Strauss: trag; 1/; 105 min; 3 s, c, 3 t, bar, 3 bs, ch; LO; B & H

Deidamia, G. Handel: com; 3/5; 3 s, t, bar, 2 bs, ch; 94

Deirdre, L. Stein: trag; 1/2(1); 90 min; 2 s, m-s, c, t, bar, bs; piano; ACA

Deirdre of the Sorrows, J. Becker: trag; 1/3(1); 90 min; MO; ACA

Deirdre of the Sorrows, K. Rankl: trag; 3/; 130 min; Ox

Deux Journées, Les, L. Cherubini: com; 3/; 150 min; 8 char, ch; Pr

Doctor Faustus Lights the Lights, M. Kupferman: com; 3/6(3); 120 min; 5 s, m-s, t, bar, bs, ch, ballet; Pr

Drumlin Legend, The, E. Bacon: com; 3/(2); 135 min; 9 char, ch; C3

Eastward in Eden, J. Meyerowitz: dr; 3/5(1); 109 min; 16 char; MO; C36

Empty Bottle, The, M. Kalmanoff: myst; 3/(3); 120 min; 7 char; Op

Evangeline, O. Luening: dr; 3/(3); 105 min; s, 2 t, bar, bs, ch; MO; ACA

Favorita, La, G. Donizetti: trag; 4/5; s, t, bar, bs, lesser, ch; MO; Ri

Fille de Mme. Angot, La, C. Lecocq: com; 3/(3); 150 min; 6 char; B & H

Fille du Regiment, La, G. Donizetti: com; 2/; 2 s, t, bs, lesser, ch; MO; Ri

Finta Giardiniera, La, W. Mozart: com; 3/(3); 120 min; 7 char; Pr

Finta Semplice, La, W. Mozart: com; 3/(3); 7 char; SO; Ri

Fra Diavolo, D. Auber: com; 3/; s, m-s, 2 t, bar, 3 bs, ch; MO; Ri

237

Gazza Ladra, La, G. Rossini: com; 3/4; s, m-s, t, 2 bs, ch; LO; Ri

Giulietta, H. Erbse: dr; 4/; 9 char, ch, ballet; LO; Pet

Godiva, M. Kalmanoff: dr; 3/(4); 120 min; 13 char; Op

Griffelkin, L. Foss: folk tale; 2/(4); 120 min; 15 char; Fi

Háry János, Z. Kodály: play with songs; Prol, 2/4, Epil; 4 char, 9 lesser; LO; B & H

Hugh the Drover, R. Vaughan Williams: ballad; 2/(2); 120 min; 9 char, ch; G Sc

Intermezzo, R. Strauss: com; 2/; 3 s, t, 2 bar, 6 lesser; MO; B & H

Involuntary Thief, The, G. Rossini: com; 3/4(2); 90 min; col, m-s, 2 t, bs-bar, bs; 241

Jacob and the Indians, E. Laderman: dr; 3/(2); 150 min; s, m-s, t, 2 bar, bs, ch; S or LO; ACA

Joseph, E. Méhul: bib dr; 3/(1); 150 min; m-s, 8 men, ch; Pet

Junipero Serra, W. Hively: hist dr; 1/(1); 90 min; MO; ACA

Kittiwake Island, A. Wilder: com; 2/(2); 105 min; 3 char, ch; MO; G Sc

Klüge, Die, C. Orff: fairy tale; 90 min; s, t, 2 bar, 2 bs, 3 lesser; LO; AMP

Kumana, E. Kanitz: com; 2/5; 120 min; 7 char; Wa

Lancelot and Elaine, A. Lora: dr; 3/(6); 165 min; 2 s, m-s, t, bar, bs, ch; LO; ACA

Landara, E. Zimbalist: lyr dr; 3/(4); 140 min; s, t, bar, bs; C60

Land Between the Rivers, The, C. van Buskirk: folk trag; 2/(1); 120 min; s, c, 3 t, 5 bs, ch; C52

Legend of Sleepy Hollow, The, A. Lora: dr; 2/(5); 105 min; s, m-s, t, 2 bar, bs, ch; piano; ACA

Liebe der Danaë, Die, R. Strauss: dr; 3/; 4 s, m-s, c, 3 t, bar, lesser, ch; LO; B & H

Linda di Chamounix, G. Donizetti: dr; 3/; s, c, 2 t, bar, 2 bs, ch; MO; Ri

Lodger, The, P. Tate: melodr; 2/; 128 min; s, m-s, t, 2 bar, bs, 4 lesser, ch; Ox

Lucrezia Borgia, G. Donizetti: trag; Prol, 2/5; s, t, bs, lesser, ch; MO; Ri

Moon and Sixpence, The, J. Gardner: dr; 3/; 4 s, 2 m-s, c, 5 t, 2 bs, ch; Ox

Nightingale, The, J. Clokey: Chin tale; 150 min; col, 4 char, 7 sp, ch; Bi

Open the Gates, D.-K. Lee: bib dr; (4); 150 min; 8 char, ch; C32

Pêcheurs de Perles, Les, G. Bizet: dr; 3/4(4); col, t, bar, bs, ch; TW

Pénélope, G. Fauré: 3/; s, m-s, 2 t, 2 bar, ch; LO; Pr

Petruchio, H. Groth: 3/(3); 100 min; s, 2 t, 2 bar, bs; C19

Pirata, Il, V. Bellini: trag; 2/6; 2 s, 2 t, bar, bs, ch; MO; Ri

Play of Daniel, The: 13th-cent mus dr; 3 s, 4 t, 5 bar, 2 bs, sp, 2 mu, ch; SO; Ox

Puritani, I, V. Bellini: trag; 3/5; col, t, bar, bs, lesser, ch; MO; Ri

Reign of Terror, S. Pimsleur: 4/(4); 180 min; 2 s, c, 4 t, 4 bar, 6 bs, ch; LO; ACA

Ritorno d'Ulisse in Patria, Il, C. Monteverdi: dr; 3/; 150 min; 12 char, ch; SO; Pr

Robe of Pearls, The, J. Kaufman: Chin tale; 2/(2); 150 min; 4 char, 4 sp; 397

Rumpelstiltskin, J. Clements: fairy tale; 90 min; 3 sp, 6 char, ch; SO or piano; Ox

Rusalka, A. Dvorák: fairy tale; 3/; 2 s, c, 2 t, bar, bs, ch; MO; B & H

Scarecrow, The, N. Lockwood: fant; 2/5(2); 120 min; 16 char, ch; SO; ACA

Schwanda, the Bagpiper, J. Weinberger: folk dr; 2/5; s, m-s, 2 t, bar, bs, 8 lesser, ch; LO; AMP

Shanewis, C. Cadman: Indian dr; 2/(2); 90 min; 2 s, c, t, bar; Mor

Smoky Mountain, E. Hunkins: folk dr; 1/2(1); 90 min; 2 s, m-s, 2 t, bar, bs, sp, ch; Fi

Snow Queen, The, K. Gaburo: fairy tale; /6(1); 115 min; 28 char; C17

Tale of Two Cities, A, A. Benjamin: melodr; /6; 3 s, c, 2 t, 2 bar, bs, lesser, ch; LO; B & H

Tarquin, E. Krenek: trag; 2/9; 150 min; 4 char; C29

Telemachus, M. Holmes: dr; 3/6(1); 90 min; s, s or t, 2 t, bar, bs-bar, bs, 6 lesser; ch; LO; C21a

Through a Glass Darkly, E. Norden: dr; 1/(1); 105 min; 2 s, c, t, 2 bs; C43

Tiefland, E. d'Albert: dr; Prol, 2/; 150 min; s, t, bar, 8 lesser, ch; LO; AMP

Touchstone, The, G. Rossini: com; 2/(1); 140 min; 94

Town Musicians of Bremen, C. Metcalf: com; 2/(3); 90 min; 28 char, ch; C35

Trial, The, G. von Einem: trag; /9(4); 120 min; 4 s, m-s, 5 t, 7 bar, 5 bs, sp, ch; AMP

Tripoli, G. Mongeluzzo: 4/(3); s, t, bar, ch; C38

Voyage to the Moon, J. Offenbach: farce; 4/; 3 s, t, bar, bs, lesser, ch; MO; 196B

War and Peace, S. Prokofiev: epic dr; 5/11; LO; Le

White Wings, D. Moore: fant; 2/(2); 120 min; 16 char, men's ch; C39

SHORT OPERAS

Abstract Opera #1, B. Blacher: /7(7); 25 min; s, t, bs, ch; AMP

Alcottiana, A. Singer: hist com; 3/(1); 38 min; 10 char; C49

Alone I Stand, R. Martinelli: dr; 1/(1); 5 char; C34

L'Amante in Trappolo, A. Pedrollo: com; 1/; 35 min; s, m-s, t, bar, bs; SO; B & H

Anachronism, The, A. Franchetti: com; 1/(1); 35 min; col, t, bar; C16

Annie Laurie, Lawrence-Lee: dr; 1/5(3); 45 min; 7 char, ch; Har

Apollo and Persephone, G. Cockshott: com; 1/(1); 26 min; s, t, bs; 294

Archy and Mehitabel, G. Kleinsinger: com; 1/(1); 30 min; 3 char, ch, sp; C26

Aria da Capo, C. Burnham: fant; 1/(1); 50 min; s, 2 t, bar, bs; C7

Aria da Capo, B. Fore: fant; 3/(1); 45 min; 5 char; MCA

Atsumori, C. Lawrence: dr; 1/(1); 45 min; s, bs; C31

At the Boar's Head, G. Holst: hist dr; 1/(1); 50 min; s, m-s, 2 t, 5 bar, 2 bs; No

Audition, The, A. Goodman: 1/; 45 min; s, m-s, 2 t, bar, bs; SO; Pr

Baby Doe, M. Di Julio: folk dr; 2/4(4); 70 min; 8 char; ch; C12

Bad Boys in School, J. Meyerowitz: farce; 1/(1); 40 min; 3 s, c, t, 3 bar; C36

Bald Prima Donna, The, M. Kalmanoff: fant; 1/(1); 60 min; s, col, c, t, bs-bar, bs, sp; B & H

Barber of New York, The, A. Vernon: folk com; 1/(1); 70 min; s, c, 3 t, bar, ch; MO; Pr

Bartleby, W. Flanagan: 2/(1); 60 min; boy s, t, 2 bar, sp; SO; ACA

Beckoning Fair One, The, G. and E. Keckley: com; 1/(1); 60 min; s, c, t, bs; C25

Beyond Belief, T. Canning: com; 1/(1); 60 min; s, t, bar, bs; C9

Bianca, H. Hadley: com; 1/(1); 60 min; 2 s, m-s, 2 t, 2 bar, 3 bs; Fl

Birthday of the Infanta, The, R. Nelson: trag; 1/(1); 45 min; s, m-s, t, bar; C42

Black Roses, E. Chisholm: myst; 1/(1); 20 min; 2 s, m-s, 2 t, 2 bar; C10

Blonde Beggars, The, J. Offenbach: com; 1/(1); 3 char; Fre

Boney Quillen, H. Haufrecht: folk dr; 1/3(1); 30 min; 2 s, 2 c, t, 3 bar, ch; MO; ACA

Boor, The, M. Fink: com; 1/; C15

Boor, The, U. Kay: com; 1/(1); 40 min; s, t, bar, 2 mu; SO; AMP

Boston Baked Beans, G. Kubik: fable; 1/(1); 20 min; 2 char; Ch

Brothers, The, G. Antheil: dr; 1/(1); 60 min; s, m-s, c, t, 2 bar, bs; C2

Canek, H. Wells: Yucatan dr; 1/(4); 30 min; 8 sp, 2 char; MO; ACA

Captain Lovelock, J. Duke: com; 1/(1); 40 min; 3 s, 3 c; Fi

Carmina Burana, C. Orff: opera-oratorio; 70 min; s, t, bar, 2 ch; LO; AMP

Cask of Amontillado, The, J. Perry: horror dr; 2/(1); 30 min; m-s, t, bar; So

Celebration, The, L. Maury: com; 1/(1); 30 min; 2 s, c, 2 t, bar, 2 bs; SO; B & H

Chanson de Fortunio, Le, J. Offenbach: com; 1/(1); 45 min; 7 s, t, sp; MO; Pr

Charley's Uncle, D. Ahlstrom: com; 1/(1); 5 char; C1

Cinderella, E. Norden: fairy tale; 3/(2); 75 min; 2 s, m-s, 2 bar, t; C43

Circus, The, E. Chudakoff: com; 1/(1); 20 min; 3 char; C11

Clock, The, V. Rieti: dr; 2/(2), Epil; 60 min; s, c, 2 m-s, t, bar, bs, 2 lesser; LO; C45a

Committee, The, M. Doran: /9(9); 45 min; 2 s, c, 2 t, 2 bar, 2 bs; C13

Cooper, The, T. Arne: com; 1/; 55 min; s, t, bar; piano or SO; AMP

Coventry Nativity, D. Moe: Christmas tale; 1/(1); 60 min; 9 char, ch; C37

Cupid and Death, M. Locke: 1/(1); 60 min; 6 char; St

239

Cupid and Psyche, A. Vernon: com; 1/4 (3); 60 min; s, m-s, t, bar, bs; SO; Pr

Cupid Has the Last Word, A. Ponchielli: com; 1/(1); 30 min; 6 char; Bl

Curious Fern, M. Kupferman: com; 1/3; 55 min; 3 s, 2 m-s, t, bar; SO; Pr

Dark Side, The, P. Pisk: trag; 1/(1); film proj; 50 min; s, bar, ch; MO; ACA

Dark Sonnet, E. Chisholm: horror dr; 1/(1); 12 min; s or c; C10

Dark Waters, E. Krenek: trag; 1/(1); 56 min; 7 char; C29

Darling Corie, E. Siegmeister: folk dr; 1/(1); 45 min; s, m-s, t, 2 bar, 2 bs; Ch

Devil to Pay, The, C. Coffey: com; /Prol, 8(3); 11 char, 2 sp; Wat

Devin du Village, Le, J. Rousseau: com; 1/(1); 3 char, ch; Ka

Dinner Engagement, A, L. Berkeley: /2; 60 min; 2 s, 2 c, 2 t, bar; SO; G Sc

Djamileh, G. Bizet: com; 2/(1); 60 min; m-s, t, bar, sp, ch; Pet

Don Fortuno, H. Forrest: com; 1/(1); 40 min; s, m-s, t, 2 bar; piano, strings

Donna è Mobile, La, R. Malipiero: com; /3; 50 min; 2 s, m-s, t, bar, 1–2 bs-bar, buf bs; LO; AMP

Dowser, The, A. Franchetti: pastoral; 1/(1); 35 min; s, t, bar, bs; C16

Dreams in Spades, S. Hovey: com-fant; 1/3(2); 55 min; 2 s, c, 3 lesser (t, bar, bs), ch; SO; Te

Drunkard Reformed, The, C. Gluck: com; 2/(2); 7 char, ch

Duped Cadi, The, C. Gluck: com; 1/(1); 30 min; 6 char; Sen

Easter Guest, The, K. Roy: (2); 40 min; m, t, bar, bs; C46

Egon and Emily, E. Toch: com; 1/(1); 15 min; col, sp; AMP

Enchanted Pear Tree, The, H. Overton: com; 1/4(1); 45 min; s, m-s, t, bar, ch; SO; ACA

Eve of Adam, J. Duffy: romance; 1/; 60 min; 15 char, sp; C14

Experiment, The, P. Schwarz: dr; 1/(1); 40 min; s, t, 2 bar, bs; C47

Farce du Contrabandier, Le, P. Pascal: farce; 1/(1); 20 min; 3 char; Du

Farce de Maître Pathelin, La, H. Barraud: com; 1/; 40 min; s, 2 t, bar, bs; SO; B & H

Farmer and the Fairy, The, A. Tcherepnin: Chin fant; 1/; 45 min; s, t, sp; SO; Mar

Fatal Oath, The, B. Koutzen: melodr; 1/(1); s, m-s, t, bar; C28

Fenimore and Gerda, F. Delius: 1/11; 2 s, m-s, t, bar, bs, 9 lesser, ch; LO; B & H

Fiesta, D. Milhaud: dr; 1/; 21 min; s, 2 m-s, c, 2 bar, 2 bs, chil; SO; Pr

Financier et le Savetier, Le, J. Offenbach: com; 1/; 4 char; SO; Pr

Fisherman, The, T. Scott: 2/(1); 70 min; s, m-s, 3 t, bar, bs; SO; ACA

Fisherman and his Wife, E. Rapoport: fairy tale; 1/(8); 60 min; 2 s, 2 t, bar, bs; MO; ACA

Fisherman's Wife, The, L. Stein: fairy tale; 1/(1); 70 min; 2 s, m-s, c, t, bs; MO; ACA

Flaminio, Il, G. Pergolesi: com; 3/(1); 7 char; Mort

Forever Rembrandt, E. Zador: com; 1/(1); 40 min; 10 char; AMP

Fortunato, M. Gideon: trag farce; /3(3); 60 min; 4 s, m-s, t, 4 bar, ch; SO; ACA

Game of Cards, A, A. Franchetti: dr; 1/(1); 23 min; s, t, bar, bs; C16

Garden of Artemis, The, D. Pinkham: myth; 1/(1); 25 min; s, c, bar or bs, ch; SO; ACA

George, I. Mopper: com; 1/(1); 46 min; s, m-s, t, bs-bar; SO; C40

G.I. Joe, E. Rapoport: 1/(1); 60 min; s, t, bar, bs; MO; ACA

Glittering Gate, The, P. Glanville-Hicks: dr; /1(1); 30 min; t, bar; SO; ACA

Goodbye to the Clown, E. Laderman: 1/(1); 45 min; s, m-s, t, bar, bs; SO; Pr

Grand Slam, A. Vernon: parody; 1/(1); 25 min; s, m-s, t, bar, bs; SO; Pr

Happy Ending, The, W. Wolf: com; 1/(1); 75 min; s, c, t, 3 bar, 3 bs, sp; MO; B & H

Happy Prince, The, V. Raines: fairy tale; 1/(1); 40 min; s, bar; C45

Harpies, The, M. Blitzstein: fant; 1/(1); 50 min; 2 s, m-s, c, t, 2 bar; Mo

Holy Night, The, L. Underwood: sacred fant; /11(3); 65 min; 10 char, ch; C51

Hunted, The, M. Mailman: hist dr; 1/; 5 char; C32a

Hunting of the Snark, E. Laderman: 1/(1); 45 min; s, m-s, t, 2 bar, 2 bs; SO or LO; ACA

Husband at the Door, A, J. Offenbach: com; 1/; 2 s, t, bar; SO; Pr

If Men Played Cards, C. Garland: sat; 1/(1); 15 min; 2 t, 2 bar; C18

Ile, B. Laufer: dr; 1/(1); 60 min; s, 2 t, 3 bar; SO; ACA

Impresario Embarrassed, The, D. Cimarosa: com; 2/(1); 6 char; Sie

In the Name of Culture, A. Bimboni: sat; 1/(1); 70 min; 5 char, ch; Fi

Introduction, The, R. Williams: com; 1/(1); 15 min; s, t, bar; C57

Intruder, The, R. Starer: 1/; 50 min; 2 s, c, bar, bs; SO; Pr

Job, L. Dallapiccola: sacred dr; 1/; 45 min; 2 s, 2 m-s, 2 t or bar, bs-bar, sp ch; LO; AMP

Joiner, The, B. Wiley: com; 1/7; 75 min; s, t, 2 bar, 14 sp, ch; piano; B & H

Judgment Day, P. Berl: dr; 1/(1); 70 min; 6 char, ch; C5

Juggler of Our Lady, U. Kay: dr; 1/(1); 50 min; s, boy s, 2 m-s, c, 3 t, 4 bar, 3 bs, ch; SO; ACA

Krapp's Last Tape, M. Mihalovici: dr; 1/; 55 min; bar; SO; Pr

Lady to Raffle, J. Offenbach: com; 1/(1); 45 min; s, 2 t; SO; Pr

Leonce and Lena, E. Zeisl: fant; 3/11; 15 char; C59

Lima Beans, D. Townsend: com; 1/(1); 25 min; s, t, bar; SO

Livietta and Tracallo, G. Pergolesi: dr; 2/(1); 2 char, 2 mu; Con

Look and Long, F. Wickham: 1/(1); 5 char; 294

Love Charm, The, P. Allen: melodr; 1/(1); 60 min; 2 s, t, bar, bs, ch; Map

Love in Transit, R. Arnell: 1/; s, m-s, t, bar, mu; Pr

Love Triumphant, D. Cimarosa: com; 1/(1); 30 min; 5 char; Al

Love's Sacrifice, G. Chadwick: pastoral; 30 min; 6 char; Bi

Magic Fish, The, P. Neeld: fant; 1/(1); 4 char; C41

Mamselle Figaro, P. Allen: com; 1/(1); 60 min; s, t, bs-bar; Map

Man on the Bearskin Rug, The, P. Ramsier: com; 1/(1); 26 min; s, m-s, bar; SO; B & H

Marriage by Lanternlight, J. Offenbach: com; 1/(1); 35 min; 3 s, t; Pr

Maypole, The, A. Franchetti: ballet-opera; 1/(1); 22 min; 2 s, c, bar; C16

Medea, R. Di Giovanni: trag; 1/(1); 60 min; s, c, t, bar, ch; C11a

Meeting, The, J. Meyerowitz: dr; 1/(1); 24 min; 5 char; C36

Midnight Duel, The, L. Kondorossy: lyr dr; 1/(2); 45 min; s, 2 c, 2 t, 2 bar, bs; C27

Milda, P. Allen: fairy tale; 1/; s, c, t, bar, ch; Map

Mon Ami Pierrot, S. L. M. Barlow: 1/(1); 75 min; s, m-s, t, bar, ch; SO; ACA

Monastery, The, P. Allen: dr; 2/(2); 60 min; s, bar, 3 bs, ch; Map

Monkey's Paw, The, C. Hamm: melodr; /3(1); 30 min; s, c, t, 2 bar; C20

Morte dell'Aria, La, G. Petrassi: trag; 1/(1); 30 min; 11 char, ch; AMP

Mother, The, J. Wood: fant; 1/5(1); 35 min; s, m-s, 2 c, bar, ch; SO; ACA

Mozart and Salieri, N. Rimsky-Korsakov: fant; 1/(1); 45 min; t, bar, sp, ch (opt); SO; B & H

Necklace, The, W. Bornstedt: tragi-comedy; 1/(1); 50 min; 3 s, 2 bar; C6

Necklace, The, L. Ratner: tragicomedy; 1/4(3); 40 min; s, m-s, bar; Pr

Night at Sea and Day in Court, E. Gyring: dr; 2/12(4); 80 min; 2 s, m-s, t, 2 bar, 2 bs; SO; ACA

Nitecap, The, C. Burnham: 1/(1); 35 min; s, c, t, bar, sp; C7

Noces, Les, I. Stravinsky: com; 1/(1); 25 min; 4 char, ch; G Sc

Omelet, The, L. Delibes: com; 1/(2); s, 4 t, bs; SO; Pr

Opera, Opera, M. Kalmanoff: com; 1/(1); 30 min; s, c, t, 2 bar; Fi

Oracle, The, B. Lees: dr; 1/(1); 60 min; s, m-s, 3 t, 2 bar, bs; SO; B & H

Ordeal of Osbert, The (Otherwise Engaged), A. Davis: com; 1/(1); 40 min; s, 2 t, 2 bar, bs; SO; B & H

Parfait for Irene, A, W. Kaufmann: com; 3/(1); 75 min; 15 char; C24

Pepito's Golden Flower, M. Caldwell: dr; 1/(1); 50 min; 9 char; C8

Poison, F. Hart: psych dr 1/(1); 45 min; s, 2 bar; SO; ACA

Port Town, J. Meyerowitz: com-dr; 1/(1); 2 s, m-s, c, bar, bs, 5 lesser, ch; SO; Mar

Prankster, The, R. Wykes: com; 1/(1); 30 min; 2 char; C58

Princess, The, A. Franchetti: lyr dr; 1/(1); 20 min; 2 s, c, bar; C16

Princess Who Talked Backward, The, R.

241

Marcus: com; 1/(1); 30 min; 7 wom; C33

Privilege and Privation, J. Becker: sat; 1/(1); 60 min; 7 men, male qt; SO; ACA

Professor, The, W. Isaacs: com; 1/(1); 50 min; 6 char, ch; C22

Provincial Episode, A, M. Wald: folk dr; /2(1); 45 min; 8 char, 6 sp; C55

Purgatory, H. Weisgall: dr; 1/; 35 min; t, bs; SO; Pr

Quiet Game of Cribble, A, M. Kalmanoff: operina; 1/(1); 35 min; s, bar; Op

Rajah's Ruby, The, S. Barab: com; 1/(1); 45 min; 2 s, t, bar, bs; SO or MO; B & H

Rapunzel, L. Harrison: fairy tale; 1/(1); 40 min; s, c, bar; SO; So

Red Riding Hood, H. Simmons: fairy tale; 3/(3); 90 min; s, m-s, c, t, bar; C48

Research, The, W. Kaufmann: com; 1/(1); 25 min; s, t, bar; C24

Romeo and Juliet, B. Blacher: trag; /3(1); 65 min; s, 2 c, 2 t, bar, bs, ch; AMP

Rossignol, Le, I. Stravinsky: lyr dr; 3/; 50 min; 2 s, c, t, bar, 2 bs; LO; B & H

Sailing of the Nancy Belle, The, A. Davis: com; /3(1); 30 min; s, t, bs, ch; SO; B & H

Scandal at Mulford Inn, The, W. Byrd, Jr.: com; 1/(1); 35 min; s, c, 2 t, 2 bar, 2 bs; SO; B & H

Signor Bruschino, Il, G. Rossini: com; 1/; s, m-s, 2 t, 4 bs; SO; Ri

Simoon, E. Chisholm: melodr; 1/(1); 50 min; s, t, bar; C10

Sterlingman, K. Roy: sat; 1/; 45 min; s, t, bar, bs; SO; Pr

Stronger, The, H. Weisgall: trag-melodr; 1/(1); 28 min; col, mu; Pr

Sunday Costs Five Pesos, C. Haubiel: com; 1/(1); 35 min; s, c, t; CPr

Sweet Betsy from Pike, M. Bucci: com; 1/(1); 25 min; s, m-s or t, bs-bar; MTI

Swing, The, L. Kastle: dr; 1/(1); 13 min; s, bar, sp; Te

Thief and the Hangman, The, A. Ellstein: dr; 1/; 2 wom, 6 men; 386

Thirteen Clocks, M. Bucci: fairy tale; 1/; 60 min; 4 men, 2 wom, ch; 1–2 piano; MTI

Three Blind Mice, J. Verrall: com; 2/(2); 30 min; 2 s, 2 m-s, c, t, bar, 2 bs; C53

Three Short Operas: L'Abandon d'Ariane; La Délivrance de Thesée; L'Enlèvement d'Europe, D. Milhaud: satires on myths; SO; AMP

Three Sisters Who Were Not Sisters, D. Ahlstrom: sat; 1/(1); 33 min; 5 char, ch; 294

Three's Company, A. Hopkins: com; /3; 60 min; s, t, bar; piano; G Sc

Tom Sawyer, J. Elkus: com; 1/7(1); 60 min; s, c, bs; No

Transposed Heads, The, P. Glanville-Hicks; fant; 1/6; 75 min; s, t, bar, 2 sp, ch; SO; AMP

Tree that Trimmed Itself, The, G. Kleinsinger: Christmas tale; 1/; 40 min; 6 char; C26

Trial of Lucullus, The, R. Sessions: 1/; 3 s, c, t, 3 bar, bs, 10 lesser, ch; MO; Mar

Trip in the Country, A, M. Peragallo: /3; 35 min; s, m-s, t, bar or bs, 4 chil, ch; LO; AMP

Triple Sec, M. Blitzstein: sat; 1/(1); 18 min; 20 char; AMP

Triumph of Punch, The, A. Vernon: com; 1/(1); 70 min; col s, m-s, c, 2 t, bar, bs-bar, bs; SO; Pr

Tub, The, R. White: 1/(1); 30 min; s, c, t, bar; C56

Unicorn in the Garden, The, R. Smith: sat; 1/; 25 min; 4 char; G Sc

Unicorn, Gorgon, and Manticore, The, G.-C. Menotti: madrigal fable; 1/; ch, d; SO; Ri

Vida Breve, La, M. de Falla: 2/4; 67 min; 3 s, 2 m-s, 2 t, 2 bar, bs; AMP

Village Romeo and Juliet, A, F. Delius: dr; /6; s, t, 3 bar, 18 lesser, ch; LO; B & H

Voice, The, L. Kondorossy: fant; 1/(1); 25 min; s, t, ch; C27

Voices for a Mirror, M. Kupferman: fant; 1/3; 55 min; 2 s, m-s, bar; SO; Pr

Volpone, G. Antheil: com; 3/(2); 15 char; C2

Wedding Knell, The, J. Verrall: dr; 1/(1); 40 min; s, c, bar, bs; ACA

Weeping Widow, The, M. Rosenthal: com; 1/2(1); 50 min; s, t, bar, sp, ch; SO; Pr

Willow Tree, The, C. Cadman: 1/; 25 min; s, c, t, bs; SO; Pr

Wise and the Foolish, The, K. List: fant;

1/(1); 30 min; s, bar, 4 sp, mu, sp ch; SO; ACA

Wish, The, G. Antheil: fant; 1/4(2); 55 min; 2 s 2 t, 2 bar, bs; C2

You Never Know, B. Koutzen: com; 1/(1); 30 min; s, t, bar; SO; C28

Zanetto, P. Mascagni: 1/(1); 60 min; s, m-s or t; AMP

Key to Some Composers of Unpublished Operas

C1. Ahlstrom, David; c/o After-Dinner Opera, 550 Fifth Ave., New York 36, N.Y.

C2. Antheil, George; c/o ASCAP, 575 Madison Ave., New York 22, N.Y. (deceased).

C3. Bacon, Ernst; Syracuse Univ. Music Dept., Syracuse, N.Y.

C4. Baylor, Murray; Knox Coll., Galesburg, Ill.

C5. Berl, Paul; 250 W. 85th St., New York 24, N.Y.

C6. Bohrnstedt, Wayne; Univ. of Redlands, Redlands, Calif.

C7. Burnham, Cardon; Dept. of Music, Bowling Green State Univ., Bowling Green, O.

C8. Caldwell, Mary; 474 S. Arroyo Blvd., Pasadena, Calif.

C9. Canning, Thomas; Eastman School of Music, Rochester, N.Y.

C10. Chisholm, Erik; S.A. College of Music, University Private Bag, Rondebosch, C.P., South Africa.

C11. Chudakoff, Edward; Oberlin Conservatory of Music, Warner Hall, Oberlin, O.

C11a. Di Giovanni, Rocco; c/o William Spada, 119 W. 78th St., New York 24, N.Y.

C12. Di Julio, Max; 2525 Oak St., Denver, Colo.

C13. Doran, Matt; Ball State Teachers Coll. Opera Workshop, Muncie, Ind.

C14. Duffy, John; address unknown.

C15. Fink, Myron; Cornell Univ. Ithaca, N.Y.

C16. Franchetti, Arnold; Pleasant Valley, Lyme, Conn.

C17. Gaburo, Kenneth; McNeese State Coll., Lake Charles, La.

C18. Garland, Charles R.; Univ. of Missouri, Columbia, Mo.

C19. Groth, Howard; Arkansas State Teachers Coll., Conway, Ark.

C20. Hamm, Charles; College-Conservatory of Music, Cincinnati, O.

C21. Hoiby, Lee; 200 W. 108th St., New York 25, N.Y.

C21a. Holmes, Markwood; Kansas State Coll., Pittsburg, Kans.

C22. Isaacs, Wilbur; 520 W. 122nd St., New York 27, N.Y.

C23. Jarrett, Jack; Univ. of Florida, Gainesville, Fla.

C24. Kaufmann, Walter; Indiana Univ., Bloomington, Ind.

C25. Kechley, Gerald; Univ. of Washington, Seattle, Wash.

C26. Kleinsinger, George; 134 Yale, Roslyn Heights, Long Island, N.Y.

C27. Kondorossy, Leslie; 3397 E. 139th St., Cleveland, O.

C28. Koutzen, Boris; 51 Cedar Ave., Pleasantville, N.Y.

C29. Krenek, Ernst; 10424 Punyon Ave., Tujunga, Calif.

C30. Kreutz, Arthur; Univ. of Mississippi, University, Miss.

C31. Lawrence, Charles; Univ. of Washington, Seattle, Wash.

C32. Lee, Dai-Keong; 245 W. 104th St., New York 25, N.Y.

C32a. Mailman, Martin; Eastman School of Music, Rochester, N.Y.

C33. Marcus (Winokur), Roselyn; 523 E. 14th St., New York 9, N.Y.

C34. Martinelli, Rodolfo; 15 W. 44th St., New York 36, N.Y.

C34a. Mennini, Louis; Eastman School of Music, Rochester, N.Y.

C35. Metcalf, Clarence; Vermilion Museum, Vermilion, O.

C36. Meyerowitz, Jan; 27 Morningside Ave., Cresskill, N.J.

C37. Moe, Daniel; Univ. of Denver, 400 Grant St., Denver, Colo.

C38. Mongeluzzo, Gaetano; Tripoli Opera Players, 4174 Gleane St., Elmhurst, Long Island, N.Y.

243

C39. Moore, Douglas; Columbia Univ., ·New York 27, N.Y.

C40. Mopper, Irving; 505 West End Ave., New York 24, N.Y.

C41. Neeld, Peggy; c/o Contemporary Opera, 16 Sedgwick Road, West Hartford, Conn.

C42. Nelson, Ronald; Brown Univ., Providence, R.I.

C43. Norden, E. Lindsey; Churchville, Pa. (deceased).

C44. Phillips, Burrill; 207 E. High St., Urbana, Ill.

C45. Raines, Vernon; Coll. of Emporia, Emporia, Kan.

C45a. Rieti, Vittorio; 309 East 69th St., New York 21, N.Y.

C46. Roy, Klaus G.; Catalogue of American 20th Century Chamber Music, Newton, Mass.

C47. Schwartz, Paul; Kenyon College, Gambier, O.

C48. Simmons, Homer; Box 635, Sunland, Calif.

C49. Singer, André; 545 W. 111th St., New York 25, N.Y.

C50. Smith, Hale; 2331 E. 88th St., Cleveland 6, O.

C51. Underwood, Lucas; Coll. of the Pacific, Stockton, Calif.

C52. Van Buskirk, Carl; Indiana Univ., Bloomington, Ind.

C53. Verrall, John; c/o American Composers Alliance, 2121 Broadway, New York 23, N.Y.

C54. Vernon, Ashley (pseudonym for Kurt Manschinger); 344 W. 72nd St., New York 23, N.Y.

C55. Wald, Max; c/o ASCAP, 575 Madison Ave., New York 22, N.Y.

C56. White, Raymond; Martin St., Cambridge, Mass.

C57. Williams, Ronald; Indiana Univ., Bloomington, Ind.
Winokur, Roselyn Marcus; 523 E. 14th St., New York 9, N.Y.

C58. Wykes, Robert; Washington Univ., St. Louis, Mo.

C59. Zeisl, Eric; 1348 Miller Drive, Hollywood 46, Calif.

C60. Zimbalist, Efrem; Curtis Institute of Music, Philadelphia, Pa.

Indexes

KEY TO ABBREVIATIONS

A: alto
ACA: American Composers Alliance, 2121 Broadway, New York 23, N.Y.
A Ka: Alfred A. Kalmus, 24 Great Pulteney St., London W1, England
Al: Lorenzo Alvary, 205 W. 57th St., New York 19, N.Y.
Amer: American
AMP: Associated Music Publishers, Inc., 1 W. 47th St., New York 36, N.Y.
approx: approximately
arr: arranged, arrangement
assn: association
B, b: bass
B & H: Boosey & Hawkes, Inc., 30 W. 57th St., New York 19, N.Y.
BB: Bote & Bock, Berlin, c/o Associated Music Publishers, Inc., 1 W. 47th St., New York 36, N.Y.
Ba: Ballard & Co., Paris, France
bar: baritone
BH: Breitkopf & Härtel, c/o Associated Music Publishers, Inc., 1 W. 47th St., New York 36, N.Y.
Bi: C. C. Birchard, 221 Columbus Ave., Boston, Mass.
bib: biblical
bklt: booklet
Bl: Henry Bloch, 170 W. 73rd St., New York 23, N.Y.
BMI: Broadcast Music, Inc., 589 Fifth Ave., New York 17, N.Y.
Br: Broude Brothers, 56 W. 46th St., New York 36, N.Y.
bs: bass
bs-bar: bass-baritone
bs cl: bass clarinet
bs drum: bass drum
bsn: bassoon
buf: buffo
c: contralto

Ca: A. & G. Carisch, Milan, c/o Boosey & Hawkes, Inc., 30 W. 57th St., New York 19, N.Y.
Car: Carlvi Music Co., 815 N. La Cienaga Blvd., Hollywood 46, Calif.
cb: string bass
cent: century
Ch: Chappell & Co., Inc., RKO Bldg., New York 20, N.Y.
ch: chorus
char: characters
Che: J. & W. Chester, Ltd., 11 Great Marlborough St., London W1, England
chil: children
Chin: Chinese
chor: chorus
Chou: Choudens, Paris, France
cl: clarinet
col: coloratura
coll: college
com: comedy
comp: composer
Con: Contemporary Music Corp., address unknown
conc: concert
cont bsn: contra bassoon
CP: chorus parts
CPr: Composer's Press, c/o Sesac, 10 Columbus Circle, New York 19, N.Y.
CS: chorus score
d: dancer
dept: department
dial: dialogue
Dit: Oliver Ditson, c/o Theodore Presser Co., Bryn Mawr, Pa.
dr: drama
dram: dramatic
Du: Durand, c/o Elkan-Vogel Co., Inc., 1712 Sansom St., Philadelphia 3, Pa.
e: English

ed: edition
El-V: Elkan-Vogel Co., Inc., 1712 Sansom St., Philadelphia 3, Pa.
En: Enoch, Paris, France
Eng hrn: English horn
epil: epilogue
E Sc: E. C. Schirmer, Boston, Mass.
Eu: Eulenberg, c/o C. F. Peters Corp., 373 Fourth Ave., New York 16, N.Y.
f: French
fant: fantasy
Fi: Carl Fischer, Inc., 56–62 Cooper Sq., New York 3, N.Y.
Fl: Harold Flammer, Inc., 251 W. 19th St., New York 11, N.Y.
fl: flute
Fra: Frank Music Corp., c/o Music Theatre, Inc., 119 W. 57th St., New York 19, N.Y.
Fre: Samuel French, Inc., 25 W. 45th St., New York 36, N.Y.
FS: full score
g: German
Ga: Galaxy Music Corp., 2121 Broadway, New York 23, N.Y.
Ger: George Gershwin Pbl. Co., RKO Bldg., New York 20, N.Y.
Gr: H. W. Gray, 159 E. 48th St., New York 17, N.Y.
G Sc: G. Schirmer, Inc., 4 E. 49th St., New York 17, N.Y.
h: Hungarian
Ha: Dolores Hayward, 83 Pomeroy, Madison, N.J.
Har: Harms, Inc., 488 Madison Ave., New York 22, N.Y.
Heu: Heugel, Paris, c/o Theodore Presser Co., Bryn Mawr, Pa.
Hi: Highgate Press, c/o Galaxy Music Corp., 2121 Broadway, New York 23, N.Y.
hist: historical
hrn: horn
i: Italian
inc: including
introd: introduction
Ka: Edwin F. Kalmus Music Library, 421 W. 28th St., New York 1, N.Y.
L: long
Le: Leeds Music Corp., 322 W. 48th St., New York 36, N.Y.
Li: libretto
LO: large orchestra
lyr: lyric
Map: Alfred J. Mapleson Music Library, 129 W. 29th St., New York 1, N.Y.

Mar: Edward B. Marks Music Corp., 136 W. 52nd St., New York 19, N.Y.
MCA: Music Corp. of America, 598 Madison Ave., New York 22, N.Y.
Me: Merion, c/o Theodore Presser Co., Bryn Mawr, Pa.
melodr: melodrama
Mer: Mercury, c/o Theodore Presser Co.. Bryn Mawr, Pa.
Met: Metropolitan Opera
Mi: Mills Music, Inc., 1619 Broadway, New York 19, N.Y.
min: minutes
MO: medium orchestra
Mo: William Morris Agency, Inc., 1740 Broadway, New York 19, N.Y.
Mor: Edwin Morris, 35 W. 51st St., New York 19, N.Y.
Mort: Mortari, Italy, c/o Boosey & Hawkes, Inc., 30 W. 57th St., New York 19, N.Y.
MPH: Music Publishers Holding Co., 488 Madison Ave., New York 28, N.Y.
m-s: mezzo-soprano
MS: miniature score
MTI: Music Theatre, Inc., 119 W. 57th St., New York 19, N.Y.
mu: mute
mus: music
Mus. Amer.: *Musical America*
myst: mystery
No: Novello, c/o H. W. Gray, 159 E. 48th St., New York 17, N.Y.
ob: oboe
Op: Operation Opera, 881 Tenth Ave., New York 19, N.Y.
opt: optional
orch: orchestra
orig: original
O Tr: other translations
Ox: Oxford University Press, Inc., 417 Fifth Ave., New York 16, N.Y.
P: parts (orchestra)
Pe: Peer International Corp., 1619 Broadway, New York 19, N.Y.
perc: percussion
Pet: C. F. Peters Corp., 373 Fourth Ave., New York 16, N.Y.
Ph: Philharmonia, c/o Associated Music Publishers, Inc., 1 W. 47th St., New York 36, N.Y.
picc: piccolo
PPC: Program Pbl. Co., 1472 Broadway, New York 36, N.Y.
Pr: Theodore Presser Co., Bryn Mawr. Pa.

prem: premiere
prep: preparation
proj: project
prol: prologue
psych: psychological
pt: part
publ: published
P-Yes: piano version authorized by composer
qt: quartet
r: Russian
rent: rental
Ri: G. Ricordi & Co., 16 W. 61st St., New York 23, N.Y.
Ru: Fred Rullman, Inc., 1425 Broadway, New York 18, N.Y.
S, s: soprano
sat: satire
sax: saxophone
Sch: B. Schott, c/o Associated Music Publishers, Inc., 1 W. 47th St., New York 36, N.Y.
Scu: Scudder Productions, Bonville, Vt.
Se: Sesac, 10 Columbus Circle, New York 19, N.Y.
Sen: B. Senff & Co., c/o Hans Riedel, Uhlandstrasse 38, Berlin W 15, Germany
Sh: short
Si: Silver, Burdette Co., Morristown, N.J.
Sie: Sieber, c/o Hans Riedel, Uhlandstrasse 38, Berlin W 15, Germany
sn drum: snare drum
SO: small orchestra
So: Southern Music Pbl., Inc., 1619 Broadway, New York 19, N.Y.
Son: Sonzogno, c/o Associated Music Publishers, Inc., 1 W. 47th St., New York 36, N.Y.
sp: speaker
sp ch: speaking chorus
spin: spinto
St: Stainer & Bell, c/o Galaxy Music Corp., 2121 Broadway, New York 23, N.Y.
SZ: Suvini Zerboni, Milan, c/o Associated Music Publishers, Inc., 1 W. 47th St., New York 36, N.Y.
T, t: tenor
T1: Royal Opera House, Covent Garden, London WC 2, England
T2: Sadler's Wells Theatre, Roseberry Ave., London EC 1, England
T3: London Opera Club, 37 Kingswood Court, West End Lane, London NW 6, England
T4: City Opera Club, 7 Ravenna Road, London SW 15, England
T5: Opera Studio, British Broadcasting Corp., Broadcasting House, London W1, England
T6: Oxford Univ. Opera Club, Trinity Coll., Oxford, England
T7: Glasgow Grand Opera Society, Glasgow, Scotland
T8: Music Society, Univ. College, Gower St., London, England
T9: Canadian Broadcasting Corp., Montreal, P.Q., Canada
T10: Walter Ducloux, Univ. of Southern California, Los Angeles, Calif.
T11: Edward J. Dent, see publisher in question
T12: Joseph Machlis, 310 E. 55th St., New York 22, N.Y.
T13: Boris Goldovsky, 183 Clinton Road, Brookline, Mass.
T14: M. & E. Radford, St. Anthony-in-Roseland, Portscatho, Cornwall, England
T15: Ruth & Thomas P. Martin, 219 W. 13th St., New York 11, N.Y.
T16: Alfred D. Morgan, 210 W. 70th St., New York 23, N.Y.
T17: Owen S. Rachleff, 2406 Quentin Road, Brooklyn 29, N.Y.
T18: E. B. Lonner, 40 Tucker Ave., San Francisco 24, Calif.
T19: Gil Gallagher, 157 W. 13th St., New York 11, N.Y.
T21: Mary Jane Matz, 105 Main St., Matawan, N.J.
T22: Central Opera Service, 147 W. 39th St., New York 18, N.Y.
T23: Frank Merkling, 239 E. 79th St., New York 21, N.Y.
T24: Rosamund Chapin, New Boston Inn, New Boston, Mass.
T25: Clifford Bair, Wake Forest Coll., Wake Forest, N.C.
T26: Sylvan Levin, 7 E. 78th St., New York 21, N.Y.
T27: Mrs. Farber England, Hotel Dover, 687 Lexington Ave., New York 22, N.Y.
T28: John Bloch, 74 East Way, Mount Kisco, N.Y.
T29: Robert A. Simon, 151 W. 86th St., New York 24, N.Y.

T30: Milton Feist, 262 W. 107th St., New York 25, N.Y.

T31; Henry Reese, 2310 Vasanta Way, Hollywood, Calif.

T32: William Murray and Hibbard James, address unknown.

T33: Edward Eager, 70 Valley Road, New Canaan, Conn.

Te: Templeton Pbl. Co., Division Shawnee Press, Inc., 157 W. 57th St., New York 19, N.Y.

timp: timpani

TMC: Tracy Music Co., 18 Newbury St., Boston, Mass.

Tr: translation

trag: tragedy

trans: transposed

trb: trombone

trp: trumpet

TW: Tams-Witmark Music Library, 115 W. 45th St., New York 36, N.Y.

UE: Universal Edition, c/o Associated Music Publishers, Inc., 1 W. 47th St., New York 36, N.Y.

Univ.: University

vcl: violoncello

vers: version

vla: viola

vln: violin

voc: vocal

VS: vocal score

Wa: Constance Wardle, 360 W. 55th St., New York 19, N.Y.

Wat: Jonathan Watts, c/o H. Baron, 50 Christchurch Ave., London NW6, England

We: Weintraub Music Co., 853 Seventh Ave., New York 19, N.Y.

Wein: Josef Weinberger Ltd., 33 Crawford St., London W1, England

wom: woman, women

xyl: xylophone

PERFORMING COMPANIES

Alabama

AUBURN
1. Alabama Polytechnic Institute
BIRMINGHAM
2. Civic Opera Association, 2519 Lanark Road
3. Birmingham Conservatory of Music, 8th Ave. and 11th St.
4. Jean Golden Opera Workshop, 2100 7th Ave. North
5. Howard Coll.
MOBILE
6. Mobile Opera Guild, Inc., P.O. Box 2218, Springhill Station
MONTEVALLO
7. Alabama Coll.
UNIVERSITY
8. Opera à la Bama, P.O. Box 2876

Arizona

FLAGSTAFF
9. Arizona Playmakers
SCOTTSDALE
9A. Scottsdale Chamber Opera Co.
TEMPE
10. Arizona State Coll. Opera Workshop
TUCSON
11. Tucson Civic Chorus
12. Univ. of Arizona

Arkansas

CONWAY
14. Hendrix Coll.
15. State Teachers Coll.
EUREKA SPRINGS
16. S.W. Federation of Music Clubs, Lyric Opera Workshop

FAYETTEVILLE
17. Univ. of Arkansas Opera Workshop
SEARCY
19. Harding Coll. Faculty

California

BAKERSFIELD
20. Bakersfield Coll.
BERKELEY
22. Berkeley Evening School Opera Workshop, 2211 Grove St.
23. Company of the Golden Hind, The Playbox, 1505 San Pablo Ave.
24. Univ. of California Opera Workshop
CLAREMONT
26. Scripps Coll. Choral Club
COMPTON
28. Compton Junior Coll.
FRESNO
29. Fresno State Coll.
GLENDALE
29A. Glendale Dept. of Adult Education, Opera Workshop
GOLETA
30. Univ. of California, Santa Barbara Coll. Opera Workshop
LOS ANGELES
31. Los Angeles Bureau of Music
31A. Los Angeles Chamber Symphony
32. Los Angeles City Coll. Opera Studio, 855 N. Vermont
32B. Los Angeles Conservatory of Music
33. Euterpe Opera Reading Club, 406 N. Cliffwood Ave.
34. Fujiwara Opera Co., 8580 Sunset Blvd.

251

35. Greek Theatre, 2700 N. Vermont Ave.
36. Guild Opera Co., 427 West 5th St.
37. Herbert Weiskopf Opera Workshop, 122 N. Gramercy Pl.
37B. Hollywood Reading Club, 545 St. Andrew's Pl.
38. Immaculate Heart Coll.
39. Los Angeles Adult Education School Opera Workshop
40. Morse M. Preeman, Inc., 737 South Hill St.
41. Occidental Coll. Music Dept., 1600 Campus Road
42. Palisades Players
43. Pepperdine Coll. Opera Workshop, 1121 West 79th St.
44. The Purple Onion
46. S.W. Civic Chorus
46A. Theatre Unlimited
47. Univ. of California at Los Angeles, 405 Hilgard Ave.
48. Univ. of Southern California
48A. Vine Street Studio Opera Workshop

LOS GATOS
50. Montalvo Foundation

MONTERREY
51. Peninsula Coll.

OAKLAND
52. Mills Coll.

PALO ALTO
53. Leland Stanford Univ.

PASADENA
54. City Coll.

PIEDMONT
55A. East Bay Opera League, 260 LaSalle Ave.

REDLANDS
56. Community Music Assn.
57. Univ. of Redlands

RIVERSIDE
58. Riverside Opera Assn., P.O. Box 629

SACRAMENTO
59. Sacramento State Coll.
60. Saturday Club Celebrity Series, 1312 K St.

SAN DIEGO
61. California Western Univ. Opera Workshop, 3902 Lomaland Dr.
63. San Diego State Coll., Music Dept.

SAN FRANCISCO
64. Cosmopolitan Opera Co., 265 Post St.

66. Golden Gate Opera Workshop, YMCA, 273 Sanchez
68. Olivier and Portcaro Productions
69. The Opera Ring, 3006 Clay St.
70. Pacific Opera Company, 1069 Market St.
70A. St. Boniface Arts Center, 133 Golden Gate Ave.
71. San Francisco Children's Opera, 410 Argvello Blvd.
71A. San Francisco Little Opera
72. San Francisco Opera Assn., War Memorial Opera House
73. State Coll.
74. San Francisco Symphony

SAN JOSE
75. San Jose State Coll.

SANTA BARBARA
76. Music Academy of the West, 1070 Fairway Road
77A. Univ. of California

SANTA MONICA
77B. Santa Monica Civic Opera Assn., 1322 10 St.

STOCKTON
78. Coll. of the Pacific Opera Workshop, Coll. of the Pacific, Conservatory of Music

Colorado

ALAMOSA
79. Adams State Coll. of Colorado

ASPEN
80. Aspen Institute of Music

BOULDER
81A. Univ. of Colorado Opera Workshop

CENTRAL CITY
82. Festival, Central City Opera House Assn.

COLORADO SPRINGS
83. Theatre Singers, 115 N. Nanonteh

DENVER
85. Greater Denver Opera Assn., 1636 Logan St.
85A. Lyric Theatre
86. Red Rocks Amphitheatre
87. Univ. of Denver School of the Theatre

GRAND JUNCTION
88. Fine Arts and Wednesday Music Club, 2010 Kennedy Ave.

GREELEY
88A. State Coll.

STEAMBOAT SPRINGS
90. Perry-Mansfield Camp

Connecticut
HARTFORD
91. Chamber Song Ensemble
92. Conn. Opera Assn.
92A. Friends and Enemies of Modern Music
92B. Hartford School of Music, 834 Asylum Ave.
94. Julius Hartt Coll., 187 Broad St.
NEW HAVEN
96. New Haven Symphony
96A. Pierson Coll., Yale Univ.
97. State Teachers' Coll.
97A. Yale Univ. School of Music and Drama
STRATFORD
97B. American Shakespeare Festival Theatre and Academy
97C. Community Players
STORRS
97D. Connecticut Univ. Opera Workshop
WESTPORT
97E. White Barn Theatre
WILTON
98. Wilton Playshop

District of Columbia
WASHINGTON
99. Recreation Dept.
100. Dept. of the Army
103. National Symphony, 1779 Massachusetts Ave.
104. Opera Society of Washington, Inc., 1745 K St.

Delaware
WILMINGTON
106. Wilmington Opera Assn., 807 East Matson Run Pkway.

Florida
GAINESVILLE
106A. Univ. of Florida, Div. of Music
JACKSONVILLE
107. Jacksonville Coll. of Music Opera Workshop, 4227 Peachtree Circle E.
LAKELAND
108. Women's Club

MIAMI
109. Junior Opera Guild and Univ. of Miami Opera Workshop, 625 S.W. 29th St.
110. Opera Guild of Greater Miami, 625 S.W. 29th St.
TALLAHASSEE
110A. Florida State Univ. School of Music
TAMPA
111. Sun State Opera Federation, 2201 Central Ave.

Georgia
ATHENS
112. Univ. of Georgia
ATLANTA
113. Opera Arts Assn., 1720 Peachtree St. N.W.
EMORY UNIVERSITY
115. Emory Univ. Opera Theatre

Idaho
MOSCOW
120. Univ. of Idaho Opera Workshop
NAMPA
121. N.W. Nazarene Coll.

Illinois
BLOOMINGTON
122. Illinois Wesleyan Univ. School of Music
CARBONDALE
122A. Southern Illinois Opera Soc. (S.I.U.)
CHICAGO
124. All Children's Grand Opera
124A. American Conservatory Opera Workshop, Kimball Hall, 306 S. Wabash
125. American Opera Co., 712 Kimball Hall, 306 S. Wabash
126. Bethany Union
127. Chicago Conservatory Opera Workshop, 64 E. Van Buren
127A. Chicago Park District Opera Guild, 425 E. 14th Blvd.
127B. Chicago Symphony
127C. Cosmopolitan School of Music Opera Workshop
127D. De Paul Univ. Opera Workshop, 1415 E. 57 St.
128. Educational Music Bureau

253

129. Fine Art Opera, 1306 Roscoe St.
129A. Hull House Opera Workshop, 7041 South Bennett Ave.
129B. International Society for Contemporary Music
130. The Lyric Opera of Chicago, 20 Wacker Dr.
131. Lakeview Musical Society
133. Musicians' Club of Women
135. Opera Repertoire Guild
136. Opera Theatre of Chicago, 228 S. Wabash Ave.
137. Pirmyn Chorus
137A. Roosevelt Coll. Opera Workshop
138. Univ. of Illinois

DECATUR
138A. Millikin Univ.

EVANSTON
140. Northwestern Univ. School of Music

MOLINE
142. Quad City Music Guild

MONMOUTH
143. Monmouth Coll.

ROCK ISLAND
145. Augustana Coll. Opera Workshop

SPRINGFIELD
146. Junior Coll.

URBANA
147. Univ. of Illinois Opera Workshop

Indiana

BLOOMINGTON
148. Univ. of Indiana School of Music

EVANSVILLE
149. Evansville Philharmonic, 350 Court St.

GREENCASTLE
150. DePauw Univ. Opera Workshop

INDIANAPOLIS
150A. Arthur Jordan Conservatory of Music, Butler Univ.

MUNCIE
150B. Ball State Teachers' Coll. Opera Workshop

ST. MARY–OF–THE–WOODS
152. St. Mary–of–the–Woods Coll.

VALPARAISO
153. Valparaiso Univ.

Iowa

CEDAR FALLS
154. Iowa State Teachers' Coll. Opera Workshop

DES MOINES
155. John Dexter
156. Drake Univ. Choral Dept.

DAVENPORT
157. Tri-City Symphony, 2915 Middle Road

GRINNELL
159. Grinnell Coll.

INDIANOLA
160. Simpson Coll.

IOWA CITY
161. State Univ. of Iowa, School of Fine Arts, 943 Iowa Avenue

WAVERLY
162. Wartburg Coll.

Kansas

EMPORIA
163. State Teachers' Coll.
164. Coll. of Emporia

LAWRENCE
165. Univ. of Kansas

MANHATTAN
166. Kansas State Coll.

PITTSBURG
168. State Teachers' Coll.

SALINA
170. Marymount Coll.

WICHITA
172. Univ. of Wichita Opera Theatre
173. Symphony Orchestra, 105 W. 2nd St.

Kentucky

BARBOURVILLE
174. Union Coll.

BOWLING GREEN
175. Western Kentucky State Teachers' Coll.

LEXINGTON
175A. Univ. of Kentucky Opera Workshop

LOUISVILLE
176. Kentucky Opera Assn., Garden Court, Alta Vista Road
177. Univ. of Louisville

Louisiana

BATON ROUGE
177A. Civic Opera
178. State Univ. School of Music

MONROE
179A. Northeast State Coll.

254

NEW ORLEANS
179B. Experimental Opera Theatre
179C. Loyola Univ.
179D. Dillard Univ.
180. New Orleans Opera House Assn., 420 St. Charles St.
180A. Newcomb Opera Workshop, Dixon Hall, Tulane Univ.
181A. Ursuline Coll.
182. Xavier Univ. Opera Workshop, Palmetto and Pine
RUSTON
183. Louisiana Technical Institute Opera Workshop, Box 322, Tech Station
SHREVEPORT
185. Civic Opera Assn., 1464 Texas Eastern Bldg.

Maine
BRUNSWICK
186. Bowdoin Coll. Dept. of Music
KENNEBUNKPORT
187. Arundel Opera Theatre, Inc., Drawer 311

Maryland
ANNAPOLIS
187A. St. John's Coll.
BALTIMORE
188. Baltimore Symphony Orchestra, 800 Cathedral St.
189. Civic Opera Co., 510 Tower Bldg.
190A. Hilltop Musical Co.
191. Junior College
192. Museum of Art, Charles and 31st Streets
193. Peabody Conservatory, 1 E. Mount Vernon
COLLEGE PARK
193A. Univ. of Maryland

Massachusetts
AMHERST
193B. Amherst Coll. Masquers
194. Community Opera Co., 119 Blue Hills Rd.
BEDFORD
195. Whittredge Clark
BOSTON
196. Annual Arts Festival
196A. Boston Conservatory
196B. Boston Opera Group
197. Boston Univ. School of Fine and Applied Arts, Commonwealth Ave.

197A. Longy School of Music
198A. New England Conservatory, 290 Huntington Ave.
199. Joseph Timbler
BROOKLINE
202. New England Opera Theatre, 120 Amory St.
CAMBRIDGE
203. Dunster House, Harvard Univ.
203A. Lowell House Musical Society
FALMOUTH
203B. Oberlin College G & S Players, Highfield Theatre
LENOX
205. Berkshire Music Centre
MEDFORD
206. Tufts Univ.
NEWBURY
207. Tracy Music
NEWTON
209. Newton Coll.
NORTHAMPTON
209A. Smith Coll. Opera Workshop
SPRINGFIELD
210. Springfield Opera Co., 154 Orange St.
STOCKBRIDGE
211. Indian Hill Music Workshop
STURBRIDGE
211A. Summer Festival
WALTHAM
212. Brandeis Univ.
WILLIAMSTOWN
212A. Williams Coll.
DUXBURY
214A. Plymouth Rock Summer Co.

Michigan
ANN ARBOR
215. Univ. of Michigan School of Music
DETROIT
216. Grand Opera Assn., 820 Ford Bldg.
218. Michigan Opera Co., 3363 Gratior
218A. Tuesday Musical Society
218B. Wayne Univ. Theatre Group, 3424 Woodward Ave.
EAST LANSING
219. Michigan State Univ.
FERNDALE
220. South Oakland Symphony
FLINT
220A. Civic Opera, 2226 Nolen Drive

255

GRAND RAPIDS
221. Grand Rapids Symphony, 1435 Alexander St.
HANCOCK
223. Suomi Coll.
INTERLOCHEN
225. National Music Camp
KALAMAZOO
226. West Michigan Coll. of Education
MUSKEGON
227. Civic Opera House Assn.

Minnesota
BEMIDJI
228. State Teachers' Coll.
COLLEGEVILLE
229. St. John's Univ. Opera Workshop
DULUTH
230. Symphony Orchestra, 704 Alworth Bldg.
MINNEAPOLIS
232A. Minneapolis Symphony
233. Univ. of Minnesota Opera Workshop
ST. PAUL
235. Civic Opera Assn., Rm. 305, Auditorium Bldg.
236. Opera Workshop
ST. PETER
236A. Gustavus Adolphus Coll.

Mississippi
JACKSON
237. Belhaven Coll.
237A. Opera Guild, 2030 Southwood Road
WASSON
239. Copiah-Lincoln Junior Coll.

Missouri
CANTON
240. Culver-Stockton Coll. School of Music
COLUMBIA
241. Stephens Coll.–Burral Opera Co.
242. Univ. of Missouri
KANSAS CITY
244. Kansas City Philharmonic, 1217 Walnut St.
245. Univ. of Kansas City, 5100 Rockhill
MARYVILLE
247. N.W. Missouri State Coll.
NEVADA
248. Cottey Coll.

PARKVILLE
249. Park Coll.
ST. LOUIS
249A. Central Grand Opera Assn., 7049 Maryland Ave.
250. Fontbonne Coll., Wydown and Bigbend Blvds.
251A. Mary Institute
252. Midwest Grand Opera Assn., 6251 Delmar Blvd.
253. Municipal Opera, 1876 Arcade Bldg.
254. Washington Univ. Opera Workshop
254A. Xavier Coll.

Nebraska
LINCOLN
258. Nebraska Wesleyan Univ.: Pinewood Bowl Assn., 50th and St. Paul
259. Univ. of Nebraska School of Fine Arts
OMAHA
261. Ed Patton Music Co.

Nevada
LAS VEGAS
263. Las Vegas Opera Assn.

New Hampshire
PIKE
264. Lake Tarleton Opera Players

New Jersey
BLOOMFIELD
265. Suburban Concerts, Inc., 31 Clarendon Rd.
HACKETTSTOWN
268. Centenary Junior Coll.
PASSAIC
270. Passaic Symphony
TRENTON
270B. Columbus Boychoir School, Inc., Box 350, Rosedale Road
270C. Princeton Univ.
UPPER MONTCLAIR
270D. State Teachers' Coll. Opera Workshop

New Mexico
ALBUQUERQUE
272. May's Music Shop

256

273. Univ. of New Mexico Opera Workshop
PORTALES
274. Eastern New Mexico Univ. Opera Workshop
SANTA FE
275. Sante Fe Opera Assn., Box 1654

New York

BINGHAMTON
278. Tri-Cities Opera, Inc., 219 Harding Ave., Endicott
BROOKLYN
279. Brooklyn Coll. Light Opera Guild, Boylan Hall, Bedford Ave. and Ave. H
279A. Pennybridge Opera Co., 182 Clinton St., Brooklyn Heights
BUFFALO
281. Philharmonic Orchestra, Kleinhans Music Hall, 370 Pennsylvania Ave.
282. Univ. of Buffalo Opera Theatre, 3435 Main St.
CHAUTAUQUA
283. Chautauqua Opera Assn., Chautauqua, N.Y.
FLUSHING
285A. Queens Coll. Opera Workshop, Bryant High School, 65–30 Kasena Blvd.
FREDONIA
286. State Univ. Teachers' Coll.
GARDEN CITY
287. Adelphi Coll. Opera Workshop
GENESEE
288. State Univ. Teachers' Coll.
HEMPSTEAD
288A. Hofstra Coll. Music Dept., Fulton Ave.
HUNTINGTON
289. Township Theatre Group
ITHACA
289A. Ithaca Coll., 322 West State St.
289B. Cornell Univ.
290. Civic Opera Group, 208 Muriel St.
KATONAH
290A. Westchester Friends of Music
LARCHMONT
292. Larchmont Women's Club
NEW YORK CITY
293. Actor's Opera, 324 West 77th St. (zone 24)

294. After-Dinner Opera Company, 550 5th Ave.
294A. All Arts Assn.
295. Amato Opera Theatre, 126 W. 23rd St.
296A. American Lyric Theatre
297. American Opera Society, 171 W. 57th St.
298. Ansonia Opera Circle, Broadway at 74th St.
299A. Barnard College
301. B'way Grand Opera Assn., 1425 Broadway
301A. Circle in the Square, Sheridan Square
302. Columbia Univ. Opera Workshop, Rm. 601, Journalism Bldg.
303. Community Civic Opera, 111 W. 57th St.
304. Community Opera, Inc., 40 E. 81st St.
306A. Cooper Union and AGMA
308. Empire Opera Co., 166 W. 72nd St.
308A. Empire State Festival, 501 Fifth Ave.
309. Finch Junior Coll. Music Dept., 52 E. 78th St.
309A. Fine Arts Opera, 601 W. 112th St.
310. Fleetwood Singers, 412 W. 56th St.
311. Walter Franklin Troupe
313. Godino Opera Studio, 949 West End Ave.
313A. Robert Goss Co.
314. Greenwich House Music School, 46 Barrow St.
315. John Harms Chorus
316. Henry Street Settlement, 466 Grand St.
317. Hunter Coll. Opera Assn., 695 Park Ave.
318. Inst. of Vocal Arts, 63–22 Booth St., Forest Hills 74
319. Inwood Chamber Opera Players, 60 Thayer St.
320. William Grant Isaacs
321. Juilliard Opera Theatre, 130 Claremont Ave.
321A. La Puma Opera Workshop, 250 W. 91st St.
321B. Kappa Mu Epsilon
321C. Lemonade Opera
322. Little Opera Co., 240 W. 72nd St.
323. Little Orchestra Society, 111 W. 57th St.
324. Long Island Opera Co., Inc., Box 112, New Hyde Park, L.I.

324A. Kathryn Long Trust
325. Lyric Festival Co.
325A. Manhattan Opera Guild Co., 549 W. 163rd St.
326. Manhattan School of Music, 238 E. 105th St.
327. Mannes Coll. of Music, 157 E. 74th St.
328. Master Inst. Opera Dept., 310 Riverside Drive
329. Metropolitan Opera Assn., 147 W. 39th St.
330. Mozart Concert-Opera Group, 111 W. 57th St.
330A. Music in Our Time
331. National Opera Club, 375 Riverside Drive
332. N.B.C. Opera Co., 30 Rockefeller Plaza
333. N.B.C.-TV Opera Co., 30 Rockefeller Plaza
333A. New School for Social Research, 66 W. 12th St.
334. New York City Opera Co., 130 W. 56th St.
335. New York City Light Opera Co., 130 W. 56th St.
335A. New York City Symphony
336. New York Coll. of Music, 114 E. 85th St.
337. Patricia Neway Opera Workshop, 509 W. 59th St.
338. Opera 56-57-58-59, 148 Bleecker St., Apt. 19
338A. Opera Futures
339. Opera Guide Theatre Co., 612½ W. 144th St.
340. Opera Players, 490 West End Ave.
341. L. Petri Opera Group, 147 E. 80th St.
343. Punch Opera Co., Box 751, Grand Central Station
343A. Queens Coll. Opera Workshop, Bryant High School, 65–30 Kasena Blvd.
344. Rossini Opera School, 50 Central Park West
345. Second Equinox Music Co.
346. Settlement Opera, 160 W. 73rd St.
347. Stadium Concerts, Inc., 50 W. 57th St.
347A. Stott Vocal Art Studio
348. Symphony of the Air, 200 W. 57th St.
349. Theatre de Lys, 121 Christopher St.
350. Third Street Music School, 55 E. 3rd St.

350A. Tolibia Opera Showcase, Labor Temple, 242 E. 14th St.
351A. Walton Youth and Community Center, 196th St. and Jerome Ave.
353. YMHA Symphonic Workshop, Lexington Ave. and 92nd St.
354. Carl Yost Mastersingers

PORT WASHINGTON
355. Port Washington Opera Co.

POTSDAM
356. State Teachers' Coll.

POUGHKEEPSIE
357. Vassar Coll. Experimental Theatre

ROCHESTER
358. Eastman School Theatre
359. Opera under the Stars, 330 Wilmot Rd.

SCHROON LAKE
361. Colony Opera Guild

STONYBROOK
363. Stony Brook Festival Orchestra

SUFFERN
364. Rockland Lyric Theatre

TARRYTOWN
365. Marymount Coll.

WARRENSBURG
366. Green Mansions Summer Theatre, Warrensburg or 40 W. 77th St., New York, N.Y.

WHITE PLAINS
367A. Westchester Friends of Music

WOODSTOCK
368. Turnau Opera Players, Woodstock, or 250 Riverside Drive, New York, N.Y.

North Carolina

BREVARD
369. Brevard Music Centre

BUIE'S CREEK
370. Campbell Coll.

CHAPEL HILL
371. Univ. of North Carolina Dept. of Music

CHARLOTTE
372. Brodt Music Co.
373. Charlotte Opera Assn., Box 6224

CULLOWHEE
374. Western Carolina Coll.

GREENSBORO
374A. Greensboro Opera Assn.
375. Univ. of North Carolina Women's Coll.
375A. Music Theatre Repertory Group

HIGH POINT
376. Music and Arts Centre
RALEIGH
378. National Grass Roots Opera Foundation, Box 1406
WAKE FOREST
380. Wake Forest Coll. Opera Workshop
WILMINGTON
381. Thalian Assn.
WINSTON-SALEM
382. Piedmont Opera Co., 2211 Buena Vista Rd.

North Dakota
FREEMAN
384. Junior Coll.
MINOT
385. State Teachers' Coll.

Ohio
ATHENS
386. Ohio Univ. Opera Workshop
BEREA
387. Baldwin-Wallace Conservatory
CANTON
388. Civic Opera Assn., 309 33rd St., N.W.
CINCINNATI
389. College Conservatory, Highland and Oak Sts.
390. Music and Drama Guild, 2650 Highland Lane
391. Summer Opera Assn., 5th and Vine Sts.
392. Cincinnati Civic Symphony, 603 St. Paul Bldg., 111 E. 4th St.
CLEVELAND
394. Cafarelli Opera Co., 2836 Corydon Rd.
395. Cleveland Institute Opera Dept., 3411 Euclid
397. Karamu Theatre, 2355 E. 89th St.
398. Musicarnival, 4401 Warrensville Center Rd., Warrensville Heights
398A. Music School Settlement
399. Western Reserve Univ.
COLUMBUS
400. Capital Univ.
401. Coll. of St. Mary of the Springs
402. Columbus Symphony, 55 E. State St.
403. Lyric Theatre Group, 151 S. 17 St.
404. Ohio State Univ. School of Music

DELAWARE
404A. Ohio Wesleyan Univ. Opera Dept.
GRANVILLE
405. Denison Univ. Music Dept.
406. Gerald Kelly
HIRAM
407. Hiram Coll.
MARIETTA
409. Marietta Coll.
NEW CONCORD
409A. Muskingum Coll.
OBERLIN
410. Gilbert and Sullivan Players
411. Oberlin Conservatory Opera Laboratory
OXFORD
412. Miami Univ. School of Fine Arts
PAINESVILLE
413. Lake Erie Coll.
TOLEDO
415. Toledo Orchestra, 401 Jefferson Ave.
WOOSTER
415A. Coll. of Wooster
YELLOW SPRINGS
416. Antioch Coll.
YOUNGSTOWN
417A. Junior Coll.
419. Youngstown Univ. Music Dept.

Oklahoma
CHICKASHA
420. Oklahoma State Coll. for Women
GOODWELL
422. Panhandle A. & M. Coll.
NORMAN
424. Univ. of Oklahoma
OKLAHOMA CITY
425. Oklahoma City Univ. Opera Workshop
TULSA
428. Benedictine Heights Coll.
429. Tulsa Opera, Inc., 1610 S. Boulder
429A. Univ. of Tulsa Opera Workshop

Oregon
EUGENE
431. Douglas C. Brinkman
432. Univ. of Oregon School of Music
MCMINVILLE
433. Linfield Coll.

259

PORTLAND
434. Byron Hoyt
435. Civic Opera Assn., 420 Corbett Bldg.
435A. Portland School of Music

Pennsylvania

GLENSHAW
436. Glenshaw Players

LANCASTER
437. Lancaster Opera Workshop, 404 N. Duke St.

LATROBE
438. St. Vincent's Coll.

PHILADELPHIA
439. Academy of Vocal Arts, 1920 Spruce St.
440. American Opera Guild, Presser Bldg., 1714 Chestnut St.
441. Co-Opera Co., 316 W. Roosevelt Blvd.
441A. Curtis Institute, Rittenhouse Square
442. Dra-Mu Opera Co., 1205 Walnut St.
443. New Opera Co., S.E. 18th and Pine
443A. Philadelphia Chamber Opera
443B. Philadelphia Grand Opera Co., 1422 Chestnut St.
444. Philadelphia Orchestra
444A. Settlement Music School, 416 Queen St.
445. Univ. of Pennsylvania

PITTSBURGH
446A. Carnegie Institute of Technology
447. Chatham Coll. (formerly Pennsylvania Coll. for Wom.)
448. Civic Light Opera Assn., 429 Diamond St.
449. Pittsburgh Opera, Inc., 1522 Farmers Bank Bldg.

READING
450. Music Club

WAYNESBURG
451. Waynesburg Coll.

Rhode Island

NEWPORT
451A. Newport Music Festival, 15 Gibbs Ave.

PROVIDENCE
453. Convivio Cultural Club

South Carolina

ANDERSON
454. Anderson Coll.

BEAUFORT
454A. Beaufort Choral Society

COLUMBIA
455. Columbia Lyric Theatre

GREENVILLE
456. The Bob Jones Univ. Opera Assn.
456A. Furman Univ.

SPARTANBURG
457. Converse Coll. Opera Workshop
457A. South Carolina Music Festival
457B. South Carolina Opera Workshop

South Dakota

ABERDEEN
458. Northern State Teachers' Coll.

FREEMAN
459. Junior Coll.

Tennessee

CHATTANOOGA
460. Chattanooga Opera Assn., 805 Barton Ave.

MARTIN
461A. Univ. of Tennessee

MEMPHIS
462. Memphis Opera Theatre, Inc., 112 Clark Place
463. Memphis State Coll.

NASHVILLE
464. Nashville Symphony Assn., Hermitage Hotel

OAK RIDGE
465. Oak Ridge Community Playhouse

Texas

AMARILLO
466. Amarillo Symphony, Box 2552

ARLINGTON
467. Civic Chorus

AUSTIN
468. Univ. of Texas Coll. of Fine Arts

BAYTOWN
470. Lee Coll.

BEAUMONT
471. Beaumont Opera Workshop, 410 Iowa St.
472. LaMar State Coll. of Technology

CANYON
472A. West Texas State Teachers' Coll. Opera Workshop

DALLAS
474B. Community Opera Guild
474C. Dallas Civic Opera

475. Dallas Lyric Theatre, Scott Hall, 1501 Simons Bldg.
476. Southern Methodist Univ. School of Music
477. Dallas Symphony Orchestra, 3409 Oak Lawn Ave.

DENTON
477A. Texas Woman's Univ.
478. North Texas State Coll. Opera Workshop

FORT WORTH
478A. Civic Opera Assn., 750 W. 5th St.
479. Fort Worth Opera Assn.
479A. Texas Christian Univ., Division of Opera

HOUSTON
480. Houston Civic Theatre
481. Houston Grand Opera Assn., Inc., 3003 Louisiana
482. Univ. of Houston Opera Workshop

KINGSVILLE
483. Teachers' Coll. of Arts and Industries

LUBBOCK
484. Texas Technical Coll.

MARSHALL
485. Civic Symphony

SAN ANTONIO
487. Grand Opera Festival, 916 Maverick Bldg.
489. Trinity Coll.

TYLER
490. Tyler Junior Coll.

WACO
491. Baylor Univ. Opera Workshop
492. Grass Roots Opera Group

WICHITA FALLS
493. Wichita Falls Symphony Orch., Inc., Hamilton Bldg.

Utah

LOGAN
494. Utah State Agricultural Coll., Fine Arts Dept.

PROVO
495. Brigham Young Univ.

SALT LAKE CITY
496. Univ. of Utah Music Dept.
496A. Utah Opera Theatre
497. Utah Symphony, 55 W. 1st St. South

Vermont

BURLINGTON

497A. Trinity Coll. Music Dept.
498. Univ. of Vermont, Dept. of Music, 70 Williams St.

Virginia

FREDERICKSBURG
499A. Mary Washington Coll., Summer Music School

FARMVILLE
499B. Longwood Coll.

HOLLINS
500. Hollins Coll.

LYNCHBURG
501. Grass Roots Opera Theatre, 1210 Norwell St.
501A. Lynchburg Coll. Music Dept., 3766 Fort Ave.

NEWPORT NEWS
502. Newport News Operatic Society, 3408 West Ave.

NORFOLK
502A. William and Mary Opera Workshop, Hampton Blvd. and Bolling Ave.

RADFORD
503. Radford Coll.

RICHMOND
503A. Virginia Union Univ.
503B. Virginia Arts Guild

STAUNTON
504. Mary Baldwin Coll.

Washington

BELLINGHAM
505. Light Opera Co.
506. Western Washington Coll. of Education

COLLEGE PLACE
508. Mrs. Morris Taylor

LONGVIEW
509. Korten's Inc.

PARKLAND
510. Pacific Lutheran Coll.

PULLMAN
511. State Coll. Opera Workshop

SEATTLE
511A. Cornish School
512. Little Opera House Assn., 702 23rd Ave. N.
513. Northwest Grand Opera Assn., 1624 4th Ave.
514. Seattle Civic Opera Assn., 1920 7th Ave. W.

515. Seattle Symphony Orch., Inc., 601 Orpheum Bldg.
516. South Pacific Coll.
517. Thalia–Allied Artists, Inc., 235 White Bldg.
518. Univ. of Washington Opera Theatre
SPOKANE
518A. Holy Name Coll.
WHITE SALMON
520. Elks Community Chorus

West Virginia

BUCKHANNON
520A. West Virginia Wesleyan Coll.
CHARLESTON
521. Civic Chorus, 309 19th St., S.E.
CLARKSBURG
522. Opera Guild, 339 Washington Ave.
MORGANTOWN
523. West Virginia Univ. School of Music
WHEELING
524. Oglebay Institute Opera Workshop

525. Symphony Orchestra

Wisconsin

MILWAUKEE
526. Florentine Opera Co., 2004 E. Edgewood Ave.
MADISON
527. Univ. of Wisconsin School of Music
527A. Civic Music
RACINE
528. Univ. of Wisconsin
RIPON
529. Ripon Coll.
STEVENS POINT
529A. Wisconsin State Teachers' Coll.
WAUSAU
530. Lucille Hanson
WAUKESHA
531. Waukesha Opera Guild, 522 Center

Canada

533. Stratford (Ont.) Festival

INDEX BY COMPOSERS

L in parentheses following the name of an opera means that it is classified herein as long, Sh that it has been classified as short. LO means that a large orchestra is required, MO a medium orchestra, and SO a small orchestra (see p. 7 for more specific information).

mermoor (L) LO, 89; Rita (Sh) MO, 214

Engél, Lehman. Malady of Love (Sh) SO, 197; The Soldier (Sh) SO, 224

Falla, Manuel de. El Retablo de maese Pedro (Sh) SO, 213

Flotow, Friedrich von. Martha (L) LO, 96

Floyd, Carlisle. Slow Dusk (Sh) MO, 223; Susannah (L) LO or MO, 136; Wuthering Heights (L) MO, 156

Foss, Lukas. The Jumping Frog of Calaveras County (Sh) SO, 192

Gay, John. The Beggar's Opera (L) SO, 34

Gershwin, George. Porgy and Bess (L) LO, 116

Giannini, Vittorio. Beauty and the Beast (Sh) MO, 168; Blennerhasset (Sh) MO, 169; The Taming of the Shrew (L) LO or MO, 138

Giordano, Umberto. Andrea Chénier (L) LO, 19

Gluck, Christoph Willibald von. Alceste (L) MO, 18; Armide (L) MO, 25; Iphigénie en Aulide (L) MO, 81; Iphigénie en Tauride (L) LO, 82; Orfeo ed Euridice (L) MO, 107

Gounod, Charles. Faust (L) LO, 62; Le Médecin malgré lui (L) MO, 99; Roméo et Juliette (L) MO, 127

Grétry, Alexandre. Les Deux Avares (Sh) SO, 175; Richard Coeur de Lion (L) MO, 121

Handel, George Frideric. Acis and Galatea (L) SO, 15; Giulio Cesare in Egitto (L) MO, 75

Haydn, Franz Joseph. Der Apotheker (Sh) SO, 166; La Canterina (Sh) SO, 172; Il Mondo della luna (L) MO, 103

Hindemith, Paul. Hin und Zurück (Sh) SO, 190; Let's Build a Town (Sh) SO, 193; Mathis der Maler (L) MO, 97

Hoiby, Lee. The Scarf (Sh) SO, 219

Holst, Gustav. Savitri (Sh) SO, 218

Humperdinck, Engelbert. Hänsel und Gretel (L) LO, 78; Die Königskinder (L) LO, 84

Ibert, Jacques. Angelique (Sh) SO, 165

Johnson, Lockrem. A Letter to Emily (Sh) SO, 193

Kastle, Leonard. Deseret (L) LO, 48

Krenek, Ernst. The Bell Tower (Sh) SO, 168

Kupferman, Meyer. In a Garden (Sh) SO, 191

Kurka, Robert. The Good Soldier Schweik (L) MO, 76

Leoncavallo, Ruggiero. Pagliacci (Sh) LO, 207

Levy, Martin. Escorial (Sh) SO, 184; Sotoba Komachi (Sh) SO, 225; The Tower (Sh) SO, 230

Liebermann, Rolf. School for Wives (Sh) SO, 221

Martinu, Bohuslav. Comedy on the Bridge (Sh) SO, 175; The Marriage (Sh) MO, 199; What Men Live By (Sh) MO, 233

Mascagni, Pietro. Cavalleria Rusticana (Sh) MO, 172

Massenet, Jules. Manon (L) LO, 93; Le Portrait de Manon (Sh) MO, 210; Thaïs (L) LO, 140; Werther (L) LO, 152

Mennini, Louis. The Rope (Sh) SO, 215

Menotti, Gian-Carlo. Amahl and the Night Visitors (Sh) SO, 163; Amelia al Ballo (Sh) LO, 164; The Consul (L) SO, 44; Maria Golovin (L) LO or MO, 95; The Medium (Sh) SO, 201; The Old Maid and the Thief (Sh) SO, 206; The Saint of Bleecker Street (L) LO, 129; The Telephone (Sh) SO, 229

Meyerowitz, Jan. The Barrier (L) SO or LO, 32; Esther (L) MO or SO, 58

Milhaud, Darius. Les Malheurs d'Orphée (Sh) SO, 198; Médée (Sh) LO, 200; Le Pauvre Matelot (Sh) SO, 208

Mohaupt, Richard. Double Trouble (Sh) MO, 180

Montemezzi, Italo. L'Amore dei tre re (L) LO, 19

Monteverdi, Claudio. I Combattimento di Tancredi e Clorinda (Sh) SO, 174; La Favola d'Orfeo (Orfeo) (L) LO, 63; L'Incoronazione di Poppea (L) SO, MO, or LO, 80

Moore, Douglas. The Ballad of Baby Doe (L) MO, 27; The Devil and Daniel Webster (Sh) SO, MO, or LO, 176; Gallantry (Sh) SO, 186; Giants in the Earth (L) MO, 73

Mopper, Irving. The Door (Sh) MO, 180

Mozart, Wolfgang Amadeus. Bastien and Bastienne (Sh) SO, 167; La Clemenza di Tito (L) MO, 42; Cosi fan tutte (L) MO, 47; Don Giovanni (L) LO, 52; Die Entführung aus dem Serail (L) MO, 57; Idomeneo (L) MO, 80; Le Nozze di Figaro (L) MO, 106; L'Oca del Cairo (Sh) MO, 204; Der